CAMBRIDGE LATIN AMERICAN STUDIES

EDITORS
DAVID JOSLIN   JOHN STREET

3

THE MEXICAN REVOLUTION, 1910–1914

THE DIPLOMACY OF
ANGLO-AMERICAN CONFLICT

THE SERIES

1 SIMON COLLIER. *Ideas and Politics of Chilean Independence, 1808–1833*

2 M. P. COSTELOE. *Church Wealth in Mexico: A Study of the 'Juzgado de Capellanías' in the Archbishopric of Mexico, 1800–1856*

3 PETER CALVERT. *The Mexican Revolution, 1910–1914: The Diplomacy of Anglo-American Conflict*

THE MEXICAN REVOLUTION, 1910-1914

THE DIPLOMACY OF ANGLO-AMERICAN CONFLICT

BY

PETER CALVERT

Lecturer in Politics, University of Southampton

CAMBRIDGE

AT THE UNIVERSITY PRESS

1968

Published by the Syndics of the Cambridge University Press
Bentley House, P.O. Box 92, 200 Euston Road, London, N.W. 1
American Branch: 32 East 57th Street, New York, N.Y. 10022

© Cambridge University Press 1968

Library of Congress Catalogue Card Number: 68–12056

Standard Book Number: 521 04423 5

Printed in Great Britain
at the University Printing House, Cambridge
(Brooke Crutchley, University Printer)

CONTENTS

Preface   *page* vii

Maps   ix, x

Introduction   1

PART I REVOLUTION

1 Díaz   15

2 The Fall of Díaz   49

3 Madero   85

PART II COUNTER-REVOLUTION

4 Recognition   131

5 Indecision   167

6 Decision   190

7 Indiscretion   216

8 Non-recognition   254

Conclusion   285

Bibliography   306

Index   317

PREFACE

This is not a history of the Mexican Revolution. Inevitably, since the actual events of the period are in many cases confused and uncertain, and it has been possible to bring both recent and fresh evidence to their interpretation, it does offer new conclusions about those events, in general, implicitly rather than explicitly. Similarly, the financial interests involved have been dealt with from their own standpoint, but only in so far as there is any ground for belief that they did influence the making of foreign policy.

The work is based almost entirely on contemporary manuscript sources, memoirs, etc., from Great Britain and the United States, many of which have here been employed for the first time. The British side of the Anglo-American dialogue has not previously been presented comprehensively; the occasion of its presentation enables the American side, for the first time since the opening of the State Department files, to be reconsidered as a unity. The Wilson period is therefore related to its antecedents under Taft. Recent published work on Mexico, to which acknowledgement has been made where appropriate, has been incorporated. For the work itself, and the conclusions it presents, I am solely responsible.

I am gratefully indebted for permission to use and to cite material from manuscript collections to: Mr William Jennings Bryan, Jr., for the papers of William Jennings Bryan; the Viscount Cowdray, T.D., for the papers of Weetman Dickinson Pearson, first Viscount Cowdray; Mr Jonathan Daniels, for the papers of Josephus Daniels; the Trustees of the late Rebekah Knox Tindle, for the papers of Philander C. Knox; and Mr Arthur H. Page, for the papers of Walter H. Page.

This research was carried out under a State Studentship from the Northern Ireland Ministry of Education, for whose help and assistance, and that of the William Waldorf Astor Foundation in enabling me to visit Mexico, I wish to express my sincerest gratitude.

I should like to record my special thanks to Professor Sir Denis

Brogan, who supervised and gave inspiration to the work, and to the Editors of the Cambridge Latin American Studies, for their helpful advice and criticism.

My thanks are also extended to Dr Harold Blakemore, Professor Lewis Hanke, Professor R. A. Humphreys, and Dr John Lynch for advice on bibliography; to Srta Berta Ulloa for guidance to the Mexican archives; to the Brookings Institution, the Hispanic Foundation, and the Institute of Historical Research, for research facilities; to the staffs of all the libraries I have used, for their help; to Miss Diana Marshallsay, who compiled the index; to Miss Ann Carr, who typed the principal manuscript, and to my wife, for her patience, sympathy and encouragement.

NOTE ON ABBREVIATIONS

The following conventional abbreviations have been employed in citations throughout:

FO	Foreign Office Papers, London.
GFM	German Foreign Ministry Archives.
SDF	State Department Files.

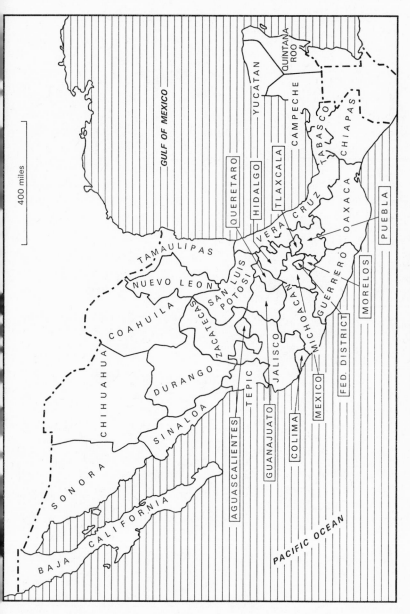

Map I Mexico: States and Territories, 1910–14

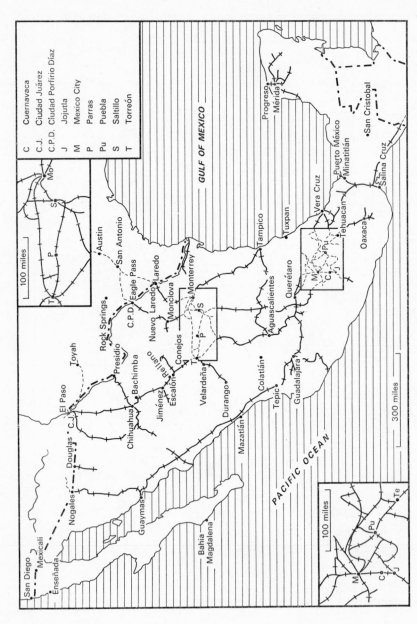

MAP 2. Mexico: Places and Communications 1910–14

Legend:
- C — Cuernavaca
- C.J. — Ciudad Juárez
- C.P.D. — Ciudad Porfirio Díaz
- J — Jojutla
- M — Mexico City
- P — Parras
- Pu — Puebla
- S — Saltillo
- T — Torreón

GULF OF MEXICO

PACIFIC OCEAN

100 miles

300 miles

100 miles

San Diego · Mexicali · Ensenada · Nogales · Douglas · C.J. · El Paso · Toyah · Rock Springs · Presidio · Bachimba · Chihuahua · Jiménez · Escalón · Rellano · Conejos · Velardeña · Durango · Mazatlán · Bahía Magdalena · Guaymas · Colatlán · Tepic · Guadalajara · Aguascalientes · Querétaro · Tampico · Tuxpan · Vera Cruz · Puerto México · Minatitlán · Salina Cruz · Oaxaca · Tehuacán · San Cristóbal · Mérida · Progreso · San Antonio · Austin · Eagle Pass · Nuevo Laredo · Laredo · Monclova · Monterrey

x

INTRODUCTION

This book is about Great Britain, the United States and Mexico. For all three, 1910 marked in some sense the end of an era, and in the three years that followed, they were to be linked in such a way as to force the two Great Powers to reconsider their relationship, and the third power to develop influence upon events beyond its natural expectation. This is the story of those events. To explain how they came about, it is helpful first to recall the condition of each country at that time.

In Great Britain[1] the end of an age is clearly defined by the death of King Edward VII in May, and in the politics of the new age Mexico did not loom large. With the largest majority since the Great Reform Bill, and more than half its term still to run in the parliament elected in 1906, the Liberal government of H. H. Asquith found its measures consistently blocked in the House of Lords. The principle of limitation had been accepted by them since 1894. It was only now that the Chancellor of the Exchequer became the leader of those who sought to make use of it. The 'People's Budget' of 1909 became the opening action in a social revolution, for it established the bargaining power of the forces seeking the liberation of women, the right to industrial organization and the security of the welfare state.

It was the second of the two General Elections of 1910 which was to give to this internal reform the added dimension of international significance. It confirmed that the Irish Nationalists could demand independence as a price of their support for the means to grant it; the government that had just granted dominion to South Africa being willing in principle to do so. It marked the end of the dominance of Chamberlainite 'imperialism' as a bipartisan policy. The fall of Balfour in 1911 and his replacement as leader of the

---

[1] It is assumed here and throughout that the reader will normally have a basic working knowledge of Great Britain and the United States. For those unacquainted with the political history of Great Britain during this period, general reliance may be placed on George Dangerfield, *The Strange Death of Liberal England, 1910–1914* (London, 1936, reprinted New York, 1961), and Colin Cross, *The Liberals in Power, 1905–1914* (London, 1963). Barbara Tuchman, *The Proud Tower* (London, 1965), is a more recent work in the field of social history, not cited here.

Unionist party by the Scots-Canadian, Bonar Law, was a consequence. Together these factors accelerated the growth of fanaticism among the Unionists. Spurning the chance, which the further weakening of the Liberals' position by by-election losses gave them, to make a counter-offer to the Irish, they chose the path of extremism, and initiated in their support of Sir Edward Carson and the Orangemen of North-east Ulster a policy of appealing to armed force. In this, they were to be successful, and by 1914 the country was on the point of civil war.

That they chose to do this in a Europe of hostile alliances made up a complex task for any Foreign Secretary. Not only did these alliances exist, and the annual manœuvres of the Great Powers make clear the likelihood of conflict, but the dissolution of the Ottoman empire gave rise to continual opportunities for provocation or the taking of offence. The basic fact in British diplomacy was that Britain's own security was at stake. Security depended on the Home Fleet and, after the opening of the Anglo-French Naval Conversations in 1911, on mutual agreement with the French for a common defence against a naval attack. An attack might come at any time. The First Sea Lord, when Winston Churchill was at the Admiralty, never went more than twenty minutes from a telephone. And though it could only come from one direction, the provocation might occur anywhere. Avoiding this eventuality was, however, the concern of the Foreign Office. There, until the outbreak of the First Balkan and Italo-Turkish Wars of 1912, actual attack was held to be potential rather than immediate, and planning to meet it contingent rather than actual.

As Foreign Secretary, Sir Edward Grey was well qualified to maintain this policy. The task demanded from him personally a degree of integrity proof against the unrestrained parliamentary and press attacks of the day, the confidence of the Prime Minister, stability of purpose, and discernment and detachment in the making of diplomatic moves or responses. All these Grey possessed in a high degree. They enabled him to maintain those elements of the country's policy which he had inherited while making adjustments to changing circumstances with which his opponents have since found themselves substantially in agreement.

Introduction

The basic element in the situation was the Entente with France, inherited from Balfour. This was the main line of defence against the German system of alliances. To it, in 1907, Grey concurred in the addition of the Entente between France and Russia, to which, on account of its autocratic government, many of his colleagues were opposed. The second element was the maintenance of the Anglo-Japanese Alliance of 1902, an offensive and defensive alliance against any hostile attack, intended on the British side as their safeguard against war in the Pacific or Indian Oceans. At its first revision in 1905 the Alliance was modified to exclude the eventuality of war between Japan and the United States. Good relations with the United States were considered by Grey to be not just a strategic necessity to conserve Britain's naval strength for the North Sea, but a positive end in themselves. He was fully aware that feeling there was by this time actively hostile to both Japan and Russia, traditionally friendly to France, but outspokenly active on behalf of Germany, and always liable to be swayed by dramatic outbursts of feeling in sympathy with the Irish cause.

The United States too were undergoing a process of change. For them, it reached a turning point in June 1910.[1] The days of Theodore Roosevelt, of drama and energy in the White House, of the New Nationalism in power though as yet without a name, were over. William Howard Taft, lawyer, former Governor of the ex-Spanish territory of the Philippines and former Secretary of War, had then been President for over a year. In that year he had failed to secure Republican promises of a lower tariff and taken an imprudent stand in lending his authority to the Payne–Aldrich bill. Further, in the Ballinger–Pinchot clash he had taken the part of Ballinger, his Secretary of the Interior, against the spokesmen for conservation of natural resources. These were the first steps, in the eyes of progressive Republicans, towards abandoning Roosevelt's policies and allowing himself to become the

[1] The author is particularly indebted in this passage to Eric F. Goldman, *Rendezvous with Destiny, a History of Modern American Reform* (New York, 1960, revised edition abridged by the author); and would particularly recommend as guides to the political history of the United States in these years George E. Mowry, *The Era of Theodore Roosevelt and the Birth of Modern America* (New York, 1958), and Arthur Stanley Link, *Woodrow Wilson and the Progressive Era 1910–1917* (London, 1954).

prisoner of the 'old guard', the big-business element within the Republican party. Taft refused to acknowledge the good intentions of the 'insurgents'. The return of the ex-President in June 1910 from his celebrated safari became the stimulus for the crystallization of their opinion around his leadership. Roosevelt's ideas, however, had advanced further in the time than Taft's had come to differ from his own while in office. The natural 'progressivism' of Taft in turn became his greatest liability when ebbing support made him increasingly dependent upon the conservatively minded. In this state of tension the mid-term elections of November 1910 resulted in a substantial victory for the Democrats and the end of years of Republican dominance.

Nevertheless, the full impact of the internal crisis had yet to be felt. Only in 1911 was there to be an open break between the two men, and the termination of the battle for control over the House of Representatives by the limitation of the power of the Speaker. Meanwhile, the results of diplomatic moves gained unusual significance from the tense situation.

Taft had inherited a policy of 'disciplining' the smaller Caribbean countries, the unhealed wound in Colombia resulting from Roosevelt's part in the secession of Panama, and a tradition of fear and hostility in Latin America which, outside Mexico, was then of recent growth. He began a policy of rapprochement by exchanging state visits on the frontier with President Díaz of Mexico in 1909, becoming the first President of the United States to set foot outside its boundaries during his term of office. He showed himself willing to come to a settlement with Colombia, though without making any apology for his predecessor, and for the time being nothing came of it. He had continued the Rooseveltian policy, though without military action, in securing the compliance of the smaller countries with their obligations. As far as Mexico was directly concerned, however, the rapprochement begun by the exchange of the visits was to be extended into a project to secure reciprocal trade treaties (known as 'Reciprocity', for short) with that country and with Canada. All this should be seen in a context in which the United States saw itself as having no major immediate preoccupation and able to engage in a general 'tidying up' of relations with other countries. Outside Latin America two aspects should be mentioned here. An Immigration Treaty with Japan in 1911 was designed to reduce tensions in California and the Pacific States, where Republican 'insurgency' was strong. And a proposal for Arbitration Treaties with Great Britain and France was being advanced in what was considered a clear climate to eliminate the last vestige of possibility that wars could occur between them. In the very first of these negotiations, therefore, they excluded that possibility.

It is clear, then, that Anglo-American relations were generally in a healthy state.[1] Controversy over the rights to off-shore fishing off the coast of Newfoundland was of importance in Maine and New England but not an emotive issue, and it was already clear that it could and would be resolved. The Panama Canal was still three years from completion and the question of the tolls to be charged still lay in the future. Canadians suspected that Reciprocity was viewed by many Americans as a first step to annexation, but they had not yet had the provocation to reject the treaty by their rejection at the polls of the Laurier government. In England ex-President Roosevelt had been acclaimed. He had attended the funeral of King Edward, been awarded an honorary degree by the University of Cambridge, and spoken at Guildhall in praise of British imperialism.

This speech, which had unofficially been shown to Grey before delivery, departed from diplomatic form without being at all undiplomatic. In its praise of British achievement in India and Egypt it offended many Americans but was well received in Britain. It could not, however, be received with complacency, since its theme was that the British grip had relaxed since Cromer's time. This was, and is, a matter of opinion. What is significant about the incident is the way in which it illustrates that by 1910 the idea was clearly accepted on both sides of the Atlantic that the

[1] The definitive work on the history of Anglo-American relations for all periods is Harry Cranbrook Allen, *Great Britain and the United States: a history of Anglo-American relations, 1783–1952* (London, 1954). Three major studies cover aspects of the critical period out of which the better relationship which is the basis of this study emerged. They are: William L. Langer, *The Diplomacy of Imperialism 1890–1902* (New York, 1951); Alexander E. Campbell, *Great Britain and the United States 1895–1903* (London, 1960); Lionel M. Gelber, *The Rise of Anglo-American Friendship* (New York, 1938).

possession of colonies entailed the practice of a coherent policy called 'imperialism'.

The misleading quality of this assumption was nowhere better illustrated than by the British possessions in the Americas. In the years immediately following the enunciation of the Monroe doctrine (1823) these had been expanded in a desultory manner. The Falkland Islands had been abandoned by Spain and had been settled by the Admiralty as a base for repairs and a coaling station. Most of the Caribbean islands had been acquired from other European powers as diplomatic counters in return for concurrence in various European wars, as was British Guiana. The pirate settlement of Belize had been removed as a danger to commerce by its re-establishment as the colony of British Honduras, it having become as much independent of Spain by its own efforts as Mexico or Guatemala. All these changes had been accepted, not always with pleasure, by successive United States governments.

In the 1840s and 1850s, then, there arose a new self-consciousness in the United States, where unplanned expansion gave way in 1846–9 to the deliberate acceptance of 'Manifest Destiny'. This was signified in the revitalization that accompanied it of the words written for President Monroe. Concern was shown about the settlement of the boundaries and status of British Honduras. Opposition was voiced to the extension of British protection to the local ruler of the Mosquito Coast of the Republic of Honduras, and in 1860 the protection was withdrawn. The fact that this withdrawal took place in 1860, however, scarcely acts as proof that it was done by way of British acceptance of the Monroe doctrine, and in fact it was not.[1]

Thereafter, on the other hand, the doctrine that neither Britain nor any other European power should seek to extend her possessions on the American continents came to be tacitly accepted. In turn, United States diplomacy advanced to the position of demanding open acceptance. In 1895 Richard Olney, as Secretary of State, made the most extreme exposition of this case in his 'Twenty Inch Gun' Note: the note that asserted the right of the

[1] For the enunciation, growth and expansion of the Monroe doctrine, see: Dexter Perkins, *A History of the Monroe Doctrine* (Boston, 1955).

United States to enforce compulsory arbitration of the dispute over the boundary of British Guiana with Venezuela. Significantly, much of the exasperation over this incident on the British side arose from surprise that there was a boundary dispute at all, that there was a Venezuelan case to be met, and that the United States could be so obtuse as not to realize that Britain was already in full concord with her fellow Anglo-Saxons on their rightful place in the world.[1]

Then, in 1898, the United States, having subdued a continent, turned to expansion overseas. A deliberate choice was made of the path of imperialism, and in Britain it was welcomed as such.[2] In turn, it obscured for the United States the lessons of the much longer period of British expansion that had preceded it.

British governments of the mid-nineteenth century had thought in terms of trade, rather than of territory. They represented the interests of a country which was still the world's largest manufacturing centre. They had only to leave its economy open to the world, and in default of other, nearer influences it tended to pull the economies of less developed areas into complementarity with it. In due course technical advances enabled other countries to develop their natural resources, as in Germany and Japan, but even the rise of German industry did not remove the dependence of agricultural Denmark on the British market. This relationship held good for certain Latin American countries, for Chile during the nitrate boom or for Argentina after the invention of the refrigerated ship.[3] The growth of the United States did not substantially alter it.

It did, however, affect deeply the economies of Central America, whose tropical agricultural products became marketable for the first time. In turn, these countries were enabled to develop import trade, and a growing volume of trade tended to become centred on the United States. This developed a reciprocal interest in the Caribbean area which led the United States governments to regard it as their sphere of influence. Since no great

[1] Campbell, pp. 40, 44.
[2] Reflected, for example, in Kipling's adjuration to 'take up the White Man's Burden'.
[3] Cf. George Pendle, *Argentina* (London, 1961), p. 83, for statistics of British investment in Argentina in 1939.

British interest had developed in the area as a trading concern, and could not be encouraged to do so,[1] this view was not easily challenged until after 1900.

The problem that then arose was twofold. On the one hand, the United States had developed a new interest in the Caribbean based on the annexation of Puerto Rico, the extension of a protectorate over Cuba, and the construction of the Panama Canal. On the other, this strategic interest made them conscious of potential sources of foreign intervention, of which the most important were European investments. The largest sector of investment in South America at the time was in communications and public utilities and was well rewarded and comparatively stable. In the Caribbean it was in the bonds of the short-lived governments. If they fell or were replaced, it implied suspension of debt service and frequently repudiation. Nor could the money be easily recovered, since it had seldom been reinvested in productive activities.[2]

It was difficult enough to recover debts where money had been so invested. For reasons of national security, investment in business was normally subject to clauses restricting the right to legal remedy, either by enforcing recourse to the national courts, or by demanding the surrender in a 'Calvo clause' of the right of recourse to a foreign government.[3] In the course of ensuring that their rights were made known, European subjects were frequently, accidentally or otherwise, deprived of life, liberty or property. The regular duties of foreign diplomatic personnel in the area included negotiating compensation for such losses and ensuring that domestic remedies were available as far as possible.

In the event of repudiation of national debts, however, there was no intermediate level on which discussion could be con-

[1] Consuls' reports throughout the period reiterate the same charges.
[2] Herbert Feis, *Europe the World's Banker 1870–1914* (New Haven, Conn., 1930), ch. I.
[3] The Calvo clause was devised by an eminent Argentine lawyer as a practical device to prevent the practice by the Great Powers of the collection of debts by force of arms, which was formally denounced by the Argentine government in the Drago doctrine (1898). Countries were advised to enforce by internal law the incorporation of the clause in all contracts made with foreigners, and most Latin American states did so. By it, the foreigner renounced resort to his own government and accepted forfeiture of his rights in the event of doing so. E. M. Borchard, 'Calvo and Drago Doctrines', *Encyclopedia of the Social Sciences*, III.

ducted. These cases became direct challenges to the survival of successor governments, and they were resisted as such. With the new strategic concern of the United States, this rapidly became the prime interest of American diplomacy. In 1903 President Roosevelt indicated his displeasure at a joint British, French and German naval expedition to recover debts from Venezuela. He could do no more, as he lacked the means to enforce his will. With the expansion of the United States fleet already under way, in the following year he felt himself able to proclaim a warning. He did not, however, warn the Great Powers not to recover their debts, even by forcible means. Instead he warned the Caribbean republics not to incur them unless they were prepared to have the United States constrain them to comply with their obligations. The warning gained strength from interventions in the Dominican Republic and Cuba.[1]

It was clear in Britain, at least to the staff of the Foreign Office, that if this was to be the attitude of the United States, it was not one with which British governments could legitimately quarrel. For some years, at least since 1895, they had taken the attitude that the hegemony claimed by the United States implied reciprocal obligations. In this spirit, the Caribbean Fleet was reduced to one squadron.[2] From a strategic position this was certainly the only possible decision. But from the position of the investors, represented by the Council of Foreign Bondholders, there appeared to be no guarantee that the United States would maintain their interests satisfactorily. When the Taft administration adopted the policy of the conscious use of United States financial power to forestall the need for dependence on British capital—the policy that became known as 'dollar diplomacy'—they voiced a warning. The United States had asked for participation in the Chinese Loan of 1909 and subsequently in the financing of a railway in Manchuria. The Council objected that there were only two

[1] This calculated use of force was the policy which became known as that of the 'Big Stick'.
[2] Practical calculations were relevant here. The necessary concentration on maintaining the naval supremacy of the Home Fleet in the Channel prevented Britain from embarking on a race for supremacy either in the Caribbean or in the Far East, where naval primacy passed to the Japanese.

countries in the world in 1909 which owed money to their members and had refused to make a settlement. One was Guatemala, where revenues originally apportioned to the British loan had been reappropriated to a later American one. The other was the United States itself, or, rather, nine of its Southern states (for which, in international law, the Federal government was solely responsible). The implications were inescapable, and it is of interest to note that, though the Guatemalan debt was settled some years later, the debt of the United States is still extant at the time of writing.[1]

The position in Mexico was unlike that in the Central American states for both the United States and Great Britain. It was intimately bound up with the character of that country's régime, and the régime was in turn bound up with the country's proximity to the United States.

The history of Mexico has been a troubled one.[2] In its modern form it is largely the creation of the Spanish conquerors and settlers who made of New Spain the northern third of the Empire of the Indies. It was they who first developed ordered government outside the Valley of Mexico and the 'Core' region of high tableland which was under Aztec–Toltec rule in 1519. They established outposts in the two other regions found in part within the modern limits of the republic: the *tierra caliente*, or fever-ridden marshland and swamp round the coast, stretching southwards into the jungles of Yucatán (where the Maya civilization had collapsed before their arrival), and the deserts of the north. These they dotted with towns far to the north, through the dry hills and plains of Coahuila, Durango and Chihuahua; over the Río Grande into Texas, over the Río Colorado into California.

These three regions, tableland, jungle and desert, make up modern Mexico, but the country of today is less than half the area of New Spain in 1810, when on 16 September the village priest Manuel Hidalgo del Castillo proclaimed its independence in the name of the Indians who lived there before the Spaniards came.

---

[1] Corporation of Foreign Bondholders, *Fortieth Annual Report of the Council . . . for the year 1913* (London, 1913).
[2] The standard history of Mexico in English is Henry Bamford Parkes, *A History of Mexico* (London, 1962). The specialized literature in English, however, is scanty.

Independence cost twelve years and the lives of thousands of Indians to secure: in the process, the descendants of the Spaniards (*criollos*) reasserted their primacy, and those of mixed blood (*mestizos*) were ignored. The short-lived empire of Iturbide resulted only in the loss of Central America, and in 1824 Mexico became a republic with a war veteran, General Guadalupe Victoria, as President.

When he retired in 1828 he was the last President for fifty years to serve a full term. Mexico first entered on almost thirty years of pillaging by transient phantoms dancing around the extraordinary and disastrous figure of Santa Anna; in turn President, exile, dictator, conspirator, hero and buffoon. To Santa Anna Mexico owes the secession of Texas, the Mexican War with the United States of 1846-8, and the loss, *inter alia*, of California, Nevada, Arizona, New Mexico and part of Colorado. His sale for private profit of the Gadsden strip in 1853 ended Mexico's losses and his own career. The Liberals who overthrew him went on to wreak vengeance on the Church for its alliance with militarism in the Wars of the Reform, to secularize education, confiscate church lands, and make a fresh start at organized government under the Constitution of 1857.

This Constitution, though much more advanced than its predecessors, had less chance to become established. In 1858 the Conservative President Ignacio Comonfort, on leading a revolt against his own régime, in the search for dictatorial power, was replaced by the great civilian and Liberal Benito Juárez, a purebred Indian from the State of Oaxaca, and he in turn had to face a new threat from Europe. The French Emperor Napoleon III saw in the events leading up to the American Civil War the opportunity to carve a glorious name in the American continent. His pretext was a debt-collecting expedition to Mexico, in which the British government at first agreed to join.

The history of this debt went back to the earliest days of the Republic, when the new state had been forced to borrow for its basic needs. It could do so only at exorbitant rates and of the sum borrowed the greater part never reached its shores. The British effort to recover it was half-hearted to begin with, and they withdrew as the imperial ambitions of their ally became manifest. For seven years, Mexico's civilian President led the guerrilla attack on the French protectorate headed by the Emperor Maximilian. Then, under the eyes of a reunited and angry United States where a vast army, until disbanded, was temporarily out of work, the French troops withdrew. The emperor was shot, and Juárez resumed the interrupted second term he had acquired by his own emergency order in 1864.

It was Juárez, therefore, who introduced re-election to Mexican politics. His term renewed in 1868 and 1872, his last days shadowed by unsuccessful rebellion, he died naturally in 1872 and was succeeded by another civilian. But this event was not prophetic. What the future had in store was thirty-four years of unchecked dictatorship, ended only by the great upheaval which began in 1910, and left ruins. Out of these ruins emerged the political, economic and social structure of Mexico today. It is the first three years of that Revolution to which this study is devoted.

PART I

REVOLUTION

CHAPTER I

DÍAZ

Anglo-American conflict in Mexico did not begin with the Revolution. Diplomatic rivalry is as old as the Republic itself, and the resulting conflicts date back to the Monroe doctrine and the ministry (1824–9) of Joel Poinsett, first United States minister to Mexico. The first stage of these conflicts came to an end when the empire of Maximilian, which Britain had recognized, collapsed. Diplomatic relations between Britain and the restored republic of Benito Juárez were severed, not to be resumed until 1883.

Accordingly, during the Restoration period, the expanding industry of the United States enjoyed a unique opportunity for trade and investment in Mexico. When a young Liberal general and hero of the French Wars named Porfirio Díaz seized power in 1876 on a platform of 'no re-election', he did not check the process. It was under the Presidency of his *compadre*, Manuel González, from 1880 to 1884, that the rapprochement with Great Britain took place. González had sworn to return the Presidential chair to Díaz at the conclusion of his term, but such was the agitation and manœuvring of the supporters of each President that Díaz determined not to run the risk again. The 'no re-election' amendments to the 1857 Constitution were gradually annulled, and Díaz remained President without question until 1904.[1]

In that year Díaz was seventy-four, and pressure from his entourage had become so insistent for him to provide for the succession that the Presidential term was extended to six years and the new post of Vice-President created. Once again, the aging President took no chances. He selected a man notorious for his extreme personal unpopularity. This was Ramón Corral, who

---

[1] Biographical details from James Creelman, *Diaz, Master of Mexico* (New York and London, 1911); David Hannay, *Diaz* (London, 1917); and Carleton Beals, *Porfirio Diaz, Dictator of Mexico* (Philadelphia and London, 1932), which is as hostile as the first two are eulogistic.

hitherto had been Secretary of *Gobernación*, or the Interior, a post involving the utmost reliability and subservience.

Díaz was first and foremost a soldier. His government was basically a dictatorship, upheld by the federal army, by the police in the cities, and in the country areas by the *rurales*—a rural para-military police force under the direct control of the President. The Constitution of 1857 was still upheld in theory and formally to a large extent in practice, but constitutionalism was used as a shield for the government and not as a platform for the exercise of the popular will. The legislature was the President's creature: its members were nominated by the President and returned in elections 'made' by the government, as was traditional in Mexican history. The judiciary, appointed by the executive, was permitted to be astonishingly corrupt so long as it used its procedural methods to delay undesirable cases and gave judgement according to the government's will.

Except in the early years, however, the dictatorship (to which Professor Cosío Villegas has given the attractive name of *Por-firiato*) was not especially harsh, except in dealing with cases of military rebellion. Freedom of speech, as such, was not en-couraged, but it was not punished. A licensed opposition was maintained both in Congress and in the press, but open opposition outside its ranks was allowed. Control was maintained by leader-ship as much as by coercion, and by playing off factions against one another.

Of course, this alone would not explain the stability of the régime. Its motto of *pan o palo* ('bread or the stick') presupposed the existence of bread, in prospect if not in actuality. Its aim was to couple dictatorship with scientific and technological progress, and the fact that this was achieved in any degree was unique in Mexico up to that time and unparalleled elsewhere in Latin America until our own time.

The group of able and brilliant men under the *Porfiriato* who first set out to make of Mexico a modern state were known as the *científicos*. They founded their programme on the Positivism of Auguste Comte because of the new assurance it offered. Positivism had attained popularity in lay circles after the Laws of the Reform had removed clerical influence from education. It was basically authoritarian.[1] It was optimistic. It was 'scientific'—and its adherents thus claimed to be 'scientists' in government.

They believed that political stability depended on financial stability, that financial stability could be obtained through a programme of economic development financed by foreign capital, and that this capital could be retained permanently by confidence in the political stability it produced.[2] This stability would also increase productive resources by stimulating immigration. It would be a self-sustaining process, in the course of which Mexico would progress directly to modern capitalism without the need for a long period of capital accumulation.

The *científico* doctrine became the official programme of the *Porfiriato* around 1892, as its expositors were taken into high office.[3] Of these the most celebrated, as well as the most significant, was José Yves Limantour, who became Secretary of *Hacienda* (Finance). Limantour was born in 1855 of French refugee origin and inherited a sizeable fortune from his father, including important holdings of land in the future business district of the city of Mexico.[4] On his achievements alone he was a remarkable figure. He contrived as a matter of course a balanced budget and developed a flexible and powerful banking system to finance development. In 1904 he placed the world's largest silver-producing country on the gold standard. In 1907 he carried out in the United States' nearest neighbour the vast merger that brought the bulk of the American-owned railways into national ownership. Finally in 1909–11 he succeeded in refunding the National Debt on a 4 per cent basis, at that time unparalleled in Latin America.

These were the peaks of *científico* achievement and they were

[1] But see Charles Curtis Cumberland, *Mexican Revolution: Genesis under Madero* (Austin, Texas, 1952), p. 11, where the author holds that up to 1901 the *científicos* upheld limited democracy, switching to upholding the dictatorship for the sake of maintaining foreign concessions.

[2] Beals, p. 327.

[3] México, Fondo de Cultura Económica, *México: Cincuenta Años de Revolución, III: La Política* (Mexico, 1961), p. 500.

[4] Edward I. Bell, *The Political Shame of Mexico* (New York, 1914), pp. 83–5; Edith Louise Coues O'Shaughnessy, *Diplomatic Days* (New York and London, 1917), pp. 35–6.

remarkable, even if their utility might be questioned today. Others of the group carried out the programme in the legal field, drawing up the new commerce law, banking law, and railway code, and revising other laws on the Napoleonic model, so that the structure of Mexican law was adapted to the demands of industrialization and the desire of investors to secure holdings in private property.[1] Others again operated the new banking system, became legal advisers to business enterprises, and were appointed governors of states, thus extending and safeguarding the system throughout the country. In return for their labours most of them became very rich.

To some extent, of course, the *científicos* became victims of their own beliefs. They genuinely believed that they had made revolution impossible. Yet in their success they were progressively influenced by creolism—a tendency to elevate the Hispanic strain in Mexican history and to decry the predominant Indian strain and with it the Indian tradition.[2] They were so successful in attracting American capital that it became desirable for Limantour to encourage European capital to balance it. Positivist doctrine did not allow for the Mexicans' elemental fear of themselves succumbing to the fate of Texas and California, and this fear destroyed any real hope that immigrants would choose to settle in the desert north.

But it was their wealth that stimulated the greatest criticism. *Científico* became a by-word for corruption among reformers. In fact, while it would obviously never be possible to prove that they were *not* corrupt, the scale on which their legal revolution enabled them to make legal gains was so immense that, for the principals at least, there would have been little point in ordinary corruption. It was axiomatic that the foreigner in Mexico should be treated with the utmost scrupulousness. In return, he need not behave other than scrupulously. If his agents chose to make money 'on the side', or had recourse to bribery on his behalf, that was another thing again.

The accusations made against the *científicos* in turn affected those

[1] Beals, p. 328.
[2] Indian 35 per cent, *mestizo* 50 per cent. Cumberland, p. 4.

who were favoured by them. By 1910 it was the Europeans, and particularly the British, who were under attack, so rapid had been the increase in their holdings in Mexico since the restoration of relations.

It is difficult to assess just what these holdings amounted to. The estimate normally quoted is that made at the beginning of 1912 by Marion Letcher, United States consul at Chihuahua. He calculated the total invested wealth of Mexico in U.S. dollars at $2,434,241,422. Of this he believed almost half ($1,057,770,000) was 'American' investment and an eighth ($321,301,800) 'British'. 'Mexican' capital accounted for $792,187,242, with the balance shared between French, German and Belgian interests.[1] But the figure of 'Mexican' investment obviously bears no relation to the total stake of Mexicans in their own country: for example, in land, houses, public buildings and the like, for which there was no possible basis for an estimate, and the figure refers only to public companies organized under the laws of Mexico. This being so, there must necessarily be doubt as to the validity of Letcher's other estimates.

J.W. R. Macleay, British chargé d'affaires in Mexico at the end of 1909, estimated British investment in 1909 at almost twice the Letcher figure, following the opinion of *The South American Journal*. Its estimate, he noted, tallied closely with that of Senator Elihu Root, a former Secretary of State, given in evidence before the Foreign Affairs Committee of the United States House of Representatives. The former figure was £135,000,000 (say U.S. $675,000,000) and the latter U.S. $700,000,000.[2] The reason for the disparity between these and Letcher's figures is clear: the former refer to the *origin* of the investment where the latter refer to its (nominal) *control*.

In 1913 William Young, Liberal M.P. for Perth, East, and director of William Young & Co., merchants and bankers in London and Mexico, claimed that much of the so-called 'American' investment in Mexico at the time was in fact British investment

[1] Ernest Gruening, *Mexico and its Heritage* (London, 1928), p. 559.
[2] Reginald Thomas Tower–Sir Edward Grey, 6 January 1910, no. 4 Confidential. FO 371/926 file 2609.

2-2

in companies incorporated in the United States.[1] There is very good reason to suppose that this is correct in the main, though a certain amount of British investment may also lie concealed in companies of Mexican registration. So great is the disparity between origin and control, however, that its explanation can only be sought in the United States. In the words of Feis, 'the available amount of American capital was increasing at a prodigious rate, yet the British investment in the United States was never greater than in 1913',[2] while at the same time British investment in French, German and Belgian companies was small. Accordingly American investment in Mexico at this time must have been little greater—if not less—than British investment. *The Times South American Supplement* of 30 May 1911 believed that (excluding the public debt) they were 'about equal'.

On the other hand, British trade with Mexico was considerably less than American, and was relatively static between 1907 and 1910, while American trade, until political difficulties intervened, was more than holding its own.[3]

British investment was concentrated in the field of railways, mining, industry and land colonization projects, a significant fraction of which were the Canadian enterprises of Dr Fred Stark Pearson, the promoter of public utilities with which William Young, M.P., was closely associated. American investment was equally significant in railways, mining and land colonization, and larger in oil, but less marked in public utilities. French investment was paramount in government securities and banking. German investment, though small, was growing in all fields, but the primary German effort went into trade.[4]

Despite *científico* hopes, however, this investment, great as it was in bulk, did not modernize the Mexican economy, but merely superimposed a modern sector on the basic subsistence

[1] *The World* (New York, hereafter cited as *The World*), 15 February 1913; see also letter by W. H. Allen of Brooklyn to *The World*, Tuesday, 22 July 1913. *The Times*, Wednesday, 5 November 1913, claimed that in 1910 American and British investment was equal, at about £50 millions (say United States $250 millions) each.
[2] Feis, footnote to p. 13. Figures, *ibid.* p. 23.
[3] *The Mexican Year Book, 1912*, p. 11.
[4] Alfred Tischendorf, *Great Britain and Mexico in the Era of Porfirio Diaz* (Durham, N.C., 1961), especially pp. 66–7, 90–1 and footnote; Feis, p. 55.

economy. Although the government enjoyed the power of almost total control over the modern sector through a most sophisticated banking system,[1] it lacked means to influence the economy as a whole. The gap between rich and poor widened, accelerated after 1904 by the adoption of the gold standard,[2] but basically because of the nature of the dictatorship itself.

Land held since pre-Spanish times in common ownership by village communities (*ejidos*) was thrown open to 'denunciation' and enclosure by plantation owners (*hacendados*) or foreign corporations. More than a quarter of the land surface of Mexico passed into the hands of not more than 834 men.[3]

Unruly elements were deliberately reduced to peonage, and thousands died in the toil of the *henequén* (sisal) plantations in Yucatán and the penal settlements of southern Veracruz or Quintana Roo. The alternative was the *ley fuga*—the custom by which inconvenient prisoners were shot 'trying to escape'.[4]

Common rights in the subsoil, including vital water supplies, were replaced in the Mining Law of 1884 by the concept of private ownership of irreplaceable minerals being vested in the ownership of the surface.[5] In the poorest parts of the country, rich foreign colonies suddenly appeared, offering high wages which might cease at any time when the deposits ran out.

Much time and effort were wasted in colonization in the arid north, which, except for a few Mormon colonies in Durango, was a total failure. It aroused xenophobia among the displaced *peones*.[6]

Of all these factors in the growth of pre-revolutionary discontent, it was agrarian revolt against enclosures that was to have the most significance for the internal history of Mexico. But it

[1] *The Mexican Year Book, 1913*, p. 40.

[2] Walter Flavius McCaleb, *The Public Finances of Mexico* (New York and London, 1921), pp. 177, 182.

[3] Charles Wilson Hackett, 'The Mexican Revolution and the United States, 1910–1926' (Boston, Mass., 1926), in *World Peace Foundation Pamphlets*, IX, no. 5, p. 340.

[4] Hackett, p. 341; John Kenneth Turner, *Barbarous Mexico: an Indictment of a Cruel and Corrupt System* (London, 1911); Channing Arnold and Frederick J. Tabor Frost, *The American Egypt, a Record of Travels in Yucatan* (London, 1909), especially ch. XIX; Francisco Indalecio Madero, *La sucesión Presidencial en 1910* (Mexico, 1911), tercera edición, pp. 147–8.

[5] Beals, p. 328; cf. Todd Downing, *The Mexican Earth* (New York, 1940), p. 208.

[6] Moisés González Navarro, *La colonización en México, 1877–1910* (Mexico, 1960), pp. 63, 89.

was the Mining Law of 1884 that had most diplomatic importance, because of its intimate connection with the growth of the
foreign-owned oil industry.

Three remarkable men were prominent in the early growth of
the Mexican oil industry: Henry Clay Pierce, Edward Lawrence
Doheny, and Weetman Dickinson Pearson.

Paradoxically enough, the Mexican oil industry originated in
the United States—not, as Alfred Vagts implies and the new school
of Soviet historians delight in emphasizing, with the abortive
explorations of Cecil Rhodes and the London Oil Trust in the
1880s.[1] The early period of frenetic drilling on the Pennsylvania
fields had led to the creation of the marketing organization known
as the Standard Oil Company, and it was a so-called 'fake independent' subsidiary of this company, the Waters Pierce Oil
Company, that first brought the oil industry to Mexico in 1885.
At the start it enjoyed a total monopoly of the Mexican market,
drawing its crude oil from the Pennsylvania fields until 1900, and
thereafter from the East Coast and Corsicana fields of Texas.[2]

The Standard Oil Company, however, though it controlled
80 per cent of the stock of Waters Pierce, could not control Henry
Clay Pierce himself.[3] 'His aggressive tactics and extremely high
profits concerned members of the Domestic Trade Committee [of
Standard Oil] from the early eighties onward, but Pierce rarely
heeded their suggestions.' He was 'an aggressive individualist'
and could never be 'persuaded to work as a member of a team'.[4]
In the atmosphere of reform at the turn of the century Waters
Pierce was accordingly one of the most vulnerable points of the
attack on the oil monopoly, and in 1900 it was ousted from the
State of Texas. The company was subsequently reincorporated in

[1] Alfred Vagts, *Mexico, Europa und Amerika unter besonderer Berücksichtigung der Petroleumpolitik — eine wirtschafts-diplomatische Untersuchung* (Berlin–Grunewald, 1928), p. 140.
[2] Ralph W. and Muriel E. Hidy, *Pioneering in big business, 1882–1911: History of the
Standard Oil Company, New Jersey* (New York, 1955), p. 128.
[3] Biographical sources: *Who Was Who in America*, I; John T. Flynn, *God's Gold—the
story of Rockefeller and his times* (London, 1933), pp. 240–2, 424. Flynn is unreliable and,
for example, gives Pierce's date of death as 1923 instead of 1927.
[4] Hidy, pp. 448–9; see also Allan Nevins, *John D. Rockefeller, the heroic age of American
enterprise* (New York, 1941), II, p. 530.

Missouri, and regained access to Texas for a time on the understanding that its connection with the Standard Oil had been
severed. It was finally expelled in 1909 when an investigation of
the company in Missouri revealed that Pierce's affidavit to this
effect was false.[1]

It was also in 1900 that Doheny, only eight years after his dis-
covery of oil in Los Angeles, was invited to prospect for oil in
Mexico by the then President of the Mexican Central Railway,
who promised to ensure that any oil discovered would be pur-
chased for locomotive firing.[2] As the railway had, until then, used
American coal, Doheny was offered a large market outside the
control of Waters Pierce. Significantly, he chose to purchase a
hacienda on which to make his first borings, so that, while his title
to the surface was undisputed, his title to the subsoil rested on the
Mining Law of 1884. On 14 May 1901 the first strike on the Ebano
field made Mexico an oil-producing country, and for five or six
years Doheny's company was the only substantial producer.

Real difficulties now arose for Doheny. The Board of the
Mexican Central Railway refused to honour the promise that had
been made on their behalf, and Doheny was forced to concentrate
on asphalt production to keep his business going. Then, after the
nationalization of the railways, he secured his contract, and came
to an agreement with Waters Pierce to supply crude oil to their
refinery at Tampico.[3] In 1906–7 his interests were reorganized into
three groups under a holding company, the Mexican Petroleum
Company, formed under the laws of the State of Delaware.[4] By
this time a rival potentially even more powerful on the distribution side was already in the field.

Weetman Dickinson Pearson,[5] head of the world-famous con-
tracting firm of S. Pearson and Son Ltd, had first visited Mexico in
1889 and had been impressed by the country's great potential for

[1] Flynn, p. 424.
[2] Vagts, pp. 141–2; the President of the Mexican Central Railway was Albert Alonzo
Robinson (1844–1918).
[3] Hidy, p. 464. [4] Vagts, p. 147.
[5] Biography follows John Alfred Spender, *Weetman Pearson, First Viscount Cowdray,
1856–1927* (London, 1930); see also Robert Keith Middlemas, *The Master Builders*
(London, 1963), and Desmond Young, *Member for Mexico: A Biography of Weetman
Pearson, First Viscount Cowdray* (London, 1966), which incorporate new material.

the engineer. He had subsequently been invited by President Díaz to tackle the most intractable problem the country had to offer, the building of the Grand Canal which today drains the Valley of Mexico. In the decade that followed, his firm, which also constructed the Dover harbour works and the Thames tunnel in England, and the Hudson River tunnels in the United States, as well as much else, turned Vera Cruz into a modern harbour, installed drainage, waterworks, electric light and tramways there, reconstructed the Tehuantepec National Railway across the fever-ridden Isthmus, and built terminal works at Salina Cruz and Puerto México (Coatzacoalcos). So great was his prestige that the Tehuantepec National Railway was built and operated by a partnership between his firm and the Mexican government.

It was in April 1901 that Pearson decided on an impulse to secure an option on all oil land in the vicinity of a seepage at San Cristóbal in the Isthmus, and enter the oil business. His interest was welcomed by a government that was becoming increasingly sensitive about the effects of a possible monopoly of American capital in any given sphere. From the start he determined to create a vertical organization, in direct competition both with Doheny as a producer and with Pierce as a distributor. Not content with this, he sought to create his own transportation company also and a distribution network in Great Britain which would challenge the monopoly of the Anglo-American Oil Company, the Standard Oil's oldest overseas subsidiary.

By this time, Pearson's relations with Díaz, and hence with the Mexican government, were very close. He lived for several months in every year in Mexico, enjoyed the respect and confidence of the most influential men of the nation, and was a wealthy and important figure in his own right. (In his own country he was Liberal M.P. for Colchester, and, though a back-bencher, a prominent figure in his party.) Having chosen to extend his operations in oil northward in Mexico after the Isthmus fields had proved disappointing, he sought and received concessions in 1906 to seek for oil in public, unoccupied, government-owned lands. These lands extended over large tracts of the states of Veracruz, San Luis Potosí, Tamaulipas, Tabasco and Chiapas.

The decision to acquire these concessions was momentous. They gave Pearson rights to exploit oil deposits which proved highly productive. They averted a clash with Doheny over buying oil-bearing territory privately. They avoided the complications of the Mining Law of 1884. They emphasized the great power and prestige of the British firm. Equally they aroused great envy, gave Pearson's enemies and rivals an ideal opportunity for allegations of corruption, and caused the *Porfiriato*'s enemies to promise a close scrutiny of the terms of contract.

Pearson could not have hoped to attain a monopoly of oil production. It is clear that he did not attempt to obtain one of oil distribution. He met with Pierce from time to time up to June 1906 and negotiated for an agreement. In that month, however, Pierce notified Pearson that his firm was building a new refinery. It was evident that he would fight for his monopoly. At first both men played for time, for Pierce hoped to wear Pearson down by delay, but in 1908 the latter opened a price-cutting 'war' which reduced oil prices to a fraction of their former height in a matter of months. The struggle continued throughout 1909 and 1910, and even then showed no sign of coming to an end.

At the beginning of the Revolution in November 1910, Pearson (Lord Cowdray since 16 July) had invested millions without significant return. His first great strike, the *Dos Bocas* well, had burnt out at a total loss. He had had to buy crude to supply his British contract, and he was selling at a loss in Mexico. A month later he was the proprietor of the largest 'gusher' known at that time, Potrero del Llano No. 4, which was successfully capped after sixty days and yielded more than a hundred million barrels in eight years. But, as proprietor, while it was still unharnessed, he 'was working in the thick of it as hard as any ordinary labourer, simply living on and in oil'.[1]

In accordance with the nature of his concessions, Cowdray's

---

[1] Sir Thomas Beaumont Hohler, *Diplomatic Petrel* (London, 1942), p. 170. This most important source was published in wartime, and suffers badly both from printers' errors and from shortage of paper, but seems in general surprisingly accurate for its late date.

For the comparable work involved at Tehuantepec, see: Edward B. Glick, 'The Tehuantepec Railroad: Mexico's White Elephant', *Pacific Historical Review*, XXII, no. 4 (November 1953), pp. 373–82.

Revolution

company, the *Compañía Mexicana de Petróleo 'El Águila'*, S.A.
(popularly known as the Aguila Co.), was not just a Mexican
company but a semi-official corporation under the Mexican
government. It was incorporated with a capital of 30,000,000
Mexican pesos (£3,000,000) in shares floated on the London
market in May 1910. Its Board at that time contained no members
of the Mexican government,[1] and, though it included many
prominent and influential Mexicans in close connection with the
government, none was in a position which could directly benefit
the company's activities. In other words, the standards observed
were at least as high as those prevailing in Great Britain at that
time.

These directors naturally held substantial shares in the company.
This gave rise to charges like John Lind's that there was 'record
evidence of the corruption fund distributed by Lord Cowdray
to the officials in power at the time his oil concessions were obtained and the transfer made to the Aguilar [*sic*] Oil Company'.[2]
In fact, these two events occurred at different times, and, while
such a distribution is not totally defensible, it is neither illegal nor
unusual. Furthermore, even during the years of turmoil in Mexico
when Cowdray was under constant attack, he was never at any
time shown to have been involved in corruption, nor was his
name ever associated with public scandals such as were created by
Pierce's connection with a United States Senator from Texas or
Doheny's with a United States Secretary of the Interior.[3]

The British chargé d'affaires in Mexico at the time when
Cowdray was being subjected to the press attacks engineered by
Pierce in Mexican, British, American and French journals in order
to destroy his reputation and frighten off potential investors in his
company has placed his opinion on record.[4] 'There was some

[1] *The Mexican Year Book, 1911*, p. 220. See also Anglo-Mexican Petroleum Products Co.
Ltd, *Mexican Fuel Oil* (London, [1914]).
[2] John Lind–Secretary of State, Telegram, 5 December 1913, 2 p.m. SDF 812.00/10,077.
[3] See J. Leonard Bates, *The Origins of Teapot Dome: Progressives, Parties, and Petroleum,
1909–1921* (Urbana, Ill., 1963), and Samuel Hopkins Adams, *Incredible Era: The Life
and Times of Warren Gamaliel Harding* (Boston, Mass., 1939). Doheny contributed
heavily in later years to the Obregón government, and may well have been forced to do
so because he was known to have contributed before. John Ise, *The United States Oil
Policy* (New Haven, Conn., 1926), p. 383.   [4] Spender, p. 168.

ground for believing the fall of the Díaz administration was desired by the American oil interests who considered that Cowdray
was being unduly favoured, a thing of which I personally could
find no trace despite diligent enquiry', he wrote. 'I never knew
whether Cowdray actually bribed any of the Mexicans, but it is
my firm conviction that he did not. He sometimes gave valuable
presents and he appointed prominent Mexicans to positions which
did not involve much work in his businesses, but I believe he acted
throughout in an entirely honourable and straightforward way.'[1]

Put in perspective, this industrial battle, the propaganda war,
and even American irritation at the attempts of the *científicos* to
maintain the independence of the Mexican economy from the
attraction of *el Coloso del Norte* were only part of a general
disillusionment with the Díaz régime in the United States.

Popular opinion there by 1909 was running strongly against
'big business'. The Taft administration was carrying 'trust busting'
to new heights, although it appeared to be becoming too well
entangled with the same institutions. Meanwhile, the 'muckrakers'
had turned their attention to the excesses of the trusts outside the
limits of the continental United States. Revelations of the state of
slavery in which so many Mexicans lived had awakened the
American conscience.[2] That Americans should be in partnership
with such a system seemed an offence in itself.[3]

The wave of anti-Japanese hysteria that swept through the
United States after the Russo-Japanese war[4] was also manifesting
itself in periodic fear of a Japanese–Mexican alliance. The 'Yellow
Peril', as the Kaiser dubbed it, even affected Great Britain, in spite
of the Anglo-Japanese alliance. Signs of Mexican concern at the
spread of American influence in the Caribbean, therefore, were
interpreted easily in the United States as indications of hostility.
Popular hostility, at least, did exist, and exist widely, but governmental hostility was, on the whole, discreetly veiled.

[1] Hohler, p. 173.
[2] See note 4, p. 21 above. Turner's book was serialized in *The American Magazine* and
achieved great publicity. But compare Creelman, pp. 405-9, for a (self-condemning)
defence of the system.   [3] Turner, pp. 213 ff.
[4] Thomas Andrew Bailey, *Theodore Roosevelt and the Japanese–American Crises* (Stanford,
Calif., 1934).

In these circumstances, the Díaz régime was placed in a very difficult position by the increasing vigour of United States interposition in the affairs of the Caribbean countries. It came to a head in Nicaragua in 1909. José Santos Zelaya, the dictator of Nicaragua, was a violent and erratic personality, with a characteristic contempt for the Great Powers and an ambition to revive the former Central American Republic. His neighbours had already banded themselves together by treaty to regulate interposition among themselves. At least one of their predecessors had been assassinated on Zelaya's orders. But in 1909 he finally went too far by ordering the execution of two United States citizens, Groce and Cannon.

The reaction of the United States government was immediate and violent. The signal was given for the outbreak of a Conservative revolution. The units of the United States fleet in port at Bluefields indicated unmistakably that they would prevent any attempt to halt it, while the Secretary of State announced that the revolutionaries, in the view of the United States, embodied the true will of the people of Nicaragua.[1] Zelaya fled, whereupon his appointed successor, the interim President Madriz, claimed legitimacy.

At this unexpected turn the revolution was checked. But the Mexican government, alarmed at the downfall of a ruler sympathetic to them, whom they had backed as a counter to United States encroachment, had shown their hand by sending a gunboat to rescue Zelaya and granting him asylum in spite of United States representations.[2] The United States government's reaction was disproportionate alarm, and the Díaz régime, for the first time for many years, became conscious of a resurgence of nationalist feeling in their own country. Between these two reactions, it found itself for once at a loss to know which way to turn.

---

[1] Dana Gardner Munro, *The Five Republics of Central America* (New York, 1918), ch. XI. For a representative Mexican view see Juan Pedro Didapp, *Los Estados Unidos y nuestros conflictos internos* (Mexico, 1913), p. 18, where the author claims that the United States overthrew Zelaya because he would not grant concessions demanded by American firms.

[2] Federico Gamboa, *Mi Diario: Mucho de mi Vida y Algo de la de Otros*, v, Segunda Serie, II (Mexico, 1938), pp. 118–21, 177. See also Tower–Grey, 23 August 1910, no. III. FO 371/928 file 32395.

Subsequently the Japanese phobia in the United States was given a new *raison d'être* when the lease of a coaling station in the Bahía Magdalena by an American concern was allowed to lapse, because the Díaz government had found Mexican feeling against it to be too strong.[1] The lapse of the concession was interpreted as implying that it was to be granted instead to the Japanese, who were supposed to be planning an invasion of the south-western states, and did in fact hold a number of small fishing concessions on the Bay. Meanwhile, Japanese immigrants were evading the 1907 'Gentlemen's Agreement' by entering the United States across the Mexican frontier. It was enough to give colour to the invasion stories and to revive the neurotic agitation against Japanese settlers in California.

No Mexican–Japanese alliance existed. The régime of Díaz, despite the chauvinism of some of its military members,[2] was much more sympathetic to the United States than any popular successor was likely to be. This sympathy was reflected most markedly in the circle that surrounded the pretender to the dictatorship, General Bernardo Reyes, whose reputation as a 'strong man' was based on a few punitive campaigns and a spell as a brutal and bloodthirsty Governor of Nuevo León. At the beginning of 1910 he was in exile. His candidature for the Vice-Presidency had been destroyed by the President with the aid of the *científicos*. Contenders outside the dictatorial party were able to point to his enforced retirement as an example of the way in which the Constitution of 1857 had been abrogated. The most important of these contenders was Francisco I. Madero, a wealthy landowner from Parras, Coahuila, and a member of one of the most powerful financial families in northern Mexico.[3]

Madero was generally considered to be the eccentric of the family. Small in stature—only five feet four inches—with a prominent forehead and small beard, his appearance was

[1] F. de la Colina, *Madero y el Gral. Díaz* (Mexico, 1913), pp. 39–40.
[2] Mexico, *Annual Report*, 1909, compiled by J. W. R. Macleay, enclosed with Tower-Grey, 6 January 1910, no. 4 Confidential. FO 371/926 file 2609.
[3] Biographical details from Stanley Robert Ross, *Francisco I. Madero, Apostle of Mexican Democracy* (New York, 1955); Cumberland, *passim*; Madero, *La sucesión Presidencial*, preface.

unimpressive. He had been educated in the United States and in France, but had disappointed his relatives by his lack of interest in finance, although he had a talent for agriculture and had taken over one of the family's *haciendas* with conspicuous success. His main interest was in politics, and he was an admirer of American democracy and French liberty. He was not against Díaz personally —in fact, he rather admired him—but he was against his system.

The Madero family was conspicuous among the great families of the age of the *Porfiriato* for eschewing the advantages of political connections and concentrating on making money in trade and agriculture. Evaristo, the family patriarch who died in 1911, had been governor of his state, but that had been under Manuel González. Evaristo and his descendants, though nominally *Porfirista*, had been too friendly with Limantour to be well regarded by the suspicious octogenarian President and were too conscious of the power of the government to be tolerant of any activities which might upset the delicate balance of suspicion. Francisco I. Madero did receive the support of a few of the junior members, notably his brother Gustavo, and some of his uncles were sympathetic, especially Ernesto Madero, who ran the family bank. But on the whole his first efforts met with ridicule both within his family and in government circles.

This reaction was strengthened by his eccentricities, although they were to prove to be his strength as much as his weakness. He was a vegetarian and a believer in homoeopathy, performing many well-attested cures on residents of his *hacienda*. He had a profound belief in the goodness of man, a trust in the democratic process, a desire to better the lot of the humble, which had led him to seek the cure for their physical and moral ills, to improve agriculture, and to run his *hacienda* as a family in itself. It was this belief that led him into politics; it was also this that gave him immense popularity in his own state. He was also a convert to spiritualism, apparently through reading a book of his father's.[1]

[1] Francisco Indalecio Madero, 'Mis Memorias', in *Las Memorias y las mejores cartas de Francisco I. Madero. Selección y líneas prologales de Armando de María y Campos* (Mexico, 1956), p. 21.

This gave him confidence in his knowledge of the future, a sense of being predestined, and—in one specific prophecy—a promise that he would one day occupy the Presidential chair. He had other qualities which were easily overlooked: a remarkably persuasive personality, and a great sincerity, and he was knowledgeable about his native territory.

He began his efforts in 1905 by founding a Democratic Club to contest the gubernatorial elections, and went on in the next three years to contest other elections, which of course he was not permitted to win. Meanwhile he extended his clubs throughout Mexico, an activity which was not prohibited. In 1908, the year in which Díaz rashly expressed his approval of democratic opposition in an interview with an American journalist, Madero produced a book, *La sucesión Presidencial en 1910*, which was a skilful indictment of the political failure of the dictatorship and a manifesto of some basic ideas on reform. On this basis he founded a national party, the Anti-re-electionist party, with the slogan 'Effective suffrage; no re-election!', and prepared to contest the Presidential elections. He toured the country, gaining sufficient sympathy among local officials to enable him to reach the people.

Meanwhile Díaz had let it be known that he would again choose Corral to be his Vice-President. The formalities of nomination were observed. Boldly the Anti-re-electionists also held a convention in the capital itself. Although many did not dare to come or were detained, that convention nominated Madero for President and Dr Francisco Vázquez Gómez for Vice-President.[1] Subsequently Madero called upon Díaz and obtained from him the cryptic, but in no way discouraging, statement that 'the people should choose between them who should hold the power'. Nevertheless, difficulties continued to be placed in his way, and, when Madero wrote to the President to complain of them, he was told that the President could not interfere with the sovereignty of the states and, though disturbances were unlikely, Madero would find his surest safeguard against them in the law.

Ten days later, on the night of 6 June, Madero was arrested at

[1] Tower–Grey, 20 April 1910, no. 53, and 28 April 1910, no. 58. FO 371/927 files 15185, 17377.

Monterrey and lodged in the city gaol, charged with shielding another man from arrest.[1]

The evidence suggests that this was not the result of a local excess of zeal, but the deliberate decision of the government.[2] It was a serious blunder. The governor of the Federal District confided to the British minister that in the elections the vote for Madero and Vázquez Gómez was surprisingly high, indicating dissatisfaction among provincial officials. He also regarded as a valid indication of the unrest the fact that in the capital, at least, a very large number (over 50 per cent) had taken the trouble to vote, though the official returns showed the customary overwhelming majority everywhere for the government.[3] The Anti-re-electionists even dared to petition the Chamber of Deputies to invalidate the election on the grounds of influence by threats, violence and fraud.[4]

There was unrest throughout the country, particularly among the *peones* of Yucatán, who rioted and were savagely suppressed.[5] Madero had nothing to do with this. His friends had secured his release on bail following the election, and subsequently he fled to the United States convinced, against his own principles, that the only way that the dictatorship could be overthrown was by armed force.[6]

The last weeks of peace were splendid ones. The centenary of

[1] Tower–Grey, 28 May 1910, no. 71. FO 371/927 file 20979. See also Francisco I. Madero–Sr. Gral. Porfirio Díaz, 14 June 1910. Archivo de D. Francisco I. Madero (henceforth cited as Archivo Madero), caja no. 1, hojas 0063–7.

[2] Tower–Grey, 8 June 1910, no. 75. FO 371/926 file 22219 and minutes.

[3] Tower–Grey, 15 July 1910, no. 93. FO 371/927 file 27883.

[4] Tower–Grey, 27 September 1910, no. 132, and 28 September 1910, no. 134. FO 371/927 files 37059, 37061.

[5] The Foreign Office did not believe this when they were first questioned about it in the House on 28 April 1910, and the Parliamentary Under Secretary of State, Mr McKinnon Wood, incautiously revealed in advance that it would be possible to make representations to the Mexican government if a report from the British Consul at Progreso, Yucatán, proved that slavery did exist. For the sake of the (unpaid) Consul, it was then necessary to keep the nature of his report secret. The whole incident was handled remarkably clumsily in view of the other scandals of the same sort that at the time were still matters of recent public concern: the treatment of the Congolese under Leopold II's rule, the Putumayo atrocities, and the affair of the 'red cocoa' grown in the Portuguese islands of San Thomé and Principe, and imported into the British empire by the very respectable firm of Cadbury's. The correspondence may be found under FO 371/927 files 15142, 16964, 21684, 27886, 31975, 33232, 33267.

[6] Tower–Grey, 8 October 1910, no. 142. FO 371/927 file 38616.

Mexican independence from Spain was being celebrated throughout September and the *Porfiriato* held a festival in its own honour. Special ambassadors arrived from all parts of the globe; led by Prince Henry of Prussia, who presented the statue of Humboldt which today stands outside the *Biblioteca Nacional*, they brought bulky masterpieces of art to grace the capital. The Díaz régime exhibited its monumental pride by inaugurating a fine new gaol and lunatic asylum. Warships of all nations, except one, crowded into Cowdray's new harbour at Vera Cruz to show the pacific intentions of their masters. The exception was Great Britain which took no part in the celebrations owing to national mourning for the late King Edward VII.[1]

Britain's absence was not the only discordant note. Limantour was not present; he failed to return from Paris, where he had gone to refund the National Debt. Rumours of changes in the septuagenarian cabinet were persistent. Disturbances in the streets of the capital, almost unknown for thirty years, broke out. And the Mexican Ministry of Foreign Affairs was watching the progress of events in Nicaragua with alarm and concern.

Something of this concern was shared by the Foreign Office in London.

The régime of President Madriz had, despite all obstacles, come very near to suppressing the revolt. It probably would have done so had it not been for the direct threat of intervention issued by the American naval commander in Nicaraguan waters, but, with the strength of the American-backed Liberals growing daily in Nicaragua, it crumbled rapidly during the summer months. The Mexican government hoped by offering to mediate to restrain United States influence in the area. Their hopes were frustrated by the flight of Madriz while the issue still remained in doubt.

As the British minister in Mexico observed, this débâcle meant that United States influence had replaced Mexican influence in Nicaragua. At the same time, he added, this did not mean that

[1] The Germans were especially conspicuous. See Tower–Grey, 17 September 1910, no. 126. FO 371/928 file 35682.

there were any visible signs in Mexico of less hostile feeling in Central America towards the United States.

Foreign Office comment on his despatch raised a whole series of vital questions as to the nature of American foreign policy, quite apart from the revealing series of vignettes it offers of British views upon it.

'The United States will find it far more difficult to establish the protectorate they are aiming at over Central America, than they did with the case of Cuba and Santo Domingo', wrote O. G. Sargent,[1] then a junior clerk in the American Department. 'If they are to obtain their object without bloodshed, they will have to show much more tact and continuity than is usually visible in their foreign policy. The collapse of the Republican Party, which is not impossible, and the advent to power of the Democrats, might shatter the whole policy and give the C.A. Republics a new lease of misspent independence.'

Rowland Sperling, an assistant clerk, enunciated the first principle of British policy towards the change. 'Our chief duty is to see that British trade in Central America is not prejudiced by the extension of U.S. political influence.' Neither the Superintending Under Secretary, Louis Mallet, nor the Permanent Under Secretary of State, Sir Arthur Nicolson,[2] made any comment, but Sir Edward Grey evidently felt impelled to enlarge on Sperling's remark.

'These small Republics will never establish decent govt. themselves—they must succumb to some greater and better influence and it can only be that of the U.S.A.', he wrote. 'We cannot compete with that and must obtain the best terms we can as occasion offers for vested British interests and commercial oppor-

---

[1] Latterly Deputy Under Secretary, 1939–45, and Permanent Under Secretary of State, October 1945 until retirement in 1949. Sir Robert Bruce Lockhart, *Friends, Foes and Foreigners* (London, 1957), pp. 187–98, describes him from a personal viewpoint, and says of him: 'Of all the Permanent Under-Secretaries of the Foreign Office he alone, in my opinion, possessed in full measure the three requisite qualities of the highest diplomatic official . . .'

[2] Harold Nicolson, *Sir Arthur Nicolson, Bart., First Lord Carnock: A Study in the Old Diplomacy* (London, 1930), is devoted almost entirely to *Grosse Politik*, and makes no mention of the Mexican question, but is indispensable both for the character of its subject and for the principal preoccupations of the Foreign Office throughout this period.

tunities. The more we can support the U.S. contention for the open door in other parts of the world the stronger our position will be morally in contending at Washington for the open door in Central America. A strong position morally is not everything but it is not without some value.'[1]

Sargent's prediction about the advent of the Democratic party on the American domestic scene received striking confirmation at the mid-term elections three months later, when the Republicans lost control of the House of Representatives and of many states in the Midwest. They were to benefit from the division between the so-called progressives and the 'Old Guard' of their opponents, which had been growing deep during the primaries.

Thus, for President Taft, foreign policy was at this stage submerged in the far more vital issues of the tariff, and in the electoral struggle itself. What the policy was tended to be obscured by the confusion inherent in its intermittent application. The lack of tact of which Sargent complained arose principally when it was necessary to take drastic action to make up for weeks, or months, of indolence.

Taft was, first and foremost, a lawyer. So was his Secretary of State, Philander C. Knox, and no less than five other of the nine members of his cabinet. Consequently the ideal of the rule of law was even more in the forefront of his mind than is customary with American statesmen. To Taft and Knox the first essential of foreign policy was that it should be in accordance with the law— that is, in accordance with both domestic law and international law, as far as it then existed. This had two important consequences. Before November 1910 the President did not, and after that date he could not, think in terms of altering the domestic law to suit his policy. And, provided a policy that was commended to him was in accordance with the principles of the law as he saw them, it was likely to be adopted regardless of its merits as a policy.

Then again, Taft had the lawyer's concept of a neat and tidy world in which it was the duty of the Great Powers to act as

---

[1] Tower–Grey, 23 August 1910, no. 111 and minutes. FO 371/928 file 32395. See also Percy F. Martin, 'British Diplomacy and Trade', *The Quarterly Review*, ccxv (October 1911), no. 429, pp. 442 ff.

'policemen' within their respective spheres of influence. If governments failed to pay their just debts, or in other ways departed from the principles which the Powers chose to lay down for them to follow, the Powers had a right to intervene. Within these limits Taft was a man of peace. He was no pacifist, for he believed that armed intervention and the waging of war in a just cause were quite 'legal'. He would not resign his right, as he himself saw it, to continue diplomacy by other means, but, on the other hand, he would not initiate military action if he could avoid it. Conveniently, the Constitution appeared to him to indicate that Congress must be the sole initiator of military policy; his duty as Commander-in-Chief was merely to have armed forces in readiness for such tasks as Congress might direct.

He also tried hard to find an effective alternative to military force. With Knox, he adopted that policy of making use of the power of money which had been proposed by the Assistant Secretary of State, Huntington Wilson. This was the policy which became known to friends and foes alike as 'dollar diplomacy'. On the occasion of the convention between the United States and the republic of Honduras in January 1911 the *Washington Post* published an editorial, the typescript of which Knox filed with the papers relating to the highlights of his office as Secretary of State.

'The Monroe doctrine, under its modern interpretation, does not compel the United States by any means to protect extravagant and improvident governments from the just claims of European or other creditors', it stated. 'But when an American republic is on the brink of bankruptcy, no friendlier or politically wiser action could be taken by the United States than to seek, through the instrumentalities of American capital, by one stroke to remove all question of European intervention, and at the same time to start the country concerned upon the road to progress, peace and prosperity.'[1]

There can be no doubt that this represents the belief of Knox himself that his department, and the administration, were pursuing a policy essentially beneficent and moral. It was the course

[1] 'Dollars vs. Bullets', filed in Knox Papers, XIII, folio 2123.

that they attempted to pursue in Nicaragua. But here events took a different turn. The interim government had been persuaded to give way to an elected President, the Conservative Adolfo Díaz. His accession to power was the signal for the Liberals to attempt a counter-revolution, and the new President found it expedient to appeal to the United States for the support of a corps of marines. The services of these last called for some financial return, and in settlement the State Department presented terms which amounted to agreement to a comprehensive political and financial protectorate. But this agreement was not yet settled when Knox left office.

However benevolent their intentions, the incurable tendency of Taft to blunder and Knox to let opportunity slip from his grasp enabled the opponents of the administration to present its policy in the worst possible light. The opposition, like the policy itself, reflected the deep significance of peace in contemporary American thought, and always for the best of motives. The policy which the administration saw as one of peace, the Democrats and Progressives saw as one of gain, dictated by and for the benefit of the financial interests.

Even without the disadvantage of a largely inactive head, the State Department was small for the tasks it sought to handle. During fourteen years of Republican administration the department had been slowly moving towards a general agreement that all but top appointments should be based on merit and that there should be a civil service standard of appointment. This had brought about a consensus of opinion and degree of common effort which should not be underestimated. It remained, however, a political body, with its own network of links with Congress and with the press. Its decisions were subject to the pressures of the internal political situation in a way that the routine decisions of the Foreign Office were not.

As far as Mexico was concerned the differences between the United States and Great Britain were conspicuously ones of geography. To the Foreign Office, Mexico had little political or strategic significance, and, despite its commercial importance, it therefore only justified, up to 1910, the maintenance of a Second

Class Legation.[1] To the State Department, Mexico was a neighbouring power, conterminous, potentially hostile, and the seat of one of the United States' eleven embassies.

The American embassy in Mexico, therefore, was particularly significant. Taft appointed to it Henry Lane Wilson,[2] of the state of Washington, a man who was something of an unknown quantity: that rarity, a political appointee who had become a career diplomatist. With his appointment the newcomer inherited two privileges of special importance: he was *ex officio* dean of the diplomatic corps, and he was the sole foreign representative enjoying the right of direct access to the head of state.

Wilson was fifty-two at the time of his arrival in Mexico. A former lawyer and journalist, he had made a fortune in banking and real estate operations in Spokane, and lost most of it in the Panic of 1893. It was natural that he should be interested in a diplomatic career; his father had been United States minister to Venezuela, and he had been offered the same post by President Harrison. In 1897 with some assistance from his brother John Lockwood Wilson,[3] then United States senator from Washington, he was accordingly appointed minister to Chile (1897–1905). There 'he received credit for greatly improving relations between Chile and the United States, and for having prevented war between Chile and Argentina'.[4] He then served in Belgium from 1906 to 1910.

His transfer to Mexico in the latter year was said to have been due to the Guggenheim copper interests as much as to his brother's political connections; both of them, perhaps significantly, came through the Secretary of the Interior, Richard A. Ballinger. If

[1] Tower, in fact, advised the Foreign Office on the eve of his departure to give his successor the local rank of ambassador, but Grey felt that they could do no more than raise Mexico to the status of a first-class legation. Tower–Grey, 31 December 1910, *Annual Report, 1910*. FO 371/1149 file 1574. See also Martin, 'British Diplomacy and Trade'.

[2] Biographical details from *Dictionary of American Biography; The New York Times*, 23 December 1932, obituary; Henry Lane Wilson, *Diplomatic Episodes in Mexico, Belgium and Chile* (London, 1927), *passim*.

   In citations referred to throughout as Wilson; Huntington Wilson and Woodrow Wilson being thus distinguished.

[3] Wilson, John Lockwood (1850–1912), lawyer, senator and publisher.

[4] *The New York Times*, 23 December 1932.

this influence meant much to him, he was far from likely to be predisposed in favour of a Madero, for the Guggenheim interests had since 1906 been in direct collision with those of the Madero family in the area of Torreón.[1]

The basis of his career was therefore political. While he did not abuse his office for private profit in the manner of his predecessor, he gathered around him many of his predecessor's clique, all of whom were closely connected with important interests, headed by the controversial Judge Wilfley, who had served under President Taft in the Philippines as his Attorney-General. Furthermore, Wilson's nervous and excitable disposition and love of words speedily led him into difficulties.[2] His knowledge of Spanish seems to have been rather limited,[3] but this was not the reason why he did not endear himself to the Mexicans.

There is strong evidence for believing that Wilson was not only a sufferer from poor health, but, at any rate at this stage of his life, an habitual drinker.[4] He was a creature of moods. His writing often shows the forcible emphasis of a weak character who is conscious of his weakness. Where he did not have accurate information, his natural nervousness directed him towards bluster, and certainly during his early days in Mexico he was very conscious of his lack of sources of information. It does not appear that his information became any more correct as the situation became more confused. Rather, he ceased to exercise the faculty of selection over the hundreds of rumours current in his circle. His task was made no easier by the fact that he was surrounded by men with an axe to grind, and was himself the focus of the complaints of some 40,000 resident Americans, many of whom, he believed with some truth, were scheming for his removal.[5]

[1] Foregoing from Bell, pp. 129-30, 137. Gruening, p. 561, is based on Bell.

[2] Tower–Grey, 14 April 1910, no. 48. FO 371/927 file 15017.

[3] Tower–Grey, 20 August 1910, no. 110. FO 371/928.

[4] Ramón Prida, *La Culpa de Lane Wilson, Embajador de los E.U.A., en la Tragedia Mexicana de 1913* (Mexico, 1962), p. 24. 'Henry Lane Wilson era esencialmente un ebrio. Es decir, era un hombre a quien gustaba beber y sentía placer no solo en saborear el alcohol, sino que se deleitaba en ponerse en el estado de semiinconsciencia del ebrio consuetudinario . . .'

[5] The effects of a continued state of alarm and uncertainty in revolutionary circumstances cannot be underestimated. The tragic fate of George B. Schmucker, American Consul at Enseñada, Baja California, who succumbed to a nervous breakdown on 26 May 1911,

Something of this seems to have been apparent to Knox, if not to the President. Knox himself, however, was frequently absent from the Department of State for reasons of health. When he was present, his natural indolence and rigidity of mind led to a tendency to let matters drift, except in a few fields of policy in which the Secretary of State was interested, of which Mexico was not one. The British ambassador in Washington, James Bryce, who was a charitable man, rapidly grew impatient with him. As early as 28 March 1910 the ambassador told Grey in a private letter about the Manchurian railways that Knox was 'either too old or too lazy to apply his mind to the subject, and to try to learn'.

'No country but the U.S. could get on under such conditions', he declared. 'As President Taft said a few days ago "Providence takes care of children, lunatics and the United States".'[1]

As a result of the weakness of the President and Secretary of State, the Assistant Secretary of State, Huntington Wilson, was allowed a singularly free hand. It was unfortunate that Huntington Wilson, like his namesake, believed in a policy of military intervention. Nor was that his only disadvantage for the office. 'Wilson is the *bête noire* of the Diplomatic Corps, as he is tactless and insincere', Count Bernstorff once wrote to a friend. 'If you get any information out of him at all it is sure to be false. Moreover he is the typical representative of "Dollar Diplomacy".' It may be added that he also had connections with the Guggenheim interests. It was Bernstorff's belief that he would take advantage of disturbances in Mexico to force the adoption of a Reciprocity Treaty similar to the one being negotiated for Canada, with the result that both countries would shortly be converted into economic dependencies of the United States. Here too there was a parallel with Nicaragua.[2]

The State Department files for the early part of 1910 are, for

indicates the hazards very clearly. See Lowell L. Blaisdell, *The Desert Revolution, Baja California, 1911* (Madison, Wisconsin, 1962), pp. 112–14, 163–5, 195.

[1] James Bryce–Grey, 28 March 1910. Sir E. (Viscount) Grey's State Papers, United States, Public Record Office, London (henceforth cited as Grey Papers).

[2] Johann Heinrich, Graf von Bernstorff, *The Memoirs of Count Bernstorff* (London, 1936), pp. 86–7, quoting Bernstorff–Freiherr von dem Bussche Haddenhausen, 24 March 1911.

whatever reason, far from informative, even though in his first year of office Taft had been sufficiently interested in Mexico to visit it.[1] The ambassador was more critical of Madero than of the information about him which he received from the circles near to Díaz. Yet when the centenary ceremonies were drawing to a close, he sent a 'Special and Confidential' despatch to the Secretary of State, saying that it was 'imperatively necessary' that he 'should not further delay' in bringing to his knowledge 'information of the exact conditions' in Mexico.

He praised the achievements of the régime, while stating bluntly that it was an autocracy, but he had to warn the Department that affairs were 'rapidly approaching a crisis'. The President was aging, and he had consistently found the *científicos* on the other side in every case in which he had had to defend American interests.

In defending these cases . . . [he added significantly], I have sometimes knowingly exceeded the limits of my diplomatic character and have assumed dangerous personal risks, but I have thought and shall continue to think that in a country where such peculiar conditions exist there is no refuge for an American citizen whose clear and just rights are being taken away from him except recourse to the power and influence of his government through its diplomatic representative.

This attitude he noted to be 'the greatest source of danger in the relations of the two countries and likely to be productive of unpleasant consequences' for himself at any time.[2] But the Secretary of State never apparently questioned this clear statement of Wilson's intention habitually to exceed his powers.

The next greatest source of danger was the general dislike of Americans, which gave rise to 'almost daily' invasions of their rights. Events were to prove that here, at least, the ambassador did not exaggerate. On 9 November riots in the capital greeted the news that a Mexican had been lynched in Rock Springs, Texas. The American flag was insulted. Passions began to overflow into anti-government demonstrations. Wilson notified the Mexican government that he would hold them responsible for

[1] Macleay, *Annual Report, 1909.*
[2] Wilson–Knox, 31 October 1910, Special and Confidential. SDF 812.00/355.

further incidents.[1] The then Subsecretary of External Relations, Federico Gamboa, has left his own account of this interview. Wilson, he recorded, spoke 'in an intemperate tone and with the arrogance of a proconsul'. The only argument that calmed him was the one that the government could not be responsible for incidents that had taken place in bars 'or other worse places'.[2]

Later, the ambassador's feelings were further soothed by the President, 'deeply grieved' and 'very indignant', who promised him that future outbreaks would be 'mercilessly repressed', and pointed out as an afterthought that revolutionaries were known to be buying ammunition in Texas, Louisiana and California. 'I consider troubles as ended', concluded Wilson,'... unless populace should be further inflamed by report of lynching in Oklahoma.'[3]

Oddly enough, Wilson made no report on the activities of these self-same revolutionaries. Yet only a week later their revolution had begun and all the 'merciless repression' the régime could command had to be reserved for them.

In London, there was even less warning of the onset of the revolution. The British minister in Mexico, Reginald Tower, was due to depart for Buenos Aires. His first telegram reporting the outbreak, dated 19 November, was minuted 'Hardly worth reporting by tel. No reason is given for the riots'.[4] His first written report was comprehensive and accurate though. It began, 'I have the honour to report that what might have been a revolution appears to have been promptly taken in hand by the Authorities.'

It appeared that the government had long been aware that, from his headquarters in San Antonio, Texas, Madero had be-

---

[1] Taft was confident that the government would not fail to safeguard American interests. See William Howard Taft–Philander C. Knox, Telegram, 10 November 1910; Knox–Taft, Telegram, undated. SDF 812.00/358.

[2] Gamboa, pp. 199, 200. Gamboa is not entirely fair to the ambassador, whose son had been threatened during the riots. See Baron von Richthofen, German chargé d'affaires–Reichskanzler von Bethmann-Hollweg, 2 December 1910, no. 45. GFM 12/14 Mexico no. 1, Bd. 26, no. A 20936.

[3] Wilson–Secretary of State, Telegram, 14 November 1910, 8 p.m. SDF 812.00/379.

[4] Tower–Grey, 19 November 1910, Telegram no. 9. FO 371/928 file 42201.

come the focus of a vast, if ill-defined, network of revolutionary preparations. Commissions had been issued by him as head of a 'provisional government', and a general call made throughout the Republic for an uprising on 20 November.

On 16 November the government had struck first, making numerous arrests and capturing incriminating documents, including the general plan for the rising. Faced with these facts, revolutionaries elsewhere saw their only chance of success in rising at once; giving the effect of a series of disconnected riots, and allowing every opportunity to the government to suppress them piecemeal.[1] At no time during the first week did it appear that the situation had got out of control,[2] and by 26 November Tower was so confident that all was over that he began to sum up. The revolutionary movement had 'been marked by an absence of cohesion or organization'. Money had been 'lavished' haphazardly, and risings had been 'permitted' to occur on consecutive days. It was clear that Madero's plans, matured on United States soil, had miscarried, and that little more would be heard of revolutions, 'for the moment at least'. '*La paix règne à Varsovie*', he concluded.

Members of the Foreign Office noted that Tower had also reported Díaz aging, Corral mortally ill, the cabinet 'so old as to be unfitted for the stress of departmental work', and the 'future . . . veiled in obscurity'. They could not be as confident as the minister. Sir Edward Grey remarked laconically: 'That part of gratitude, which consists in an expectation of favours to come is necessarily weak as regards a man of eighty. President Diaz's position cannot therefore be as strong as it was.'[3]

Tower devoted a separate report to the influence of the *científicos* and the defects of their policy, which he predicted would lead to the establishment of a United States 'protectorate' in Mexico as well as in Nicaragua. Of the American Department in the Foreign Office, E. H. J. Leslie considered that it was quite likely, while G. S. Spicer, the acting head of the department,

[1] Tower–Grey, 19 November 1910, no. 165. FO 371/928 file 44082. Madero–revolutionary forces, Telegram, n.d. Archivo Madero, caja no. 1, hoja 0080.
[2] Tower–Grey, 23 November 1910, no. 168. FO 371/928 file 44218.
[3] Tower–Grey, 26 November 1910, no. 169. FO 371/928 file 44885.

expected that Mexicans would attempt to restrain United States influence. But Louis Mallet went uncontradicted when he wrote: 'If America wants to intervene, a pretext will be found.'[1]

Meanwhile, a Maderista army continued to survive in the mountainous terrain of the state of Chihuahua, led by a young farm hand named Pascual Orozco. Though defeated in a pitched battle on 11 December, his forces were able to escape from the heavily armed federals, tied as they were to railway lines of communication. On 29 December Tower had to report that little progress had been made towards reducing them, and that the revolutionaries seemed to be gaining strength daily.[2]

In fact, during these first six weeks of the revolution, nothing seems to have been further from the minds of the Taft administration than establishing a protectorate over Mexico. Neither the State Department nor the Department of Justice had been able to collect sufficient evidence to prevent Madero from crossing the frontier into Mexico after he had received news of the first outbreaks; this despite a plea from the ambassador.[3] When the evidence provided by the Mexican government was received, the Solicitor to the State Department, Joshua Reuben Clark, Jr., maintained that it proved only that the revolutionaries had been engaged in 'mere trade in arms, ammunition and other articles of contraband'. This, according to the rules of international law, was even in time of war to be 'considered legal and subject to no penalty save the loss of the goods if captured in the trade'.[4] And this was not even a time of war.

However, when Madero found himself unable to make contact with other revolutionary groups and was forced to retreat across the frontier, convinced that the attempt had totally failed, the Department of Justice issued general instructions for his

---

[1] Tower–Grey, 28 November 1910, no. 170 Confidential. FO 371/928 file 45254.
[2] Tower–Grey, 29 December 1910, no. 188. FO 371/1146 file 1573/1573.
[3] Wilson–Secretary of State, Telegram, 21 November 1910. SDF 812.00/444.
[4] Memorandum by Joshua Reuben Clark, 1 December 1910; Knox–Wilson, 14 December 1910, no. 167. SDF 812.00/447. Clark subsequently served as Under Secretary of State, 31 August 1928 to 20 June 1929, during which time he was author of the Clark Memorandum rejecting accretions to the original Monroe doctrine in relation to Latin America; and as special ambassador at the Inauguration of President Ortiz Rubio, February 1930. Ambassador to Mexico, 1930–3.

arrest.[1] These instructions were not carried out, as the Mexican government seemed unable to comprehend that the United States was not an autocracy. Numerous notes delivered at the State Department, none of which contained any evidence of an actual infringement of a United States statute, aroused only irritation.[2]

In Mexico, however, the ambassador could—and did—secure the suppression of a newspaper for publishing anti-American articles. Yet on the whole his natural pessimism proved a temporary advantage. Though he believed, as did Tower, that by 25 November the movement had been suppressed,[3] he warned Washington that it had been much stronger than was supposed, and it had been handled so badly by the government that a well-organized movement under a good leader could well have succeeded.[4] He cannot, therefore, have been especially surprised when by the end of the year it had become apparent that the revolution had come to stay.

By this time, Tower had submitted his last report on its progress. On 16 January he left Mexico, leaving as chargé d'affaires Thomas Beaumont Hohler,[5] who had arrived on 5 January to take up the duties of first secretary.

Hohler was then just forty years of age, and already was known as 'the Stormy Petrel'. Thus, he had arrived in Constantinople in 1894 just before the Armenian massacres of that year, and, after spells in St Petersburg (1897–9) and Cairo (1899–1901), he was transferred as second secretary to Tokyo, where he remained throughout the Russo-Japanese War. Subsequently, as chargé d'affaires in Addis Ababa, he had succeeded in the delicate mission he had been set of persuading the Emperor Menelik to appoint his successor—an action which subsequently led to some ten years of civil war. In 1908 he returned to Constantinople as first secretary, and saw at close quarters the overthrow of Abdul

---

[1] J. A. Fowler, Assistant Attorney-General–Secretary of State, 30 November 1910. SDF 812.00/520.

[2] Francisco León de la Barra–Knox, 10 December 1910, no. 422; Knox–de la Barra, 29 December 1910, no. 371. SDF 812.00/559, 586.

[3] Wilson–Secretary of State, Telegram, 25 November 1910, 10 a.m. SDF 812.00/474.

[4] Wilson–Knox, 26 November 1910, no. 272. SDF 812.00/517.

[5] Biographical sources: *Foreign Office List, Who Was Who 1941–1950*; Hohler, *passim*.

Hamid and the Young Turk revolution—an experience which, like his extended period of responsibility in Addis Ababa, was to stand him in good stead in Mexico.

From the beginning, in a period for which American reports are scanty, his despatches were critical of the capacity of the government and exhibited a proper distrust of official information.[1] At the beginning of February the spread of the revolutionary movement began to bring in reports that armed men had been seen in the vicinity of British enterprises. Considerable alarm was caused when the wires on the main railway line to the north were cut in several places, yet Hohler was careful to add: 'But they committed, so the director of railways tells me, no wanton damage, their object being evidently not to destroy property but merely to embarrass the Government and render the line unworkable.'

A mining engineer had a similar story to tell of a brief rebel occupation of a British mine at Tamanil. '. . . During their occupation, the rebels were scrupulous about maintaining order, punishing theft, enforcing the drink regulations, etc., with much more vigour and efficiency than had been the custom of the local Jefe Politico [Prefect].'

I beg to call your attention particularly to these last few words [Hohler ended]. Wherever the rebels have been successful so far, they have shown marked care in preserving order and in respecting property. While discontent is shown against various points of the present administration, there are evident signs that the mass of the people are entirely opposed to any continued disorder, whilst foreigners and their property have so far enjoyed almost complete immunity from molestation.[2]

In American eyes, if foreigners enjoyed immunity at all, it did not extend to citizens of the United States. The alarm, it seems, was first raised by General Harrison Grey Otis, a 'regular' Republican best known for his proprietorship of the *Los Angeles Times* and

[1] Hohler–Grey, 25 January 1911, no. 11; 1 February 1911, no. 13 Confidential. FO 371/1146 file 1573/4513, 5446.
[2] Hohler–Grey, 23 February 1911, no. 27, FO 371/1146 file 1573/8519; Hohler–James Bryce, 6 February 1911, Papers of James Bryce, Viscount Bryce of Dechmont, Bodleian Library, Oxford (henceforth cited as Bryce Papers), USA 31 folio 83.

his war against syndicalists and labour unions. On 30 January he complained to Richard Ballinger, Secretary of the Interior, that the presence of insurgents at Mexicali, Lower California, threatened the work on the dam on the Lower Colorado river which, by treaty with Mexico, was being built on the Mexican side of the border by United States engineers. He called for the President to send troops to the border, ready to despatch to the works.[1] It should be noted that this outbreak in Lower California was from the beginning somewhat apart from the main stream of the revolution. The movement was linked closely with the syndicalist groups of Los Angeles which Otis so much detested, and had, on the face of it, so much reason to detest. It was linked especially with the International Workers of the World. The aim of its leaders, the brothers Flores Magón, was to set up a socialist republic. Fatally handicapped from the beginning by lack of organization and the attraction such a movement held for cranks and publicity hunters, the sporadic skirmishes in Lower California attracted an absurdly disproportionate amount of attention from the West Coast press and contributed powerfully to the belief that Mexico was seething with revolutionary turmoil. This was still far from being the case.[2]

The President was already concerned about the policing of the border, having held a conference with the Secretaries of the Treasury and of War and the Attorney-General to discuss the matter. Knox objected strongly to the advice that the Attorney-General had given, and even more to the fact that he had issued instructions to the American consul at the frontier town of Ciudad Juárez, who was also an F.B.I. agent in El Paso, Texas, which went well beyond the State Department's position on the interpretation of the neutrality laws.

I moreover believe the President to be well aware [he wrote] of the serious doubt whether this Government could relieve the Government of Mexico of the undoubted duty itself to guard its frontier, without

---

[1] Copy of General Harrison Grey Otis–Ballinger, 30 January 1911, in Ballinger–Secretary of State (7 February 1911). SDF 812.00/742.
[2] Blaisdell. See Grace Heilman Stimson, *Rise of the Labor Movement in Los Angeles* (Berkeley, Calif., 1955), for background, including details of the McNamara dynamite plot.

going to lengths which would, to say the least, savor of the reverse of that well-ordered neutrality which would comport with the well founded policy and duty of the United States.[1]

Henry Lane Wilson wrote to Knox on 8 February that revolutionary outbreaks, weak in themselves but alarmingly frequent, were spreading, though usually (curiously enough) at 'points remote from consular observation'. He expected extensive cabinet changes shortly, including perhaps the replacement of the Secretary of External Relations, Enrique C. Creel,[2] by the Mexican ambassador at Washington, Francisco León de la Barra, who would then become second in line of succession to the Presidency. Creel, Wilson considered, had proved 'a disappointment', lacking in experience and having tendencies to anti-Americanism. He considered it was becoming increasingly evident that 'the directing power and force of the Díaz Administration' was Limantour, now at last on his way back from Paris. Limantour was currently having talks in New York with the revolutionary agent, Francisco Vázquez Gómez, and members of the Madero family. The family themselves were meanwhile being subjected to 'a regular system of persecution'.[3]

As the month wore on, further disturbing signs were noted, but had not resolved themselves into a pattern. A prominent Mexican made an anti-American speech. Ballinger reported that insurgents had gone so far as to seize supplies for the dam. The Guggenheim-owned American Smelting and Refining Company smelter at Velardeña was visited by revolutionary troops. A special ambassador left for Washington, as also did Henry Lane Wilson travelling on personal business.[4] And plans were made at the State Department for a series of notes to be addressed to the Mexican embassy, beginning on 8 March.[5]

[1] Memorandum by Secretary of State to Attorney-General, 2 March 1911. SDF 812.00/780.
[2] See George Creel, *Rebel at Large: Recollections of Fifty Crowded Years* (New York, 1947), pp. 77–8.
[3] Wilson–Knox, 8 February 1911, nos. 154, 157 Confidential. SDF 812.00/797, 796.
[4] Wilson–Knox, 15 February 1911, no. 162; Ballinger–Knox, Telegram, 23 February 1911; Charles M. Freeman, U.S. Consul Durango–Knox, 14 February 1911, no. 158. SDF 812.00/814, 827 and 831.
[5] Memorandum: J. R. Clark–W. T. S. Doyle, 8 March 1911. SDF 812.00/843.

CHAPTER 2

THE FALL OF DÍAZ

On that very day (8 March) the President of the United States ordered the mobilization of 20,000 men in the area of Texas adjoining the Mexican border. No advance notice was given, either to Mexico or to the press. The announcement of the action gave 'manœuvres' as the only reason, so imagination was given full play, and there was wild speculation as to the meaning and further intentions of the administration. Bryce's telegram announcing the deed caused a special irritation in London.

'State Department maintains this has no relation to Mexican affairs,' Bryce reported, 'and it is just possible that mobilisation is not intended as a demonstration. [The] step has, however, caused much wild talk, such as that Mexican Government is on point of collapse, and that mobilisation is due to British representations for protection of foreign interests. Embassy is replying to enquirers that it has no knowledge of any such representations.'

On this report, the acting head of the American Department, G. S. Spicer, commented acidly: 'It is impossible for the State Dep[artmen]t to maintain that a mobilization of this nature has no relation to Mexican affairs, while it is scarcely friendly to us to let the report spread that mobilization is due to our representations.' He urged that a denial be made and drafted one in the form he suggested. But Sir Arthur Nicolson, the Permanent Under Secretary, modified the draft into a form which carefully avoided any implication of either approval or disapproval of the action itself; stating simply that reports of British representations were 'wholly without foundation'.[1]

In the United States, however, *The World* which had given the interpretation most prominence, stating even that it had been accepted 'as fact' by the London *Morning Post*, was unwilling to withdraw. On 9 March it twice asserted—on the front page—that representations had been made, going even further in claiming

[1] Bryce–Grey, 8 March 1911, Telegram no. 41 Confidential. FO 371/1146 file 1573/8670.

that Mexico had agreed to the mobilization. On an inside page it carried the Foreign Office denial, but said of it: 'The Foreign Office officials speak in such diplomatic terms that their statements are not necessarily convincing.'[1]

Meanwhile, at the British legation in Mexico, Hohler had received a copy of Bryce's telegram. Bryce had suggested (as did the American press) that the move might be due to secret information that Díaz was seriously ill; having informed London that similar 'wild talk' had been circulating in Mexico, though 'the Pearson firm', i.e. the Aguila Co., had denied making any representations, he wrote a personal letter to Bryce.

He dismissed the theory of Díaz's illness. 'I really do not believe Díaz is unwell', he wrote. 'Last Friday he was quite wonderful, and after presenting him with a letter from the King with every solemnity, we had no end of jokes and anecdotes.'

Hohler suggested another possibility in the light of the news which by now would have had time to reach him—that there were heavy naval concentrations off the east and west coasts of the United States coinciding with the mobilization on land, and ships were also coming north. He maintained that this was planned as a demonstration to Japan.[2]

This interpretation, though incorrect, as we have seen, was not far-fetched. As recently as 21 December 1910, Tower had felt it necessary to transmit to the Foreign Office a lengthy despatch on the situation that would arise in Mexico in the event of a Japanese–American war. 'The continued material success of the Tehuantepec Isthmus Railway, giving increased trade facilities between Europe and the Far East, via the American continent, is a

---

[1] *The World*, 8 and 9 March 1911.
[2] Hohler–Grey, 9 March 1911, Telegram no. 3. FO 371/1146 file 1573/8788. Hohler–Bryce, 9 March 1911, Bryce Papers USA 31 folio 118. The story seems to be devoid of foundation that the mobilization was ordered because the American government had come into possession of a copy of the alleged secret Mexican–Japanese Treaty which had been stolen from Limantour in Paris by a German agent and communicated to Henry Lane Wilson. See Horst von der Goltz, *My Adventures as a German Secret Service Agent* (London, 1918), pp. 80–99; also Barbara W. Tuchman, *The Zimmermann Telegram* (London, 1959), pp. 35–7, for evidence that the Japanese scare at the time of the manœuvres was manufactured by the German Military Attaché in Washington, Herwarth von Bittenfeld. Bernstorff eventually had to ask for Herwarth's recall on the ground that he was exceeding his powers (Franz von Papen, *Memoirs* (London, 1952), p. 15).

new factor to be reckoned with', he warned London, 'and it may well be assumed that, in the event of war between the United States and Japan, the forces of the latter would be tempted immediately to land troops to seize and control the railway.' He did not feel it necessary to state that this would involve the British interests in part ownership of the railway, namely S. Pearson and Son, in a most embarrassing predicament.

The presence of Japanese naval vessels in Mexican waters—though on a 'courtesy' visit—and the notorious fact that the Japanese were systematically surveying the Mexican coast, certainly gave rise to interest and concern in some high official quarters in the United States; the United States ambassador had gone so far as to speak to President Díaz about these activities. The President has said candidly that if the Japanese launched a *coup de main* the tiny Mexican navy could never prevent it, and that the only Power which could 'check' the Japanese on the American continent was the United States.[1]

On 14 March Bryce reported further details from Washington. He stated that there were still few facts on the despatch of troops to the frontier. Indeed, the insurrection had been smouldering for months, and had even been receiving aid from the United States. About this aid, the United States government, though evidently uneasy, had said nothing.

Thus the announcement, made as soon as Congress adjourned, that a large force was to be suddenly and promptly dispatched to the frontier for the purposes of undertaking military manœuvres on a large scale, came as a shock on the American public and set all tongues wagging. Wonder grew when it began to be rumoured that United States war vessels were to patrol both the Atlantic and Pacific coasts of Mexico . . . Nor was suspicion lessened by the fact that the President went to Georgia, where he meant to remain for nearly a fortnight, the Secretary of State having already departed for Florida, while the Assistant Secretary of State lost no time in catching a bad cold, which made him inaccessible to callers.

Bryce went on to say that fresh statements were afterwards 'allowed to appear' to the effect that the troop movements had

[1] Tower–Grey, 21 December 1910, no. 185 Secret. FO 371/1145 file 356.

been made to control export of arms and provide protection against 'armed incursions'. These had been received with incredulity for three reasons: the suddenness of the decision, the naval concentrations, and the fact that shell and ball cartridge had been issued to the forces instead of blanks.

'The incident', he summed up, 'is another illustration of the strange, happy-go-lucky—one might almost say unthinking—way in which the business of the State is here conducted, and which the head of the State does not think it necessary to correct. One cannot apply here any of the rules or standards applicable to European Governments.' And he added that this was not only true of United States foreign relations; 'for all Washington believe that the decision to move the troops southward was taken by the President and the Chief of Staff alone . . . Were the President a man filled with ambitious projects the mischief might be serious.'[1]

In Mexico the confusion was indescribable.[2] Henry Lane Wilson was on leave in Washington and the first secretary, Fred Dearing, a competent career officer, was in charge. The first news of the mobilization reached him in a telegram dated 7 March, 10 p.m., which asked him to assure Creel that American motives were entirely friendly. He reported forthwith that the Secretary was confident that this was the case, but that there was general belief elsewhere that the action held an ulterior motive.[3]

Meanwhile the Mexican government had become aware that United States ships were heading for their coasts, and grew alarmed. Carlos Pereyra, first secretary of the Mexican Embassy

[1] Bryce–Grey, 14 March 1911, no. 70. FO 371/1146 file 1573/10280; cf. Bernstorff–Bethmann-Hollweg, 14 March 1911, no. A 49: 'In einem europäischen Staate würde das in diesem Falle beliebte Verfuhren kaum denkbar sein, aber hierzulande muß man immer einen anderen Maßstab anlegen und das gänzliche Unerwartete für wahrscheinlich halten.' GFM 12/14 f. A 4813.

[2] The Mexicans might have been less alarmed had they known at the time how far the design for the land mobilization had exceeded performance. See Hermann Hagedorn, *Leonard Wood, a biography* (New York, 1931), II, p. 111, for Wood's comment, 26 April 1911: 'Of course, when you come down to brass tacks our division was only a skeleton, our regiments were less than half strength and had to be filled up entirely with green recruits. While everybody clapped and said, "How beautiful!" to those of us who looked behind the scenes it was clearly apparent that the real expression should have been: "How little!"'

[3] Dearing–Secretary of State, Telegram, 8 March 1911, 5 p.m. SDF 812.00/898.

in Washington, in the absence of the ambassador in New York, called upon Alvey A. Adee,[1] Third Assistant Secretary of State, and impressed upon him the extreme importance of issuing an official explanation of the naval manœuvres. This request was then transmitted to President Taft in Georgia, but, unhappily, in diplomatic cypher, for which the President did not have a key. This brought an undeserved rebuke for Adee. The message was then retransmitted through the White House. The President gave orders that the ships were only to call at Mexican ports to load coal and then to proceed north. The temperature in Mexico dropped sharply when it was realized that an invasion was not, after all, about to take place.[2] It was left to Adee and Winthrop (the President's naval aide) to invent convincing explanations for the curious evolutions of the vessels. But the real reason, the problem of whether Taft had really been planning an invasion, remained as obscure as before.

First of all, it should be said that on 7 March Taft seems to have been in an absent-minded mood. He failed, after all, to announce the resignation of Richard Ballinger to half his cabinet.[3] He had received a visit from Henry Lane Wilson, on leave in the United States on account of the illness of his mother. Wilson was most pessimistic about conditions in Mexico. 'He regarded the situation as most critical, and could not tell when a catastrophe might ensue', as Taft wrote later to Theodore Roosevelt in reply to his letter volunteering for the war (if any).

Taft goes on to describe the consequences in the terms of a man of action:

I summoned Dickinson and Wood and Meyer and Wainwright,[4] and directed them to mobilize a division of 20,000 men to the north of the

---

[1] 'Adee, a bachelor who would work at night and sleep in his office when the department's work load could not be handled in a normal day, drafted instructions, went through the morning mail, signed official correspondence, and performed other administrative duties. He served until 1924, when he died in harness at the age of eighty-two. Altogether, he had spent forty-seven years in the State Department, easing the administrative burden of twenty-two Secretaries of State.' Alexander DeConde, *The American Secretary of State, an Interpretation* (London, 1962), p. 157.

[2] William Howard Taft–Alvey A. Adee, Telegrams, 12 March 1911. SDF 812.00/921 and 922.   [3] Taft Papers, Presidential Series 8, Letterbook 24.

[4] Jacob McGavock Dickinson (1851–1928) was Secretary of War, 4 March 1909–May 1911. George von Lengerke Meyer (1858–1918) was Secretary of the Navy, March 1909

border, in order to patrol the border more effectively . . . I further directed that this force should be kept there for several months and engage in maneuvers of a useful character, and remain where it could be used should the explosion that Wilson feared take place and chaos ensue, in which case I should ask Congress to authorize me to send a force into Mexican territory to preserve American lives and property which would certainly be exposed to a great deal of danger.

Taft left the same day for Augusta, Georgia. On his way south he evidently felt his 'cover' was wearing thin, for he personally gave the statement to the press which compromised the story of 'maneuvers', and admitted for the first time that the mobilization was directed at the Mexican situation. But the news that the Mexicans were alarmed about the ships came as a complete surprise to him, he later claimed, for it meant that the orders he had given—for a naval concentration in United States waters—had been exceeded. As Taft put it:

. . . the Navy, in addition to having mobilized a force at Galveston and San Diego, had also sent a few small boats north from Panama and Central America with a view to patrolling the Mexican coast. This attracted the attention of the Mexican Government, and they invited my attention to it, and I immediately reversed the orders as to those vessels. The Navy is anxious for a contest, and has to be held in leash. However, they now understand my exact position, and I am hopeful that with Limantour's going to Mexico and adjusting matters with the insurrectos, we may avoid any further difficulty.[1]

The exact request to the navy, embodied in a letter to Secretary of the Navy George von L. Meyer from Augusta (14 March), was that they were to see 'that these small fry do not appear any more

---

–March 1913, having been Postmaster-General, March 1907–March 1909. Leonard Wood (1860–1927) was Major-General, USA, and Chief of Staff, July 1910–April 1914. Richard Wainwright (1849–1926) was Rear-Admiral, USN, and aide for operations to the Secretary of the Navy, 1910–11.

[1] Taft–Theodore Roosevelt, 22 March 1911, Personal and Confidential, Taft Papers, Presidential Series 8, Letterbook 24, p. 205; Joseph Bucklin Bishop, *Theodore Roosevelt and His Time, Shown in His Own Letters* (London, 1920), II, p. 311. Taft's statement is of particular importance since Vázquez Gómez suggests that the mobilization was due to the influence of Limantour, who dined with Dickinson the previous night. Francisco Vázquez Gómez, *Memorias Políticas (1909–1913)* (Mexico, 1933), p. 107 and footnote.

in Mexican ports' and to 'keep all . . . maneuvers to the north of the border line'.[1]

Knox, who had not been consulted, received two anxious letters from the President; the first gave news of the mobilization and the second enclosed the very full instructions Taft had sent to General Wood, commanding the forces in Texas, on 12 March. These instructions also contained a summary of his reasons.

It seems my duty as Commander-in-Chief to place troops in sufficient numbers where if Congress shall direct that they enter Mexico to save American lives and property, an effective movement may be promptly made. Meantime, the movement of the troops to Texas and elsewhere near the boundary, accompanied with the sincere assurances of the utmost goodwill towards the present Mexican Government and with larger and more frequent patrols along the border to prevent insurrectionary expeditions from American soil will hold up the hands of the existing government and will have a healthy moral effect to prevent attacks upon Americans and their property in any subsequent general internecine strife . . .

The assumption by the press that I contemplate intervention on Mexican soil to protect Americans' lives or property is of course gratuitous, because I seriously doubt whether I have such authority under any circumstances, and if I had, I would not exercise it without express Congressional approval.

A copy of this letter was also transmitted to the embassy at Mexico for the information of Henry Lane Wilson.[2]

Taft had good reason to be anxious about Knox's attitude. His military aide, Archibald Butt, recorded in a letter to his sister that Knox had already threatened to resign over the Mexican question, but that Taft hoped that Knox would endorse his action on this occasion. As Butt put it: 'He feels that he has done right, yet fears the criticism which seems inevitable . . .'[3] The criticism had not been wanting, either from indignant cabinet members, or from the press; the detailed explanation given to

[1] Copy in SDF 812.00/955.
[2] Taft–General Leonard Wood, 12 March 1911, Confidential, Taft Papers, Presidential Series 8, Letterbook 24, p. 142; Huntington Wilson–Embassy Mexico, Telegram, 15 March 1911, 9 p.m. SDF 812.00/963A.
[3] Archibald W. Butt–Clara Butt, 13 March 1911, printed in Archibald W. Butt, *Taft and Roosevelt, the Intimate Letters of Archie Butt, Military Aide* (New York, 1930), II, pp. 602–3.

Roosevelt reflects awareness of the deep gap that had already opened between the two men. Even Limantour, then in New York on his way back to Mexico, had conversed with representatives of the revolutionary party and believed that the move had been precipitated by the Guggenheim interests acting through Huntington Wilson; on 9 March he said that any crossing of the frontier would mean war.[1] The doubt and concern were further enhanced two days later when General Wood reiterated that the mobilization had no connection with events in Mexico—an announcement, in keeping with the original story, which perhaps explains the length and detail of Taft's letter to him. The confusion arose out of the secrecy, and the secrecy, Taft makes clear, was merely to avoid making the position of his ambassador untenable.

Knox, however, sent the President a very amiable reply, which was both written and copied for his files on hotel paper in longhand. It gives a rare glimpse into the character of one of the most reserved of Secretaries of State.

'Your two letters arrived about the same time', he wrote. 'There was some delay in the delivery of the first one. In this vast place such things frequently occur. They don't hustle much for people below the rank of a stock broker.'

I suppose we may look for a shindy in Congress about the Mexican situation [he continued]. What with De La Barra howling for strict enforcement of neutrality and some pronounced expression of disapproval of American aid to their insurrectos; with Wilson throwing fits about the imminence of Diaz going up in an explosion; with Americans with interests in Mexico demanding protection against real and fancied dangers and Americans with no interests in Mexico but large newspaper investments at home wanting to see the worst happen; with the Monroe doctrine constantly requiring a measure of benevolent supervision over Latin American countries to meet its logical requirements; with the delicate entente with the Latins which has been nourished and maintained largely in the past upon champaign [sic] and other alcoholic preservatives; what in view of all these and many other factors bearing on the situation is one to do upon whom responsibility rests, except his duty as he sees it upon the facts presented to him?

---

[1] *The World*, 10 March 1911.

I apprehend that if your plans work effectively to your purpose that by the time the present appropriations are exhausted their success will be demonstrated or that a situation will be revealed in which Congress cannot fail to support you.[1]

Butt tells us that the President received this letter with great relief and joy, as well as some amusement at Knox's spelling.[2] From the content of the letter, he might have been expected to express some doubt. For the letter contains at least one notable omission: it passes no judgement on the *quality* of the advice on which the President had acted. In Mexico the coincidence between Henry Lane Wilson's visit to Washington and the mobilization was not overlooked, even if Taft did take care that no definite statement linking the two was released. Some members of the American colony there even went so far as to write to Washington to say that the situation was not as bad as Wilson was likely to have painted it.[3] Nor was the press silent on these matters.[4]

Meanwhile, even in London, the Foreign Office denials had not entirely put an end to speculation. The American action brought forth a sequence of parliamentary questions. On 13 March J. R. Lonsdale (Unionist M.P. for Mid-Armagh) asked for a statement and was assured by Mr McKinnon Wood (Parliamentary Under Secretary at the Foreign Office) that there was no reason to assume British subjects to be in danger. The following day Col. T. M. Sandys (Conservative M.P. for Bootle) asked if there was any further information, and Grey referred him to the previous question. On 20 March Arthur Fell (Conservative M.P. for Great Yarmouth) asked the Foreign Secretary for an assurance

[1] Knox–Taft, 15 March 1911, Knox Papers, XIII, item 2229. There is more than a hint here that Knox, like Ambassador Bernstorff, thought that the movement was designed to force the hand of a reluctant Congress, which had baulked at Wood's previous estimates. See Bernstorff–Bethmann-Hollweg, 10 March 1911, no. A 45, GFM 12/14 f. A 4855.

[2] Butt's description of it (*Taft and Roosevelt*, pp. 604–5) is misleading. The original is quiet and humorous in tone and contains no bombast about the Monroe doctrine, nor about anything else.

[3] Under the leadership of ex-Ambassador Thompson, a further resolution purporting to give the true state of affairs was passed by the Committee of the American Colony on 17 May and transmitted to Washington. This resolution was signed by Galbraith. David E. Thompson *et al.*–President, Telegram, 17 May 1911. SDF 812.00/1842.

[4] *The World*, Friday, 10 March 1911, editorial: 'Militarism in the Dark'.

as to the safety of British subjects, and the First Lord of the Admiralty what ships were in Mexican waters; the answers to both questions were reasonably satisfactory.

Finally, on 27 March J. F. Remnant (Conservative M.P. for Holborn) asked if the Foreign Secretary would advise His Majesty's representatives in Washington to urge mediation of the Mexican question on the President of the United States. Mc-Kinnon Wood answered accurately that relations between Mexico and the United States were friendly. In a supplementary question, Earl Winterton (Conservative M.P. for Horsham) asked if it was not true that the United States government had massed troops on the frontier for the purpose of exerting pressure on the Mexican government. The Under Secretary replied that he was unable to admit that assumption, as it was admitted neither by Mexico nor by the United States.[1] But the most remarkable thing about the British reaction was the unerring precision with which in the midst of the turmoil Foreign Office officials attributed the mobilization to the ambassador's influence, and dubbed him an 'alarmist'—a description which they were to continue to use throughout his time in Mexico. This can only be attributed to accurate intelligence, and in fact Hohler, indicating that Wilson foretold 'a general upheaval', had already written:

Mr Wilson is of a nervous and somewhat excitable disposition, and his health has no doubt been affected by the great altitude of the City of Mexico. While I should be very unwilling to describe the situation in this country as satisfactory, yet I cannot but think that the view which His Excellency takes of it is somewhat exaggerated and unduly pessimistic.

Hohler had also quoted a letter from Mr P. G. Holms, British Vice-Consul in Guadalajara, concurring in his view that in general Americans in Mexico were 'suffering from a species of hysteria'. And he had added: 'I may further remark that the Americans here have little sympathy from any of the other

[1] *Parliamentary Debates*, Fifth Series (House of Commons), 1911, XXII, cols. 1839, 2200, XXIII, cols. 6, 21, 872. Subsequently Chancellor of the Duchy of Lancaster, etc., Earl Winterton visited Mexico in 1906–7 as guest of Mr W. H. M. Pearson, attended the opening of the Tehuantepec Railway, and visited Tampico in the early days of the oil-prospecting boom. *Pre-War* (London, 1932), pp. 39–57.

foreign colonies, as they have only their own manners to blame for the execration in which they are held.'[1]

Unfortunately the ambassador was not just a passive spectator, but a very active participant in events. His prophecies therefore tended to be fulfilled, when they were not mutually contradictory. As it happened, in the aftermath of the mobilization when Limantour was at last travelling south to Mexico, it was Huntington Wilson who first returned to the State Department to take charge. He proposed to the President that he be given a free hand to manipulate press opinion to bring it behind the 'strong' policy which he had evidently decided the President had intended to adopt.[2] At the same time he took a stand on the question of the suspension of constitutional guarantees which, if taken seriously, would largely have bound the hands of the Mexican government in applying the policy of suppression at all. Hohler was not concerned with this question, since he was confident that British subjects would not take part in revolutionary activities.[3]

Huntington Wilson took it 'for granted' that American citizens would have a fair trial if caught engaging in any such acts, and directed Dearing to deliver a note to that effect.[4] Certainly, Americans were warned by Presidential Proclamation to keep clear of involvement and to observe strict neutrality. But, as Henry Lane Wilson admitted, it had been American filibusters 'who had been guilty of the chief part of the destruction of the railway lines and bridges in Chihuahua, etc.'. Hohler found it difficult to see how there could be any intervention if they were caught red-handed.[5]

The ambassador was conspicuously more pessimistic on his return, basing his doubts as to Limantour's chances of success on the substantial ground that he was 'unpopular with masses'.[6] But

[1] Hohler–Grey, 11 February 1911, no. 17 Confidential, FO 371/1146 file 1573/7233; P. G. Holms–Hohler, 18 February 1911, enclosure (copy) in Hohler–Grey, 23 February 1911, no. 27.
[2] Huntington Wilson–President, 15 March 1911, Knox Papers, XIII, item 2231.
[3] Grey–Hohler, 21 March 1911, Telegram no. 8; Hohler–Grey, 21 March 1911, Telegram no. 6, FO 371/1146 file 1573/10389 and 10472.
[4] Huntington Wilson–Embassy Mexico, Telegram, 16 March 1911, 7 p.m. SDF 812.00/973A.   [5] Hohler–Grey, 22 March 1911, no. 42. FO 371/1146 file 1573/12640.
[6] Wilson–Secretary of State, Telegram, 20 March 1911, 7 p.m. SDF 812.00/1027.

Hohler found himself 'unable to find any sufficient justification for the increased degree of alarm' the ambassador showed. There had been 'no striking development' since the mobilization; nor any alarm expressed by British residents or firms. In fact, S. Pearson and Son had just placed orders for almost a million pounds worth of plant and equipment for use in Mexico. He admitted, though, that if Limantour's influence did not secure cabinet changes and reforms the situation might grow 'really serious'.

The ambassador's doubts must have seemed all the more curious since the British chargé was by now convinced that Wilson had been instrumental in securing the mobilization. He recalled that in mid-February, when Taft and his cabinet had been considering offering the Mexican government troops to suppress the revolt in Lower California at Mexicali, the ambassador had told him: 'We would, of course, like to get hold of Lower California if we decently could: not for itself, for so far as I have seen it, or heard of it, it is a desolate and miserable country, but for its strategic value. The Bay of Magdalena is very important.'[1] Hohler now expressed the hope that this aspiration had not influenced the decision, but the implication is clear that he thought it had, at least in so far as it dictated Wilson's own view. It must be said, however, that such sentiments at this time were by no means unusual, and it is not necessary to suppose that the ambassador was in fact motivated by any considerations other than the strategic; the same considerations in 1912 were to lead Henry Cabot Lodge of Massachusetts to introduce in the Senate of the United States the resolution declaring opposition to prospective Japanese colonization in the area which is known as the 'Lodge corollary' to the Monroe doctrine. For this to be achieved in the immediate context it was sufficient for the United States interests that Mexico should continue to be ruled by a stable, friendly government.

However, Wilson had already been told by Limantour that 'his ability to save the situation was problematical'.[2] He assured the State Department that the mobilization had brought good

[1] Hohler–Grey, 16 February 1911, no. 21 Very Confidential. FO 371/1149 file 8188; Hohler–Grey, 22 March 1911, no. 43 Confidential. FO 371/1146 file 1573/12641.
[2] Wilson–Secretary of State, Telegram, 22 March 1911, 6 p.m. SDF 812.00/1037.

practical results: martial law, and a general sense of the need for law and order, which he believed would spread, except to the diplomatic corps, which, he said, adhered—'with that profundity of wisdom which is usually prevalent in diplomatic bodies—to the idea that the maneuvers signify an object lesson to Japan'. The French and Italian ministers had expressed their approval. He dismissed Hohler with the phrase: 'British Chargé d'Affaires has no opinions on anything.'[1] Only three days later, however, he was again telegraphing in most pessimistic vein.[2]

Limantour had begun his programme by openly criticizing the government's policy. On the same day, 23 March 1911, the Mexican ambassador in Washington, Francisco de la Barra, was recalled and told of his nomination to the portfolio of External Relations. When he went to pay his courtesy call on President Taft it was immediately clear that this was to be no ordinary interview, for, as he told Mrs O'Shaughnessy long afterwards, the President welcomed him with the greeting: 'I think, Mr Ambassador, that you will at no distant date find yourself President of Mexico.'

This consideration could hardly have failed to strike de la Barra. By virtue of his office, the new Secretary of External Relations would be second in succession to the octogenarian President, after the mortally ill Vice-President. Even without detailed knowledge of Limantour's negotiation with the Maderistas in New York, it was apparent that events were moving to a crisis. If the prospect of de la Barra was pleasing to the government of the United States his speedy elevation was now a certainty—though it did not follow that he would receive any positive help. It is therefore vitally significant that, according to de la Barra himself, this greeting by President Taft was but the prelude to a ninety-minute discussion in which he showed the greatest friendliness and frankness in discussing the outstanding problems of the two countries.

---

[1] See above, note 2, p. 50. This seems to be conclusive as far as any belief the ambassador had a part in the 'Secret Treaty' affair goes.
[2] Wilson–Secretary of State, Telegram, 23 March 1911, 8 p.m. SDF 812.00/1048; Wilson–President, 20 March 1911 enclosed (copy) with Charles D. Norton–Secretary of State, 27 March 1911. SDF 812.00/1275.

'You may be sure that I will help you in every way compatible with justice, and the interests of the United States', Taft is said to have promised. The disposition of the Chamizal tract, formed by the shifting of the bed of the Río Grande at El Paso, and the embarrassment of the Japanese fishing rights in the Magdalena Bay, were among the topics specifically mentioned.[1]

The following night the entire Mexican cabinet resigned—the last symbolic act of power available to the aged dictator. But it was left to Limantour to form the new one. Limantour had, as Bell put it, assumed the sceptre of Díaz.[2] It remained to be seen whether he could save the *Porfiriato*, or, indeed, whether he intended to do so.

With widespread reports that Madero was advancing on Chihuahua at the head of a considerable force, alarm was growing, and there was unrest in the capital itself. American consuls were ordered by the State Department to report twice weekly on political developments.[3] In the circumstances, the new cabinet failed to command confidence, composed as it was mainly of non-entities; the exceptions being Limantour himself, and General Reyes, recalled by him from exile to take over the portfolio of War and Marine.

Limantour had staked the *científicos'* hopes, and perhaps his own, on one last resource in the struggle to retain power. He would make use of the ancient President himself, and at the opening of Congress endeavour to outbid the revolutionaries by promising to redress the grievances for which they were fighting. He would thus sweep the ground from under them,[4] and disperse them by force while they were disunited.

He was seriously mistaken in these calculations. The President's speech was equivalent to a military defeat. Even by the hand-picked Congress it was seen as an admission of weakness, and even

---

[1] Edith Louise Coues O'Shaughnessy, *Intimate Pages of Mexican History* (New York, 1920), pp. 93–7. [2] Bell, *The Political Shame of Mexico* (1914), p. 68.
[3] Wilson–Secretary of State, Telegram, 23 March 1911, 11 p.m. SDF 812.00/1049; Huntington Wilson–Consul-General Monterrey, Telegram, 25 March, 5 p.m. SDF 812.00/1085A.
[4] Hohler–Grey, 28 March 1911, no. 49 Confidential. FO 371/1146 file 1573/13582.

from those perennial ranks the loudest cheers came for the news that the government had adopted as its own the principle of 'no re-election'![1] The message was not lost on onlookers, some of whom, after the event, formed the impression that Limantour had deliberately betrayed the régime in order to preserve his own memorial in his work as Secretary of *Hacienda*.

Wilson considered that the President's speech lacked 'definiteness' though Hohler considered that it had 'scattered the clouds' —for the moment, at least—and demonstrated that the revolutionaries were only fighting for personal ambition.[2] Significantly, this was the view assiduously propagated by the paid press. The 'vigilant' measures which were used in parallel therefore failed to convince the public that the government was sincere in its promises.

As early as 3 April Wilson reported, accurately, that the situation had 'not changed' for the government, though the rebels might treat.[3] Limantour obviously wanted a speedy settlement but the Maderistas were undoubtedly less influenced by this consideration than by their own shortage of food and ammunition and the ambivalent attitude implied by the United States mobilization. On the other hand, Hohler reported this last in a telegram of 28 March as 'continued presence of U.S. army on the frontier and the completion of its preparations . . . causing increased feeling and alarm', and constituting 'a distinct danger'. The Foreign Office received this report with a caution which fortunately led them to decide not to send a ship to Mexican waters, which could have been of very little use.[4]

Wilson was confidentially informed by de la Barra of the opening of negotiations with the revolutionary party as early as 7 April.[5] The British chargé, however, was not so privileged. He realized that they must be under way when on 10 April Congress granted Corral leave of absence to go abroad for medical care, although it remained a secret that before the Vice-President did

[1] Hohler–Grey, 3 April 1911, nos. 53, 54. FO 371/1146 file 1573/14297 and 14298.
[2] Wilson–Secretary of State, Telegram, 1 April 1911, 11 p.m. SDF 812.00/1163. Hohler–Grey, 3 April 1911, no. 54. FO 371/1146 file 1573/14298.
[3] Wilson–Secretary of State, Telegram, 3 April 1911. SDF 812.00/1193.
[4] Hohler–Grey, 28 March 1911, Telegram no. 9. FO 371/1146 file 1573/11304.
[5] Wilson–Secretary of State, Telegram, 7 April 1911, 9 p.m. SDF 812.00/1241.

so he had signed his resignation for Limantour to present with that of Díaz should the time come.[1] The imminence of the President's resignation, however, was sufficiently obvious. As Hohler put it: 'Such, in fact, is the logical result of his Speech, and still more of any treating with the revolutionaries.'[2]

The situation in the country at large deteriorated also. At Mexicali, the commander of H.M.S. *Shearwater* was invited to land troops on 13 April to defend the city, the civic authorities having fled. In fact, the band of revolutionaries they dreaded did not materialize, and the troops withdrew after seventeen hours. The Mexican government's official protest was almost entirely ceremonial. But in some quarters in the United States the incident was held (notably by Senator William J. Stone of Missouri in a resolution of 17 April[3]) to be a violation of the Monroe doctrine justifying American intervention.

The following day the revolutionaries captured the border town of Agua Prieta—the first marked reverse suffered by the federal forces. This surrender was such a blow to government prestige, in Hohler's view already gravely weakened by the concessions made and the generally accepted fact that the government had entered into negotiations with Madero, that the government made a last great effort to recapture the town and was successful.

In the course of the capture, a few spent bullets had fallen on the American side of the frontier, in the streets of Douglas, Arizona. Taft had taken the unusual course of telegraphing the Mayor of Douglas to ask Americans to preserve neutrality by withdrawing from the area affected. A note to the Mexican government thereupon warned them to avoid firing on to American soil in future. But it was virtually impossible for the federal forces to observe this if they were to recapture the town, and this gave rise to fresh charges that the American government was aiding the rebels. The federal forces did not in the event avoid it. When they had recaptured the town, de la Barra made counter-charges of American interference, including allegations of firing

[1] Bell, p. 81.
[2] Hohler–Grey, 12 April 1911, no. 60 Very Confidential. FO 371/1147 file 1573/15728.
[3] S. Res. 19, 62d Congress, 1st Session (17 April 1911). SDF 812.00/3029½ [*sic*].

from the United States side, which the ambassador regarded as 'highly provocative'.[1] But no action came from the administration, and its pacific intentions could hardly have been clearer.

Nevertheless, Hohler was becoming seriously worried about the effect on the situation of the ambassador's views.

... I cannot exaggerate the degree of pessimism and alarm with which he described the situation [he wrote privately to Bryce on 14 April]. He instanced the state of affairs in the Tuxpam–Tampico district, and showed me a lot of reports from his consul at Tampico 'analysing' the situation. They were merely a collection of rumours and fearful anticipations without one single fact to support them ...

I suggested that foreign interests were being respected & the mines going on working. He said 2/3 of the American mines had had to close down. Now I beg of you to cast your eye at the enclosed bundle of mining news which I have been collecting during the last 3 weeks from the local American paper. They absolutely confirm what the English mine people tell me, and they do not bear out Mr Wilson's statements.

I will not bother you further with what he said, but I hope I have told you enough to show his state of mind. He has been ordered to send in a daily report [!] of the progress of the revolution, and if, as I suppose, he sends in all these rumours and wild stories, it must make fairly sensational reading at Washington [he concluded]. I have said that I think the situation is distinctly worse & I am going to send my reasons. But I do not think Wilson's attitude is justified by the facts, and it seems to me that, having got the army to the frontier (for I feel certain now that he must be very largely answerable for that), he is seeking to justify its presence there, and even to bring it further.[2]

Then on 17 April Hohler reported on a conversation with Limantour.

M. Limantour is ... much disturbed at the attitude of the United States as reflected in the press, and in the bearing of the United States Ambassador, of whom he spoke with great bitterness. He believes that he sends inaccurate and exaggerated reports to his Government (of the latter I have no doubt), and is thus an untrue agent between the two governments.

As regards the United States Government, he complains especially

---

[1] Wilson–Secretary of State, Telegram, 18 April 1911, 12 midnight. SDF 812.00/1391.
[2] Hohler–Bryce, 14 April 1911. Bryce Papers USA 31 folio 161. Bryce–Grey, 18 April 1911. Grey Papers USA 44.

that, while they freely allow arms to be sent across the frontier, as consistent with the freedom of trade, they will not allow arms, money or provisions to be sent to the Federal troops. In reply to representations, they said that it would be helping one side, which, as Señor Limantour said, is a semirecognition of belligerency of the insurgents.[1]

On this last point Bryce, while defending the United States position, was not entirely convincing.

I cannot believe they have willingly or wittingly done so [he wrote]. They are certainly unable to prevent the smuggling of arms along a frontier of several thousand miles, short of confiscation of such arms, and no law exists under which they could proceed to this latter drastic course. There is no evidence how far they have acted in all respects correctly according to international law; but, on the other hand, there need be no doubt that they have endeavoured to do so.

'Short of absolute necessity', he added, the administration would not intervene in Mexico. 'Still,' he recalled thoughtfully, 'a conflagration in a neighbour's house has sometimes justified interference which in normal circumstances would be burglary.'[2]

He based his opinion on the need for the American forces to move by rail, but there is no evidence that this consideration reassured the Mexicans in face of the continual qualification of the American assurances. It was absurd to suggest, as Wilson did, that the Mexican government had at the time of Agua Prieta attempted to precipitate intervention to save themselves, but no less absurd to believe that the friendship of the United States would be valued above the exigencies of domestic policies.[3]

Within days of the incident, negotiations were openly under way, the government having agreed to an armistice. Though Hohler sensed a general mood of unrest which he likened to that in Constantinople in 1908, he continued to think the ambassador pessimistic.[4] Yet, in some ways, events were outrunning Wilson's worst expectations, for he had not hitherto believed in the possibility of Díaz's resignation, and now he was forced to conclude

[1] Hohler–Grey, 17 April 1911, Telegram no. 17 Confidential. FO 371/1146 file 1573/14021; 17 April 1911, no. 63 Confidential. FO 371/1147 file 1573/16688.
[2] Bryce–Grey, 20 April 1911, no. 120A. FO 371/1147 file 1573/16610.
[3] Wilson–Knox, 26 April 1911, no. 497 Confidential. SDF 812.00/1543.
[4] Hohler–Grey, 18 April 1911, no. 66. FO 371/1147 file 1573/16691.

it might happen.[1] Hohler noted that Díaz himself was growing in unpopularity, and considered that Madero had rallied the opposition to himself largely because he alone had had the courage to stand up to Díaz in the days of his strength.[2]

A last attempt by the government to split the revolutionary ranks by denying their special commissioner, the jurist and future Chief Justice of the Supreme Court, Francisco Carbajal,[3] powers to cede the resignation of Díaz himself, nearly had its desired effect. The radicals, under their young leader, Pascual Orozco, had gone to the point of putting Madero under arrest before he conceded the majority view.[4] Then on 7 May the demands were openly refused, and the armistice itself broke. Madero, pointing to the dangers inherent in international complications should the same situation arise as at Agua Prieta, had announced his decision not to attack the frontier town of Ciudad Juárez, where he had encamped, but to march on the capital instead. In fact, his real reason was that he had been 'directed' by the spirit of Benito Juárez himself to do so.

However, at 10 a.m. the following morning, 8 May, his forces initiated an attack on the town which within forty-eight hours was completely successful. The situation was transformed in this way, because 'famine—punitive deaths by hunger occurring—was prevalent among his men, especially in Orozco's body, and, to get something to eat, they had to capture Ciudad J.', while the federal commander, after the long siege, 'had only 500 men . . . of whom 200 were down with typhoid'.[5] Madero was able to regain

[1] Wilson–Knox, 26 April 1911, 497 Confidential (see note 3, p. 66).
[2] Hohler–Grey, 22 April 1911, no. 69. FO 371/1147 file 1573/17284.
[3] Carbajal was appointed Secretary of External Relations, 10 July 1914. Serving only five days in that post, he became, on the resignation of President Huerta, President *ad interim* of Mexico from 15 July to 13 August 1914, when he resigned and fled before the advancing constitutionalist army. He was, however, subsequently allowed to return to Mexico, where he died in 1932.
[4] Philip C. Hanna–Secretary of State, Telegram, n.d., received 7 May 1911, 10.13 a.m. SDF 812.00/1648. Ramón Prida, *From Despotism to Anarchy* (El Paso, Texas, 1914), p. 30, notes also the trap set by Vázquez Gómez for the government in demanding a special commissioner and so obtaining virtual recognition.
[5] Hohler–Bryce, 27 June 1911. Bryce Papers USA 31 folios 262 ff.; see also Vázquez Gómez, p. 146, where the author claims he advised Madero not to attack the city. The revolt against Madero, he claims, occurred because he had not demanded the resignation of Díaz as well as that of Corral.

control of the troops easily and on 14 May a prolonged session of the Mexican cabinet decided that Díaz must resign.

Behind the scenes the first major British conflict with the United States—over Henry Lane Wilson—had come to a climax. From beginning to end it had been entirely secret, and it is doubtful indeed whether its subject ever came to know about it.

In Washington, the first move was made by Lord Cowdray. Through George W. Wickersham, the Attorney-General, formerly of Strong and Cadwalader, his legal advisers, he secured an interview with several members of the cabinet, and afterwards with the President himself, and complained to them about the behaviour of the ambassador.

I felt I could not so freely express myself to the President as I had done with the Members of his Cabinet whom I had met [he afterwards wrote to the Mexican ambassador in Washington], but I told him that if his representative in Mexico City reported at all to his Government in the strain that he freely spoke in Mexico, he was a source of great danger to the amicable relationship of the two countries.

He claimed that he was voicing the opinions of 'many foreigners, and also of the American Ambassador's colleagues in Mexico', who habitually found that their views of the situation conflicted with those of the ambassador.

For instance [Cowdray wrote], I told him that Mr Wilson had stated to them, or some of them, that three-quarters of the American mines in Northern Mexico were shut down in consequence of the Revolution; whereas, according to their information they could not find that a single mine was, as a fact, shut down. I attributed these expressions of Mr Wilson to his being a highly sensitive nature and believeing [*sic*] every 'cock and bull' story that he heard.

The President was not convinced, he reported. 'The President said that he knew Wilson and his brother very well, and he must admit that he had to take [their] statements with "a grain of salt"; but, on the other hand, speaking generally, he found the reports Wilson had sent to Washington were fairly confirmed from outside sources.' For this the President cited U.S. consular reports, the reports received by the British and French ambassadors at Washington, and a recent courtesy visit by the French minister in Mexico. The opinions of the French, unfortunately, are not available, but certainly it is clear that the U.S. consular and British sources are far from supporting the opinion Taft expressed to Cowdray.

Finally, after remarks indicating that he was entirely convinced the administration had no intention of resorting to armed intervention—the President himself had added the usual reservations, but Dickinson had given an absolutely unqualified assurance— Cowdray concluded his letter by saying bluntly: '. . . I was also asked by Mr Dickinson if Mr Wilson drank. I, of course, admitted that it was so rumoured. He added that it was generally known that he used to drink but it was claimed that he had now given up that practice.'[1]

The significant thing is that Bryce knew of this interview, and also of a long talk that Cowdray had had with the Attorney-General personally.

Lord Cowdray . . . [he added] told me that he had talked freely to the Attorney General and said to him that the United States Ambassador in Mexico was a highly nervous and excitable man, whose alarmist reports must be taken with much caution and in fact largely discounted. People said of him in Mexico that it was better to see him before rather than after lunch. Lord Cowdray had hoped that this need for taking the Ambassador's reports with some reserve would be conveyed to the President, and I suspect this has been done.

The following Saturday, Bryce himself was seated beside the President at the annual dinner of the American Society of International Law.

. . . He took occasion to remark to me that the state of things in Mexico had within the last few days been growing worse and caused him much concern [he reported]. In some provinces there was a condition of disorder approaching anarchy. This was reported by some of the United States consuls. I observed that our Chargé d'Affaires in Mexico did not give quite so gloomy a view of the situation, and that he had told me that hardly any British or American mines or other property had been

[1] Lord Cowdray–Manuel Zamacona, 26 April 1911. Cowdray Papers.

destroyed. The President agreed that this was so, but said that forty Americans had in one way or another been killed. I asked if they had been killed fighting with the insurgents, and he replied he thought not, that they were non-combatants. He did not however seem to be quite clear on this point . . .[1]

This report was received with approval in London. 'Just as well that Mr Taft should be made aware, if he was not so already, of the excitable and alarmist character of his Ambassador at Mexico', commented R. H. Campbell, who as a junior clerk had recently moved to the American Department. 'Very possibly Mr Wilson's pessimistic views are derived from U.S. financial interests in Mexico', suggested Spicer. 'According to Sir C. MacDonald [the British ambassador in Tokyo] who knows him,' pronounced Sir Francis Campbell, 'Mr Wilson's views would not be likely to carry much weight with his Gov[t].' And the report was passed to the Prime Minister and to Lord Morley as Lord President of the Council.

That, however, was as far as it went. The State Department was embarrassed by an exceedingly hostile interview in Santander with Ramón Corral, still Vice-President, in which he accused them of fomenting the revolution, and perhaps even more, by the satirical comment this provoked in the press.[2] The ambassador was frightened and alarmed by criticism levelled at the accuracy of his reports by the President of the Society of the American Colony in Mexico, ex-ambassador David E. Thompson, whose involvement in private business concerns as ambassador had been a matter of some scandal. Wilson wrote to the Department warning them against Thompson, while Judge Wilfley, notorious as an associate of both ambassadors, told the President how utterly unrepresentative the Society was—which was certainly true.[3] However, Wilson was seriously checked in his slide towards intervention when the diplomatic corps failed to adopt his proposals for the 'common defence' of the colonies in case of riots in the city.

He himself told the State Department that this meeting was

[1] Bryce–Grey, 1 May 1911, no. 136 Confidential. FO 371/1147 file 1573/17452.
[2] *The World*, Tuesday, 2 May 1911, editorial: 'Nothing but the Truth'.
[3] L. R. Wilfley–President, 15 May 1911, Confidential; Wilson–Secretary of State, 10 May 1911, no. 535. SDF 812.00/1802.

convoked at the request of the Italian minister, Count Massiglia.[1] But Hohler records that the ambassador put the proposals, and the Spanish, Italian and French ministers supported them. For his own part, he considered a concerted plan to be worse than useless—liable to produce the very dangers it was supposed to meet. The Foreign Office endorsed this view. 'If the British and German colonies hold aloof it will probably upset the U.S. scheme', Spicer wrote; 'this may annoy the U.S. Gov[t] but I don't see that it can be helped.'[2]

President Taft was equally unconcerned by the fact that the revolutionaries had gained a significant advantage by capturing Ciudad Juárez, for he had concluded that it was the duty of the United States to allow arms and ammunition to pass across the frontier. 'This may be,' he commented, 'but it grows out of the weakness or misfortune of the Mexican government, for which we are not responsible.'[3]

On 17 May Wilson was informed by de la Barra that the government had accepted Madero's terms.[4] A new armistice went into effect, and on 21 May a peace treaty was signed—the Treaty of Ciudad Juárez—naming de la Barra for the interim Presidency and designating all but one of the members of his cabinet.[5] The situation was uncertain, and Hohler was offered a legation guard of 250 men by the Japanese minister, which he politely declined.[6] The Japanese were particularly concerned, for the last act of the war had been the capture of the important railway town of Torreón, abandoned by the federal forces, and in the interval the scene of a ghastly massacre of Chinese residents incited by the women of the town whose laundry businesses they had displaced.[7]

Finally as Díaz, seriously ill with a septic jaw, still refused to resign, there was a serious riot in the capital itself, cut short only

[1] Wilson–Secretary of State, 10 May 1911, no. 535. SDF 812.00/1802.

[2] Hohler–Grey, 12 May 1911, Telegram no. 30. FO 371/1147 file 1573/18209.

[3] Taft–Knox, 12 May 1911. SDF 812.00/1808.

[4] Wilson–Secretary of State, Telegram, 17 May 1911, 10 p.m. Strictly Confidential. SDF 812.00/1830.

[5] Wilson–Secretary of State, Telegram, 22 May 1911, 11 a.m. SDF 812.00/1888.

[6] Hohler–Grey, 17 May 1911, no. 95. FO 371/1147 file 1573/20781.

[7] G. C. Carothers, Consular Agent Torreón–Secretary of State, Telegram, 19 May 1911, 6 p.m., 22 May 1911. SDF 812.00/1895, 1968.

by one of those torrential tropical rainstorms common at that season. In the early hours of 25 May the President finally gave way. His resignation was taken to Congress at 3.30 in the afternoon, and accepted unanimously by those very deputies who were so well accustomed to obeying his command. 'Thus ended', recorded Hohler, 'the public career of the most eminent statesman Mexico has ever known, General Porfirio Díaz.' But there was a postscript.

Preparations were made with the utmost secrecy for the departure of President Diaz, one or two Englishmen being invited to assist and giving all the aid that was possible, and he left the City by the Interoceanic Railway at 4 o'clock on the morning of 26th . . . [Hohler said]. He is staying, pending the departure of his steamer, [at Vera Cruz] in the house of an Englishman belonging to the firm of Messrs. Pearson and Son. His intention is to go to Spain on account of the language and the climate, declining for this reason the offer of a residence in England which had been put at his disposition by Lord Cowdray.[1]

John Body wrote to Lord Cowdray to tell him that Fred Adams, the firm's agent in Vera Cruz, had preceded the ex-President in another train; it was anticipated that if Adams was held up 'he would be unmolested on account of carrying a Foreign Government's dispatches' and would have time to warn the train behind. He had been one of the few to know of the plan beforehand. 'You will be surprised to know that even Mr Limantour was not aware of the President [*sic*] impending departure and he had a most unpleasant surprise yesterday when he knew of it.'[2]

The select circle of those who knew, in addition to Body and Adams, comprised E. N. Brown, President of the National Railways, General Victoriano Huerta, commanding the bodyguard, and President de la Barra, who had to be stopped from coming to the station. It also included Hohler himself, as he did not record until he came to write his memoirs.[3] Henry Lane Wilson was not

[1] Hohler–Grey, 27 May 1911, no. 110. FO 371/1148 file 1573/23268.
[2] John B. Body–Lord Cowdray, 27 May 1911, Cowdray Papers.
[3] Hohler, p. 174; cf. for praise of Díaz as a ruler, Andrés Molina Enríquez, *Los Grandes Problemas Nacionales* (Mexico, 1909), p.77: 'Se ve, pues, cuán complexa ha sido la obra del Sr. Gral. Díaz, y cuán complexa he tenido que ser su responsibilidad. Es un hombre único, que en una sola nación, ha tenido que gobernar y ha gobernado sabiamente,

among their number. He attacked the 'undignified flight' violently, being particularly critical of those who, with no thought of the harm it might cause them in the future, had helped the old man to escape. 'Since his arrival at Veracruz General Diaz, with his entire family, has been the guest of an Englishman by the name of Adam [sic], who is the confidential representative of the oil companies of which Lord Cowdry [sic] is President [sic]', he wrote, adding spitefully, and without any foundation for his charge, 'receiving thus during his last days in Mexico the hospitalities of one of the most corrupt influences among the Cientifico group but of whose iniquities he is probably not fully aware.'[1]

In view of the close connection of Lord Cowdray and his firm with the Díaz régime and the antagonism of his American competitors, charges and countercharges like Henry Lane Wilson's were in the course of the next two years to become inextricably interwoven with the conduct of British and American diplomacy in relation to Mexico. The fall of Díaz became the datum point for all future revolutionary movements, and so the sources from which Madero's revolution was financed are uniquely significant to any assessment of the association of future movements with financial interests. It is therefore important to analyse these sources.

The problem is posed for us by the conflicting testimony given before the Smith committee of the United States Senate in late 1912 and early 1913. The hearings of this committee were intended to ascertain whether or not Madero's own movement, and the subsequent revolts against Madero, had been financed from American sources. Sittings of the committee were cut short by the fall of the Madero administration. Consequently the committee did not publish a report, although the evidence was printed verbatim and Senator Smith himself has left at least his own personal impressions derived from the mass of testimony in speeches reported in the press of the day.[2]

muchos pueblos distintos, que han vivido en diferentes períodos de evolución, desde los prehistóricos hasta los modernos.' And this was written by a much more perceptive critic of the Díaz régime than Madero himself!

[1] Wilson–Knox, 31 May 1911, 610 Confidential. SDF 812.00/2037.
[2] United States. Congress. Senate. Committee on Foreign Relations, *Revolutions in Mexico*, etc. (Washington, D.C., 1913); *The World*, Saturday, 28 June 1913.

The quality of the evidence is very uneven. Much of it is hearsay, and the whole is much influenced by the course of contemporary events in Mexico, the unsuccessful efforts of Pascual Orozco and Félix Díaz to gain recognition for their movements giving rise to many claims and opinions of a tendentious nature.

Several witnesses claimed to have no knowledge of any important attempt to finance the revolution from the American side of the frontier, of whom the most significant, though not necessarily the most reliable, was Braulio Hernández, secretary of state of the state of Chihuahua while Abraham González was provisional governor, and an original revolutionary. At the time of his evidence he was a *Vazquista*, and later was one of the first to join the constitutionalist cause.[1]

This evidence is necessarily negative, and there are some very positive statements to contradict it. Some can certainly be discounted as voicing information given them by interested parties. The evidence of two in particular, however, claims special attention. Lawrence F. Converse, who had been a runner for the Maderista forces, was emphatic that Madero himself had told him that he was getting funds from the Standard Oil Company, who would 'back them to the last ditch'. And Juan Pedro Didapp, writer and publicist, formerly of the Mexican diplomatic service, lent support to this view by his disclosures of the activities of the revolutionary attorney in Washington, the lawyer Sherburne G. Hopkins.

On the complicity of the Standard Oil, Didapp was perhaps not entirely convincing in his own right, though with due allowance for exaggeration his estimate was probably not too far wrong in the case of Hopkins. 'He was in communication with all the revolutionists in America,' Didapp pointed out, 'and was connected with the Nicaragua revolution, and when Mr Ancona told me that Mr Hopkins was his attorney I understood perfectly well that the Standard Oil Co. was behind it, because I understand that all the revolutions in Latin America are planned on the eighth floor of the Hibbs Building, in Mr Hopkins's office, in Washing-

---

[1] *Revolutions in Mexico*, pp. 548 ff.

ton.'[1] From this he had 'deduced' that the Standard Oil had given the cause $5,000,000—a sum roughly equivalent to the amount the Mexican Treasury reserves had fallen between the Treaty of Ciudad Juárez and the accession of Madero.[2]

The reason for their interest, Didapp went on to say, was that their subsidiary, the Waters Pierce Co., wanted to destroy their rivals, the Aguila Company, and he told the committee that they had in fact done so, and sold out, 'because Mr Pearson [i.e. Lord Cowdray] has nothing to do with it [the Aguila Company] any more, and he was the controlling power'.

This curious misapprehension may well cause one to distrust the evidence offered on other counts, for Lord Cowdray did not part with his holdings in the Company until 1919.[3] The distinction between what Didapp really knew and what he thought he knew is made clearer, for when he was questioned on his actual relations with Hopkins he explained that he had 'forecast' the revolution in 1910.

I was introduced to Mr Hopkins by a friend of mine in Washington, in order to have him help me in any way, shape or form. I had a talk with Mr Hopkins, four or five talks with him, and Mr Hopkins plainly told me that if I would get next to the secretary of the Standard Oil Co., I would have the help of the Standard Oil Co. to overthrow Diaz . . .

I told him I did not know anybody in the Standard Oil Co. He told me, 'Well, I know the Secretary, and I am going to New York and I will talk the matter over with the secretary of the Standard Oil Co., and then you can try to see him.'

Quite what Didapp might have expected the committee to consider were his motives in this affair is very far from clear. At the

[1] According to *Who Was Who in America*, 1, Hopkins specialized 'in internat. matters and settlements with the Govt. Adviser to several Latin Am. govts.; adviser to provisional govt. of Mexico (Madero), 1911; constitutionalist govt. of Mexico, 1913–14; to provisional govt. of Mexico (de la Huerto [sic]), 1920'.

Hopkins's connection with the revolutionists who overthrew Zelaya is certain. Furthermore, his firm, Hopkins & Hopkins, seems indeed to have been involved in a long sequence of revolutions, reaching as far back as the Chilean Civil War of 1891, when they acted for the Congressional side. T. J. Lawrence–W. T. S. Doyle, 3 December 1911. SDF 812.00/2627.

[2] *Revolutions in Mexico*, pp. 458ff.

[3] Spender, *Weetman [Dickinson] Pearson, First Viscount Cowdray* (1930), p. 203.

date when this was supposed to have taken place Didapp was Mexican consul in Norfolk, Virginia, and in his evidence to the committee he had already stated that he had not in fact joined in the revolution against Díaz because he did not believe in the over-throw of the government by force. It is quite possible that he was an *agent provocateur*, which would greatly reduce the value of the evidence. Unfortunately the members of the committee did not see fit to clear up the contradiction, and in his book, *Los Estados Unidos y nuestros conflictos internos*, published in the city of Mexico in 1913, Didapp gives even less information about his own part, confining himself to an attack on 'North American capitalists', who, he said, had fomented the revolution purely for their own ends.[1]

Braulio Hernández afterwards called Didapp 'an impure liar, an insane sower of darnel'—and swore: 'The truth of God is that the revolution was fought with the abnegation and hunger of the Mexicans, with no more.'[2]

It was inevitable that the committee should cross-examine Sherburne Hopkins at considerable length, but this care did not entirely succeed in separating the question of financing the revolutionary forces from his own role as attorney; nor, perhaps, was it meant to. As attorney, Hopkins was in 'almost daily' con-tact with Gustavo Madero from October 1910 until after the fall of Ciudad Juárez, when he was summoned to Mexico in person for consultations on railroad matters and claims, in his own words 'giving them the best advice [he] knew how to give in regard to the best manner of deposing the Diaz government'. For this advice he stated that he had received the fee of $50,000, which he believed probably came from the $300,000 (Mexican $600,000) paid to Gustavo by the government of the *interinato* to settle revolution-ary debts. He was paid during his visit to Mexico.

He stated that a month after the fall of Díaz he was first em-ployed by the Waters Pierce Oil Company to 'expose' the 'crooked practices' by which, he alleged, the Pearson concessions had been obtained. After trying to maintain—somewhat un-

[1] Didapp, *Los Estados Unidos y nuestros conflictos internos* (1913), p. 12.
[2] *Revolutions in Mexico*, p. 567.

convincingly—that the sole motive behind this had been to inform the Mexican public of how their government had been run by the *científicos*, Hopkins had to admit, under close examination by Senator Hitchcock, that it was not 'for any idealistic purpose, or purpose of public benefaction', but 'among other things, to even up conditions'. He had been employed by the company, in its corporate capacity. The senators also elicited that as a result of the revolution there had in fact been no change in the status of the company, nor, for that matter, had there been any action against Lord Cowdray.

The so-called exposures were detailed in a further sitting. They are already familiar to us from their appearance in *The World*. No doubt Mr Hopkins gave them a certain air of conviction when he went on to say that he believed that Cowdray had a contract with the Standard Oil Company; he added that Doheny and Canfield were also said to have an 'understanding' with this compromising source of finance, while he put it on record that the Waters Pierce Oil Company was divorcing itself from Standard Oil and had in fact 'done more than anyone else to keep the Standard out of Mexico'.

As for the financing of the revolution, Hopkins said that he did not believe that it cost the Maderos themselves more than $400,000 gold. Others, he agreed, must have spent money derived from other sources; others had certainly 'helped themselves' to supplies of money and kind. But the aggregate cost could not have been in excess of $1,500,000 U.S. Senator McCumber was incredulous. He asked: 'And you think you can finance a successful revolution in a country of that size for less than a million dollars?' To which Hopkins replied, 'Yes.' His estimate must be taken seriously, for there can be no doubt of his connection with the revolution, even though it is certainly very doubtful whether his advice was worth the high fee paid for it.[1]

The charges of Didapp concerning Standard Oil were, however, refuted by Hopkins out of hand. Nevertheless, they had been often repeated. The amount of money supposed to have been received from 'the millionaires of Wall Street' ran as high as the

[1] *Revolutions in Mexico*, pp. 743 ff.

$14,000,000 denounced in the Orozco manifesto, though another political opponent of Madero quoted a rather more reasonable figure of $5,000,000.[1] Römer considered in 1929 that the balance of the evidence pointed to a major role being played in the revolution by American interests, especially Waters Pierce, and this view has been reiterated in the last few years by the new school of Soviet historians.[2]

Most prominent among the accusers was Henry Lane Wilson. His memoirs, published in 1927, include the following passage:

Financial assistance was obtained from certain sources in the United States and Europe, notably from Paris and Frankfort-on-the-Main. The records of the Department of Justice of the United States carry revelations connecting Gustavo Madero with an oil company doing business in Mexico and with the active agents of an arms company in Washington. Many events during the Madero régime abundantly confirmed the rumours that were in general circulation in the early stages of the revolution. With this aid efforts at organization and discipline were made, and victories of an unimportant character, largely exaggerated by the press, were gained.[3]

Wilson was naturally concerned to show the unimportance of the movement, and victories that topple governments, however trivial, can scarcely be regarded as unimportant. The reference to the arms company can be ignored, for the purchase of arms may be considered a legitimate revolutionary activity. It is the degree of connection with the oil company that demands attention.

Now the charge made by Wilson was not new. Bell had heard of it, and wrote: 'One may hear ... that the Waters Pierce Oil Company financed Madero's operations, and that a document proving this is on file at Washington. It is needless to say that the document, as described by ex-Ambassador Wilson, would fall far short of proving anything.' But Bell could have little real proof, except for his knowledge of Wilson, and although his view

[1] Letcher–Knox, 3 April 1912, no. 177. SDF 812.00/3539; Colina, p. 51.
[2] Hans G. Römer, *Amerikanische Interessen- und Prinzipienpolitik in Mexiko 1910–1914: Ein Beitrag zur Kritik des Wilsonismus* (Hamburg, 1929), p. 21 footnote; M. S. Alperóvich and B. T. Rudenko, *La Revolución Mexicana de 1910–1917 y la política de los Estados Unidos* (Mexico, 1960), pp. 88–90.
[3] Wilson, *Diplomatic Episodes in Mexico, Belgium and Chile* (1927), p. 206.

was accepted by Calcott, Vagts, Cumberland and other writers, it was by no means conclusive.[1]

The true story, as recorded in the State Department files, was certainly sordid. On 18 April 1911 a certain Mr C. R. Troxel approached two brothers, T. B. and Ed. B. Cunningham, in the Sheldon Hotel, El Paso, Texas. He 'stated that he was representing a company who would furnish the insurrectos with from $500,000.00 to $1,000,000.00 on the condition that the insurrectos would issue to his company 6% gold bonds and a certain commercial concession which his company would ask of the insurrectos'. One of the brothers was an informant for an agent of the Department of Justice, and later told the agent that he knew that Troxel was an agent of the Standard Oil Company. The brothers introduced him to a Mr J. V. Smith whom they knew to be an agent of the revolutionary party. Their discussion was held in private, at the request of Troxel, but afterwards Smith told the brothers 'that he thought the party was OK and had showed him his credentials as to who he was and also showed him a letter from John D. Archbold of the Standard Oil Company, authorizing him to make contracts'. The terms had been sent off to Madero.

The revolutionary agent explained the motives of the company.

Smith stated that the Standard Oil Co. has concession of the same nature in Mexico, but that these concessions had been cancelled by the federal government and that they were now operating through the Waters Pierce Oil Co, and that the federal government was imposing on the Waters Pierce Oil Co. by assessing them with unreasonable taxes.

The following day, in a Turkish Bath, a group including Luis Hernández considered a draft contract, and sent a telegram to Francisco Vázquez Gómez in Washington to secure his consent. After it had been signed by Madero it would have to be negotiated by him in New York.

[1] Bell, p. 48; also quoted by Wilfrid Hardy Callcott, *Liberalism in Mexico, 1857–1929* (Stanford, Calif., 1931), p. 197. Vagts, *Mexico, Europa und Amerika unter besonderer Berücksichtigung der Petroleumpolitik* (1928), p. 162 footnote; Cumberland, *Mexican Revolution: Genesis under Madero* (1952), p. 194.

Reports on all these events were transmitted to the Secretary of State by Attorney-General Wickersham on 26 April in a letter which concluded: 'I would suggest that this matter is of sufficient importance to justify its communication to the Mexican Embassy, unless for some reason you should deem it best not to act accordingly.' For some reason, the Secretary of State did not, but a copy was sent to Henry Lane Wilson on 2 May for his 'confidential information merely'.[1]

A few days later the State Department were further informed that Vázquez Gómez had advised Madero to act on the contract, and on 2 May there came a detailed report of further developments. At a meeting in the Zeiger Hotel the informant met with J. V. Smith, Luis Hernández and J. J. Bennett, and they learned from Hernández that Alfonso Madero, now staying at the Sheldon Hotel, had been appointed financial agent of the revolution in place of Vázquez Gómez, and Luis Hernández had become assistant financial agent. Hernández had the approval of Francisco I. Madero for the negotiations, and Alfonso was prepared to act on it.

The participants in the negotiations were not forgotten. Troxel was to get a commission of 5 per cent, and this was to be divided equally among them. 'It was then agreed that nothing should be said to any of the Madero [*sic*] in regard to this 5% commission, it being paid by the Standard Oil Co.' Luis Hernández had another offer. They were to receive 'all of the hides which should come from the cattle used by the insurrecto forces', but it was agreed that Troxel was not to be allowed to participate in this, nor in the monopoly of the supply of arms and ammunition to the revolutionary forces which had also been offered.

The following day they met Alfonso Madero and a telegram was despatched to Toyah, Texas, to summon Troxel, who was expected to arrive on 27 April.[2]

The State Department was at last stirred to action. On 10 April Knox saw the President and obtained his approval for the dis-

[1] Wickersham–Secretary of State, 26 April 1911, 90755–782, Confidential. SDF 812.00/1503, with Knox–Wilson, 2 May 1911, no. 323 Confidential.
[2] Wickersham–Secretary of State, 28 April 1911, 90755–789, Confidential; 2 May 1911, 90755–810, Strictly Confidential. SDF 812.00/1542, 1593.

patch of a letter to the active head of the Standard Oil Company, John D. Archbold, informing him that the Department had in its possession 'information of a most serious character' which it would have disregarded as rumour 'were it not for the fact that the information comes with such a wealth of particulars and details, including names of negotiators, the amounts involved, and the proposed terms . . .'. Archbold was briskly reminded that in the event of the revolutionaries failing to hold to their obligations the company would have no legal remedy. At the same time, the Attorney-General was asked to direct 'a vigorous investigation of the matter' to determine whether or not the neutrality statutes had been infringed.[1]

Something, undoubtedly, had already leaked out. In his famous interview on arrival at Santander on 26 April Vice-President Ramón Corral had directly charged American financial interests, and the American press had specifically referred to Standard Oil.[2] It is not unlikely that there was a leak from the company of amateur conspirators at El Paso, or from the Maderist camp before Ciudad Juárez. It is even possible that Henry Lane Wilson had passed on some or all of his confidential information to the Mexican government.

On 2 May, in the park at El Paso, Troxel met Gustavo Madero. Gustavo wanted to close the deal on the basis that the government could cancel the concessions at any time by handing back the principal. Troxel was not prepared to agree to these terms, but agreed that after five years the concessions could be cancelled at any time by paying a higher rate of interest, and Gustavo was prepared to accept this. The key question was to follow. 'Troxel asked Madero if in case they came to terms of peace they would not want the money. Madero answered that they would not, but there was no chance at this time of having peace, as the main thing in making the armistice was to enable the insurrectos to prepare arms, ammunition and finances.'[3]

Troxel then left for Austin, Texas, due to return to El Paso the

[1] SDF 812.00/1593.
[2] Wilson–Secretary of State, 29 April 1911, no. 508. SDF 812.00/1618; also 1593.
[3] Wickersham–Secretary of State, 8 May 1911, Strictly Confidential. SDF 812.00/1679.

following Tuesday, 9 May. He did not return. On 10 May Ciudad Juárez fell to the revolutionaries. On 15 May John D. Archbold wrote to Knox to deny his company's involvement, and enclosed a denial of other reports including some alleged to have been made in the British press before 4 April. A representative, Mr Wm. H. Libby, visited Washington and had two interviews with the Attorney-General, on 17 and 19 May, following which he dispatched what the company claimed to be the only exchange of correspondence with Mr Troxel: an unimportant exchange concerning some oil samples from Mexico, dated in January 1910. This, he said, was the sole relationship that any officer of the company had had with Troxel.[1]

From this, the sum of the evidence available, clear conclusions emerge which do not support the allegation of Henry Lane Wilson. First, if Troxel was in fact acting on his own, it is difficult to see what he stood to gain, unless he was in fact a spy for the Mexican government or an *agent provocateur*. This would be quite in keeping with the methods of the *Porfiriato*, but it would not implicate the Standard Oil Company. Secondly, if Troxel was a concealed agent for Standard Oil, perhaps operating on behalf of the Waters Pierce Oil Company so that the company could disclaim him with legal truthfulness, the knowledge that he was *brulé* would have been sufficient to end the negotiations for the time being. However, before Knox's letter was written, Ciudad Juárez had fallen, and, as Gustavo was said to have pointed out, once the revolutionary party was on the point of success it then attained, it would no longer need the loan.

This loan, then, was never concluded. But it is equally clear from the course of the negotiations that no previous loan of this nature had been concluded, for in that case the elaborate series of introductions and negotiations at increasingly significant levels would have been quite superfluous. Indeed, the clear need of the revolutionaries for further large sums, so well documented, would be incomprehensible.

Where, then, did the funds of the Madero revolution come

[1] John D. Archbold–Knox, 15 May 1911; Wickersham–Secretary of State, 24 May 1911. SDF 812.00/1796, 1942.

from? Bell makes it clear that, apart from the Madero family fortune on behalf of which no claims were later made on the Treasury, the principal source of money was found by Gustavo Madero, who embezzled the funds subscribed by a French company for the construction of a railway in the state of Zacatecas. This fact was well known to the Díaz government, and they naturally made it one of their main points for attack on the foundations of the revolutionary movement. It was for the repayment of this money that the *interinato* made the settlement, through Hopkins, of claims totalling some $650,000 Mexican on behalf of Gustavo Madero a matter of the first priority, and the secrecy with which it was necessarily done furnished a fresh pretext for attack by the opponents of the new régime.[1]

The State Department files do not disclose the true nature of the sources from which the revolutionary funds derived. It is now possible, however, to produce independent evidence in support of Bell's view, and evidence which is contemporary with the events described. The Madero papers have been analysed.[2] But the true state of affairs was known to at least one foreign representative, as Hohler's report of 1 April 1911 shows. 'Madero himself found about $100,000, and he obtained between $300,000 and $400,000 from various of his relatives', he reported. Gustavo's embezzlement he estimated at some $500,000, proceedings having already been initiated by the French agent for the company, M. Charbonneau. 'A certain amount', he added, 'has been obtained from American sympathisers, but they are private people and of no great consequence. There are one or two Jews in San Antonio, Texas, who have been specially active: one named Riesenberg is the principal.'[3]

One last point is interesting, without being decisive. The rumours of Standard Oil involvement in the revolution were first published in England. This does not necessarily mean that they originated there, although it may or may not be decisive that two years later the strongest belief in the theory was held by British

[1] Bell, pp. 89–94.
[2] Cumberland, pp. 131, 154.
[3] No. 52, FO 371/1146 file 1573/14296; cf. Vasconcelos, p. 261.

oil men in the Tampico area. The British popular press, like the American, was quite ready to publish rumour as fact. One cannot, by the nature of the case, be certain that the rumours originated in Mexico, but it does seem very likely.[1]

[1] Consul Miller of Tampico told the State Department on 8 May 1911 that the allegations that Waters Pierce had aided the Madero revolution were probably originated by Pearsons's. No. 261. SDF 812.00/1781.

CHAPTER 3

MADERO

British and American views of the interim government of President de la Barra differed markedly. Hohler was enthusiastic about its qualities and achievements from beginning to end.[1] This feeling was not shared by Wilson, who from the outset regarded it as potentially weak and contaminated with dangerous men and 'altruistic, if not socialistic', doctrines.[2] The former was rewarded by close contact with the administration and a friendly relationship with the President; the latter was not.

That the two men did not come into conflict over these differences must be very largely attributed to Hohler's discretion. It was less easy to conceal the fact that their views on the situation at large in the country were almost equally opposed.

Wilson saw everywhere 'rapine, violence, looting and the collapse of organized government'. He believed the states of Morelos, Guerrero, Sinaloa, Puebla and Michoacán to be 'in a state of complete anarchy'. He had become, and wished the State Department to become, 'reconciled to the view that Mexico is entering upon a long period of turbulence and political unrest, and that she will continue to be a subject and a problem' for the United States Government.[3]

Hohler reported to Sir Edward Grey that the state of the country seemed 'surprisingly good', and that the most encouraging sign was that the revolutionary party were co-operating with the government for the 'exemplary punishment of brigands'. This drew the comment from one member of the Foreign Office, C. F. J. Dormer, 'Satisfactory—a little shooting will probably stop the brigandage.'[4] The chargé had doubts, of course, about the future, and in particular about the qualities of Madero himself. But he was satisfied that the warmth of the latter's reception

[1] Hohler–Grey, 27 May 1911, no. 111. FO 371/1148 file 1573/23269.
[2] Wilson–Knox, 23 May 1911, no. 578 Confidential. SDF 812.00/1981.   [3] *Ibid.*
[4] Hohler–Grey, 29 May 1911, no. 114. FO 371/1148 file 1573/23272.

at his triumphal entry into the capital on 7 June indicated that his popularity was capable of sustaining peace until the next leader of Mexico had time to emerge.[1]

It was significant, however, that the ambassador's views were similarly modified by this spectacle. Many years later, he stated that on that day he had dictated a dispatch to his government 'predicting a continuance of the revolution and the probable ultimate downfall of the Madero government. This prediction', he added, 'was based upon the substantial ground of the natural tendencies of the Mexican masses to disorder and lawlessness and the inadequacy of the platform and the policies of Madero in meeting the tendencies.'[2] No such dispatch appears to exist. That of 13 June 1911, dealing with the triumphal entry, while reporting that Madero intended to follow no 'well mapped course' and that he was to receive the support of General Reyes, said nothing of the future.[3] That of 23 June, which does make predictions, specifically states that with the arrival of Madero dangers from the Madero revolution are to be considered at an end, while warning the State Department that there may be *new* revolutionary movements, thus clearly indicating that *at the time* Wilson did not foresee 'a continuance of the revolution'. Nor, alas! did he predict 'the probable ultimate downfall of the Madero government', but only the rise of a 'formidable opposition' to Madero himself, who had some months to go before undergoing the ordeal of the polls.[4] Finally, though the ambassador did make a prediction of a long period of turbulence on 23 May, as noted above, this dispatch was sent before Madero's entry, when the revolutionary leader was still very much an unknown quantity.

This modification, however, was confined to events in the capital. Elsewhere, the ambassador still saw 'brigandage, rapine and violence, of the most repugnant and barbarous type', that is, that involving the appropriation of 'lands, chattels and wives' of 'higher conditioned neighbours'. This view should be regarded

[1] Hohler–Grey, 8 June 1911, no. 125. FO 371/1148 file 1573/24749; see also O'Shaughnessy, *Diplomatic Days*, p. 53.

[2] Wilson, *Diplomatic Episodes in Mexico, Belgium and Chile* (1927), p. 226.

[3] Wilson–Knox, 13 June 1911, no. 654. SDF 812.00/2142.

[4] Wilson–Knox, 23 June 1911, no. 671 Confidential. SDF 812.00/2181.

with proper suspicion. A consular report bears witness that all was quiet in Tabasco at the time the ambassador was writing that it was in a state of upheaval.[1] Morelos and Guerrero were certainly beginning to stir with the agrarian ferment. The peasants there did indeed take over the properties of their (generally absentee) *hacendados*. This movement was, however, very limited in geographical extent. There was certainly no justification for Wilson writing, as he did, that disturbances of a similar kind were rife throughout the states of Veracruz, Sonora, Chihuahua, Tamaulipas, Durango and Puebla.

The ambassador tended to see too much significance in the attitudes of groups such as the old aristocracy and the Church, whose political importance the Díaz régime had kept to a minimum, and in the daily grumbles of the foreign community. But most of all his picture of the situation was distorted by his persistent belief that the interim government was 'Maderist'.[2]

Madero, the triumphant leader of the victorious revolution, was still only a private citizen. His name was the key to everything, but his supporters were a mixed lot, in which the old revolutionaries had been almost swamped by the sudden accession of opportunists and would-be office-holders, who were quite ready to pledge it to any project which caught their fancy.[3] The problem was that Madero was not in a position to 'deliver'. Bell says that 'from the day Madero entered Mexico City, de la Barra was president in name only'.[4] Unhappily this was far from true. De la Barra was not a Díaz, but he was President. He did not use his powers to prevent such characteristic innovations as freedom of the press, open political discussion, and the like. Nor did he

[1] Cf. Consul Lespinasse–Secretary of State, 18 June 1911, no. 131. SDF 812.00/2185.
[2] The whole significance of the *interinato* was that it was not Maderist.
[3] 'From Paris the white-bearded and pompous General Bernardo Reyes announced that he was hurrying back to crush the Revolution. By the time he reached Havana its progress led him instead to offer it his services. He was admitted to Mexico on pledging his loyalty to the Madero régime. Four months later when he found his presidential prospects unpromising he revolted against it' (Gruening, *Mexico and its Heritage* (1928), p. 302; see also Bell, *The Political Shame of Mexico* (1914), p. 113; O'Shaughnessy, *Diplomatic Days*, p. 37).
[4] Bell, p. 109; but see also Manuel Calero, *Un Decenio de Política Mexicana* (New York, 1920), p. 70: 'Madero no concebía el gobierno del Sr. De la Barra sino como la antecámara de su propio gobierno.'

restrain—at first, at any rate—the activities of the Maderist ministers with whom he had been 'issued' under the Treaty of Ciudad Juárez. But Madero could not exercise the powers of government on his behalf.

In the country there was hostility between the regular army and the revolutionary forces. Madero himself, with his strong belief in constitutionalism, held that the moment for armed revolt had passed with the treaty, and that his followers should now disband and return to their homes. The conservative members of the cabinet also preferred to disband the revolutionary forces, with the threat to order that they represented, and to depend on the regular army. However, many revolutionaries, notably among the cabinet the brothers Vázquez Gómez, feared that if this were permitted to happen the revolution would be betrayed and its gains speedily lost.

In this situation it was the radical Emilio Vázquez [Gómez] who, as Secretary of *Gobernación*, held the responsibility for the maintenance of public order. Instead of using the regular troops to disband the revolutionaries, as some hoped he would do, he chose to pay them off handsomely. This had unexpected consequences. Men, once disbanded, took up arms again to be disbanded a second or even third time, and the cost to the Treasury was incalculable.[1] Meanwhile, the Secretary used all his efforts to entrench the revolution in the state governments by replacing *Porfiristas* in official positions and using all the power of the government to influence the state elections. His methods worked, but at a price. The machinery of government crumbled,[2] and the dismissed employees swelled the throng of the discontented.[3]

The crisis came before the end of June over the question of the status of the person and forces of Emiliano Zapata, the leader of the agrarian revolt in Morelos. He had received a commission from Madero, and styled himself leader of the forces of the revolutionary army of the south. His men, however, because of the agrarian motives that prompted them, were less concerned

[1] Hohler–Bryce, 16 June 1911. Bryce Papers USA 31 folio 253.
[2] Hohler–Bryce, 27 June 1911. Bryce Papers USA 31 folio 262.
[3] Hohler–Grey, 4 July 1911, no. 149. FO 371/1148 file 1573/28120; 23 June 1911, no. 137. FO 371/1150 file 26877.

with spreading the doctrines of the revolution outside their home state than with overthrowing the landlords and holding and cultivating the lands they succeeded in expropriating. To conservatives, foreigners and onlookers he was therefore a 'notorious bandit'.

Madero himself, however, considered the Zapatistas to be brothers-in-arms against the tyranny of Díaz, and expected them to co-operate with him in his plans for the reforming government, which included agrarian reform. He met the southern leader and formally appointed him commander of the revolutionary forces in his state. So great was the outcry that Madero was forced to summon Zapata to the capital, where, after an interview, it was announced that he had declined the post as he had to take the waters for 'a serious gastric complaint'. Hohler, who had been among those who had lodged protests with the government on behalf of 'a Mrs Norman King, a very respectable English lady' whose hotel in Cuernavaca had been threatened with destruction, remarked drily: 'It is said that he was presented with a sum of one hundred thousand dollars to defray the expenses of his cure.'[1]

This, and other incidents, convinced Hohler that lawlessness was growing.[2] The claims commission set up by the government proved to be dilatory and inefficient, but the number of genuine cases it had to handle was surprisingly low.[3] Nevertheless it was clear that the policy of conciliation—some called it bribery—was proving an expensive failure. At this point Hohler had an interview with the President, in which de la Barra spoke very freely about the problems confronting him, and of his desire to resign.

'I expressed the strongest hope that His Excellency would not

[1] Hohler–Grey, 28 June 1911, no. 142. FO 371/1148 file 1573/27072. This incident is not recorded by Mrs King, although she does mention Hohler and speaks highly of him in connection with a similar appeal in 1915. See Rosa E. King, *Tempest over Mexico, a Personal Chronicle* (London, 1936), especially p. 285.

A sympathetic source for the life of Zapata (in English) is: H. H. Dunn, *The Crimson Jester, Zapata of Mexico* (London, 1934); see also Baltasar Dromundo, *Emiliano Zapata* (México, 1934). As Zapata's motives are traditionally represented, both by apologists and by accusers, as being economic ones, it is of more than passing interest to note that as late as 14 August 1911 his demands on the government were entirely political. Archivo Madero, caja no. 4, hoja 0938 (00101).

[2] See below, note 1, p. 90.

[3] Hohler–Grey, 7 July 1911, no. 153. FO 371/1148 file 1573/28993.

think of resigning as I told him plainly he was the one man in whom all parties, and all persons whether foreigners or Mexicans, had confidence and in whom were centred practically all existing guarantees for law and order', Hohler reported, and his concern must have been the greater for knowing that it was Emilio Vázquez who stood next in the line of succession!

He explained the extreme difficulty of the position he had been occupying, acting as a link between the Diaz Administration and the theories and ideas of Madero: he had at last definitely told Madero that his (Madero's) influence was waning and his prestige failed to provide the necessary guarantees for order, and that unless he (Señor de la Barra) was left to act with an entirely free hand, he must lay down the Presidency and cast the full responsibility for public affairs upon Madero.

Madero replied that he would unreservedly submit himself to Señor de la Barra's authority, and now His Excellency intends to adopt a new policy.[1]

Clearly this was a crucial moment in the history of the *interinato*. But what was the new policy? The full use of the powers of the government to crush brigandage, if necessary by armed force. To carry it out, significant changes would have to be made in the administration: the replacement of the Secretaries of *Gobernación* and of War and Marine, of the Chief of Police in the City of Mexico, and of the Chief of *Rurales*. By the Treaty of Ciudad Juárez all these posts had been given to revolutionaries with the exception of the Secretary of War and Marine, whom de la Barra had been allowed to appoint himself. It would therefore require all the President's skill and diplomacy to alter them without precipitating a schism with the revolutionary movement, for every step was likely to be seen as counter-revolutionary.

The Foreign Office had no doubt that de la Barra's course was the right one, while Henry Lane Wilson commented: '. . . This decision of the President might have been taken to the great advantage of the country a week or two ago.'[2] In fact, by the time he was told of it, it *had* been taken a week previously, which casts

[1] Hohler–Grey, 14 July 1911, no. 161 Confidential. FO 371/1150 file 30078.
[2] Wilson–Knox, 18 July 1911, no. 729. SDF 812.00/2230.

an interesting light on his relations with the government. But neither he nor Hohler seems to have appreciated the magnitude of the task.

'The President found many obstacles in the way of the changes which he desired to make, and which he had thought he would be able to put through in a day or two. It was three or four days before he could get rid of the Minister of War [*sic*] and that Department is now entrusted to General José González Salas, with the rank of Under Secretary', wrote Hohler on 27 July.[1] Yet de la Barra had replaced his own nominee by a Maderista! When he came to replace the Chief of *Rurales* by a *Porfirista* and the revolutionary Secretary of *Gobernación* by Alberto García Granados, who was the President's closest personal friend but had a bad reputation among the Maderistas as a reactionary, he met with even greater resistance.

The new Chief of *Rurales* was accepted by the revolutionaries only after he had visited Madero at his retreat at Tehuacán 'for the purpose of obtaining pontifical confirmation of his appointment'. Emilio Vázquez, on whom Hohler correctly laid the responsibility for what he called 'the weakness and inactivity of the Government' in face of the general unrest, was even more formidable.[2] The perseverance of the President was finally rewarded on 2 August by the receipt of his letter of resignation. This was couched in militant terms, stating clearly that he was submitting it only at the request of the President; his followers were so incensed that they marched on Chapultepec 'in arms', though Madero sent a telegram to the press commending the President's action and censuring those of the fallen Secretary, of whom Hohler wrote: 'His acts have been as illegal as any of those of the ex-President Diaz, and he has not even taken the pains to cloke them as did Diaz with the semblance of the law . . .'[3]

By this time Wilson had gone on leave. The American chargé d'affaires, Fred Dearing, wrote: 'Mr Madero also has acted with

---

[1] Hohler–Grey, 27 July 1911, no. 178. FO 371/1150 file 31154.

[2] Hohler–Grey, 3 August 1911, no. 187. FO 371/1150 file 32135.

[3] This remark is in itself significant as showing how opinions about the Díaz régime changed unconsciously after its fall. Statement by Madero, 2 August 1911. Archivo Madero, caja no. 1, hoja 0098.

much decision and discretion and given another proof of his disinterested patriotism.'[1] In fact he roundly denounced Vázquez as
one of those who had only joined the revolution when it was all
but over.[2] When the government clumsily arrested 102 of his
supporters, the ex-Secretary was decisively alienated from the
Maderist movement and headed a campaign to set up anti-re-
electionist clubs in his own name. The subsequent defeat of his
authentic revolutionary brother, Francisco Vázquez Gómez, by the
hitherto almost unknown José María Pino Suárez of Yucatán, for
the Vice-Presidential nomination of Madero's new party, the
Progressive Constitutional Party, made the breach with the radical
wing of the revolution complete.[3]

Madero, however, got very little credit for his statesmanship,
for almost at once it was his fate to come into conflict with the
'strong' policy of the new Secretary of *Gobernación*. García
Granados had dispatched three columns of troops to the area of
Jojutla, which the Zapatistas were reputed to be sacking and looting. He had had the full approval of the President. Madero had
offered to negotiate with Zapata. Hohler believed he did so to
avoid the loss of the state of Morelos at the Presidential elections;
but it is difficult to see how, if Morelos was as disturbed as his
dispatches imply, anyone could even have considered holding
elections there. In any case, motives apart, his intervention was unwelcome and the offer was rejected by the largely anti-Maderista
cabinet. Nevertheless Madero went to meet Zapata, and from
Cuautla, on 18 August, telegraphed to the President that a settlement had been reached.

This alone would have been disturbing, if not entirely unexpected, but the telegram also included a denunciation of the
General, Victoriano Huerta, who was leading one of the columns
and who, Madero claimed, had endangered his life by allowing
the troops to advance while he was crossing into Zapatista
territory. He also claimed, in a speech delivered immediately
afterwards, that Huerta was working in conjunction with General

[1] Dearing–Knox, 5 August 1911, no. 775. SDF 812.00/2268.
[2] Hohler–Grey, 10 August 1911, no. 192. FO 371/1150 file 33598.
[3] Dearing–Knox, 4 September 1911, no. 887, SDF 812.00/2345; Vázquez Gómez,
passim; Hohler–Grey, 6 September 1911, no. 205, FO 371/1150 file 37236.

Reyes to establish a tyranny. Zapata—'that most valiant and most upright soldier of the revolution'—was saving the country from this fate by opposing the generals, he said.

The sensation caused by the telegram and the speech was very great [Hohler recorded]. Although he [Madero] had no official capacity, and was treating with Zapata only in his character of a private citizen, yet as 'chief of the revolution' it was impossible for the Government to ignore his recommendation completely and it would not have been wise to attempt to do so. They were much chagrined, I understand, at finding their plans checked by the intervention of Madero, but they issued orders to the troops to advance no further . . .

For the third time the Zapatistas were solemnly disarmed. As the British chargé noted, however, even the papers which normally supported Madero seemed to 'find it a little difficult to give to him their entire approval'.[1] The American military attaché, Captain Burnside, was even more outspoken. The officers, he claimed, universally believed that Madero, as a private citizen, had been presumptuous and 'a marplot'.[2]

Hohler, however, did present the case for the apologists for Madero,[3] as Dearing did not. This is particularly interesting, since from the beginning he had been devastatingly critical of his personal characteristics.

. . . He is [a] wretched insignificant little figure of a man of very mean appearance [he wrote to Bryce]—a big head with bulging upper part while his little mean features occupy only the lower quarter of it. He is a spiritualist, a teetotaller, a vegetarian, a homoeopath, and to judge from the few minutes talk I had with him, a windbag. It is wonderful how circumstances have brought such a man as he appears to be to his present heights, and I have great difficulty in believing that he will last.[4]

He had still not changed this opinion thirty years later.[5] In contrast, Henry Lane Wilson was relatively sympathetic. The fact that the revolutionary leader had declared at a banquet that a

[1] Hohler–Grey, 24 August 1911, no. 198. 26 August 1911, no. 199 Confidential. FO 371/1150 files 35213, 35718. Madero–Juan Sánchez Azcona, 25 October 1911, Archivo Madero, caja no. 3, hoja 0517.
[2] Dearing–Secretary of State, Telegram, 23 August 1911, 6 p.m. SDF 812.00/2304.
[3] Hohler–Grey, 2 September 1911, no. 201. FO 371/1150 file 36538.
[4] Hohler–Bryce, 16 June 1911, *cit. sup.* p. 88.   [5] Hohler, p. 177.

speech made by the ambassador would be the basis of his programme when he became President, certainly had much to do
with it.[1]

He is insignificant in appearance, of diffident manners and hesitating
speech, and seems to be highly nervous and uncertain as to his course
in regard to many important public questions [Wilson had written].
He has, however, one redeeming feature—a pair of excellent eyes,
which indicate to me earnestness, truthfulness and loyalty, and, it may
be, reserves of strength and force of character which time may more
fully reveal.[2]

Madero still enjoyed this sympathy when he became President.
For at the elections in October he achieved an overwhelming
victory. His most formidable rival, General Reyes, proved to be
'a lath painted to look like iron', as Wilson put it, in the celebrated
phrase originally used of Lord Salisbury and ascribed to Bismarck.
'His campaign has revealed this flamboyant person in his true
character of an opera-bouffe soldier and patriot and his candidacy
seems to have lost the support...of the army and to have become
a by-word and a jest in the arena of politics', he wrote.[3] At
last, the best he and Emilio Vázquez could do was to leave the
country ostentatiously, which, by a coincidence, they both did on
the same day.[4]

'...It is certain, at all events, that never before in the history of
Mexico have any elections taken place under circumstances of so
much freedom and impartiality', wrote Hohler. 'They were undoubtedly, very far indeed from perfection, but they were un-
questionably a great advance on any that have gone before.'[5]

[1] L. R. Wilfley–President Taft, 11 July 1911. SDF 812.00/2224.
[2] Wilson–Knox, 11 July 1911, Confidential. SDF 812.00/2219. The ambassador's remark
about Madero's eyes is interesting in view of Bell's comment that there was 'little fire'
in them (Bell, p. 112). It is confirmed, however, by contemporary portraits, notably the
magnificent one in the Sala de la Revolución Mexicana de 1910 at Chapultepec. Bell
adds: 'The caricaturists found his beard the salient feature, but it was really very
ordinary, a plain, small beard of a brownish tinge, a little lighter than his hair, [and] in
appearance and manner he was the reverse of impressive'; and admits that, although he
was one of the few people who had heard Madero's 'curbstone' lectures before 1909, he
was still at a loss to account for his magnetism.
[3] Wilson–Knox, 22 September 1911, Confidential. SDF 812.00/2384.
[4] They also both went to the United States, but their subsequent revolts were in no way
connected, though equally futile.
[5] Hohler–Grey, 4 October 1911, no. 217. FO 371/1150 file 41409.

Wilson, on the other hand, though he said at the time only that 'little comprehension of voting methods existed', came to the conclusion after the vote of the Electoral College was known that the election of Pino Suárez had been secured 'by the exercise of methods closely resembling those of General Diaz during his regime'.[1] The ambassador, it seems certain, had hoped that de la Barra, who had been nominated for the Vice-Presidency against his will by the Catholic party, would remain under the new government as a conservative influence, while it was well known that the Yucatecan held views much more radical than those of Madero. Hohler summarized the weakness of the case Wilson put forward as fact:

Señor Madero is being hotly criticised in the press for so warmly espousing the candidature of Señor Pino Suarez for the Vice Presidency, but the criticism seems to me feeble, for the critics can bring forward no case of the candidature being pressed by force or illegal means, and are therefore driven to describe the 'imposition' of Pino Suarez as a 'moral illegality'.

With no further untoward incident,[2] Madero was sworn in as President on 6 November 1911.

Even before reaching the capital, Madero had shown goodwill towards foreign interests and had said that he would welcome an increase of American investment. In the words of Mrs O'Shaughnessy: 'It sounds almost too reasonable to be true',[3] was the general American reaction. It was, of course, widely believed, even among Americans, that his movement had been financed from American sources. Then doubts began to reappear, from a different direction. Madero might want more American investment. But would he be strong enough to safeguard it?

Significantly, after Madero's intervention in the operations

---

[1] Wilson–Secretary of State, Telegram, 2 October 1911, 2 p.m.; Wilson–Knox, 27 October 1911, no. 1034 Confidential. SDF 812.00/2393, 2453.

[2] Hohler–Grey, 16 October 1911, no. 221. FO 371/1150 file 41409. But see Hohler–Grey, 28 October 1911, no. 231 Confidential, FO 371/1150 file 44893; Wilson–Secretary of State, Telegram, 28 October 1911, 1 p.m., SDF 812.00/2443; Hohler–Grey, 7 November 1911, no. 239, FO 371/1150 file 47274; cf. Prida, *From Despotism to Anarchy*, p. 68.

[3] O'Shaughnessy, *Diplomatic Days*, p. 55.

against Zapata, Dearing wrote: 'Business men express anxiety and certain of my colleagues seem to feel that everything else being equal they cannot trust him to guarantee foreign lives and interests as against the unintelligent demands of the proletariat.'[1]

In the British case, these demands took the form of requests for the annulment of Lord Cowdray's concessions, and this feeling of hostility towards interests closely identified with the old régime was carefully cultivated by Waters Pierce. Yet John B. Body was able to write to Lord Cowdray on 14 June: 'I have naturally been most anxious to ascertain the feeling of the new party towards us, and am assured that it is not unfriendly. Quite the contrary is the case with the Bancaria.'[2]

Those members of the cabinet of particular concern to the company were all Maderistas: Ernesto Madero, Secretary of *Hacienda*, Lic. Rafael Hernández, Secretary of Justice, Lic. Manuel Calero, Secretary of *Fomento*, and Manuel Bonilla, Secretary of Communications. Of these, Ernesto Madero, uncle of the revolutionary leader, had sat on the same Mining Board with Body and was intimately known to T. J. Ryder, Cowdray's general manager at Tampico, while Rafael Hernández, Madero's cousin, was also known to Body. Calero was the only real problem. 'You will remember that the latter is Doheny's legal representative in this City', Body reported, 'and that you met him when we were in New York last June and I am anxious now to know how we shall be treated by his Department.'[3] On the other hand, Calero was also nephew to Señor Luis Méndez, legal adviser to the British legation, where he was later to take refuge at a critical moment in Mexican history, so that he was certainly not anti-British. A vain, handsome, arrogant, ambitious and unstable personality, who had a reputation as a 'trimmer', he was in any circumstances a difficult person with whom to establish good relations. But he was not close to Madero, who had sent forward his name on his

[1] Dearing–Knox, 26 August 1911, no. 849. SDF 812.00/2318.
[2] The *Bancaria* was the private banking organization of the *científicos*, then in the process of retreat from Mexico via New York and Havana. See Bell, p. 106. Body's sentence is ambiguous, but probably simply means that the *Bancaria* was not popular with the new régime.
[3] John B. Body–Cowdray, 14 June 1911, Body–Cowdray, 27 May 1911. Cowdray Papers.

political reputation alone. It would be the relatives of Madero who carried the real weight in the government.

Body's letter was still in the post when on 18 and 22 June Cowdray was heavily attacked in the columns of *The World* and other American, as well as Mexican papers, allegedly on information from a Maderista source. He was accused of having bribed prominent Mexicans in the formation of the Aguila Company by a free issue of shares at a meeting on 1 April 1910. The reports were exceedingly detailed and apparently circumstantial; purported minutes were quoted verbatim, and names mentioned.[1]

Body issued a denial, which also covered the allegation that a special dividend of 8 per cent had been paid to the holders of these shares while others had received nothing. In fact, on the first payment of dividend in 1911 all holders of the preference shares received 8 per cent.[2] It was also suggested that the directors of the Aguila Company had used improper influence to secure control of the National Railways, from which they then secured contracts for the supply of lubricating oil and for railway construction; however, examination of the Railways Board shows that in 1911 it included only three members of the Aguila Board, as against—for example—three members of that of Waters Pierce![3]

In this connection the names of Henry W. Taft of the firm of Strong and Cadwalader and George W. Wickersham, Attorney-General of the United States, were also mentioned. Thus Cowdray was defended, quite incidentally, by an unexpected champion.

After seeing the article [in the *Mexican Herald*] I immediately sent for the representative of the Waters Pierce Oil Company [Ambassador Wilson told President Taft] and informed him that if any further mention was made of persons connected with your Administration I should deem it my duty to make public a Secret Service report furnished me by the Department, which recites the evidence of the financial relations between the Revolutionary Party and the Standard

---

[1] The names mentioned were those of the original members of the Board.
[2] *Mexican Year Book, 1912,* p. 162.
[3] The Aguila members were Guillermo de Landa y Escandón, President of the Aguila Company, Lic. Luis Elguero, and Lic. Luis Riba y Cervantes. The Waters Pierce members were Henry Clay Pierce himself, his son Arthur Clay Pierce, and Henry S. Priest (*Mexican Year Book, 1911,* pp. 167, 220).

Oil Company. Since this interview, nothing has appeared in the *Herald* of this objectionable character, and I am of the opinion that nothing will appear.

Henry Lane Wilson was not entirely disinterested, of course. He had also shown his dislike of Sherburne G. Hopkins, when that industrious intermediary had arrived in the capital with Madero, and the feeling had been reciprocated.[1] Yet, as we have seen, he had no evidence. The report that he had been sent was for his eyes only. No deal had ever been concluded. Why then did the threat work? Purely, perhaps, because it showed that the ambassador was well aware that Waters Pierce was behind the attacks, and any unnecessary divergence from the wishes of the United States government could be very damaging to the American company at that time, when its relations with Standard Oil were under close scrutiny in American courts. From the diplomatic point of view, it is even more revealing, for it shows the lack of concern of the ambassador for the maintenance of friendly relations with foreign, non-American interests.

Meanwhile, Cowdray arrived in Mexico on his annual visit, and set to work to establish good relations at the highest level. On 26 August he had an interview with Madero himself, at which the only other person present was Body.[2] Madero had no hesitation in saying that 'concessions which had been given by the old government would be properly respected', though 'in future all contracts would be open to all and given to the best bidder'. In fact Madero, though obviously eager to explain 'some of his policies regarding education and uplifting of the peon class', was evidently on the defensive.

Mr Madero assured Lord Cowdray that his party had no relations with the Standard Oil, and that the money they had got for the revolution was entirely Mexican; that his father had raised loans on his property and that the total cost of the revolution had only been $350,000 gold [Body wrote]. They would look with suspicion, he said, on the entrance of the S.O. into Mexico, and he hoped therefore we would not

[1] Wilson–Taft, 17 July 1911. Taft Papers, Series 2, 1662 (Henry Lane Wilson, US Ambassador to Mexico).
[2] Cowdray Papers.

sell out to these people, although he acknowledged he had no right, nor had the Government, to prevent our doing so. Lord Cowdray expressed his opinion that the Aguila Company, with its Government concessions, must always remain a Mexican Company. He explained further that it might be necessary to get other funds, possibly through a combination of forces with the Gulf Refining or Texas Company in order to assist in the selling of our products . . .

In fact both of these companies were Standard Oil subsidiaries, and, in the event, it was to be from Standard Oil itself (after the dissolution of its empire) that Cowdray received his aid. It was, however, achieved then as a straight commercial deal, without any transfer of stock. Cowdray went on to speak of the recent articles, 'undoubtedly instigated' by Pierce, and of how he had broken the Waters Pierce monopoly.

Mr Madero replied that he was aware that our entrance into this business had been a good thing for the country, and that such competition was welcomed. He said that he had not read any of the articles referred to. Lord Cowdray explained that the newspapers had coupled his (Madero's) name with statements that he was ready to even cancel our concessions when he came to power, and had generally made use of his name quite freely in bolstering up their assertions about the Aguila Company and Lord Cowdray. Mr Madero said that he authorised us to contradict these statements, or we might send him the articles referred to and he would do so through the press. He again assured us that our concessions, and all concessions granted by the late Government, would be duly respected, and foreign capital encouraged to come to Mexico.

Madero's statements at this interview amounted to a repetition of views he had already expressed in public. On the basis of them, it is clear that the company would be satisfied that they would not be subjected to arbitrary proceedings. Madero did not even say, as was later suggested, that his approval of the company's position was conditional on an examination of the concessions proving that they had been legally obtained.

Cowdray had immediate proof of Madero's good faith. News of the meeting could not be kept secret from the watchful eyes of

Waters Pierce agents. On 29 August the Maderista paper, *La Nueva Era*, published an article based on a garbled account of it taken, significantly, from the *St Louis Post-Dispatch*. It stated that Cowdray had come to pay homage to Madero, recognizing his strength. But the new régime, it said, would have no favourites and Cowdray's concessions had received no guarantees. Madero could well have followed the path of expediency and allowed this account to stand. Instead he responded with a lengthy declaration which made his position entirely clear.

Much has been said lately in the foreign Press and has frequently been copied in our own [it said in part] to the effect that the new Government has the intention of making an investigation into the petroleum concessions granted to the house of Pearson and that this investigation has as its goal the revocation or restriction of those concessions. In this context I wish to state now, once and for all, that it has never entered into my plans to do such a thing, since I know that there is nothing irregular in the Pearson concessions and that those concessions were granted legally.

While we are dealing with this question, it is very relevant to declare, as I do now, that comprehending as I do the fact that our rich country needs capital and foreign immigration for its development, it would not be convenient to place obstacles in the way of either coming into the country and, on the contrary, one of the principal cares of my programme of government will be that of favouring within the limits of the most exact legality, the implementation of new industries, great businesses of all kinds and, in general, foreign capital investments of all kinds, since if it is certain that the natural riches of the republic are immense, it is not less so that to develop them we need foreign capital.

I wish to say with all necessary emphasis, that Foreign Capital will be guaranteed (*amparado*) by the same strict safeguards and will have the same security under any government of which I have the control, as it received under the old régime and is receiving at present.

As regards the honourableness of Lord Cowdray I believe that that is a point which does not admit of question, and I do not consider his influence in this country to be mischievous, as the paper with which I am dealing imagines, but on the contrary, I believe that his firm has been a considerable factor in the advancement of the country.

In consideration of all the foregoing, I have said to Mr Pearson that I wish him to continue in this country his petroleum and other businesses, since he has brought here a great quantity of capital and destroyed the petroleum monopoly which formerly existed in the republic.[1]

All the evidence, therefore, indicates that, by the end of the *interinato*, Cowdray had not only established good relations with the Madero circle, but was confident that they were strong enough to resist future attacks.

The public events of the Madero administration form an apparently clear and straightforward pattern. In fact much of what has been written on the nature of the régime under which they occurred is misleading, and some is almost entirely untrue.

The problem is one of historiography, and it is this. The Madero government foundered abruptly, if not entirely without preliminary warning. It had, throughout, been characterized by a degree of licence in public criticism and abuse remarkable by any standard. Then, within a week of his deposition, Madero himself died in circumstances which cast the utmost suspicion on the next government. This, in turn, became the focus of international attention, and ultimately disapproval, so that its supporters were more than ever concerned to depreciate the currency of the powerful ideas Madero had let loose.[2]

On the other hand, the emergence of the ultimately successful constitutionalist movement, led by Venustiano Carranza and incorporating the most radical elements among those who had formerly supported Madero, gave rise to a desire to emphasize a continuity with the past which would support the claim of the movement to be the legitimate government of the country. This, of course, it was not. The figure of Madero was elevated to an impossible stature; the deficiencies of his government conveniently forgotten. Still, the constitutionalist view of Madero did not go unchallenged in the memoirs of those who had taken part in politics in his time: neither by opponents, such as Ricardo García

[1] T. J. Ryder–Lord Cowdray, 4 November 1911, Cowdray Papers. Cutting from *La Nueva Era*, 29 August 1911, and typescript statement, undated, initialled C. B., filed with press publications and cuttings, Archivo Madero, rollo 18, hojas 15706, 15707/8.
[2] E.g. Rafael Aguilar, *Madero sin máscara* (Mexico, 1911); 'Pirra-Purra', *La parra, la perra y la Porra* (Mexico, 1913).

Granados or Henry Lane Wilson, nor by early supporters who had separated from his party before his fall, such as Francisco Vázquez Gómez and Manuel Calero.[1]

When in the 1920s men started to write in Marxist terms in Mexico, Madero was still seen as the first great leader of the Revolution, but was subtly reduced in political significance. He was considered to have failed to appreciate the nature of the 'socio-economic' forces that propelled his revolutionary followers. The existence of contemporary and earlier political movements and leaders in the struggle against Díaz was emphasized; their failure and his success were alike 'played down', and his motivation, so remote from an explanation in purely material terms, was misunderstood. Madero's death alone remained as a monument, a symbol of the vileness of the counter-revolutionary forces that supplanted him.[2]

Outside Mexico the development was less involved. British authors took their views from American sources. Americans, with an astonishing unanimity, took theirs from the standpoint of Woodrow Wilson. The Wilsonian view of Mexico assumed an almost total ascendancy, once the last survivors of Wilson's contemporaries had ceased to have their—admittedly often equally misguided—say.

Madero, naturally, comes out of the process more enviably than his opponents. At least he appears a weak but well-meaning democrat, while they appear as bloodthirsty traitorous ruffians. The most astounding errors of fact, often directly attributable to contemporary politicians or reporters, survive in the general works, while the writings of recent American scholars, who have done so much in the last ten years to get to the truth, have yet to be incorporated into the textbooks. Meanwhile the picture is one

---

[1] Ricardo García Granados, *Historia de México desde la Restauración de la República en 1867, hasta la Caida de Huerta* (Mexico, 1956), II; remainder as cited. Francisco Bulnes, *The Whole Truth about Mexico—President Wilson's Responsibility* (New York, 1916), like its author, is *sui generis*.

[2] The general trend of Mexican historiography is well illustrated by *México: Cincuenta Años de Revolución*. As far as the Marxist critique is concerned, it should be said that the latest work in this field, Friedrich Katz, *Deutschland, Diaz und die mexikanische Revolution; die deutsche Politik in Mexiko 1870–1920* (Berlin, 1964), is a scholarly work, extensively supported by original sources, and does not exhibit the faults of its predecessors.

of reversed dates, interchanged actors, and unchecked guesswork. Even without these errors, however, the impression of events in Mexico can be rendered entirely misleading by placing them outside their Mexican context. When this is done, the picture of a struggle of interests, of a revolutionary upheaval, of social, economic and political changes, and, still more, of the diplomatic exchanges of which these events were the centre, is completely distorted.

This book is not a history of Mexico. The view of internal events it presents differs from previous interpretations in the main implicitly rather than explicitly. It is concerned in detail with the diplomatic mesh that surrounded the events. The final warning, therefore, in considering the course of events after the accession of Madero, is that it will become increasingly important to suppress the historical foreknowledge of things to come. The First World War, the Russian Revolution, the League of Nations—in retrospect, these powerful historical magnets distort the last years before 1914 into strange, fanciful shapes.

The internal history of the Madero administration has been well documented by Charles Curtis Cumberland and Stanley Robert Ross. No warning is therefore necessary for a modern reader against viewing it solely as a series of abortive revolts. Unhappily it was this aspect of it that made the deepest impression on foreign onlookers.

There were at least five of major significance. General Reyes crossed the border from the United States within a month of Madero's installation, wandered aimlessly for a few days, failing to attract any response from the people, and was arrested and sent to gaol in the City of Mexico. At the beginning of March 1912, Pascual Orozco, who had been sent to Chihuahua to maintain order, organized a revolt, rallied the disaffected garrisons of the north, and defeated the former Secretary of War and Marine, General González Salas, in the field.[1] General Huerta was

[1] Francis Stronge–Sir Edward Grey, 8 June 1912, no. 228. FO 371/1394 file 158/26774. General Salas committed suicide in the train bearing him away from the battle, apparently under the mistaken impression that he had lost his entire artillery train to the rebels.

appointed as his successor. Meanwhile Emilio Vázquez Gómez launched a radical revolt which proved a complete failure.

Huerta spent a considerable time in preparation for his campaign, and clearly aimed to amass overwhelming superiority before commencing operations. This decision was to avoid the mistake of González Salas of rushing unprepared into the disaster of Escalón. It imposed an interminable strain on the political prestige of the administration, but proved fully justified. Within the space of two months, at the battles of Conejos (12 May), Rellano (22/23 May) and Bachimba (3 July), Huerta inflicted progressively heavier defeats on the Orozquista forces, until they broke up in disarray and fled to the mountains of Sonora.

In October, soldiers in barracks at Vera Cruz, led by General Félix Díaz, nephew of Porfirio, pronounced against the government, but were crushed in less than four hours' desultory fighting by the federal General Beltrán, while Díaz himself was imprisoned. Finally, throughout the period, the agrarian revolt of Zapata continued and developed by the promulgation of the *Plan de Ayala* into an open war against any government that did not place sweeping agrarian reform at the head of its priorities.

On 9 February 1913 a military coup in the capital, led by General Reyes and Félix Díaz, placed counter-revolutionary forces in command of its principal strongpoint. The bombardment that ensued occupied the remaining ten days of the administration's existence, and, under the cover of it, it was General Huerta who emerged as the new ruler of Mexico. The rise of General Huerta, therefore, was the most important event of Madero's period of office.

Victoriano Huerta[1] was born at Colotlán, in the state of Jalisco, on 23 December 1854. Fortunate as a boy to be selected for a cadetship at the Chapultepec Military College, he was unfortunate to find himself on the losing side of the battle that gave the

---

[1] Biographical details from Louis C. Simonds, 'Victoriano Huerta—a sketch from life', *The Atlantic Monthly*, CXIII (Boston, 1914), p. 721; William L. Sherman and Richard E. Greenleaf, *Victoriano Huerta, a Reappraisal* (Mexico, 1960). Seeing Huerta for the first time on 17 August 1911, Mrs O'Shaughnessy described him as '*muy hombre*, a broad shouldered, flat-faced, restless-eyed Indian with big glasses, rather impressive' (*Diplomatic Days*, p. 102). The so-called *Memorias del Gral. V. Huerta* ([Barcelona], 1915) are clearly apocryphal.

Presidency to Díaz. Under the new régime he was employed on the geographical survey for twenty years, before leading punitive campaigns successfully in 1895, 1901 and 1902. For the last he received promotion to the rank of Major-General, but it is clear that he continued to be distrusted by Díaz, for from 1907 to 1910 he was absent on leave from the army as an engineer at Monterrey.

We have already seen how de la Barra chose him to escort the ex-President in his flight, and subsequently employed him in the campaign against Zapata, where Madero had chosen him as a principal target in his accusations of treachery. Huerta offered his resignation to the government as a result of this affair, but reconsidered it after correspondence and a meeting with Madero. At a banquet on the occasion of the new President's inauguration, he publicly reproved him for his former distrust of the army. Less than five months later he was in supreme command of the federal forces for the first time.

Bachimba set the seal on a well-deserved military reputation. Within the confines of the cumbrous machine inherited from the *Porfiriato*, based as it was on a garrison strategy, heavily dependent on rail transport and seriously lacking in cavalry, he had secured a notable victory. With the civilians, even with Madero himself, his position was less happy, though in Madero's case the blame appears to be Huerta's own.[1] He was criticized for delay, for failing to capture Orozco himself, and for failing to account for some million and a half pesos. (His style of living was so modest that it is unlikely that he embezzled these last himself.) On the other hand, he too had cause for complaint, for his promotion to Divisional General came tardily. Yet until the last coup he remained loyal to the government.

It must be remembered that then (as to this day, in many other countries) in Mexico the first loyalty of the soldier was to the army. It would be hard indeed to say that there was a difference in kind, rather than in degree, between the view of a Mexican general of the period on the place of the soldier in the state and

[1] Sherman and Greenleaf, *Victoriano Huerta, a Reappraisal* (1960), pp. 55–6. Madero–Victoriano Huerta, 22 June 1912, expresses full confidence in him while dismissing a number of specific complaints as due to misunderstanding. Archivo Madero, caja no. 2, hojas 0445 y 0487–8.

Revolution

those of many of his European contemporaries, though there was
certainly a historical difference. Generals were loyal to the government in power as long as their interests were not infringed. If the
Mexican generals had little enthusiasm for civilian rule, they
nevertheless gave Madero's administration a fair chance.

They made no move to aid Reyes. Orozco they did not help;
he was an ex-revolutionary, and not one of themselves. When
Félix Díaz rose in Vera Cruz it seemed to many that it was inevitable that the generals would give him their support. But
General Beltrán, having brought up his forces, gave ceremonial
notice of his intention to take the city—and duly did so.[1]

Beltrán's success was received with a storm of abuse, but it was
the fact that Madero refused to grant Díaz his life that influenced
the army. It was saved instead on a timely technicality by the
aged and conservative Supreme Court, and this infringement of
the tradition by which high officers enjoyed a virtual right of
revolt was not forgiven.[2] Even Díaz had not broken the rule—he
had anticipated the revolts before they occurred, while most
former rulers of Mexico, however ruthless or tyrannical, and
however violently overthrown, had in some way been given the
opportunity of going into exile or otherwise escaping the ultimate
penalty.[3] Only from this time did the other generals join hands
against the government. And still Huerta remained aloof.

It is a short step from the belief that the Standard Oil Company financed the Madero revolution to the belief that its rivals

[1] The charge that Beltrán misused the white flag does not stand up to examination of the
evidence supplied by Consul W. W. Canada, who believed it. W. W. Canada–Knox,
23 October 1912, no. 768. SDF 812.00/5424.
[2] This follows Stronge–Grey, 2 November 1912, no. 318. FO 371/1395 file 158/49016.
Others claim that it was Madero who extended clemency to Díaz, e.g. Bell, pp. 232–3,
but the most that can be said for this is that Díaz's prosecutor did not demand the death
sentence (Cumberland, p. 204). Madero, in fact, specifically refused to exercise clemency
after the court martial on the ground that when he had done so previously it had been
attributed to weakness (The World, Monday, 28 October 1912; Schuyler–Secretary of
State, Telegram, 27 October 1912, 12 noon, Confidential. SDF 812.00/5358). In view
of subsequent events particular interest may be attached to the protestations of loyalty
in Victoriano Huerta–Madero, 14 December 1912, and A. Blanquet–Madero,
3 December 1912, copies of which are in Archivo Madero, caja no. 2, hojas 0489,
0490.
[3] Of the five put to death, Iturbide had tried to set himself above the officer caste, while
Maximilian was a foreigner in Mexican eyes, supported by foreign force, to whom
Robles Pezuela and Miramón had betrayed Mexico.

financed the movements against Madero. The agrarian agitation of Zapata may, for this purpose, be disregarded, as the poverty of the movement and its methods of literally living 'off the land' were and are well known. Nor is there any indication of the nature of the support given to General Reyes's expedition. The ludicrous nature of his failure would seem to suggest that he had very little, or, since he was a rich man, none, lacking as he did the support of the other military exiles who aided him and Félix Díaz a year later.

Both attempts of Félix Díaz were intended to be military coups following the classical patterns of subversion. Though this meant that the government was expected to pay for its own downfall, it must certainly have necessitated an adequate display of financial strength, and probably some direct bribery. Conspirators, naturally, do not leave written records of these forms of activity, and even the Felicista Carlos Toro is vague on such matters.[1] There were, however, persistent rumours that a large cheque had been subscribed to the cause from *científico* circles in Paris. This is quite possible. It does not follow that anyone but the exiles subscribed towards it. Great reliance, both at Vera Cruz and in the capital—too much, in fact—was placed on the name of Díaz and on the rewards to be expected by the soldiery under his rule.[2] General Mondragón, organizer of the second attempt, was an extremely wealthy man from the sale of patents and perquisites under the *Porfiriato*, and his self-seeking was so open as Huerta's Secretary of War and Marine that he was dismissed.[3]

The counter-revolutionary movement headed by Orozco alone demanded finance on a grand scale, and a great deal is known about its methods.[4] The military force with which Orozco began his revolt was substantially clothed and armed by the federal government while it was still hoped that he would remain loyal. It was then backed by the Terrazas family in the state of Chihuahua,

[1] Carlos Toro, *La caída de Madero por la revolución felicista* ([Mexico], 1913).
[2] And also, in the Vera Cruz case, to negotiating for foreign recognition.
[3] *The World*, Tuesday, 24 June 1913.
[4] Letcher–Secretary of State, Telegram, 23 March 1912, 1 p.m.; 20 March 1912, no. 166; 31 March 1912, no. 175. SDF 812.00/3353, 3424 and 3525. See also Calero, p. 95; Prida, *From Despotism to Anarchy*, p. 82.

and received considerable aid from other *hacendados* in sympathy with the old régime. Despite this, the movement was very soon in need of money, and met this need by forced loans from banks in the area which it controlled and semi-voluntary loans from the Chihuahua Chamber of Commerce. These were, by their nature, 'public', and the total sum expended must have been near the $2,000,000 mentioned during the Smith committee hearings, where the contrast with the sums expended by the Maderistas a year earlier did not go unnoticed.

Certainly large numbers of United States citizens were involved in the Orozco movement, and some of them contributed money to the cause.[1] Only once, however, do we find Lord Cowdray charged with rendering assistance, and this in a report to the State Department from Saltillo by Consul Holland, which was reported by him as a rumour 'without in the least subscribing to it'.[2]

Bell, who ascribes to the Pearson interests considerable influence against the Madero government, does not go so far. He makes considerable play with the wish of Cowdray to 'unload' on the Mexican government his part share in the Tehuantepec Railway, the Maderista promise to curtail his privileges, and the supposed fact that he had no 'friends at court'.[3] But he also points out (though as proof of Madero's diplomatic skill) that in the autumn of 1912 the Tehuantepec negotiations were expedited by express order of the President, while we know now that the question of privileges had been amicably settled by August 1911 and that Cowdray had at least one very important 'friend at court' in the person of Ernesto Madero. The Pearson interests had little to gain, and a great deal to lose, by a further change of government.

Only at one brief moment did the firm play an important role in the diplomacy of the period, and that was for and on behalf of the Madero government. On 11 March 1912 Enrique C. Creel

[1] An exception should be made here to mention the allegation of the German spy, Horst von der Goltz, that it was Germany which backed Orozco through the agency of Consul Kueck of Chihuahua, President of that Chamber of Commerce that offered so much to Orozco's cause (Von der Goltz, pp. 231–3).
[2] Philip E. Holland–Secretary of State, 17 July 1912, no. 83. SDF 812.00/4468.
[3] Bell, pp. 124–9, 191.

telegraphed to Lord Cowdray, who happened to be visiting New York, that local American firms were cabling their principals in the United States to press for the prohibition of the introduction of munitions of war into Mexico through El Paso, Texas, and thus to the Orozquistas. Cowdray called in his legal adviser in the United States, Henry Taft, who discussed the question with his brother, the President, and Attorney-General Wickersham.

At first the President replied that no action could be taken. On telephoning him later, however, Henry Taft was told that the question was that very day (12 March) receiving the attention of the Senate Foreign Relations Committee, and that the President would be in favour of the Joint Resolution which they had proposed. When the law was amended, no time would be lost in carrying his wishes into effect. In the evening he was further assured that everything would be done to hamper the export of arms, which was permissible under the law as it stood.

Bryce was fully informed at all stages of the negotiations, and exerted his own pressure, and in Mexico T. J. Ryder did not fail to ensure that Ernesto Madero was kept fully informed. On 19 March, after the ban had gone into effect, the Secretary of *Hacienda* cabled his thanks to Cowdray for his co-operation, and expressed himself equally appreciatively to Creel. Full credit in the matter was given to Bryce.[1]

Of course, as the correspondence makes entirely clear, Lord Cowdray did not initiate the move. Interestingly enough, it is not at all clear who did, if anyone, apart from Senator Root himself, whose name is deservedly remembered in connection with the Joint Resolution, and who received the thanks from Mexico that was his due. But it is the most striking proof of Cowdray's good relations with the government, which continued to the last.[2]

Henry Lane Wilson was convinced from the first that Mexico could only be ruled by the methods of Porfirio Díaz. His attitude towards Madero, which continued to be benevolent during the

[1] Cowdray Papers.
[2] Cowdray Papers; Root Papers, 1912; Philip C. Jessup, *Elihu Root* (New York, 1938), II, p. 254.

early months of his Presidency, was openly based on the belief that Madero could be educated to become what he considered was the proper type of Mexican ruler; that he was ready to reconcile 'his peculiar political creed and the program of the revolution with the prevalent conditions and the stern necessities of the hour', and that he would be 'compelled by the force of circumstances to more and more revert to the system implanted by General Díaz, thus paying mute and tardy but eloquent tribute to the wisdom of his great predecessor'.[1]

There was a turning point, when the ambassador's attitude changed from one of doubt as to the practicality of the Maderista doctrines and concern to set them right, to dislike of the movement and of its leader and a readiness to further moves to eliminate either. It can be located at the beginning of September 1912.

It coincides neither with one of Wilson's trips to Washington, nor with the government's quarrel with Manuel Calero, nor with the Vera Cruz uprising. Calero, whom Madero had chosen as Secretary of External Relations, soon fell out with the Vice-President, and had to be transferred to the Washington Embassy. He has been very close to Wilson, and Bell suggests that he reported from Washington that Madero had been manœuvring there for Wilson's removal as ambassador at Mexico.[2] Wilson, however, indicates that he only learned of such efforts after Madero's fall.[3] It was only subsequently that his dislike changed to hatred, and this seems to rule out a straightforward personal motive.

In fact, Wilson was on leave in the United States from May to July 1912, and again from October 1912 to January 1913. In his absence Montgomery Schuyler, first secretary, was chargé d'affaires. He was a scholar who had been one of the first professional recruits to the State Department in 1902. His reports show an identical change between the two periods; his later ones being in every way as severe and critical of the government as Wilson's own, and his disgusted comments on the failure of the Vera Cruz uprising betraying a startling degree of commitment.[4]

[1] Wilson–Knox, 30 November 1911, no. 1103, Confidential. SDF 812.00/2601.
[2] Bell, p. 146. [3] Wilson, pp. 234–5.
[4] Schuyler–Secretary of State, Telegrams, 16 October 1912, 3 p.m.; 23 October, 1 p.m. SDF 812.00/5253, 5333.

Since Schuyler shared neither the nerves nor the idiosyncrasies of his chief, the explanation must be political, not personal, and due to the belief that anti-American forces had taken the upper hand in the government and with Madero himself. What is significant is that Schuyler did not take over the ambassador's apparent immunity from reprimand for exceeding his powers.[1]

The State Department, with Fred Dearing now at the newly formed Bureau of Latin American Affairs, was suspicious of the embassy reports throughout the period. Up to January 1913 this was a negative suspicion—a belief that they gave 'too dark a picture', in the words of Huntington Wilson at the time of the Orozco rebellion.[2] In that month Knox for the first time suggested in so many words that there were signs that the ambassador was trying to force the Department's hand.[3] In fact, as we have seen, Wilson had tended to do this from the outset; what Knox should have been concerned about was the difference in degree.

The ambassador's return to Mexico on 6 January 1913 followed a personal disaster of great magnitude. On 5 November 1912 the party by which he had been appointed to his office had been defeated at the polls. The following day his brother, the former Republican senator, died suddenly in Washington, D.C. Overnight the ambassador, himself a sick man, found his career in the balance. It must have seemed to him that only a great diplomatic coup could save it. Fate presented him with the opportunity. He took it—and found that he had earned an infamous reputation which was, to a large measure, unjustified.

The State Department was largely responsible for his getting into this position. The weird consistency of the administration's Mexican policy, which appeared remarkably incoherent to Mexicans, would have been difficult even for an exceptionally gifted diplomatist to convey.

It opened inauspiciously on 6 February 1912 with a second mobilization on the frontier, in response to the disturbances that preceded Orozco's revolt. This time it was carried out with the

[1] Department of State–Schuyler, Telegrams, 23 October 1912, 7 p.m., 8 p.m. SDF 812.00/5294.
[2] Huntington Wilson–President, 17 February 1912. SDF 812.00/2881 B.
[3] Knox–President, 27 January 1913, Confidential. SDF 812.00/7229 A.

Revolution

concurrence of the Secretary of State and without the publicity that had attended the previous 'exercises'. But within days the movement of troops was common knowledge in Mexico, bringing about a rapid loss of confidence in the government at a most critical moment.[1]

Nevertheless, no threat emerged to United States citizens until the insurgents began to close in on Ciudad Juárez, with the obvious intention of taking it. The problem was that which had arisen when Madero decided to turn towards the capital—that of the danger to the inhabitants of El Paso. This time, however, it was election year, and it was the President who wanted to send troops across the frontier to help the federal forces keep the rebels off, while Huntington Wilson advised that it would endanger fewer Americans if the inhabitants of El Paso were asked to withdraw from the probable area of fire.[2]

When the time came the action taken was quite different. The news reached Washington at 9 p.m., and it was Joshua Reuben Clark, Solicitor to the State Department, who dictated the two telegrams in reply. The first was a brief message to Consul Edwards at Ciudad Juárez telling him informally to advise both General Campa, commander of the insurgents, and the federal commander, of the serious consequences that would follow any firing across the line. The second was to the embassy at Mexico, directing Wilson to advise the Mexican government of 'the absolute necessity that there be no firing into American territory at El Paso'. It went further, asking them to require their commander to withdraw to take a defensive stand elsewhere if they thought it best 'in view of the peculiar situation existing and the possible eventualities'. This was a straightforward invitation to abandon the city.[3]

---

[1] Bell, pp. 153ff. *The World*, Thursday, 4 April 1912, editorial, 'A mysterious coincidence', attributed the mobilization to a need to assist the new Naval Appropriation Bill through a hostile Congress.

[2] Wilson–Secretary of State, Telegram, 24 February 1912, 3 p.m., Urgent and Confidential; reply to Huntington Wilson–Wilson, Telegram, 24 February, 11 a.m., and followed by Huntington Wilson–President, 24 February 1912. SDF 812.00/2884, 2884A.

[3] Memorandum by Fred Dearing with Huntington Wilson–Consul, Ciudad Juárez, Telegram, 26 February 1912, 11 p.m., and Huntington Wilson–Wilson, 26 February, 11 p.m. SDF 812.00/2912.

Fred Dearing took these telegrams to the White House. 'The President read them,' he recorded afterwards, 'approved them at once, and remarked "You know I am not going to cross the line. That is something for which Congress will have to take the responsibility." He then added "But I suppose it will do no harm to threaten them a little".'[1]

Taft was wrong. It did a great deal of harm. The Mexican government took the threat seriously and ordered the evacuation of the city. The rebels were installed on the border, their cause was strengthened, and the United States assumed a moral obligation towards the Mexican government that their action had done so much to weaken. For at first they pleaded the legalistic argument that they had no right to prohibit the export of arms unless a state of belligerency was proclaimed.[2]

Next Taft issued a proclamation calling on United States citizens not to interfere in the internal affairs of Mexico.[3] This aroused nothing but irritation. Then the ambassador announced that large areas of Mexico were unsafe, and advised American citizens to leave them. Since no other power did likewise, it was assumed by many that this heralded a United States invasion.[4] Wilson, however, had told the State Department that the British and other foreign ministers had been contemplating something similar, and Huntington Wilson had laid the responsibility for the move on the embassy's judgement of local conditions.[5] He did not reckon on the capacity of the ambassador for exceeding his instructions, for the latter laid the responsibility in his statement to the press on the Department itself, and then gave the Department an ingenuous explanation.

[1] Memorandum by Fred Dearing, *loc. cit.*
[2] Huntington Wilson–Wilson, Telegram, 1 March 1912, 7 p.m. SDF 812.00/2959.
[3] *By the President, a Proclamation*, 2 March 1912. SDF 812.00/3005 C.
[4] Bell explains that the Americans themselves interpreted the warning to leave as a prelude to intervention *because* no other power took similar steps. It seemed to them that the danger to be feared was one to them alone, which was only likely to be the eventuality of an armed landing (Bell, p. 171).
[5] Wilson–Secretary of State, Telegram, 1 March 1912, 6 p.m. SDF 812.00/3000, indicates that Stronge was 'contemplating' such a move. The authorization was given in Huntington Wilson–Wilson, Telegram, 2 March, 2 p.m., SDF 812.00/3005 D, and timed to harmonize with the Presidential Proclamation referred to above.

'In using the words "Department of State" instead of "the Embassy" I was conscious of the technical error [he wrote] but believed the change wise on account of the misinterpretations which were being put upon the President's proclamation and also to take out of the notice the appearance of an estimate of conditions based solely on the opinion of the Ambassador.'[1] But this, of course, was just what it was.

Nevertheless, the ambassador genuinely believed that he was doing what he could to support the government, and welcomed Senator Root's Joint Resolution when, at last, it appeared, showing in the most unmistakable way that the United States government really was concerned to do just that.[2] But, as always, the Mexican and American views of the action conflicted. What Wilson considered a 'great and substantial benefit', the Mexicans regarded merely as a fair return for having to surrender Ciudad Juárez. When Taft used threats, the Mexicans obstinately persisted in taking them literally—lacking, perhaps, Taft's phlegmatic confidence that no firebrand in Congress was going to place him and the country in a state of war. It is only fair to add that at this time Wilson was well in advance of his government in even understanding that no thanks were to be expected, and that, as in his confidential report of 20 March, he was at this juncture both calm and optimistic about the chances of the government.[3]

The disaster of Escalón, irritation at the government's determination to make American railway employees pass a language test in Spanish, and other disputes were overshadowed by the Orozquistas' insistence on trying to blackmail the United States government into recognition. But internal American politics seem to have dictated the appearance of a 'firm line' with the Mexican government, when on 15 April identic notes were sent to them and to the rebels, demanding protection of United States interests in a minatory tone which caused almost as much offence in government circles as the fact that the rebels were treated as

---

[1] Wilson–Secretary of State, Telegram, 4 March 1912, 4 p.m. SDF 812.00/3048. See also Huntington Wilson–Wilson, Telegram, 3 March, 8 p.m. SDF 812.00/3005 D.

[2] *The World*, Thursday, 14 March, and Friday, 15 March 1912.

[3] Wilson–Knox, 20 March 1912, no. 1320, Confidential. SDF 812.00/3365.

their equals.[1] All the same, it received a polite but firm reply. The
diplomatic exchange, as such, was inconclusive, for it was not
followed up. What was significant was that it revealed that the
ambassador had made a number of emendations of his own in the
text of the note. One paragraph, indeed, had been entirely re-
written, and on it Dearing minuted that it had been drafted
originally as the ambassador had made it, but was altered in the
authorized text because as it originally stood it was felt that 'it
would only cause anger'.

Furthermore, it was Wilson who had inserted a passage 'quoting
to the Foreign Office the instructions sent to Consul Letcher',
while elsewhere he had made some alterations, as he claimed, 'to
give the document greater clearness'. The Solicitor commented
on this: 'Isn't it about time to suggest that the Ambassador is not
our instructor in English Grammar and Rhetoric—and that "we
want what we want when we want it"?'

In view of this, it is perhaps fortunate that he could not hear
Wilson's real views and reasons. The ambassador had told the
German minister, who had asked him whether the newspaper
reports of the note were authentic: 'In substance it is, but not
verbally. The instructions didn't come in cipher but en clair. It
repeats itself, it contains all the points, but repeatedly. It has been
written by a lawyer, but by a badly educated lawyer. I am just
working out a note much shorter but which will cover all the
points.'[2]

On 1 May Henry Cabot Lodge, a strong supporter of Theodore
Roosevelt, made a speech in the United States Senate drawing
attention to the supposed dangers of the extension of Japanese
influence in the Magdalena Bay area. It was then that he introduced the resolution which was subsequently adopted by the
Senate, and is known as the Lodge corollary to the Monroe
doctrine, already mentioned above. In it he extended the claim

[1] Wilson–Secretary of State, Telegram, 13 April 1912, 8 p.m.; Knox–Wilson, Telegram,
18 April, 5 p.m. SDF 812.00/3590. Text of notes in SDF 812.00/3593A. Comment in
Wilson–Secretary of State, Telegram, 15 April 1912, 9 p.m. SDF 812.00/3602. Also
Wilson–Secretary of State, Telegram, 17 April, 9 p.m. SDF 812.00/3634.
[2] Wilson–Knox, 17 April 1912, no. 1364; notes to foregoing: Huntington Wilson–
Wilson, 1 May 1912, no. 804. SDF 812.00/3690. Hintze–Bethmann-Hollweg, 17 April
1912, no. A33. GFM 12/15 f. A7682.

made by the United States to have the right to prevent intervention in Latin America to cover the case of an Asian nation and
a foreign company as opposed to a foreign government. Though
not adopted until August, it was throughout this period seen by
Mexicans as a constant menace to the national independence of
Mexico. And the initial speech was followed almost at once by
the expulsion of two Americans from Mexico for supplying arms
to Orozco; an operation in which, the government noted, members of the embassy circle were implicated. Together these acts
aroused the highest suspicion of the real motives of the United
States.[1]

When, therefore, every diplomatic effort was made in Washington to prevent the federals recapturing Ciudad Juárez by force
of arms, thus adding to the delay of Huerta's campaign,
there was some reason to fear that concerted intervention was
afoot.[2] Ships were sent to Mexican ports, and complaints made
to the government that the rebels were disarming American
residents to get arms for themselves. The great achievements of
Huerta's campaign, by which even Ciudad Juárez had been recovered without incident, were speedily forgotten.[3]

Apparently independently, the State Department then embarked on a new *démarche*. In a note proposed to the President
on 28 August, authorized by him on the 2nd and sent to Mexico
on the 3rd, but not delivered until 15 September, the United
States government ordered the 'government which in Mexico

[1] *The World*, Thursday, 2 May and Thursday, 4 April 1912; Bell, pp. 201–2.

[2] Wilson–Secretary of State, Telegrams, 22 April 1912, 9 p.m.; 4 May, 5 p.m.; Schuyler–
Secretary of State, Telegram, 19 June, 9 p.m., and series of preceding correspondence.
SDF 812.00/3685, 3800, 4245, 4310.

Schuyler–Secretary of State, Telegram, 20 June, 10 p.m.; T. D. Edwards–Secretary
of State, Telegrams, 20 June, 23 June and 5 July. SDF 812.00/4258, 4251, 4274, 4359.

[3] The ambassador called it 'an exhibition of impotence'. Wilson–Secretary of State,
Telegram, 1 August 1912, 4 p.m. SDF 812.00/4537. The ambassador attributed this
expression to Consul Letcher of Chihuahua. The consul's reports, however, give a
more favourable impression than this isolated phrase would seem to imply. This is
particularly significant in view of the clear desire of the ambassador to channel all
consular reports through the embassy, which led to a dispute with Consul General
Shanklin. The latter was temporarily suspended, and his transfer decided upon, but the
President decided personally to return him to his post. See Bell, pp. 173–4; Taft–
Huntington Wilson, 22 March 1912; Taft–President William Arnold Shanklin,
Middletown, Conn., 26 March 1912; Taft–Wilson, 15 April 1912. Taft Papers,
Presidential Series 8, XXXIV, f. 418; XXXV, ff. 39, 341.

controls business' [*sic*] to make its northern frontier secure by placing garrisons of specified numbers in specified places. It further included a long bill of complaints about the treatment of Americans and their interests which, as Bell indicates, were not only spurious, but must have been known to the ambassador to be spurious.[1]

In a stylish, efficient reply the Secretary of External Relations, Pedro Lascuráin, a lawyer, not only dealt with these points but presented the case for an administration in substantial control of the country, which was conscious of its duties both at home and abroad, and which conformed to them.[2] He had replaced Calero earlier in the year and was also responsible for the reply to the April note. The original note, however, was not published by the Department of State, though, in the circumstances, it was not hard for the public to guess at its substance, for there had been an interview between President Taft and Ambassador Calero on 8 September, after which the ambassador had made a spectacular journey back to Mexico bearing with him a verbal message to his President.

This impression, however, was misleading. The President, it seems, was much more sympathetic to the Madero administration than the Department of State. As recorded by Calero, his impression of the interview contrasts with the drama his expedition lent to the occasion and thereby to himself.

In substance [he wrote] Mr Taft told me that his desire for the success of our President's administration was very sincere; but that, since the impotence of the administration was palpable, with great risk to foreign interests in Mexico, he exhorted me to convince President Madero that it was a serious international necessity that such a situation should change. Mr Taft added that while he was President, the American

---

[1] Bell, pp. 225–7.

[2] Huntington Wilson–Wilson, Telegram, 2 September 1912, 1 p.m.; Wilson–Knox, 28 August 1912, no. 1618 Confidential. SDF 812.00/4785 A, 4899. Mrs O'Shaughnessy states positively that the reply was written by Lascuráin, and she tended to sympathize with it (*Diplomatic Days*, pp. 251–3). Yet as late as 4 December 1912 Montgomery Schuyler, advising the State Department to let Lascuráin know during his visit to the United States that his reply would not be 'overlooked', said he believed it had been written by Calero (Schuyler–Secretary of State, Telegram, 4 December 1912, 2 p.m. SDF 812.00/5645).

government would remain deaf to the call of those who were asking for intervention; but that, on the other hand, he, as President, had to see that the interests of foreigners in general, not just as those of Americans, did not continue to suffer from the inadequacy with which the Mexican government gave them the protection to which they were entitled.[1]

Once again the *démarche* was not followed up, despite the Felicista sympathies of Schuyler, and his predictions of further disorder. Far from breaking out again, as Schuyler predicted, this last continued to decline everywhere from then until the coup of 9 February.[2]

Reyes had not yet entered Mexico when the new British minister took charge of the legation on 8 December 1911.

Francis William Stronge[3] was born on 22 November 1856, a younger son of Sir James Stronge, Bart., of Tynan Abbey, Co. Armagh, and brother of the fifth baronet. He entered the Diplomatic Service as an attaché in 1878 and had reached the rank of minister in 1906 on his appointment to Bogotá. His arrival in Mexico, delayed by his need to convalesce from a serious operation and receive treatment for arthritis, coincided unavoidably with Hohler's departure on leave for personal reasons, and the latter did not return to Mexico until 12 June 1912, 'embittered', as he later put it, 'by domestic losses and distress'. Stronge recorded the position on his arrival in a personal letter to Spicer, which indicates strikingly how not all the trials of taking up a new post were diplomatic ones.[4]

As you know [he wrote], Hohler had to leave a few days after my arrival, and I am only feeling my way. I hope therefore that you will forgive me if some of my despatches should be a little sketchy. There is much work, for Canadian lawyers and others pour out their woes at enormous length, and the state of the country, though improving,

[1] Calero, *Un Decenio de Política Mexicana* (1920), p. 102.
[2] The last consular reports before the *Decena Trágica* show almost complete calm throughout the country.
[3] Biographical details from *Foreign Office List*, *Who Was Who, 1921–1930*. Some of the following has appeared in Peter A. R. Calvert, 'Francis Stronge en la Decena Trágica', *Historia Mexicana*, xv, no. 1, julio–septiembre 1965, pp. 47–68.
[4] Stronge–G. S. Spicer, 27 December 1911 (Personal) filed with FO 371/1396 file 1449.

gives rise to much correspondence . . . We are only camped in the Legation, for the Govt. furniture has not yet been sent out, and our own bedroom stuff is only now being unpacked. Much time has been spent in fighting the bugs, which have taken possession of some of the bedrooms in almost incredible numbers. A minor misfortune was a severe earthquake a few days ago. The house rocked like a boat at sea, but beyond a crack in the porch and a bulge in my study fireplace no damage seems to have been done. Of course I was in terror lest all the English servants should give warning, but they have behaved very well.

From his later experience of him Hohler wrote this sympathetic appreciation of the man and the minister:

Stronge was a charming old gentleman, well read, writer of excellent despatches, but he seemed incapable of making up his mind [he recalled]. He had a hesitating manner and a stammer, an untidy beard and hairy nose and ears, and to see his parrot nibbling at his ears was a grotesque spectacle.

Despite these serious disadvantages which made him a very indifferent British representative—although he would have been an excellent University Don—I was very much attached to him but differed from him in practically every opinion he had or decision he took. His wife was neither intellectual nor interesting, but a source of continual amusement. She had developed a philosophy (quite incomprehensible which she induced some of the unfortunate secretaries in the Mexican Foreign Office to translate into Spanish) that had something to do with a belief that plants thought.[1]

Henry Lane Wilson was, for a man who could never resist making an obvious sally, almost equally complimentary. He described Stronge as

a Belfast [sic] Irishman, who though of sufficiently sedate years had recently married an Irish lady of respectable maturity. Both Sir [sic] Francis and Lady Stronge were amiable people, anxious to be on good terms with all the world and to meet the exigencies of the diplomatic protocol. Sir Francis had a consuming passion for parrots, and one gathered somehow the suspicion that they participated in his councils. Whether in drawing room, at table, or in the chancellery, one of them was always present, perched upon His Excellency's shoulder and mingling affably but insistently in the conversation.[2]

[1] Hohler, p. 178.   [2] Wilson, pp. 181–2. Stronge was knighted in 1915.

Stronge considered the ambassador and his wife to be 'pleasant, hospitable people' and personally popular. The embassy demanded heavy work from its head. 'Besides this,' Stronge recorded, 'there has lately [April 1912] been a good deal of illness in his family, and, as he is of a very nervous temperament, he suffers much from the constant strain, which he is said to relieve by the use of stimulants.' By nature a pessimist, he felt that he had to take a lead in affairs, but his government was unwilling to take the responsibility. 'The result of all this is that Mr Wilson is torn in two directions and his acts and language seem vacillating and contradictory. He seems to favour drastic measures more than any of his colleagues, but to be anxious that they should make the first move and that he should appear to be exercising a restraining influence.'

Stronge found that he had more in common with the new German minister, Rear-Admiral von Hintze, of whom he wrote: 'I find him very frank and straightforward in business, and a most pleasant companion. In diplomatic matters in which his colleagues are concerned he endeavours, as far as possible, to remain in the background, and if he speaks at all it is always in favour of moderation and caution.'[1]

Von Hintze was already one of those figures who inspire legends. He had been a career officer in the newly formed Imperial German Navy, having entered it at the age of eighteen in 1882 and subsequently passed through the Naval Academy. He had been Flag Lieutenant to Vice-Admiral von Diedrichs, commanding the East Asiatic Cruiser Squadron in 1898. In the celebrated incident at Manila Bay in that year, he was the officer who bore the message to Admiral Dewey which the American conceived to be insulting. His rise thereafter in the imperial favour was rapid. He was promoted to Corvette Captain commanding S.M.S. *Kaiser Wilhelm II* in 1901, and appointed marine attaché to St Petersburg in 1903. In 1905, it was he who ordered a German torpedo-boat to Kronstadt to rescue the tsar if need arose, and is said to have advised the stern suppression of the Revolution, subsequently gaining high favour at court. This was paralleled by

[1] Stronge–Grey, 10 April 1912, no. 116. FO 371/1397 file 17956.

rapid promotion to Captain, appointment as ADC to the Kaiser in 1907, and ennoblement in 1908.

He had become a key figure in the Kaiser's personal system of diplomacy, recognized by his appointment in the same year to the personal rank of military plenipotentiary. His removal from that post in 1911, allegedly as the result of an indiscreet remark, was not followed by any diminution of favour, for he was promoted Rear-Admiral and appointed to Mexico—a sign not just of the German government's interest in that country, but of the Kaiser's personal interest. His subsequent career, like its antecedents, belonged to *Grosse Politik*, but it exhibited the same qualities described by Stronge as moderation and caution.[1]

Moderation and caution were the key to Stronge's own character. Though not naturally optimistic, he did not consider the Madero government's chances of survival dim, but noted with concern both the spread of Orozco's rebellion and the degree of hatred that prevailed against Americans, which one British consul likened to 'the hatred of the Chinese for the missionary: if I knew of any stronger hatred', he wrote, 'I would endeavour to express it by a still stronger measure'.[2] Stronge gave a copy of this report to the ambassador, from whose hands it found its way to the State Department files.[3]

It appears, however, that at the time of his proclamation, President Taft was in fact considering the possibility of intervention

[1] Biographical details from Eric Dombrowski, *German Leaders of Yesterday and To-day* (New York, 1920), pp. 262–70; *Der Grosse Brockhaus* (Leipzig, 1931), VIII; *Encyclopaedia Britannica* (London, 1963), XI.

In his memoirs (p. 222), Hohler wrote of him: 'Well before the War Admiral von Hintze's appointment in so out-of-the-way place [*sic*] as Mexico had indicated that the German Government wished to pay particular attention to Mexican affairs. Von Hintze's mother was English and he spoke English, and one or two other languages perfectly. He was small, inquisitive, a pleasant colleague; he entertained well and I used to enjoy his company.'

But cf. Nicolson, *Sir Arthur Nicolson, Bart., First Lord Carnock* (1930), pp. 293–4, 312 footnote, for a less favourable view, based on his activities in Russia.

[2] Stronge–Grey, 24 February 1912, no. 24. FO 371/1392 file 158/10523 encloses P. G. Holms–Stronge, 19 February 1912, no. 1, copy of which (extracted) in Wilson–Secretary of State, 1 March 1912, no. 1287. SDF 812.00/3070.

[3] This is virtually the only document from British sources to find its way into American files during the period down to the fall of Madero, although there are several examples of the reverse process. Guadalajara, with its large British colony, was one of the few significant places in Mexico with no U.S. consul.

in Mexico seriously enough to sound Bryce unofficially about the possibility of a joint move. It was equally seriously debated in London from the standpoint of its hazards.

Leslie was most concerned about the danger to European residents, and suggested that it would be best not to answer the dispatch. Spicer concurred.

In spite of the desire of H.M. Gov^t to meet the wishes of the U.S. Gov^t wherever possible I cannot but feel that any such intervention on our part might create a most inconvenient precedent [he minuted]. Similar revolutions may occur in any of the big republics of S. America in which our interests are quite as great as they are in Mexico, & yet we should be powerless in such cases to interfere without the approval of the U.S.—or rather without their invitation. In any case we should not I presume intervene unless other European powers were similarly invited & once Europe collectively began to intervene the consequences cannot be foreseen.

He ended by pointing out that the War Office was unlikely to be able to send a sufficient body of troops for such a purpose. This theme was developed by Sir Louis Mallet. His verdict was: 'I should think that HMG would hardly even consider the question of sending troops to Mexico & I am surprised that Mr Taft should have made it. A madder enterprize could not be conceived.'

Mr Acland,[1] Sir Arthur Nicolson, Sir Edward Grey and the Prime Minister did not dissent from this view.[2]

It was next the turn of the Mexican government to ask for British aid in their relations with the United States. Equally unofficially, Calero approached Stronge to complain of the action of the United States government in not cutting off the supply of arms to Ciudad Juárez. Though the official Foreign Office view was, 'We cannot interfere', we have seen that unofficially Bryce did convey these views to the administration, and, when news reached London of the joint resolution, it was very definitely welcomed. 'If this resolution is acted upon it should be a long step in the direction of preventing the U.S. from being used as the

---

[1] Francis Dyke Acland replaced Mr McKinnon Wood as Parliamentary Under Secretary at the Foreign Office on 24 October 1911, on the promotion of the latter to the Treasury.
[2] Bryce–Grey, 4 March 1912, no. 61 Very Confidential. FO 371/1392 file 158/10938.

Madero

jumping off ground for revolutions in Central America & Mexico', Spicer wrote.[1]

The Foreign Office made no comment on the proposal to notify areas of disturbance, either when it was first raised in Washington or when Stronge reported that the ambassador was considering it and, although there did not yet seem to be sufficient grounds, he proposed to follow suit 'should necessity arise'.[2] When he actually asked for permission to do so, however, Spicer suggested that such action would forfeit the right to hold the Mexican government legally responsible. C. J. B. Hurst gave as his opinion, as Assistant Legal Adviser, that this would be the case.

If the condition of affairs in the country is such that British subjects can only remain at their stations at the hazard of their lives, they ought to be advised to withdraw [he concluded], but the last teleg. of Mr Stronge . . . states that the reports are more reassuring, and the mere fact that the U.S.A. have taken this course scarcely seems conclusive as to its necessity. The U.S. Gov^t may have ulterior motives.[3]

But Stronge had already had to act to avert panic, and his message to British consular officers was a masterpiece. It read: 'US citizens have been notified to leave certain disturbed districts . . . You should advise British subjects stating that the measure is precautionary and of local application only, and that all is quiet in Mexico City.'[4]

The general move to arm the members of the foreign colonies after these warnings produced a disagreeable but rather petty quarrel between Stronge and Wilson over Stronge's interpretation of Wilson's views. The incident occurred at a dinner party when a member of the American colony, with the ambassador's concurrence, suggested that the Powers should send marines to Mexico. The ambassador said 'that he only waited a request from any two of his colleagues representing Great Powers in order to

[1] Stronge–Grey, 11 March 1912, Telegram no. 7; Bryce–Grey, 14 March 1912, Telegram no. 33 Urgent, and minutes. FO 371/1392 file 158/10677, 11122.
[2] Stronge–Grey, 2 March 1912, Telegram no. 4. FO 371/1392 file 158/9294.
[3] Stronge–Grey, 3 March 1912, 11.06 p.m., Telegram no. 5. FO 371/1392 file 158/9295, and minutes.
[4] Stronge–Grey, 5 March 1912, Telegram no. 6. FO 371/1392 file 158/9768.

take the initiative'. Stronge was left with the clear impression that he had been sounded officially, and, in reporting the incident to London, added that he had later told the ambassador that the suggestion would be disastrous.[1]

The Foreign Office, approving this view, repeated Stronge's telegram to Washington, where Bryce mentioned it to the President. Consequently, Wilson received a sharp rebuke from the State Department. To this he responded indignantly, saying that he had taxed Stronge for sending 'such peculiar information' to his government. From him Wilson secured his admission that he had been misled. Then, he claimed, Stronge had asked him to dictate a correct version of the matter and he had refused to do so. At this, Stronge had drafted a further telegram which was still 'not wholly' accurate, 'but which he said that he was obliged to word in such a manner as not to stultify himself'.[2] Not too much importance should be attached to this last charge; the effect of a telegram in the ambassador's characteristic style upon the Foreign Office is very hard to imagine. Furthermore, it is very hard to see how the message Stronge did send could have been worded to 'stultify' its sender, for it added, as confirmation of Stronge's interpretation, that the German minister had been approached by the same American 'alleging concurrence of the Ambassador'.[3]

[1] Stronge–Grey, 1 April 1912, Telegram no. 13. FO 371/1393 file 158/14027.

[2] Huntington Wilson–Wilson, Telegram, 3 April 1912, 6 p.m.; Wilson–Secretary of State, Telegrams, 3 April, 9 p.m.; 4 April, 6 p.m. SDF 812.00/3484A, 3485, 3493. Stronge–Grey, 2 April 1912, no. 100 Confidential, FO 371/1393 file 158/16355, reports the original incident and the steps taken by Stronge to confirm it in great detail. The penultimate paragraph is of special interest: 'Mr Schuyler, the newly arrived Secretary to the United States Embassy happened to be dining with me the same evening, and I took occasion to explain to him that it was very disagreeable to me to find myself at variance with his chief, whom I liked personally, that I would greatly prefer to work in accord with the American Embassy and that the last thing I wished was, in any way, to oppose American political influence or interests here. In the course of conversation which ensued Mr Schuyler said that the Ambassador was of a very nervous temperament, and that he was completely overwrought [*sic*]. He also told me, in strict confidence, that, just before leaving Washington, he had been told, he did not know why, that he must be prepared to take charge at any moment.'
    On the report closing the incident Spicer minuted: 'The incident is not important, but from what Mr Stronge says in his desp. No. 100 it certainly looks as if the U.S. Ambassador had really wished to bring about the landing of an international force, without however wishing to appear as the instigator of the idea' (FO 371/1393 file 158/16359).

[3] Stronge–Grey, 5 April 1912, Telegram no. 15. FO 371/1393 file 158/14426.

The story seems to be true as it stands, and the ambassador reacted violently precisely because he knew that he was playing a lone hand. It was in this sense that it was received in London. 'It looks as if the United States were contemplating some move or other', wrote R. H. Campbell. 'President Taft, to our surprise, made a somewhat similar suggestion the other day. Perhaps they would like to interfere, but want the onus of doing so to fall on others.'[1] But once the matter had developed into an incident, it was, of course, impossible to tell where the real responsibility lay.

Stronge had already accurately summarized the danger presented by the ambassador. '. . . I think it would be impossible for any Government to maintain itself here, in face of the open, or even concealed hostility of its powerful neighbour', he had written on 23 March. 'The American Ambassador assures me that he is doing his best to support the Madero Government, and he has given me some proof that this is so. His views are, however, so pessimistic that I think his Government might easily conclude that it was useless to compromise the future by supporting a lost cause.'[2]

Nevertheless, when the American note of 15 April appeared, Bryce reported: 'I see no reason to think that President Taft has changed the view he has consistently held and proclaimed, that armed intervention by the United States in Mexico ought, if possible, to be avoided.'[3] Stronge, however, considered that it made intervention a 'possible contingency'.[4] In view of the fact that the *Mexican Herald* persistently hinted that there was European pressure for intervention at the time, it is interesting to find that what was in fact being discussed in London was the withdrawal of the legation staff before American intervention took place, so as to avoid another Peking siege.[5]

Before the federal successes redressed the balance, Stronge

[1] Stronge–Grey, 5 April 1912, Telegram no. 15. FO 371/1393 file 158/14426, minute.
[2] Stronge–Grey, 23 March 1912, no. 78 Confidential. FO 371/1393 file 158/14832. Rather more alarming, perhaps, was the belief that Wilson seemed to hold that the arms ban was absolute. Had this been the case, the federal forces would have been hamstrung. Stronge–Grey, 22 March 1912, no. 76. FO 371/1393 file 158/14830. Also Bryce–Grey, 16 April 1912, no. 106. FO 371/1393 file 158/17495.
[3] Bryce–Grey, 16 April 1912, no. 106. FO 371/1393 file 158/17495.
[4] Stronge–Grey, 20 April 1912, no. 136; 27 April 1912, no. 150. FO 371/1393 file 158/19133, 20261.   [5] Stronge–Grey, 20 April 1912, no. 136, minutes.

himself was very gloomy about the government's prospects and tended to lay the blame for the continued tension on the President himself. He felt that, whatever might be the results of events in the north, some means would be found to 'bring about his suppression or retirement'.[1]

From then on, however, he was consistently optimistic. With the revival of rumours of intervention in September he reported:

... Mr Wilson still takes a very pessimistic view of the situation. He is apparently much under the influence of a small group of Americans of chauvinistic views who disseminate reports of disturbances in various parts of the country, and lay stress on the dangers of the political situation. I happen to know also that Mr Wilson has himself given news to the 'Mexican Herald' which was afterwards proved to be so exaggerated as to be altogether misleading.

And of the American complaints, he said: 'Personally I believe that the present state of affairs is very much what was to be expected, and that things will gradually improve, unless they should be disturbed by some unforseen incident.'[2] Even the revolt of Félix Díaz did not shake this opinion. Although he tried in his private capacity to intercede for Díaz's life,[3] he was not satisfied, as he said that many supposed, 'on very insufficient grounds, that a Diaz would know by instinct how to deal with brigands, and give the country the peace it so earnestly desires'. Had Díaz succeeded, he said, he could see nothing for the future but 'a long series of pronunciamientos which would, in the long run, have led to foreign intervention'.[4]

On the eve of Wilson's return to Mexico, rumours of intervention were again so persistent that Bryce felt it necessary to refute them. But ironically there was for the first time a real danger of a move towards a 'strong' policy in Washington. Taft, smarting under defeat at the polls, with nothing to lose and no immediate challenge to meet, wrote to Knox on 14 December: 'I am getting to a point where I think we ought to put a little

[1] Stronge–Grey, 3 May 1912, no. 163. FO 371/1394 file 158/21402.
[2] Stronge–Grey, 11 September 1912, no. 282. FO 371/1395 file 158/40142.
[3] Schuyler–Secretary of State, Telegram, 27 October 1912, 12 noon Confidential. SDF 812.00/5358.
[4] Stronge–Grey, 2 November 1912, no. 318. FO 371/1395 file 158/49016.

dynamite in for the purpose of stirring up that dreamer who seems unfitted to meet the crisis in the country of which he is President.' There seem an unconscious irony in the fact that the man who was writing was the man who had just proved so thoroughly unfitted to meet the crisis in his own country.

Once the decision to meet Lascuráin was taken, with Henry Lane Wilson's encouragement, it is clear that the Mexican was able, at least for the moment, to satisfy the administration. But in Mexico, doubt remained.[1]

Stronge was unhappy about the condition of the country. He noted that Schuyler was considering a proposal by which the United States would cut off the supply of funds to Mexico 'from the fountain head'—an interesting harbinger of events to come. Later he added that Wilson was attempting to use the German minister, under the pretext of exacting retribution for the 'Covadonga Massacre' (a local incident in which some five German traders lost their lives), for a fresh mandate for exerting pressure on the government.[2] Although Wilson by then regarded the government as 'hopelessly incompetent', and attached more importance —perhaps correctly—to the instability in the provinces than to the stability in the capital, Stronge later wrote: 'My own opinion was that if the Army could be conciliated and serious financial trouble avoided (and both seemed possible) the Madero Government would drag out its existence to the end of its term.'[3]

But this was not to be.

[1] Bryce–Grey, 6 January 1913, no. 2; Stronge–Grey, 30 December 1912, no. 344. FO 371/1670 files 2231, 2273. Taft–Knox, 14 December 1912, Personal. SDF 812.00/5697.
[2] Stronge–Grey, 3 January 1913, no. 1; 22 January 1913, no. 19 Confidential. FO 371/1670 files 2973, 5657.
[3] Stronge–Grey, 17 March 1913, no. 73 Confidential. FO 371/6269 file 1672/15911.

PART II

COUNTER-REVOLUTION

CHAPTER 4

RECOGNITION

The rising of Félix Díaz and Bernardo Reyes in the capital on 9 February 1913 was a *coup manqué*. The National Palace was to have been secured by treachery before Reyes arrived to take charge of it. Owing to the personal bravery of Gustavo Madero, and the loyalty of General Villar and a handful of troops, it was recovered for the government even before the news had spread that it had been lost. Reyes, confidently stepping towards the Palace in the face of what he believed was a purely formal warning not to do so, was felled by a bullet from the first salvo.

Díaz was more fortunate. Failing to gain control of any significant area of the city, he and his men—cadets from the Military College at Tlalpam—fell back on their principal objective, the arsenal or Ciudadela, and secured possession of it after a brisk exchange of rifle fire.[1] Following the pattern he had already established at Vera Cruz, he then proceeded to defend essentially static lines and to open negotiations with anyone who seemed inclined to listen to him. For the rest, Díaz had to rely on military loyalties and civilian non-involvement. He was not disappointed.

The problem for the government was to regain control of this one point with troops whose loyalties were an uncertain quantity. Unfortunately, General Villar, whose allegiance was beyond question, had been severely wounded in the retaking of the National Palace. It was there that the President, who had ridden in from Chapultepec on a white horse, took the decision to appoint General Victoriano Huerta in his place as military commander.

Huerta proposed two methods for the reduction of the Ciudadela. Wave upon wave of *rurales* were sent in frontal attack against the fortress. They were infallibly mown down by the concentrated fire of the machine guns they faced. Meanwhile an aimless bombardment was conducted by the artillery on both

[1] Stronge–Grey, 21 February 1913, no. 41. FO 371/1672 file 6269/13385.

sides; the Ciudadela was hit once by a federal shell, but both sides did a vast amount of damage to civilian property in the residential and business areas of the city. No real advance was made towards the capture of the Ciudadela—in fact the Felicista forces, heavily provisioned during the night with several waggon-loads of supplies that somehow managed to evade the vigilance of the federal sentries, eventually emerged from their fortress, which, whatever its real strength, was still virtually unscathed, and captured the YMCA. This last, by then in a very bad state of repair, was of little value as a strategic objective.

The attack began on 11 February and continued for eight days, during which time the apparent turns and changes in the military position were solemnly reported and the dispatches were headline news in Britain and America. The reporters cannot be blamed for not realizing at the time that the battle was not a real one; after all, it was being fought with live ammunition, and there were real casualties. Forty-four civilians were killed, including four Americans.[1] But it was not a real fight. Díaz had actually met Huerta on the first day of the battle, and from then on it was only a question of precisely how the government was to fall.[2]

The determining factor was the influence of the United States and how it was to be exerted. At the first news of trouble the President had ordered the now customary concentration of military and naval forces; in particular preparations for an expeditionary force which rapidly took shape at Galveston. To the administration this seemed to be a policy of restraint. To the Mexicans it was a cause of serious alarm, and the opponents of the government were not slow to place the responsibility for continued disorder on Madero himself. The State Department believed that Díaz might suppress the persistent disturbances in the provinces where Madero could not;[3] their reaction to a well-meant proposal of mediation by John Barrett, the Director-General of the Pan-American Union, was so hostile that it even seemed that they welcomed the upheaval as an excuse to intervene.

---

[1] Prida, *La Culpa de Lane Wilson*, p. 42. These figures were taken from the *Registro Civil*. See also Cumberland, *Mexican Revolution: Genesis under Madero* (1952), p. 258.

[2] Ross, *Francisco I. Madero, Apostle of Mexican Democracy* (1955), p. 291.

[3] Memorandum, W. T. S. Doyle–Secretary of State, 12 February 1913. SDF 812.00/6092.

In fact, they officially released a telegram from Henry Lane Wilson in which the proposal was denounced in unmeasured terms.[1] It seems that in the confusion the Department were prepared to attribute a degree of responsibility to the ambassador which, as we have seen, in the previous month they would not have done. The attitude of the ambassador towards the Mexican government was thereby given an official sanction which his propensity for exceeding instructions made extremely hazardous.

Nevertheless it is only fair to say that the Department kept him on as tight a rein as they knew how. He was refused 'instructions of a firm drastic and perhaps menacing character' on the 12th, and 'control . . . over the American ships and marines' on 15 February.[2] They remained oblivious to a clear hint on 14 February that he had been menacing Lascuráin with American might and discussing with him the possibility of the President's resignation.[3] But the same day Knox formally advised the ambassador to withdraw if the embassy was in danger, pointing out that the situation was by no means without precedent. The ambassador clearly did not wish to withdraw because it would have destroyed his *raison d'être* for making demands on the government.[4]

The Department behaved with propriety in informing Wilson at once of the full text of Madero's telegram complaining of his behaviour, while at the same time demanding a full explanation for the circumstances described in the concurrent Mexican note. But they showed no signs of concern over the ambassador's faithfully reported and growing involvement with General Huerta, whom Wilson expected to 'take steps . . . towards terminating the situation' after 16 February. This was a phrase that could only mean one thing, as Wilson afterwards never entirely denied: the overthrow of the government. No doubt could have remained after the ambassador's telegram of 17 February, which ran as follows:

[1] Wilson–Secretary of State, Telegram, 14 February, 1 p.m. SDF 812.00/6151.
[2] Wilson–Secretary of State, Telegram, 11 February, 6 p.m.; Knox–Wilson, Telegram, 12 February, 5 p.m.; Wilson–Secretary of State, Telegram, 14 February, 11 a.m.; Knox–Wilson, Telegram, 15 February, 4 p.m. SDF 812.00/6092, 6149.
[3] Wilson–Secretary of State, Telegram, 14 February, 2 p.m. Confidential. SDF 812.00/6153.   [4] Knox–Wilson, Telegram, 14 February, 7 p.m. SDF 812.00/6170 A.

General Huerta has just sent his messenger to me again to say that I may anticipate some action which will [1 cypher group omitted] Madero from power at any moment and that plans were fully matured, the purpose of delay being to avoid any violence or bloodshed. I asked no [1 cypher group omitted] and made no suggestions *beyond requesting that no lives be taken except by due process of law*. [My italics.]

Wilson was ingenuous. The fact that he had made any condition could only have been interpreted as tacit acceptance, even as encouragement. It is not necessary to see it in a more sinister light. Though he later described the *ley fuga* as a 'process' in reference to the death of Gustavo Madero, whether or not he considered it 'due process of law' will never be known, but the ambiguity was probably slovenly thinking, not deliberate incitement to murder.[1]

Wilson's attitude has been very thoroughly documented and annotated from within days of its culmination. There can be no doubt that it was based on a dislike of Madero and his government which had grown to such proportions that, in the name of peace, he exerted every power at his command to bring about their overthrow. Indeed, from his own dispatches and later speeches, not to mention his own memoirs, it is apparent that he considered this overthrow, and the settlement afterwards to which he was a party, to be a major diplomatic victory for his country.[2] The tragedy was that the government he helped to overthrow was far more satisfactory to the real interests of the United States than any that could be expected to follow it. Its anti-Americanism existed largely in his imagination, and in the settlement he was merely the instrument of the ineptness of Díaz, the military power of Huerta, and the weariness of the civilians.

Wilson believed that a Díaz could once again bring firm

[1] Wilson–Secretary of State, Telegram 16 February, 12 midnight, Confidential. SDF 812.00/6186; Wilson–Secretary of State, Telegram, 17 February, 4 p.m. SDF 812.00/6225; Wilson–Secretary of State, Telegram no. 14, 19 February, 5 p.m. SDF 812.00/6264. See also Querido Moheno, *Mi actuación política después de la Decena Trágica* (Mexico, 1939), pp. 13–14; Knox–Wilson, Telegram no. 21, 21 February, 2 p.m., SDF 812.00/6294 A.
[2] See American Academy of Political and Social Science, *Annals*, LIV—'International Relations of the United States' (Philadelphia, Pa., 1914), pp. 148 ff.; Wilson, p. 282; *The World*, Friday, 7 March 1913; and Mexico (City) Committee of the American Colony, *Facts*, etc. (Mexico, [1913]), pp. 8–12, representative of opposed views on his actions and the ambassador's own; also: Luis Manuel Rojas, *La Culpa de Lane Wilson en el Gran Desastre de México* (Mexico, 1928), 1 (no other published).

government to Mexico. But Díaz failed even to reach power, Huerta failed to achieve the pacification of the country, and Wilson himself was branded as a monster and dismissed with ignominy. It is impossible not to see him as a tragic figure. For the first time in his Mexican career he had been too optimistic.

It should be said that *at the time* his attitude corresponded to almost unanimous reports in the American press. Editorial comment differed within narrow limits but the actual news sources, though differently treated by more or less imaginative sub-editors, were substantially the same, no doubt owing much to the Associated Press and *Mexican Herald* network closely linked to the embassy.[1] Díaz was erroneously reported from the beginning to have virtual control of the city.[2] Madero was given the full blame for trying to suppress the revolt.[3] The most sensational example, however, was the false report which gained banner headlines everywhere on Saturday, 15 February, that Madero had already resigned and that de la Barra was again to become provisional President. The credence given to this even by the leading papers would be beyond belief if the report on which it was based had not commanded the highest confidence. It was, in fact, ascribed to the British legation.[4]

Throughout the *Decena Trágica*, as the period is known, the American ambassador, whether threatening the President with intervention, calling on him to resign, negotiating with Félix Díaz in the Ciudadela, arranging a cease fire, or endeavouring to get in touch with General Huerta, claimed to be acting in the name of the diplomatic corps. Manuel Márquez Sterling, the then Cuban minister, has indicated that for these purposes the corps consisted only of European representatives, in particular the British, German and Spanish ministers. The Latin American representatives were either not consulted, or they were faced with a *fait accompli*.[5]

---

[1] *The New York Times*, Thursday, 13 February 1913, editorial: 'Our duty towards Mexico'; *The World*, Tuesday, 11 February 1913, editorial: 'A Warning to Mexico'; Wednesday, 12 February 1913, editorial: 'Mediation not Intervention'.

[2] *The New York Times*, Monday, 10 February 1913.

[3] *Ibid.* Wednesday, 12 February 1913.

[4] *Ibid.* Saturday, 15 February 1913.

[5] Manuel Márquez Sterling, *Los últimos días del presidente Madero (Mi gestión diplomática en México)* (Havana, 1917), p. 371: 'Le estorbaban al Embajador los ministros que no se

The Spanish minister, it is generally agreed, was in a special position. His colony was exceptionally large, and the members of it were to all intents and purposes indistinguishable from Mexicans. Their dangers, therefore, were particularly great, and the minister himself, who had once in his life undergone a similar terrifying experience at the Siege in Peking, was determined at any cost to ensure that such a situation would not recur.[1]

It has long been assumed the British and German ministers were men of such weak fibre that they just did what the ambassador told them. How this view could have arisen is rather obscure. The subsequent career of von Hintze was one of remarkable initiative and independence, while Stronge, for all his eccentricities and his donnish manner, was a man of very decided views. Either of them might have supported the ambassador for other reasons: in von Hintze's case perhaps to establish authoritarian rule, or in Stronge's perhaps for economic reasons, but the fact is that they have not been accused of doing so.

Naturally the figure of Henry Lane Wilson, claiming as he did to be leading a group, attracted the principal share of the blame. William Bayard Hale,[2] for example, in his mission on behalf of President Wilson, was naturally mainly concerned with the part of the American ambassador, whom he considered to have betrayed democracy. Reporting that he 'took the topsy-turvy view that the President, by not surrendering instantly to the mutineers, was responsible for the bloodshed', he shows, however, that chance too played a part in forming his assessment of the ministers.

This view was congenial to the Spanish Minister, and to it were won the British and the German ministers. The Spanish and German

plegaron a su criterio en la primera junta; y de un gesto imperativo, suprimía la representación, en México, a los menos, de tres cuartas partes del planeta.' See also William Belmont Parker, *Cubans of To-day* (New York, 1919), p. 579.

[1] *Enciclopedia Universal Ilustrada, Europeo–Americana,* XIV. Señor Cologan is said to have been of Irish extraction. Peter Fleming, *The Siege at Peking* (London, 1959), pp. 102–3. See also *ibid.* pp. 145–7, 251 footnote.

[2] Baker describes him as 'a brilliant journalist who was, however, temperamentally unfitted for such a task' (*Woodrow Wilson, Life and Letters,* vol. IV, p. 243). Despite this judgement, his report seems to be substantially accurate. Hale had been author of Wilson's campaign biography, but subsequently became a paid propagandist for the German embassy and finally broke with Wilson publicly (*Dictionary of American Biography,* VIII).

ministers are not now in Mexico, but I have had the honour of meeting
the British minister, and am obliged to say that I never met an individual
whose character so absurdly belied his name [he wrote]. Mr Stronge is
a silly, stuttering imbecile, the laughing-stock of the whole city, which
regales itself with nothing more to its perennial delight than daily stories
of Mr Stronge and the parrot by which he is constantly attended.[1]

It is curious that Hale must have had access to documents
which would have led him to question this view. But he was not a
professional investigator: his task was to ascertain Wilson's part,
and, by the time he had completed his report, Stronge had already
been transferred to Chile. But the publication by Isidro Fabela of
these documents—copies of messages from Stronge to the ambassador—now raises the question of their significance, as well as
the question he poses: 'Did the Foreign Office then have any
information relating to the arbitrary conduct of its diplomatic
representative in Mexico? Because to have had knowledge of that
act would have been a motive more than sufficient for stripping
him of his important office.'[2]

The first is dated 10.20 p.m., Wednesday, 12 February 1913. It
runs:

If I could get over to you I doubt very much whether I could get back.
I associate myself with you and my colleagues in any measure you
may take to put an end to the present state of things.

The second is dated 14 February 1913:

Mr Brenchley has just told me that you had privately urged Mr
Lascurain to get some members of the Senate together who should
impose the resignation of President Madero.

I entirely concur in the course you have taken which seems to me to
be well adapted to bring to an end this intolerable situation.

The third is dated 15 February 1913. It has a particularly interesting history, for Wilson quoted it verbatim in a telegram to

[1] William Bayard Hale, Memorandum, 18 June 1913. SDF 812.00/7798½ [sic]. This has
not been published in full in English, but a full text in Spanish translation, with com-
mentary, may be found in John P. Harrison, 'Henry Lane Wilson, el trágico de la
decena', *Historia Mexicana*, VI, no. 23, enero–marte 1957, pp. 374–405.
[2] Isidro Fabela, *Historia Diplomática de la Revolución Mexicana, I, 1910–1917* (Mexico,
1958), p. 87.

Washington dated 9 p.m. of the same day. On 26 February he further telegraphed the Department to transmit Stronge's request that the 'letter be not published nor made a part of the record as it was a personal expression of views'. Knox told him to inform Stronge that this would be done, but, although the communication was not published, it remained on the files.

Mr de la Barra is here [it began]. From what he tells me Madero's final decision as regards resignation will largely depend on the reply he receives from President Taft.

I gather that he would or at least might resign in face of a threat of immediate intervention.

A fourth note is not dated. It is headed *Private—Most Confidential*, and reads:

As you are, of course, aware the Minister of Foreign Affairs becomes the head of the Administration in default of the President and Vice President.

Now I have good reason to believe that if Mr Madero were induced to resign and to put Mr Lascurain in the position of provisional President, the latter would receive the cordial support of persons of great political influence and reputation...

I may add that although Mr Lascurain does not belong to the Progresista party, he has necessarily been brought in close contact with its principal leaders, and would therefore find less difficulty in dealing with them than any other man (not actually belonging to the party) who has taken part in recent politics.

Two of the ambassador's replies to these missives survive in written form. Both are dated 17 February. The one in reply to Stronge's note of the 14th says:

In this connection it may be of interest to you to know that President Madero caused a very false, wicked and misleading telegram to be sent to Washington in which, among other things, he attempted to convey the impression that our joint, friendly and unofficial action in suggesting his resignation was a formal act of Diplomatic Corps instigated by this Embassy. Von Hintze, learning of this yesterday, was very indignant and has advised his Government of the falsity of this Government's statement. I am informed that you have done the same...

The internal contradiction in this message is not resolved, least of all by the other reply, which deals with something entirely different.

I have your letter relative to the desirability of having Mr Lascurain succeed to the executive functions in the event that there should be a default [it begins]. I esteem Mr Lascurain very highly but fear that he would not be strong enough for the part as my experience for the last few days has shown me that he is vacillating and prone to fall in a highly nervous state.

Reports have just come to the Embassy that Huerta is the virtual prisoner of his officers in the Palace. This story, while not confirmed, may possibly account for his failure to keep the appointment which he himself made with me for yesterday. The story is that these officers are in direct communication with Diaz and are advising him how to direct the destructive fire which he is making.

If I can do anything for you I shall be very glad to place my services at your disposition.[1]

The context in which these messages were written is clearly of the first importance. Yet there is little that has been published that casts any more light on Stronge's motivation during this period—even Hohler, to his great regret, was absent on a visit to Guatemala and El Salvador during the crucial days, and did not return until all was over.[2] The truth has to be extracted from Stronge's own telegrams and reports to the Foreign Office, and from the lengthy memorandum, written partly at the time and partly from memory, in which he described the events of the period.[3]

On the first news of the rising Stronge, in common with most of the other representatives, went to the United States embassy, where they arranged for the ambassador to apply for protection

---

[1] Wilson–William Jennings Bryan, 12 March 1913, no. 1901, Annexures 17, 25, 31, 48, 49 and 50. SDF 812.00/6840.

[2] Hohler, *Diplomatic Petrel* (1942), p. 181. His journey was, however, not without its excitements. During his visit to El Salvador he arranged to meet President Araujo, but, on his way to the interview, a little late, he heard the noise of the President being shot (4 February 1913). Because of the coup in Mexico, the news of President Araujo's death on 9 February did not officially reach that city until 24 February, by which time Mexico had had three Presidents. Mexico thereupon recognized the new President of Salvador (México, Secretaría de Relaciones Exteriores, *Boletín*, xxxv, nos. 2, 3 and 4, 28 February 1913, p. 110).

[3] Stronge–Grey, 21 February 1913, no. 41. FO 371/1672 file 6269/13385. All quotations covering period to 18 February 1913 from this source unless otherwise cited.

for the foreign colonies. In the afternoon they gathered again and were told by Wilson that Díaz had sent a messenger to him 'with a request that the Diplomatic Body would use its influence with the Government to induce them to yield, as he held the town and he wanted to prevent unnecessary bloodshed'. The same messenger had also been to the Palace to suggest that joint measures be taken to protect the colonies. However, when Madero assented and dispatched the head of the police, General Figueroa, to the Palace, Díaz had the latter arrested.[1] In the presence of the Corps, Wilson then spoke to Lascuráin, but 'the response . . . though courteous, was so unsatisfactory' that the diplomatists decided that they were 'justified in applying to General Díaz'. But Díaz later 'replied that he could give no guarantees, and that that was the affair of the constituted Government'.[2] This proved, if proof was needed, that Díaz did not hold the town as he had claimed.

It was certainly late in the evening when Stronge dispatched his first telegram on the outbreak. It reported severe street fighting and gave credence to the belief that the majority of the troops in the city had gone over to Díaz, which was not the case. After detailing arrangements made to secure foreigners against mob uprising, it concluded: 'I learn this moment by telephone from Spanish Minister that the President and Minister have just escaped [sic] from the palace leaving General Humerta [sic] in possession. If this is true an arrangement between military chiefs seems probable.'[3]

No further official telegram reached the Foreign Office from Mexico until the morning of 15 February, though unofficial communication was secured through a Mr Woodcock, the assistant manager of the Galveston–Vera Cruz Cable Company, and a British subject. This is the more curious since Stronge indicates

---

[1] He was released unharmed at the end of hostilities.

[2] Compare Wilson–Secretary of State, Telegram, 9 February, 7 p.m. SDF 812.00/6058, which emphasizes that Wilson contacted the Secretary of External Relations only *after* the emissary from Díaz had asked him to persuade Madero to resign. The ambassador stated that he 'was unable to take any action as he had no credentials' and 'would not assume any responsibility except with the approval of entire Diplomatic corps'. The envoy then returned with credentials.

Lascuráin's actual reply—'that he would do all he could'—does not seem unreasonable in the circumstances.

[3] Stronge–Grey, 9 February 1913, Telegram no. 8. FO 371/1671 file 6269/6269.

that the city was quiet on Monday, 10 February, and his day passed in arranging for a guard of British subjects. He also agreed, on an inquiry from Mr Body, of S. Pearson and Son, to take the Vice-President into the legation if his life was in danger.

Madero's mysterious departure from the Palace, it is now well known, was to motor to Cuernavaca to secure reinforcements from the loyal troops of General Ángeles, the most distinguished Mexican artillerist of his day. He stayed the night in Mrs King's hotel, under the protection of the British flag, and returned to the capital the next day.[1] Meanwhile the square round the Palace was entrenched, and Huerta sent out troops for the protection of the colonies, as Stronge bears witness.

Once the firing had begun, the legation (the new building on the Paseo de la Reforma which had been completed by S. Pearson and Son just before the coronation of King George V) was in a particularly exposed position, and separated from both the embassy and the cable office by the width of the avenue itself. Nevertheless, it was there that de la Barra chose to take refuge. It is clear that his presence was worth little from the point of view of information, for most of the rumours he reported were incorrect. But he did not waste his time, for he spent some of the interval writing letters to the President and General Díaz offering to mediate. Wilson, who had meanwhile been told by Díaz that his position was strong, did the same.

When firing was resumed early on 12 February, telephone communication with the embassy and other legations was cut off. Nevertheless, Manuel Calero was able to join de la Barra in sanctuary, while notes summoning de la Barra to a meeting of senators and Stronge to a meeting of the diplomatic corps were delivered. Stronge was unwilling to run the risk of being marooned at the embassy, leaving the ladies at the legation on their own. Accordingly, as we have seen, he sent a note in reply associating himself with the actions of his colleagues. Though apparently rash in the breadth of its terms, it is clear that its author did not envisage the ambassador acting except in accord with the corps.

[1] King, pp. 107-11. The President also sought aid from Zapata, but it was refused.

When later he learnt that Wilson, von Hintze and Cologan were making fresh representations for protection he did join them in time to accompany them to the Ciudadela. By this time the legation was in the centre of heavy fire, apparently as the result of the siting of federal cannon in the vicinity. Stronge, through Lascuráin, succeeded in having these moved, but was told by the Foreign Office, through Woodcock, the following day: 'You should inform the Mexican Govt. that HMG will hold them responsible should injury befall you or your staff. You should on no account incur any risk which could be avoided & if possible should leave the Legation for safer quarters. Ships are being sent to Vera Cruz.'[1]

In the early hours of 14 February 'General Ángeles came to invite Mr de la Barra to go to the Palace, but the latter had gone out early before the firing began to see his wife', Stronge recorded. 'I gave the General his address.' De la Barra had taken refuge, he said, because his life was in danger from the Maderistas; yet Stronge gave his address to the best-known Maderista general. The minister informed the Foreign Office that he believed that the summons indicated that the government wished to come to some arrangement with the rebels.[2] It seems clear that this suggestion originated from de la Barra himself and that it was he who by passing on this view to the press created the false story that Madero had already resigned. At 10.30 in the evening, after a further day of bombardment, cars went from the embassy, and Stronge and Wilson were joined there by the German and Spanish ministers. It seems clear that the rest of the corps was not summoned.

Mr Wilson then told us that he had called us together as he thought the time had come for us to take some further action [Stronge wrote afterwards]. He had, himself, told Mr Lascurain, who had come to him for advice, that if he would allow him to speak quite privately, he felt bound to say 'that Madero must get out', and Mr Lascurain, who was in an almost distracted state and had no other solution to propose, had accepted his view. We discussed the matter until nearly three in the

---

[1] Grey–Mr Woodcock, 12 February 1913, Telegram. FO 371/1671 file 6269/6876.
[2] Stronge–Grey, 14 February 1913, Telegram no. 9. FO 371/1671 file 6269/7447.

morning, and finally decided that Mr Cologan, the Spanish Minister, should go to the Palace as soon as it could be arranged, and after making an appeal to the President's feelings of patriotism should suggest to him as a private hint from himself and his colleagues of the United States, Germany and England that his resignation would simplify the situation and lead the way to peace. The exact wording of the communication we left to the Spanish Minister in whose tact we had every confidence.

It is clear, since this meeting lasted into 15 February, that Stronge's note to Wilson dated 14 February must have been written *before* he went to the embassy. He was therefore aware beforehand what the meeting was likely to be about, since he knew and had approved of Wilson's moves to get Lascuráin to put pressure on Madero through members of the Senate. It is hard to say that he was 'won' to the ambassador's view: as early as the first day of the rising he had made it clear that he believed an 'arrangement between military chiefs' could be obtained if Madero were removed. As the move was unofficial, it is not surprising that the Foreign Office was told merely: 'Situation at legation unchanged. Heavy firing continues',[1] but it was certainly misleading, if only because the federal guns had been taken away.

On 15 February Cologan was received by Madero and a delegation of senators by Ernesto Madero, who, as de la Barra reported, 'represented that the situation of the Government was not unfavourable and stated that the President had sent a telegram to Mr Taft putting matters in their true light'. Stronge continued:

I think that it was on this occasion that Mr Lascurain pointed out the great danger the country was running, and finding that his arguments were of no avail, altogether broke down. I gathered from Mr de la Barra's statements that Mr Taft's reply to the President's telegram would have a deciding influence as regards the question of resignation, and I, at once, conveyed this information to Mr Wilson in a private letter.

This was the third letter—the second being overlooked by the memorandum. Furthermore, it seems probable that the undated message, recommending Lascuráin for the interim Presidency, was sent the same day. In any case, this is the point at which

[1] Stronge–Grey, 15 February 1913, Telegram no. 10. FO 371/1671 file 6269/7448.

Stronge exceeded his duty as a representative and began to take actions designed to promote changes in the country's internal affairs.

The fact that Stronge was in communication with the embassy only by messenger makes it unlikely that he had any real knowledge of the text of the telegram dispatched by Madero to Taft. It was a plea for non-intervention, which, after stressing the strength of the government's position, indicated that its chief fear was of the landing of American marines, and that Wilson had been making threats that he could bring this about.[1] An official note delivered at Washington further accused the ambassador of using the diplomatic corps as cover for his own ends.[2] The same day, the Mexican government sent out a circular to governors of states indicating its fear of imminent American attack. It seems most probable that this was a real fear—as the behaviour of the normally staid Lascuráin indicates—and not merely an attempt to rally the country behind a failing cause. Even the State Department were sure that Wilson had in fact made the threat attributed to him.

Lascuráin's behaviour throughout the *Decena Trágica* has provoked startlingly little criticism; even Fabela, the first to depart to any extent from the long tradition of ignoring him altogether except as a cypher, criticizes him only for his role in the events leading up to the installation of Huerta as President and the subsequent death of Madero. It is not, however, the place of a Foreign Minister to side with foreign diplomatists in moves to overthrow the government of which he is a member.

[1] 'I have been informed that the Government over which Your Excellency so worthily presides has ordered that warships shall set out for Mexican coasts with troops to be disembarked to come to this capital to give protection to Americans. Undoubtedly the information which you have and which has caused you so to determine is erroneous or exaggerated ...' (Knox–Wilson, Telegram, 15 February, 12 midnight (*en clair*), quoting from Madero–Taft, Telegram, 14 February, 9 p.m. SDF 812.00/6172C).

[2] 'At the instigation of Ambassador Wilson with a part of the Diplomatic Corps one of its members was commissioned to notify President Madero that he should resign his position in order to solve the present conflict in the city. The President refused to recognise the right of the diplomatic representatives who had come together to interfere in the domestic affairs of the nation and informed them that he was resolved to die at his post before permitting foreign interference. The Ambassador, in view of local circumstances, will try perhaps to disembark marines and this will produce an unnecessary international conflict terrible consequences' (Knox–Wilson, Telegram, 15 February, 12 midnight, *loc. cit.*).

Recognition

The telegram to governors already mentioned was first reported to the State Department by Wilson on 16 February as having been received by the Governor of Aguascalientes on the previous day; this is in itself an interesting point. From the outset, the ambassador claimed that it was a deliberate falsehood on Madero's part, comparable with the telegram to the Mexican embassy in Washington, and cited as evidence a letter allegedly received from Lascuráin admitting that he had told him as early as the 14th that he had no control over the landing of marines. In view of Lascuráin's behaviour in other matters this cannot be taken as evidence of knowledge in the President.

On the contrary, there can be no doubt that Wilson had threatened the Mexican government with the eventuality that European pressure might force the United States to land troops, much as he was to do later on the occasion of the conclusion of the *Pacto de la Ciudadela*. To make better use of this non-existent pressure he had applied to Washington, as we have already seen, for permission to land United States troops on his own initiative. This permission was not refused until the 15th, the day *after* the meeting covered by Lascuráin's letter; this casts a very different light on what took place at this meeting. There can be no doubt that these manœuvres were transparent to the State Department since a memorandum attached to the White House copy of President Madero's telegram reads: 'Mr Dearing, who translated attached message, says he is confident it is the result of statement made to President Madero by Ambassador Wilson on his own responsibility.'[1]

On Sunday, 16 February there was an armistice, arranged by the ambassador and the German and Spanish ministers. Stronge, it appears, did not leave the legation, reporting to London only: 'Firing ceased since last night. Situation uncertain.'[2] In the interval

[1] For role of Lascuráin see: Fabela, *Historia Diplomática de la Revolución Mexicana*, vol. 1 (1958), pp. 103–4; Márquez Sterling, pp. 427–8. For documentation of the telegram dispute see: Wilson–Secretary of State, 16 February, 3 p.m. SDF 812.00/6181. Prida, *La Culpa de Lane Wilson*, and Wilson–Secretary of State, Telegram, 17 February, 3 p.m. SDF 812.00/6224. Madero–Taft, Telegram. SDF 812.00/6532, together with memorandum by Dearing.
[2] Stronge–Grey, [16] February 1913, Telegram no. 11. FO 371/1671 file 6269/7449.

before the armistice was broken about noon, foreigners were removed to safety.

Later on [the British minister recorded], I received a letter from Mr Wilson asking me to telegraph Mr Bryce, which I, at once, did . . . The telegram was to the effect that President Madero's telegram to Mr Taft was misleading, that Mr Wilson's reports were to be trusted, and that the resignation of Mr Madero seemed to be the only possible solution.[1]

None of these statements was in fact true, although allowances must be made for the confusion of events. Significantly, Wilson's note to Stronge is not preserved in his report to the State Department. By any standards it was a surprising message: a further attempt to put pressure on his own government to back up his threats in Taft's prospective reply to the Mexican President. Stronge may or may not by this time have read Madero's telegram—it is hard to see how he could have, without either going to the embassy or to the Palace, for no newspapers were being published.[2] He certainly could not have seen the embassy's latest reports and been in a position to testify to their accuracy.

Indeed, in the last two days of the bombardment Stronge had no part to play. The initiative for the ambassador's private meeting with General Huerta came from the German minister, and he was Wilson's only companion at it. When Huerta invited him to a further meeting, he considered inviting only the German and Spanish ministers to accompany him. However, this meeting was postponed because knowledge that Huerta intended to change sides had reached Maderista ears, and he was temporarily under arrest.

The ambassador's knowledge of Huerta's intentions after his release came through a 'confidential messenger'. This was Enrique Cepeda, officially nephew but actually natural son of Huerta, who promised the ambassador that he would be the first to be informed when the coup was successfully accomplished. There can be no doubt that the ambassador had full details of its

[1] Text of telegram in Stronge–Grey, 16 February 1913, Telegram no. 13. FO 371/1671 file 6269/7604.

[2] The *Mexican Herald* ceased publication on 15 February; the others at latest on the previous day. The ambassador claimed that the *Herald* had been suppressed (Wilson–Secretary of State, 16 February, 11 a.m. SDF 812.00/6180). It need hardly be stated that there would have been excellent reasons for its suppression.

nature in advance, for he reported it to Washington at the time it was supposed to have taken place, though it was late.[1]

The denouement was not long in coming. The firing, which continued on 17 February, had ceased on the morning of 18 February. The suspicions of Huerta's motives, which had led to his temporary custody in the Palace, had been relieved by the apparent sincerity of his protestations of loyalty.[2] At this point there came a fresh intervention by General Blanquet, notorious in Mexican history as the man who gave the Emperor Maximilian the *coup de grâce* at his execution at Querétaro. Fresh troops under his command moved into their positions as the men under the command of General Ángeles were on the point of attaining a vantage point next to the Ciudadela from where it could have been entirely demolished by point-blank fire.[3] The sympathetic reply of President Taft disclaiming intentions of intervention[4] did not affect the dangers inherent in the military situation for the federal commander. To save his own position he had to act, and under his orders Blanquet's troops arrested Gustavo Madero, the temporary commander of the police, and, around 2 p.m., the President and Vice-President. Stronge did not learn of this until he was 'sent for' by the ambassador around 4 p.m. He was therefore not implicated in the actual overthrow of the Madero government, even if he did know beforehand that it was going to happen.[5]

Late into the evening, under the auspices of Henry Lane Wilson, General Huerta and General Díaz negotiated in the

[1] Wilson–Secretary of State, Telegrams: 15 February, 7 p.m.; 15 February, 11 p.m.; 16 February, 11 a.m.; 18 February, 2 p.m. and no. 9, 18 February, 12 noon. SDF 812.00/6175, 6178, 6180 (*cit. sup.*), 6245 and 6249.
[2] Calero states positively that Madero never trusted Huerta (*Un Decenio de Política Mexicana* (1920), p. 116). At the beginning of the revolt Henry Lane Wilson believed that his loyalty was doubtful (Wilson–Secretary of State, Telegram, 10 February, 12 noon. SDF 812.00/6075). The General's name was on the list of conspirators given to Gustavo Madero beforehand, though marked with a query (Bell, *The Political Shame of Mexico* (1914), pp. 257 ff.). In fact, the plot was delayed because he refused to join it, and began when it did only because the conspirators knew word of it had leaked out (Hohler–Grey, 24 September 1913, no. 303. FO 371/1677 file 6269/46230). Ross, pp. 304–5, describes how it was the President himself who returned Huerta's pistol and had him released on 17 February.
[3] Hohler–Grey, 24 September 1913, no. 303; Bell, p. 287.
[4] *The New York Times*, Monday, 17 February; Tuesday, 18 February 1913.
[5] Stronge–Grey, 21 February 1913. On his part in the Decena Trágica as a whole, see O'Shaughnessy, *Intimate Pages of Mexican History*, p. 235.

American embassy for a settlement. Wilson finally observed that European powers might force United States intervention if one was not forthcoming.[1] It was agreed that Huerta should become provisional President while Díaz would be allowed to be a candidate for the definitive Presidency at the next elections, and this was embodied in the formal pact called the *Pacto de la Ciudadela*. But Madero was still President, though Huerta had by proclamation taken over the executive power.[2]

Not until the following day were the resignations of the President and Vice-President procured and laid before the Chamber of Deputies, who voted to accept them. With every formality, Lascuráin was sworn in as President. He appointed General Huerta as Secretary of *Gobernación* in his sole official act, and at once resigned, whereupon the Chamber accepted General Huerta as provisional President. General Díaz at his side appeared to many as the guarantee of peace and order they had so long been seeking.

At the last, the British Foreign Office were not left in ignorance of the part their emissary was playing. After telegraphing to Bryce, Stronge had brought the whole question of Madero's resignation into the open (16 February).

[?Spanish Representative] in the name of U.S. Ambassador, German Minister and myself yesterday urged President to resign [he reported].

Majority of Senate acting together have done the same I think unanimously. President remains obdurate. M.F.A. yesterday urged danger of American intervention but I gather from Mr de la Barra that the President did not fear it as he had telegraphed his version of the situation to Mr Taft. I am, as is U.S. Ambassador, adding that it seems that a threat of immediate intervention would have great weight.

The US ambassador wishes to get every possible support in forcing the resignation.[3]

---

[1] The ambassador had, of course, no warrant for such a threat (Wilson, p. 281).
[2] The agreement between the generals was a formal pact, officially entitled the *Pacto de la Ciudadela*, but popularly and correctly known as the *Pacto de la Embajada*. After Stronge's departure from Mexico Hohler transmitted to London a full account of its negotiation which other sources confirm to be extremely accurate, and which has been cited above as Hohler–Grey, 24 September 1913, no. 303. His source was Félix Díaz's interpreter.
[3] This is the original decypher of Stronge's telegram, which was subsequently emended in the Foreign Office by replacing 'am, as is' by 'have told' and 'seems' by 'seemed'. Stronge–Grey, 16 February 1913, Telegram un-numbered and minutes. FO 371/1671 file

This telegram produced the sort of debate in the Foreign Office that should really have taken place in the minds of the diplomatists in Mexico, and at the outbreak of hostilities instead of when the régime was already at the point of collapse. Despite the last paragraph it was received with calm and deliberation, and the proposals were considered on their merits.

'President Madero's resignation would be the best solution', minuted H. M. Knatchbull-Hugessen,[1] then a new entrant to the Foreign Office, recently appointed to the American Department. 'But can we help to procure it without our action being too much in the nature of an intervention; &, if we do, can we [? be sure] that Diaz will mend matters? . . . Perhaps when Pres^{dt} Madero finds that his appeal to Mr Taft has failed he will be more inclined to resign, without further outside pressure, especially if Diaz is gaining ground & feeling against him is rising.' He favoured approving Stronge's actions and advising him that he might support the United States.

Spicer, however, (rightly) remarked that it was an internal question for Mexico. 'Should Madero succeed in overcoming his opponents the position of H.M. Minister will not be improved by the advice given to resign', he observed. 'If the U.S. Amb^r likes to threaten the intervention of his Gov^t I do not see that we are in any way called upon to support him.' He recommended that Stronge be advised accordingly.

6269/7624. Compare Hintze–Bethmann-Hollweg, Telegram no. A18, r. 11.55 a.m., 17 February 1913, GFM 12/15 f. A3442:

'Amerikanischer Botschafter arbeitet unverhohlen für Diaz, hat in meiner Gegenwart zu Madero den Grund gesagt, Diaz sei proamerikanisch. Diese Parteinahme erschwert Tätigkeit des diplomatischen Corps. Regierungstruppen anfangen des Kampfes überdrüssig zu werden.

Die über Washington kommenden Nachrichten sind mit Mißtrauen aufzunehmen, weil zugunsten Diaz gefärbt.

Wirke mit allem Nachdruck nur für Schutz Deutscher, hatte mich sonst gegenüber den vielen amerikanischen Ansuchen zurück ohne anzustoßen.

Botschafter und spanischen Gesandten haben ungeregt, Madero zum Verzicht aufzufordern, englische Gesandten einverstanden, französischer Geschäftsträger hat von vornherein seine Zustimmung zu allen Schritten gegeben die wir 4 unternehmen. Ich habe erwirkt, dass lediglich freundschaftlicher Rat gegeben, Verzeiht als zeitweilige Lösung der Schwierigkeit in Betracht zu ziehen, spanischer Gesandter dazu von uns 5 ermächtig, hat diesen freundschaftlichen Rat angebracht doch nicht angenommen.'

[1] His memoirs, *Diplomat in Peace and War* (London, 1949), say little about the position in 1913.

The reply, drafted by Sir Louis Mallet with an addition by Sir Edward Grey, ran as follows:

> The situation is doubtless very critical and you are the best judge of how to deal with it but I am doubtful of wisdom of pressing resignation on Madero as the revolt is essentially a question of internal politics. I must however leave this more or less to your discretion. It would likewise be better to refrain from making any communication to the United States Ambassador which he might interpret as encouraging the military intervention of the United States Government—the sole responsibility of that must be left to the United States Government. Neither party in Mexico would presumably thank us for encouraging it.

By the time this was dispatched, at 3 p.m., 19 February, Madero was already in custody, and it would have been received about the time when Madero signed his resignation.[1] Had Stronge informed London on 14 February, when the question first arose, there is little doubt that the reply would have been the same, while had he refused to take part at all it seems likely on past performance that the ambassador's actions would have been much more moderate, lacking the shelter of the 'diplomatic corps'. But Stronge makes no attempt to represent the moves as being those of the corps. While he exceeded his authority, it is only fair to say that, although aware of Wilson's final efforts towards encouraging the military coup, he did not help.[2] And the answer to Fabela's question is that although Stronge pressed for Madero's resignation, and even urged that the United States make a threat of intervention, these actions did not amount to such an excess of duty as to require reprimand, let alone dismissal.

There was never any real question in London of *not* recognizing

[1] Allowing for time differences.

[2] Stronge–Grey, 18 February 1913, Telegram no. 14. FO 371/1671 file 6269/7950. To him the situation remained 'uncertain'. He indicates, however, that the ambassador had assured Senators that troops would not be landed if the President resigned and order was re-established. This was certainly not an accurate reflection of the policy of the State Department. Stronge knew at the time that Huerta had promised the ambassador action to end the situation (Stronge–Grey, 17 March 1913, no. 73 Confidential. FO 371/1672 file 6269/15911).

the new régime in Mexico, only of *when* recognition ought to be accorded.

At 8.01 a.m., on 19 February 1913, the telegraph operator at Buckingham Palace received a telegram addressed to 'His Majesty King of England' and signed 'Victoriano Huerta'. It read: 'Peace at last. Your subjects interests respected protected.'[1] Lord Stamfordham sent it to the Foreign Office with the comment: 'If it is from the newly elected President the King concludes a suitable reply will be sent.'

H. W. Malkin, of the Treaty Department, observed: 'I'm not aware that Huerta has been "elected" in any shape or form. He has I presume simply assumed office as the result of a successful revolution, a coup d'état . . . Surely it would be premature for The King to recognize Huerta in any way as President *yet*, which he would be doing if he answered this message.'

As yet Malkin's only source of information was a report in *The Pall Mall Gazette* stating, with much inaccurate detail, that Madero had resigned and Huerta 'proclaimed' his successor. But Huerta's telegram had in fact been dispatched the day before he became President. As things were, Spicer minuted: 'I quite agree. We have no official information of any kind with regard to the suggested seizure of the Presidency by General Huerta & it would be contrary to practice to recognize him until constitutionally elected.' Lord Stamfordham was accordingly so informed.[2]

Stronge, replying to Grey's criticism of his support for Wilson, next reported:

Resignation of Madero appeared the only means for securing the return of tranquility and consequent avoidance of the danger of intervention.

[1] Compare Victoriano Huerta–Taft, Telegram, 18 February 1913: 'I have the honor to inform you that I have overthrown this Government, the forces are with me and from now on peace and prosperity will reign. Your obedient servant', etc. SDF 812.00/6250. This was the telegram which Bryan considered to be sufficient justification for not recognizing the new government.

Curiously enough, the corresponding telegram to the Kaiser was also written in *English*, which raises an interesting question as to who wrote the original messages. It said, with a soldierly simplicity: 'War is over my compliments' (Victoriano Huerta–His Majesty Emperor, Germany Berlin, Telegram, 18 February 1913. GFM 12/15 f. A3531).

[2] Victoriano Huerta–His Majesty King of England, [18 February 1913], Telegram; Lord Stamfordham–Sir William Tyrrell, 19 February 1913, with minutes. FO 371/1671 file 6269/8275; *The Pall Mall Gazette* (London), 19 February 1913.

He and the Vice-President resigned yesterday. According to constitution, M.F.A. succeeded to the presidency. After nominating General Huerta as Minister of the Interior, he resigned and the Senate then by a practically unanimous vote proceeded to elect General Huerta as provisional president. The Cabinet which he has formed appears to be distinctly good and strong. The town remains quite quiet.

Willoughby Maycock, Superintendent of the Treaty Department, minuted:

I don't think there is anything to be done until President Huerta writes to The King notifying his election. As yet he is only *provisional* President apparently. When he is fully and regularly installed I suppose he will write to The King & it is The King's reply that constitutes the formal recognition. When his letter arrives I suppose on political grounds we sh^d probably find out what the President of the U.S. does in the way of reply ...

This was embodied in a suitable message to Stronge, at Mallet's suggestion, to let him have some word 'after the trying time he has been through'.[1]

Meanwhile the American ambassador had advised the State Department to require a guarantee from the new government of a satisfactory solution of the terms of the American note of 15 September. This suggestion was adopted, and instructions were sent on 21 February.[2] But he clearly did not intend this to prejudice the question of recognition, since he went ahead to lead the diplomatic corps at a reception on 21 February in reading a formal address. Stronge reported: 'The matter had been discussed at a meeting at the U.S. Embassy last night when it was decided unanimously that it was necessary to act without instructions as it was essential to give the new government immediate support. Moreover the legal forms had been observed in accordance with Mexican constitution.' But this still left doubt as to how far Huerta's position was legal and how far merely provisional.[3]

---

[1] Stronge–Grey, 20 February 1913, Telegram no. 17 and minutes. FO 371/1671 file 6269/8310.

[2] Knox–Wilson, Telegram no. 25, 21 February, 11 p.m. SDF 812.00/6325A.

[3] Stronge–Grey, 21 February 1913, Telegram no. 20 and minutes. FO 371/1671 file 6269/8498.

The confusion was understandable. Hohler's memoirs, with their description of the devastation of the city, reinforce the impression of bewilderment there at the sudden turn of events.

'Poor old Stronge came in for the most violent criticisms by the British colony', he wrote, 'and indeed he must have been a quaint spectacle in the midst of the firing, walking about with his head as usual through the middle of a white poncho and his vile parrot perched on his shoulder dropping its excrement and nibbling his ear.' Some of them, it appears, had appealed for aid to the American embassy. The ambassador considered this an 'undeserved rebuke' for Stronge,[1] and, indeed, in view of the exposed position of the legation during the fighting, it is difficult to see how the minister could have done more to help.

Madero and Pino Suarez were imprisoned in the palace, having been forced to resign on February 20th [*sic*], and Huerta succeeded to the Presidency under a cloak of legality [Hohler continued]. On the 22nd, the birthday of Washington, Mr Wilson gave an afternoon reception. When I arrived I found the room crowded with Diplomats, etc. I was talking to the Chilean Charge d'Affaires [*sic*] when Huerta and his Cabinet turned up. I made at once for Huerta and found him, true to his reputation, half-drunk. We three went to the sideboard and helped ourselves. I drank to the success of his future government while my Chilean friend stuttered something to the same effect. Huerta, on his side, stuttered 'D-d-d-Diez [y] O-O-O-ocho c-c-centavos una c-c-c-cuerda'. Between these two inarticulate individuals I was a good deal perplexed until I found that all Huerta wanted was eighteen centavos to buy a rope to hang Zapata. After three or four glasses of brandy his Excellency retired with his Cabinet. During that night Madero and Pino Suarez were murdered. Of course, it was alleged that a party of friends had tried to rescue them and that they were only shot in obedience to the Ley fuga, by which it is permitted to shoot any escaping prisoner. I did not believe it was Huerta who was guilty of this crime, but some of his officers. He was very drunk at Wilson's party, but I only saw him definitely under the influence of drink on one other occasion.[2]

This is the only eye-witness account that has been published of the events of that celebrated party. The belief that Huerta had

---

[1] Hohler, pp. 183–4; Wilson, p. 182.   [2] Hohler, p. 184.

returned to the Palace drunk and forthwith ordered the killing of the prisoners dies hard, and the appalling deaths of Gustavo Madero and Adolpho Basso within hours of the embassy pact had already made many fear for the safety of the deposed President and Vice-President. Márquez Sterling and Hevia Riquelme, the Chilean minister, had done all that was in their power to ensure their safety.[1] They were to have been conveyed to Vera Cruz and placed on board a Cuban warship to go into exile once their resignations had been signed. The prisoners, however, clearly recognized that their safety lay in the value of legitimacy of the new rulers, and when Pedro Lascuráin, to whom their resignations had been entrusted, conveyed them at once to Congress, he threw away their ability to bargain. The special train, which was standing waiting, was forthwith cancelled, allegedly on the grounds given by Huerta that the disturbed condition and known Maderista sympathies of Vera Cruz made the journey too risky.[2]

Thereafter they had been held in custody at the Palace until late in the evening of 22 February, when a guard came to fetch them and convey them to the penitentiary, supposedly for their greater safety. That they had only a small escort clearly indicates that no real concern was felt that they might be rescued on the way. In fact, there is clear circumstantial evidence that they were taken in motor-cars to the rear of the penitentiary, where the external lights had already been switched on, ordered to dismount, and shot down by their 'escort'. The marks of tyres and of their blood were clearly visible to anyone who cared to look the next day, and no attempt was made to conceal them.[3]

[1] Márquez Sterling, pp. 480 ff.

[2] *Ibid.* pp. 532, 548–52.

[3] Hohler–Grey, 30 September 1913, no. 307 Confidential. FO 371/1677 file 6269/48287:
'It may be of some historical interest to you to possess an accurate account of the death of President Madero and Vice-President Pino Suarez on the 22nd February last.

At 5 o'clock in the afternoon of that day a certain British subject who keeps motor-cars for hire received a telephonic message from a very rich and well-known Mexican landed proprietor named Ignacio de la Torre, who is son-in-law of General Porfirio Díaz, to send a large car at once to his house. The order was carried out, a Mexican chauffeur being in charge of the car. After a long period of waiting he was directed to proceed to the National Palace, and at 11 p.m. Madero and Pino Suarez were brought out and placed in the car, which was escorted by another containing a guard of Rurales under the command of a certain Major Cardenas. This officer had for many months been in charge of the body of men detached to protect the hacienda, near Toluca, of

Time has disclosed, with reasonable certainty, the names of those actually involved in the murder. It has been less successful in determining the responsibility for it.[1] It is clear, though, that the provisional President was in fact one of the few people with no motive for giving such orders, and witnesses claim that he was aghast on learning of the deed.[2] The man who had the best motive to order the killing of the ex-President and Vice-President was, with equal certainty, Félix Díaz, who had not yet achieved the Presidency, and to whose ambitions the deposed President, alive and in exile, could have been a major obstacle.[3] Huerta, in command of the governmental machine, had relatively little to fear, and is well known to have shown no fear. Furthermore, Díaz had a personal cause for emnity against the man who had refused to save his life when he was defeated, while Huerta, despite the slights he felt he had suffered from the Maderistas in the past, had been the last of the principal generals to decide to oppose the government.[4]

Nevertheless, Huerta blundered once the act was known. The official statement on the deaths was so palpably untrue—one Mexican claims that he disbelieved it purely because no official

Señor Ignacio de la Torre. I understand that he had a warm personal affection and admiration for General Porfirio Díaz, and had sworn to avenge his downfall.

The cars proceeded by a devious route in the direction of the Penitentiary, but they passed the main entrance and proceeded to the far side of the building where they were ordered to stop. Some firing then began, the shots passing over the top of the car; and Major Cardenas caused his two charges to descend from their conveyance. As Madero was alighting, Cardenas put his revolver to the side of his neck and shot him dead. Pino Suarez was taken up to the wall of the Penitentiary and there shot. There was no attempt on their part to escape, and it seems quite certain that there was no real attempt at rescue.

Before the car was returned to its owner a number of shots were fired into it, though at the moment of the crime it sustained no damage. The injury done to the car was subsequently paid for.

On the following day the chauffeur was called to the National Palace together with his employer, in whose presence Cardenas gave the chauffeur instructions as to what evidence to give before the judge who was to investigate the matter.

There is and will be, of course, no evidence forthcoming to show whether Cardenas acted from motives of private revenge or under instructions from some superior.'

[1] That Huerta became an accessory after the fact in shielding the murderers there can be no doubt, but this does not make him responsible for the murders.

[2] O'Shaughnessy, *Intimate Pages of Mexican History*, pp. 185–7.

[3] Sherman and Greenleaf, *Victoriano Huerta, a Reappraisal* (1960), pp. 77–83.

[4] Bell, pp. 261–3. The charge that the American ambassador was responsible for Madero's death does not stand up to examination.

statement is ever true!—that it cast grave doubts on him personally, while de la Barra, who reluctantly endorsed the official view, never recovered from the injury it inflicted on his higher reputation.

Stronge notified the Foreign Office of the deaths on 23 February, when the first story appeared in the press in London. The minister's attitude towards the official story was non-committal.[1] *The Westminster Gazette* of 24 February found it doubtful and contradictory, and in a leader commented that deaths of public men in such circumstances were not entirely unexpected. *The Times* of the same day had no doubts that the 'lame and halting story' of the official statement was a fiction and that the 'innate ferocity of Mexican politicians and military adventurers' remained 'untamed'. 'The most for which the unhappy country can hope', its leader-writer wrote scornfully, 'is the restoration of a rule not worse than that of Diaz.' The summary of this opinion published in Mexico moved Wilson to demand of the State Department that it rectify the ignorance of *The Times* correspondent in Washington, although he did not go so far as to say in what respect.[2]

On that Monday morning Stronge's report on the killings was not the only matter the Foreign Office had to consider. He had also reported that the United States ambassador 'had received instructions to the effect that a formal recognition of the new Mexican Govt. by the U.S. would be dependent on the payment of compensation to American citizens . . . and on acceptance in principle of the demands formulated in ambassador's note' of 15 September. He was told to reserve his government's position on claims.[3]

The following day a more complete report came from Mexico, recording that both General Huerta and de la Barra had given the most complete assurances that the lives of the ex-President and

[1] Stronge–Grey, 23 February 1913, Telegram no. 23. FO 371/1671 file 6269/8705.
[2] Wilson–Secretary of State, 24 February, 3 p.m. Telegram no. 33. SDF 812.00/6347. See also Bell, p. 319.
[3] Stronge–Grey, 25 February 1913, Telegram no. 25, and minutes. FO 371/1671 file 6269/8719.

Vice-President would be safe. It concluded: 'U.S. Ambassador states that he accepts the official version of death of President and Vice-President and has urged his Govt. to do so too as he thinks that the new administration will effect pacification of the country.'

'The news from the provinces is on the whole favourable so far but I feel I must suspend judgement on both points.'[1]

Wilson was very active on behalf of the new régime. He wrote to Washington:

The Secretary of the British Legation [Hohler] expressed the opinion to me today that his Government will doubtless not recognise the Provisional Government on account of the murder of Madero. This will be a great error endangering the present Government upon which the safety of all foreigners depends and I think it would be wise to have some consultations with the British Embassy . . . In spite of all the rumors which are afloat I am disposed to accept the Government's version of the affair and consider it a closed incident.[2]

Hohler's view was not that of the Foreign Office. Irwin Laughlin, the United States chargé d'affaires in London, had reported on 21 February that the Mexican minister had been told on that date by Sir Louis Mallet 'that the British Government would not recognize any president in Mexico except one chosen by the legal method of election'. On 25 February he reported further:

This morning with aid of Mexican Minister, who cleared the way for a conversation I had this afternoon with Sir Louis Mallet by saying that I might refer to the statement I reported in my February 21, 4 p.m., as to the attitude of the British Government towards the de facto Government of Mexico, Sir Louis corroborated the statement the Mexican Minister made to me on the twenty-first and said that while the British Government would continue to 'carry on' with the present Mexican Government they would make no formal recognition of a president until that official formally notified the King of his election according to the duly prescribed constitutional methods . . . Upon my inquiring

[1] Stronge–Grey, 24 February 1913, Telegram no. 26. FO 371/1671 file 6269/8950.
[2] Wilson–Secretary of State, 24 February, 7 p.m., Telegram no. 35. SDF 812.00/6353.

what action they would take in case General Huerta should notify the King of his assumption of the presidency, Sir Louis replied that the British Government would take no notice of it.

It will be seen that this statement took no account of the murder of the ex-President. It was not a factor governing the decision whether or not to recognize. The question was solely one of whether or not the government was lawfully established, and here the word 'election' became the key point for inquiry. Had Huerta been legally 'elected' by Congress, or had he to be elected by the nation?

Laughlin, as his later statements bear witness, did not see it in this light. To him the key word apparently was not 'election' but 'assumption'. He therefore took it that Mallet's statement implied that in no circumstances would General Huerta be recognized as President, and when the Foreign Office later announced that they had done so, he took a copy of this report to them and asked for an explanation of the divergence. He clearly took their reply to mean that they had changed their minds, and his report to this effect was generally thought in Washington to mean that he had been deliberately misled.[1]

In fact, Laughlin's report is undoubtedly correct, only the interpretation put upon it afterwards is wrong. Huerta did not 'assume' the Presidency of Mexico by overthrowing Madero: he merely assumed the executive power. When Madero subsequently resigned, his resignation went before Congress, and it was Congress that decreed that the Presidency had devolved upon the General through Lascuráin. Hence as far as the Presidency was concerned the constitutional forms—though not their spirit, certainly—had been fully observed, and when the Foreign Office were convinced of that fact, the conditions mentioned by Sir Louis Mallet had been fully observed.

[1] Irwin Laughlin–Secretary of State, Telegrams, 21 February, 4 p.m. Confidential; 25 February, 6 p.m. Confidential. SDF 812.00/6300, 6372. Burton J. Hendrick, *The Life and Letters of Walter H. Page* (London, 1924), I, pp. 180–1. He wrote: 'The unequivocal answer that Mr Laughlin received was that the British Government would not recognize Huerta, either formally or tacitly.' This is not true, and Laughlin's own report proves it. Similarly, Spring-Rice was not instructed to inform Washington that Great Britain 'had changed its mind', but that it had made it up, so that the 'initial mistake in the Huerta affair' was made, not by Great Britain, but by the United States.

The misunderstanding was enhanced, no doubt, by the fact that the American interpretation intruded its way into reports of the similar statement Mallet had given in response to press inquiries. On this last, Wilson telegraphed to Washington:

The Associated Press this morning announces that the British Government will refrain from recognising the present legally constituted Provisional Government and will only make recognition after the election for permanent President. This statement taken in connection with the attitude of the Legation in other matters has made a disagreeable impression on the Mexican Government and has aroused profound indignation in the British colony which is already taking active steps in rebuke of the supposed attitude of its Minister as reflected by the statement of the Government.[1]

But Stronge was simultaneously advising London:

Exact legality of General Huerta's present position is the following. Madero & Pino Suarez resigned so that Lascurain, M.F.A., became President, being duly called by Chambers to assume that office. He appointed General Huerta Minister of the Interior & then resigned. According to the constitution the Presidency then devolved on to the general & Chambers again called on him to assume it.

Knatchbull-Hugessen minuted:

See 8310 [20 February 1913, no. 17]. Mr Stronge states there that General Huerta is *provisional* president. I suppose he is in the same position as Sr. de la Barra was after Diaz's resignation in 1911. (Madero became President by election subsequently.) Sr. de la Barra notified his appointment as President in an autograph letter to the King, to which H.M. replied (27532/11). Perhaps we might telegraph to Mr Stronge to ask whether there is to be a presidential election in due course. (It has been stated in the papers that there will be.)

To this Spicer added: 'I think we can wait till General Huerta announces his election to the post of provisional President.'

Then, from the Treaty Department, Maycock made a significant objection. 'But if and when Huerta does announce to The King that he has been elected *Provisional* President, it wouldn't at all follow that The King would reply. He does not *as a rule*,

[1] Wilson–Secretary of State, 25 February, 12 noon, Telegram no. 38. SDF 812.00/6373.

write to Provisional Presidents. The case cited was exceptional & is explained by the Minute inside 27532.' This indicates that the action was taken to regularize the Mexican mission to the coronation.

'[Huerta] I understand is for the moment a sort of stop gap', he went on, 'and that there must be a general election before he is full blown & that would really be the proper time for him to write to The King.'

He thereupon drafted a telegram to Stronge which was dispatched at 6 p.m. on 26 February. It ran:

I gather from your tels . . . that Huerta's position is Provisional President only and that before he is confirmed in office there must be an election. Is that so & if so is it possible to form any idea when such election would take place. The proper time for him to write to The King is when he is finally installed and not before & you might throw out a hint to that effect. In De La Barras case the circs were exceptional owing to Coronation mission but The Sovereign does not usually expect to receive announcements from Provisional Presidents.

'My motive in suggesting the message is twofold', added the drafter of this telegram. '(1) It may prevent Huerta firing off a letter to The King to which on general grounds it is improbable we sh^d advise H.M. to reply & (2) it will afford time for things to settle down, for us to see how Huerta behaves himself, and what line the U.S. take.'[1]

However, Stronge, from Mexico, had this to say of the events of 22 February. 'I fear that there can be no doubt that the ex President & Vice-President were executed by order of military revolutionary chiefs & that story of attempted rescue is an invention', he reported. 'The crime is regarded as a necessary & inevitable measure which is likely to facilitate the pacification of the country.' In London it was merely noted that the United States seemed inclined to accept the official version, though Spicer commented: '"Murdered" would be a better word than "executed" . . .'[2]

---

[1] Stronge–Grey, 25 February 1913, Telegram no. 27 and minutes. FO 371/1671 file 6269/9098.

[2] Stronge–Grey, 25 February 1913, Telegram no. 28 and minutes. FO 371/1671 file 6269/9099.

Then on 1 March it became evident that Mr Maycock's effort to forestall the question of official recognition had failed.

Mr de la Barra informs me that General Huerta is president ad interim & according to constitutional principles accepted but not yet promulgated the ad interim president is ineligible as definitive president [Stronge telegraphed]. It is probable that the date of elections will be fixed by Congress in April next and that they will be two or three months later.

The President will announce his accession to foreign sovereigns by autograph letter in about a fortnight, thus conforming to precedent and custom to some extent implied by the laws of the country.

I endeavoured to convince the Minister that the precedent of his own case was inapplicable, but without success. He maintains that the Government must be held to be innocent of the death of the late President & said that he would resign if the investigation which would be thorough & impartial were to show the contrary. He laid great stress on the progress that had already been made in pacifying the country & on the importance to foreign interests of affording the new Government every moral support.

It is, I think, true that the accession of the new Government has been generally well received and that the outlook at present is more reassuring than for a long time past.

As regards the investigation I place little confidence in the Minister's assurances though the deception is perhaps unconscious.[1]

This report indicates clearly both the ambiguous nature of de la Barra's position under the new régime, and the coarsening of his moral fibre. Certainly he had force on his side, if he chose to use it. Foreign interests were notoriously vulnerable, and the hint of blackmail was difficult to evade because the new President had every right to write to anyone he pleased. It was for the recipients to decide whether or not they would assume the invidious responsibility of declaring an unfriendly attitude.

Spicer felt that the danger was too great to risk.

Our interests in Mexico are so enormous that it might be imprudent to risk any possible injury to them by too rigid adherence to the custom of not recognising Provisional Presidents. General Huerta's position as such seems to be regular enough, & if we irritate him needlessly

---

[1] Stronge–Grey, 28 February 1913, Telegram no. 29. FO 371/1671 file 6269/9678.

during the 6 months or more till a new President is elected he may succeed in doing our interests a good deal of harm at a period when we want to accord them all the support we can.

From the Treaty Department, W. A. Stewart, acting assistant head, assented.

Mr Maycock's minute . . . states the procedure ordinarily followed in the case of provisional Presidents, in S. & C. American States [he wrote]. The question whether or not that procedure is to be varied is a political one. But if & when General Huerta does address a letter to The King announcing his assumption of the 'provisional' Presidency, I do think it will be most desirable to find out what action certain other Powers—such as the U.S.—are taking before the King is advised to reply to it.

Sir Louis Mallet then addressed the Foreign Secretary directly.

There is truth in Mr Spicer's observations and I agree that the question of recognizing Gen[l] Huerta is a political one as to which we shall be in a better position to judge a little later [he began]. In the meantime Mr Stronge evidently thinks that HMG may refuse recognition on account of Sr. Madero's murder. You said before you left London that you did not intend to intervene in the internal strife between the rival factions and I informed Lord Cowdray—*who was seriously alarmed at rumours which had reached him from Mexico* and which I have reason to think were based on something said by Mr Hohler to effect that HMG would withhold recognition on account of Sr. Madero's murder—that this question had not even been considered by HMG & that as far as I knew, HMG would pursue the usual course & recognise as Head of the Mexican State whoever was constitutionally elected.

The murder of Sr. Madero may *possibly* be a reason against breaking our rule & recognising Huerta as Provisional President, but to give that as a reason when we have another—namely that it is against our rules to recognise Provisional Presidents, is foolish & Mr Stronge should not discuss this at all. When the letter arrives from Gen[l] Huerta announcing his app[t], then we shall be in a better position to judge what course to follow. Personally I agree with Mr Spicer that we should be guided by our interests which are very extensive, irrespective of the murder of Madero.

Sir Arthur Nicolson added: 'We should consult US Gov & those of France & Germany as to what course they pr[opose] to take.' To this Grey returned: 'Our interests in Mexico are so big that I think we should take our own line without making it dependent upon that of other Govts.' And he added to the draft telegram which Mallet had prepared, warning Stronge not to discuss the recognition question, something that clearly shows how his mind was already inclined towards the 'political' decision: 'It would be desirable to form as accurate an impression as possible whether General Huerta's administration will command confidence & create stability in Mexico. If so the sooner we recognise it the better.' To insert this he deleted a sentence that stated he was consulting the other governments Sir Arthur Nicolson had named.

Even after Stronge's report that he disbelieved the official story of the deaths of Madero and Pino Suárez the question of withholding recognition on these grounds was dismissed as irrelevant. Furthermore, Sir Edward Grey personally took the decision to act without reference to the intentions of other governments. Stronge again repeated that he considered the Mexican government to be legally constituted, and on 3 March he further alluded to the evident wish of the Mexican government to force the hand of the diplomatic corps. The same day he reported that the United States ambassador wished the British view to be communicated to Washington. Although it was decided by the Secretary of State not to do this, he equally refused once again to follow Sir Arthur Nicolson's advice to consult Washington as to their views.[1]

Grey, however, was approached by only one representative of British interests in Mexico to press for recognition. This was Mr Hamar Greenwood, then Liberal M.P.[2] for Sunderland, whose interests were principally Canadian, and who had an interview with Sir Louis Mallet.

Sir Louis Mallet explained to him the position [Grey told Stronge], and added confidentially that I was disposed to recognise the President when the formal announcement of his accession was made and that I

[1] Minute on Stronge–Grey, 4 March 1913, Telegram no. 33. FO 371/1671 file 6269/10285. Preceding quotations from minutes on Stronge–Grey, 28 February 1913, Telegram no. 29.
[2] Subsequently Chief Secretary for Ireland, 1919–22, when post abolished by treaty. Lord Beaverbrook, *The Decline and Fall of Lloyd George and great was the fall thereof* (London, 1963), observes that he was noted for his 'song and soft shoe shuffle routine'.

was in consultation with you on the subject. Mr Greenwood was greatly relieved and said that he would not trouble me in the circumstances to receive a deputation.[1]

Lord Cowdray had not pressed his view; it had been sought by Mallet for guidance.

Stronge's report on the stability of the régime arrived on 7 March. It was favourable.

It is naturally somewhat early to be able to form a very definite opinion of the prospects of General Huerta's administration, but Mr Stronge is evidently sanguine [noted Spicer]. The reestablishment of order in Mexico is of the first importance to us, & I think it cannot be doubted that we shall contribute materially to that end by recognizing a Gov^t that seems to possess the elements of stability.

Maycock introduced a new supporter for this view—one who was to be increasingly prominent in maintaining it. 'Sir L. Carden who knows a good deal of the Mexicans thinks well of President Huerta he told me', he observed. 'I expect when his letter to The King arrives it will be best to advise His Majesty to answer it, subject to what we may hear from U.S.A., Paris & Berlin, & perhaps anyhow.'

Sir Louis Mallet indicated that Mr Hamar Greenwood had approached Mr F. D. Acland, Parliamentary Under Secretary for Foreign Affairs, the previous day and had asked for an immediate announcement to be made. The Mexican minister had indicated that a telegraphic message was expected at any time. 'The President does not ask for telegraphic recognition', he added, 'but the Minister thinks that is the gist of his telegram.'

He recorded later:

Since writing the above I have spoken to the Sec. of State who authorizes me to inform the Mexican Sec^y. when he communicates the telegram from the President that as soon as the autograph letter arrives he will advise H.M. to reply to it thereby recognizing him as interim President, i.e. if the conditions are unchanged between now & then.

We are then to inform Wash'ton, Paris & Berlin & enquire their intentions.

[1] Memorandum by Sir L. Mallet, 3 March 1913. Grey–Stronge, 12 March 1913, no. 25. FO 371/1671 file 6269/10335.

As an afterthought, Grey added: 'The King should be informed of the reply.'[1]

The same day the autograph letter left Mexico. On 14 March Sir Edward Goschen notified Grey that the German government had decided not to recognize until Huerta had been elected. It was noted in London that he was not eligible for election, and Maycock stated: 'The line the Germans *have* taken is probably the line we *should have* taken in normal circs, but Political cons[ns] outweigh these.'[2] Then the Mexican minister called again, to ascertain 'when the friendly disposition of the British Gov[t] may be made public'. The Foreign Office had already notified the British ambassadors in Washington, Paris, Berlin, St Petersburg and Rome of their intention to recognize. Sir Arthur Nicolson remarked with concern: 'We seem to be going faster than other Govt[s].'[3]

On 15 March London was told that the Italian government intended merely to return their autograph letter to the Mexican Foreign Office. No further information of this nature was received until the arrival of the autograph letter, and on 31 March 1913 the ambassadors to the Powers were instructed to inform the governments to which they were accredited that Great Britain was recognizing the government of Mexico, *ad interim*.[4]

Bryce reported from Washington, in his last report on the Mexican question, that he had seen the Secretary of State after formally notifying him of the decision by note.

Mr Bryan said that he had quite understood from my note that after what had gone before the form of recognition therein mentioned must be accorded in the way it had been done but as regards the action of the

[1] Minutes on Stronge–Grey, 6 March 1913, Telegram no. 34. FO 371/1671 file 6269/10599. Stronge's written report on General Huerta, incorporating a memorandum by Hohler on the character of the new President, did not reach the Foreign Office until 25 March. It was not flattering, and the impression it created may be gathered from the minutes: by Sir L. Mallet, 'Genl. Huerta is a man of base morals, "nearly blind" and "a drunkard"', and by Sperling, 'General Huerta appears to have no redeeming qualities except that of a short way with brigands—which perhaps outweighs all others at this particular juncture in Mexico'. It did not reverse the decision to recognize. Stronge–Grey, 21 February 1913, no. 42. FO 371/1672 file 6269/13386.

[2] Sir E. Goschen–Grey, 14 March 1913, Telegram no. 52 and minutes. FO 371/1671 file 6269/11957.

[3] Grey–Bryce and others, 15 March 1913, Telegrams and minutes. FO 371/1671 file 6269/12150.

[4] Grey–Bryce and others, 31 March 1913, Telegrams. FO 371/1672 file 6269/16058.

American Government he was not able to give me any definite indication. He thought they would at any rate wait some while longer before recognising General Huerta's government.[1]

This was interpreted in the Foreign Office as meaning that the United States intended to withhold recognition, as had been previously indicated, until the question of claims had been settled. This belief was seriously and even dangerously wrong.

[1] Bryce–Grey, 1 April 1913, no. 87. FO 371/1672 file 6269/16743.

CHAPTER 5

INDECISION

On the morning after 4 March 1913 it was not apparent to anyone, except, perhaps, the incoming President of the United States,
that American foreign policy as regards relations with Mexico was
likely to change much. Two years of revolution in Mexico had
left the United States a series of decisions, actions and precedents
tending to inhibit or delimit future policy.

In particular, three decisions taken by President Taft in the last
days of his administration seemed to indicate a possible continuity
of ideas. These were the decisions not to break off relations with
Mexico or to intervene militarily, to locate forthwith such naval
and military forces under the command of the United States
that intervention could be adopted by the incoming administration without delay, and to commence diplomatic negotiations
tending towards the recognition of the Huerta government on
certain conditions. The indication by the Democratic press of a
preference for mediatory methods rather than interventionist ones
was the only straw in the wind to indicate change, and, as events
proved, it was quite misleading.

It is now well established that the incoming President had, in
fact, given very little thought to the problems of foreign relations,
and, in giving precedence to domestic action, fell naturally into
the habit of thinking of foreign policy as an extension of internal
reform.[1] Concomitant factors in shaping the development of
foreign policy were likewise internal, and inherent in the nature
of the administration which Woodrow Wilson had created.

The State Department, since the time of McKinley, had been
gradually moving towards the merit system for appointments.

---

[1] Where not otherwise cited, information on the Wilson administration from: Ray
Stannard Baker, *Woodrow Wilson, Life and Letters*, IV: '*President, 1913-1914*' (London,
1932); John Morton Blum, *Woodrow Wilson and the Politics of Morality* (Boston, Mass.,
and Toronto, 1956); Arthur Stanley Link, *Wilson—the New Freedom* (Princeton, N.J.,
1956); Harley Notter, *The Origins of the Foreign Policy of Woodrow Wilson* (Baltimore,
Md., 1937).

The evolution, however, had depended on the personal predilections of Roosevelt and Taft for orderly administration, and their informal system had not been enacted by Congress, largely for political reasons. It had not hitherto been tested by a change of party in the Executive branch, and the Democratic party's traditional belief in the 'spoils system' found no more passionate advocate in the administration than the new Secretary of State, William Jennings Bryan.[1]

Paradoxically, although the damage done to the State Department by the wholesale dismissals and changes of the following three months was exceedingly great, they cannot be held entirely responsible for the confusion which reigned in the field of Mexican affairs. Huntington Wilson was asked to remain as Assistant Secretary of State until the Department had been reorganized. It is true that he resigned just over two weeks later, sending an open letter to the President denouncing in the strongest terms the new régime and the refusal of the cabinet to take part in the Chinese Loan. As he seemed to be expected to remain at the head of the Department while Bryan went on lecture tours and his own policies were abandoned to the accompaniment of self-righteously reproving statements, this was not surprising.[2]

Alvey A. Adee remained as Second Assistant Secretary of State, specifically retained for his knowledge of more than thirty years of precedents. John Bassett Moore, the distinguished international lawyer, was persuaded to accept the special post of Counsellor, ranking even above the Assistant Secretary. However, Doyle was replaced as Head of the Latin American Department by a political appointee with no Latin American experience, Boaz W. Long, while Dearing was posted to Brussels.[3] Finally, Henry Lane Wilson was asked to remain for the time being at the embassy in Mexico, where he was joined later in the year by Nelson O'Shaughnessy, bringing with him his warrant of appointment as first secretary. O'Shaughnessy, a Republican, received his con-

[1] Warren Frederick Ilchman, *Professional Diplomacy in the United States, 1779–1939: a study in administrative history* (Chicago, Ill., 1961), pp. 119–26.

[2] Woodrow Wilson–William Jennings Bryan, 20 March 1913, Telegram. Wilson Papers, File VII, Letterbook 1, f. 285.

[3] Sir Cecil Spring-Rice–Grey, 15 August 1913, no. 188. FO 371/1675 file 6269/39431.

firmation, after two months of Democratic resistance, on the very eve of President Wilson's inauguration.[1]

The confusion was not just one of personalities, but of policies. The cabinet, to be sure, were united in repudiating what they called 'dollar diplomacy'. They were divided as to what to put in its place. As far as Mexico was concerned there was as yet no convenient parallel with the Latin America of Richard Olney's day. Only if the Monroe doctrine came to be involved was there likely to be one, and the claims to hegemony of the 'Twenty Inch Gun' Note, still unsurpassed by any assertion of Roosevelt's, seemed alien to the spirit of a non-interventionist, and even pacificist, administration.

If the new President was viewed as something of an unknown quantity from Great Britain, what was known of him was likely to meet with the sympathy of a Liberal government. When Walter Hines Page was appointed by him as ambassador to the Court of St James's, the name met with general approval. Lord Cowdray had hoped that his old friend Judge Gerard might be chosen, but he was selected for Berlin instead.[2]

As it happened, the inauguration of the new administration coincided with the replacement of James Bryce as British ambassador to Washington. His successor, Sir Cecil Spring-Rice,[3] had many friends in the United States, though he would have been hard put to it to rival the popularity of his predecessor. Unhappily, he suffered from poor health, and was confined to bed for a large part of his first year in office, during which time the

---

[1] Taft Papers, Presidential Series 2, file 3690 (Nelson O'Shaughnessy). O'Shaughnessy was subsequently detailed to Vienna, 2 September 1914, and appointed to Rio de Janeiro, 8 October 1915, but retired from the service the following year, following the publication by his wife, Edith Louise Coues O'Shaughnessy, of *A Diplomat's Wife in Mexico*. In testimony before the Foreign Relations Committee of the United States Senate on 3 May 1920 testified that he believed the Wilson policy towards Mexico to have been 'preposterous . . . brutal, unwarranted and stupid'. Sources: *Who's Who in America*; *Dictionary of American Biography*, XXI; Robert E. Quirk, *An Affair of Honor: Woodrow Wilson and the Occupation of Vera Cruz* (New York, McGraw-Hill, 1964), *passim*.

[2] Woodrow Wilson–Richard Olney, Telegram, 10 March 1913; 11 March 1913; 14 March 1913. Wilson Papers, File VII, Letterbook 1, ff. 94, 113, 196. Herbert J. Carr–Cowdray, 7 January 1913, Cowdray Papers. *Westminster Gazette*, 1 April 1913. Hendrick, *The Life and Letters of Walter H. Page* (1924), I, pp. 130-1.

[3] Stephen Gwynn, ed., *The Letters and Friendships of Sir Cecil Spring-Rice: a record* (London, 1929), especially ch. XX.

embassy was severely handicapped for lack of personnel. In any case, such is the supposed climate of Washington that he had to spend the entire summer at the summer embassy at Dublin, New Hampshire, and it is a tribute to his ability and that of the embassy staff during this time that his reports were outstandingly, even startlingly, accurate about the development of administration policy. As a close personal friend of Sir Edward Grey, he was equally well informed about British policy, but, as with all other ambassadors in Washington, he found it virtually impossible to convey information to the President. The fact that the latter had taken a self-denying vow of abstinence from attendances at public functions during his first year of office ruled out many opportunities for informal exchange of views which are so often the means of easing diplomatic friction arising from misunderstanding.

It would not be right to introduce Spring-Rice without some personal account; that of the then Austrian ambassador deserves quotation.

An Irishman, positively scintillating with wit, and a classical scholar, Sir Cecil was in every sense of the term a 'character' [he wrote, many years later]. He laid less stress on externals—clothes, ceremonial and so forth—than is perhaps becoming in a diplomat. Moreover, he was so absent-minded that his charming wife, who was the daughter of Sir Frank Lascelles, the English Ambassador in Berlin, had to remind him of invitations and was obliged in addition to make sure at the last moment that he really dressed in time and did not forget his tie or anything else of that sort. Unfortunately he suffered from asthma and probably also from a weak heart. He could not stand the scent of flowers and only accepted invitations to dinner on condition that the table should be entirely free of them. He was a gracious personality and in every sense a gentleman, a most affectionate father and the kindest of men.

Despite his sympathy, the new ambassador found it even harder to accept the Wilson administration at face value than his predecessor had found the previous administration. His personal letters to Grey reflect this. The first mention in them of the Mexican problem and the danger of intervention, on 23 June, is accompanied by the comment: 'I am quite sure that this government if it can be called a government is intensely opposed to the idea.' But a letter to Sir William Tyrrell, received in London on 7 July, went even further in describing the situation in Washington as 'worthy of a café chantant'. The State Department had succeeded in simultaneously offering provocation to Russia, France, Japan, Mexico and Germany. As for the Secretary of State— 'Bryan's chief interest is cutting Wilson's throat, as a possible second term candidate, and Wilson's chief interest, next to not having his throat cut, is to cut Bryan's as his principal rival'.[1]

Until the middle of August 1913 the sum of public knowledge of administration opinion on Mexico was extremely small. Indeed, on the basic question, the recognition of Huerta, the statements printed in the press were actually misleading, while discussion revolved in the main around the degree of guilt to be attributed to Henry Lane Wilson for his part in the February *coup*. This began with savage attacks on him in *The World* of 7 and 8 February. After the exploratory missions of Reginald Del Valle, a friend of the Secretary of State, and William Bayard Hale, they culminate in his recall on 17 July and his dismissal on 5 August.

Though it was known that the ships sent by President Taft to Mexican waters had been retained,[2] it was not clear that the administration did not intend to use them, until on 22 July Senator Fall raised the question in Congress.[3] Though the President had made a statement on 12 March, previously discussed by the entire cabinet, that the administration would take as its principles in its relations with the 'sister republics' of Latin America that 'co-operation is possible only when supported at every turn by the orderly processes of just government based upon law, not upon arbitrary or irregular force', and that 'just government rests always upon the consent of the governed', and warned

[1] Constantin Dumba, *Memoirs of a Diplomat* (London, 1933), p. 162. Spring-Rice–Grey, 23 June 1913; Spring-Rice–Sir William Tyrrell, n.d. Grey Papers.
[2] Daniels Papers: *Diary*, Friday, 7 March 1913.
[3] Woodrow Wilson–Augustus O. Bacon, 24 July 1913. Wilson Papers, File VII, Letterbook 5, f. 291. *The World*, 23–26 July 1913. Senator Bacon was then Chairman of the Senate Foreign Relations Committee.

that it would lend its 'influence of every kind to the realization of these principles in fact and practice' and would 'have no
sympathy with those who seek to seize the power of government
to advance their own personal interests or ambition', it was not
necessarily clear how this was to be applied in the specific case of
Mexico.[1] It could have meant a policy identical with those of the
powers then in the process of extending recognition.[2] Some
Democratic observers were decidedly cynical in their reactions.

The Secretary of State repeated that he had nothing to say when
reminded that the policy of the new Administration, as defined in the
statement, was similar to the policy of the late Administration, announced by Mr Taft soon after he entered the White House. It was
upon such a declaration of policy that Secretary of State Knox and
Assistant Secretary of State Wilson inaugurated their famous dollar
diplomacy [recalled *The World*'s Washington correspondent].

Certainly it was on the same day that the first report appeared
that the United States might not recognize Huerta at all. It was
not connected with the statement, however, and did not amount
to the 'lead' which *The World* subsequently complained had been
ignored when Britain's recognition was made public.[3]

A lead from Washington might have been ignored by the
European powers, but it could not have been overlooked. But
there was no lead; further official statements all gave the impression that the United States did intend to recognize Huerta, but not
just yet.[4] Statements were also allowed to appear that the administration had expected such steps as 'a sort of retaliation' for the
way in which they themselves had ignored the customary processes of consultation in withdrawing from the Chinese Loan.[5]

When the President himself made his first statement specifically
on the recognition question he said that it was 'some way off' and
might in fact never happen, but that 'the de facto Government of
Mexico would be recognised as the Provisional Government when

[1] Daniels Papers: *Diary*, Tuesday, 11 March 1913. Wilson Papers, File VII, Letterbook 2,
f. 20: 'Released for morning newspapers, March 12, 1913'.
[2] México, Secretaría de Relaciones Exteriores, *Boletín*, XXXVI, *passim*.
[3] *The World*, Wednesday, 12 March 1913.
[4] *Ibid.* Sunday, 6 April 1913.
[5] *Ibid.* Tuesday, 25 March; Sunday, 6 April 1913.

it had worked out the problem now before it—the establishment
of peace—and demonstrated to the world that it is capable of
running the republic'.[1] The following day it was reported that
Bryce had been informed 'that it made no difference to the
United States what was to be Great Britain's attitude, that the
American Government would be guided by its own judgement
and that recognition of Huerta by Great Britain would not give
the American Government any concern or interfere with its
policy'. The policy was now said to be to wait for a constitutional
election to be held after fighting had ceased.[2] Only on 17 July
was it announced that these conditions had been put to Huerta,
and had been refused.[3] The issue between the United States and
Mexico at last came into the open, and with it the probability of a
dispute with the powers that had extended recognition. It only
remained to be publicly stated that they had had ulterior motives
for doing so.

On the same day Winston Churchill, First Lord of the Admiralty,
announced in the House of Commons his Navy Plan for the
coming year. A major feature of the Plan was the provision for the
future of twelve super-Dreadnoughts, twelve cruisers, forty destroyers and other craft, all of which were to burn oil. To ensure
the necessary supply of fuel for these, as well as for the existing
destroyers which were to be converted to oil-firing, Churchill
asserted boldly that it was necessary to have a contract with a
certain large supplier. That supplier was Anglo-Mexican Petroleum Products, and the head of that company was Lord Cowdray.

To put the question in perspective it should be noted that
Churchill said that the Mexican contract would supply 'a comparatively small proportion, but still a substantial proportion' of
the navy's needs, and that it was 'an extremely advantageous
contract', and 'a necessary feature of our interim arrangements'.
While it was not insignificant, therefore, it was not a source on
which the navy would be in any sense absolutely dependent.
Furthermore, it was known already that in time of war *all* the oil

---

[1] *The World*, Saturday, 12 April 1913.   [2] *Ibid*. Sunday, 13 April 1913.
[3] *Ibid*. Thursday, 17 July 1913. This was not true.

conceivably likely to be required for the navy could (at a cost) be recovered from the Scottish shales.[1]

The announcement that the government had seen fit to make such a contract with a firm headed by a prominent member of the Liberal party who had contributed heavily to the party funds was, characteristically, flung down by Churchill as a challenge. It was a challenge, however, not to the United States government, who were to take it up, but to the Conservative Opposition, who did not.

The Marconi disclosures were at the time in full flood.[2] Among those named was the former ministerial Chief Whip, the Master of Elibank, now Lord Murray of Elibank, against whom the charges were freshly made that he had used the knowledge of a forth-coming government contract to speculate in shares for the benefit of the party funds.[3] Lord Murray was at that time in Colombia in search of oil concessions over considerable territories for the firm of S. Pearson and Son.[4] These activities, in strategic proximity to the Panama Canal,[5] were made known to the United States government on 17 April by their chargé d'affaires in Bogotá, to whom Murray had also confided his personal plans to obtain railway concessions.[6] When a rival promoter suggested to President Wilson that Murray was engaged in an attempt to outflank the Canal with a rival one through the Atrato region, using the transport clauses as cover,[7] the State Department exerted every effort upon the Colombian government to stop the draft con-

[1] *The Spectator*, CXI, no. 4438, 19 July 1913, p. 83; *Parliamentary Debates*, Fifth Series, LV, cols. 1465–82 (17 July 1913); Rt. Hon. Winston Leonard Spencer Churchill: *The World Crisis, 1911–1918* (London, 1931), pp. 89–93; *The World*, Friday, 18 July 1913.

[2] Full account in Frances Donaldson, *The Marconi Scandal* (London, 1962). See also: George Dangerfield, *The Strange Death of Liberal England* (London, 1936, reprinted New York, 1961), pp. 309–11, and biographies of Rufus Isaacs, David Lloyd George, etc.

[3] *The Spectator*, CX, no. 4433, 14 June 1913, p. 1002 ('The Newest Marconi Disclosures'); L. J. Maxse, 'From Bedford to Bogota', *The National Review*, LXII, no. 369, November 1913, pp. 409 ff.

[4] L. J. Maxse, 'From Bedford to Bogota', *loc. cit.*

[5] James T. DuBois–Secretary of State, 30 September 1912. Knox Papers, XVIII, f. 3070. For a brief account of the Costa Rica negotiations see Dana Gardner Munro, *Intervention and Dollar Diplomacy in the Caribbean, 1900–1921* (Princeton, N.J., 1964), pp. 430–2.

[6] Leland Harrison–Bryan, 17 April 1913, no. 154 Confidential. SDF 821.6363/1.

[7] Harrison–Bryan, 11 August 1913, no. 198, enclosing P. Chester Thompson–Woodrow Wilson, 9 August 1913. SDF 821.6363/7. This belief also in Miles Dobson, *At the Edge of the Pit* (Pasadena, Calif., 1914), pp. 42–53.

cession before approval, basing their plea nominally on the ground that it would create a monopoly.[1] The bill for the concession was withdrawn on 24 November.[2]

From the State Department correspondence, it is evident that the contract was killed in Colombia, not in Great Britain as Walter H. Page believed.[3] It was killed, too, not for idealistic motives, but for an openly commercial reason thinly disguised as moral. The 'strategic' argument, as far as it concerned a canal through the Atrato, had already been exploded by General Wood under the Taft administration.[4] The incident had importance in many ways, but its immediate significance lay in its relation to the developing situation in Mexico.

The scale of Murray's efforts, which was indeed immense, aroused Wilson's and Bryan's suspicions of the interests against which they had for so long battled at home; to the point at which they were even prepared to overlook the increment to their own interests if by the restraint of European competition they were allowed to range unchecked. Publicly, the President spoke of equal opportunity; privately, the State Department pressed the claims of American firms against their European rivals. No opposition came from the administration in 1914 to the entry of the Standard Oil into Colombia.[5]

It was thus easy to go on to suspect the relationship between Lord Cowdray and the British government. The publicity that

---

[1] Bryan–Thaddeus Austin Thomson, Telegram, 1 October 1913, 4 p.m.; Thomson–Secretary of State, Telegram, 3 October 1913, 6 p.m.; John Bassett Moore–Thomson, Telegram, 6 October, 6 p.m. SDF 821.6363/8, 9.

[2] Harrison–Secretary of State, Telegram, 22 November 1913, 7 p.m.; Walter Hines Page–Secretary of State, Telegram no. 114, 26 November, 5 p.m. SDF 821.6363/22, 23.

[3] Page–Woodrow Wilson, 8 January 1914. Wilson Papers Ac 3335 Box 86. See also: J. Fred Rippy, *The Capitalists and Colombia* (New York, 1931), p. 108. For an extended account of the diplomacy of the Murray Contract see: Peter A. R. Calvert, 'The Murray Contract; an Episode in International Finance and Diplomacy', *Pacific Historical Review*, XXXV, no. 2, May 1966, p. 203.

[4] Taft was prepared to buy the option on the route, but clearly only as a diplomatic way of compensating the Colombians for the loss of Panama, while removing the remotest chance of competition. This consideration, however, did not apply to a Democratic administration prepared to admit the guilt of its Republican predecessors (Knox–Taft, 29 November 1912; Knox–DuBois, 6 December 1912, Confidential. Knox Papers, XIX, f. 3257; XX, f. 3259).

[5] Moore–Isaac S. Manning, 21 November 1913, no. 71. SDF 821.6363/16. Henry P. Starrett–Bryan, 7 April 1914, no. 60. SDF 821.6363/34.

had attended Murray's efforts linked him throughout with the Marconi Affair. Was this another case of big business running government through a financial hold on the ruling party? Cowdray personally had been under attack for many years in the United States. He was a former Member of Parliament. Lord Murray was not the only figure of political interest to have been taken into his firm; Lloyd George's eldest son was another. Furthermore, the Marconi committee had forcibly revealed to the public that Lord Murray also had a brother, Captain Arthur Murray, Liberal M.P. for Kincardineshire, who had given some very unfortunate evidence to the select committee. And Captain Arthur Murray was Parliamentary Private Secretary to none other than Sir Edward Grey.

There can be no doubt that Cowdray had the opportunity of communicating his opinions through Captain Arthur Murray to the Foreign Office. But a parliamentary private secretary is a relatively small figure in the British government. Views can more readily be transmitted to those who really take the decisions in a club discussion and even then it is another question whether they are acted upon. The paradox was that in Washington the British government was criticized simultaneously for basing all its policy on financial considerations and for listening to the views of financiers. Yet of these two self-contradictory accusations it was the former that was nearer the truth.

It was an equally easy step to the belief that Cowdray's activities in Mexico were corrupt, and to the view that the British government was deliberately thwarting the wishes of the United States in Mexico. The result was that it was felt to be an incentive to re-state the Monroe doctrine's opposition to political or military penetration so that it covered financial penetration also. In all these ways, the Colombian contract seemed to act as corroboration of all suspicions Americans were to develop about the British and Mexico.

The signing of the Admiralty contract crystallized all these attitudes by providing the apparent motive for the apparent British intransigence. National defence provided so satisfying an explanation, that the blank assertion that British policy was 'writ in oil'[1] continues to appear in textbooks as if it were a statement of truth. But it was not quite so simple, and the fact that the First World War has intervened makes it seem very much more important than it was up to July 1914.

Until the beginning of July 1913 the public attitude of the United States government largely coincided with its private attitude. It took its starting-point from an almost total lack of knowledge about the internal situation in Mexico. It became concerned about the reports of Henry Lane Wilson's activities, and developed towards an emotional rejection of a régime in Mexico conceived to be founded upon murder and certainly anti-democratic in its tendencies.[2] The emergence of an armed opposition to Huerta, describing themselves as Constitutionalists, offered within days of the *Decena Trágica* an alternative force which might well supplant it. The Constitutionalists were nominally under the leadership of Venustiano Carranza. But Carranza was then only the elderly governor of the state of Coahuila; he had been legally elected to that position in the time of Madero, despite a previous spell of office under Porfirio Díaz.

Woodrow Wilson's immediate concern was the question of licensing the supply of arms to the contending parties under the Joint Resolution of 1912. On this issue he remained indecisive, and for several months arms continued to pass to both sides. The President asked the State Department for a memorandum on the question shortly after coming into office, and concluded that the action of the department had hitherto been 'prudent and entirely satisfactory'.[3] He therefore continued to use the Taft criteria in granting licences, the first aim of which was naturally to allow American citizens in Mexico to have weapons for their defence.

No check, however, was placed on export of arms to Huerta's government before July, when the President started to 'go slow'.

---

[1] This particular phrase from George Sylvester Viereck (pro-German publicist and anglophobe), *The Strangest Friendship in History: Woodrow Wilson and Colonel House* (London, 1933), p. 51.

[2] Baker, *Woodrow Wilson, Life and Letters*, vol. IV (1932), p. 237; David Lawrence, *The True Story of Woodrow Wilson* (London, 1924), p. 97.

[3] Woodrow Wilson–Alvey A. Adee, 25 March 1913. Wilson Papers, File VII, Letterbook 1, f. 392.

The supply was not cut off until after representations by Senator Augustus O. Bacon (Chairman of the Senate Foreign Relations Committee) on 23 and 26 August. Bacon emphasized that the political consequences might be serious if it became known that arms were still reaching the hands of those who might use them to kill Americans in the event of armed intervention.[1]

As far as the State Department were concerned, however, the first question was the pressure of the Huerta government for recognition. As the British example showed, it was not necessary to establish formal relations with provisional governments to carry on business on a satisfactory basis. But the American government had no such convenient custom of not recognizing provisional Presidents. They were not compelled to do so, of course. The Mexicans were the suitors, and it was unlikely that any government would attempt to blackmail a Great Power with threats to the welfare of its resident citizens when that Power was both conterminous and aggressive. What the Department, under Bryan, wished to know was whether the government had the support of the people and could therefore achieve peace. Bryan's first telegram to Mexico, on 8 March, indicated that the ambassador was to urge the use of mediation and just concessions to secure such a result.[2]

Henry Lane Wilson hastened to assure the new Secretary of State that the policy of the Department was the policy that he had been following, and, incidentally, revealed that he had been giving information from consular dispatches to the Mexican government to enable it to restore order. While discouraging this practice, Bryan did not entirely forbid it, and, indeed, allowed it by implication provided the information was purely general and verbal.[3]

Meanwhile, the Department was receiving communications calling upon the administration not to recognize Huerta, as well as conflicting information on the state of the Constitutionalist

---

[1] Bryan–Woodrow Wilson, 23 August 1913. Also Woodrow Wilson–Bryan, 4 August 1913. Bryan Papers, Special Correspondence, Box 43, ff. 157, 103.

[2] Bryan–Wilson, 8 March, 6 p.m., Telegram no. 91. SDF 812.00/6522.

[3] Wilson–Secretary of State, 9 March, 12 noon, Telegram no. 96; Bryan–Wilson, 11 March, 7 p.m., Telegram no. 97. SDF 812.00/6574.

forces. However, there were already indications that Britain was prepared to extend recognition, and, on receiving the news from London, de la Barra implied that he would prefer to hear from Washington first.[1] At this stage, the President had already received a letter from Waters Pierce circles drawing attention to an alleged involvement of Lord Cowdray with both Félix Díaz's movement and the drive for recognition. Yet Bryan's next move was to inform the Attorney-General that there no longer seemed to be any reason to withhold proceedings against people involved in opposition to the new Mexican government.[2]

On 21 March Henry Lane Wilson's lengthy report on the *Decena Trágica* reached Washington. It put forward a good case for his having acted only in a manner which might properly be expected from a diplomatic representative charged with the interests of his country. Although it could be challenged on many points even from internal evidence, it could not be criticized in detail on many points of fact that were then unknown.[3] On the other hand a letter from David Starr Jordan, peace advocate and President of Stanford University,[4] to the Secretary of State, enclosing a letter by the journalist, James H. Wilkins, indicated a continuing suspicion of the ambassador and of the motives of the financial interests in Mexico.[5] It must be said that Wilkins's letter contained nothing that could be called evidence. A moment's reflection should have convinced his correspondent that revolutions could not be prepared in two days, as he seemed to suggest.

But Wilkins's letter was not the only pointer to the existence of an unsavoury element in the régime. From Mexico Marion Letcher reported that the governor of Chihuahua, Abraham González, a heroic figure of the struggle against Díaz, had disappeared. He had last been seen being escorted south by rail in the custody of a squad of federal soldiers, and it came as no surprise to anyone when confirmation was received of his death; his body

---

[1] Wilson–Secretary of State, 11 March, 10 p.m., Telegram no. 99. SDF 812.00/6640.
[2] Stanley Copeland–Woodrow Wilson, 1 March 1913; Bryan–Attorney-General, 14 March 1913. SDF 812.00/6684, 6704A.
[3] Wilson–Secretary of State, 12 March 1913, no. 1901. SDF 812.00/6840.
[4] Edward McNall Burns, *David Starr Jordan: Prophet of Freedom* (Stanford, Calif., 1953), pp. 24–5.
[5] David Starr Jordan–Bryan, 19 March 1913. SDF 812.00/6878.

12-2

had been thrown under a train, alive or dead. A greater scandal touched the family of the President himself. Enrique Cepeda, Huerta's 'nephew', who had acted as go-between for the General with the ambassador during the *Decena Trágica*, had been rewarded with the key post of the governorship of the Federal District. A few days after his appointment, he went to the federal penitentiary, ordered a political prisoner to be led out, shot him with his own hand, and burned the body with petrol. He was hastily certified as insane and removed into protective custody, but the incident made it impossible for the régime to disclaim responsibility for political murders at the hands of agents.[1]

The ambassador, who was the only American official to be informed in advance that Great Britain had definitely decided to extend recognition, rightly told the State Department that 'a restraining influence should be exercised on England' if the United States had decided not to follow suit.[2] His advice was not taken. Normal business continued to be transacted, and inquirers were told only that no formal recognition had been made 'as yet'.[3] A source of embarrassment was removed for the Mexican government by rotating the ships standing by in Mexican ports. In fact, the State Department considered the Huerta régime to be 'the obviously responsible authority of the country', and continued to act on that premiss.[4]

The first indication that British interests were bestirring themselves to secure United States recognition of Huerta did not come until 5 May—two days after King George V's autograph reply had been formally delivered to the Mexican President. On this date James Speyer, of Speyer and Company, New York, offered to arrange a meeting with Percy Furber for John Bassett Moore. He described Furber as an 'Englishman at the head of the Oil Fields of Mexico Company, closely allied with Lord Cowdray'.[5]

[1] Wilson–Secretary of State, 26 March, 6 p.m., Telegram no. 136; Marion Letcher–Secretary of State, 24 March 1913, no. 325. SDF 813.00/6888, 6952.

[2] Wilson–Secretary of State, 31 March, 10 p.m., Telegram no. 149. SDF 812.00/6957. The phrasing was absurd but the advice basically sound.

[3] Memorandum by Alvey A. Adee, 29 March 1913. SDF 812.00/6992.

[4] Memorandum by Alvey A. Adee, 22 April 1913. SDF 812.00/7206.

[5] James Speyer–Moore, 5 May 1913. SDF 812.00/7390. Percy N. Furber's company, the Oil Fields of Mexico Co., was incorporated 27 June 1912 under the laws of West

Speyers' move involved the official status of the considerable loans inherited by the Huerta government from its predecessors. Though the bulk of these loans was held in Europe, he and other Americans were concerned about Mexico's continued financial stability and were therefore pressing for recognition.

Had the Huerta government remained patient and given no cause for provocation the existing excellent relations could have been maintained in all but name until the excitement had died down. The loans might have been safeguarded, and even increased, without formal recognition. Huerta, however, had lost patience with the long course of de la Barra's diplomacy. Furthermore, there was much truth in the saying that he had never been afraid of anything.[1] He was not afraid of the enmity of the United States, but he was not intelligent enough to realize it could be a considerable nuisance.

On 7 May he summoned Henry Lane Wilson and told him that he considered the attitude of the United States in refusing to accord recognition 'as unwise and susceptible of an unfriendly interpretation'. Up to this time the ambassador, with the concurrence of the State Department, had continued to take part in discussions on the question of outstanding claims, in which the French minister had taken the lead. The President now told him that in the circumstances the Mexican government was not prepared to settle these cases. On 10 May the President, in conjunction with the Secretary of External Relations, issued a statement that no further negotiations other than routine would be handled with the embassy, thus reducing the ambassador, as he complained, to the role of a chargé d'affaires.[2] This alienated the ambassador without impressing the United States government.

Meanwhile Speyer continued to press, both indirectly through Secretary W. G. McAdoo and directly in correspondence with

Virginia. Its board included C. W. Bowring, however, and it was capitalized in London. The Aguila Company held a mortgage on its railway and pipe to Tuxpam from its pleasingly named working site of Furbero (*Mexican Year Book, 1914*; cf. Percy N. Furber, *I Took Chances: From Windjammers to Jets* (Leicester, 1954), p. 170).

[1] King, *Tempest over Mexico, a Personal Chronicle* (1936), p. 82.
[2] Wilson–Secretary of State, 8 May, 8 p.m., Telegram no. 225; 10 May, 12 noon, Telegram no. 227. SDF 812.00/7431, 7454.

John Bassett Moore, for clarification of the administration's attitude. Noting that some Madero short-term notes were due to mature within the month, he observed that if these notes were to be paid off with the proceeds of a European loan the United States would lose much prestige in Mexico. In fact, Henry Lane Wilson had already reported that such a loan had been settled in London. Speyer now stated that he was not necessarily urging recognition, particularly as the promised Presidential election had not yet taken place, but that from his point of view, if the United States had decided that Huerta must go, the sooner he went the better. His letter was lost for over two weeks, and then answered briefly by the comment that there was no purpose in his coming to Washington for further discussions.[1]

The change in the situation was not yet evident from outside, but President Wilson had already begun to take an active interest in the question. On 19 April he had written to William Bayard Hale asking him to go to 'Central and South America' to find out what was going on 'down there'.[2] Hale agreed, and departed for Mexico. Meanwhile an old friend, Judge Delbert J. Haff of Kansas City, arranged to see Woodrow Wilson, and left a memorandum of his views. There seems little doubt that this was the first turning point in the President's policy but it may just be coincidence that Kansas City was the headquarters of Doheny's organization.

... Foreign nations are becoming restive and are seeking to undermine the influence of the United States in Mexico [Haff wrote]. The British Government has already recognised Huerta in a most marked manner by autograph letter from the King, due to the efforts of Lord Cowdray (Sir Weetman Pearson) who has the largest interests outside of American interests in the Mexican Republic. He is using his efforts to obtain a large loan in England, and I am informed that he has succeeded on condition that the English Government would recognise Huerta, which has been done. If Mexico is helped out of her trouble by British and German influence, American prestige in that country and the commerce of the United States will suffer great damage.

[1] Speyer–W. G. McAdoo, 5 May 1913; Speyer–Moore, 1 May 1913; 19 May 1913. Moore–Speyer, 20 May 1913, Telegram. SDF 812.00/7473, 7545, 7546.
[2] Woodrow Wilson–William Bayard Hale, 19 April 1913. Wilson Papers, File VII, Letterbook 2, f. 408. See also SDF 812.00/6596.

Almost identical words were used by Josephus Daniels when he came to write *The Wilson Era*, thirty years later.[1] On the face of it, the words were nonsense. Autograph letters are not a 'marked' manner of recognizing a ruler: they are the only manner. As we have seen, however, they conceal an unexpected truth. It *was* exceptional for a government such as Huerta's to be formally recognized at all by Great Britain. But recognition was not due to the efforts of Lord Cowdray; it was assumed from the moment news came to London that the government had been formed. The United States had long been undermining the position of other countries in Mexico, not the other way round. The point of this communication was that the administration did not like the existence of the Huerta government, and here was a suggestion that there was one man above all others who had the influence to maintain that government in power, and was taking the very steps that were vital to ensure that it was maintained.

Was Cowdray 'using his efforts to obtain a large loan in England'? It was, in a sense, irrelevant whether he was or not, so long as he was believed to be doing so. The results on all sides would be likely to be much the same. And the facts of the case make it especially hard to give a decisive answer.

On 9 April Huerta's minister of *Hacienda* had seen Luis Riba, attorney in Mexico City of S. Pearson and Son, and also, incidentally, Mr Hamar Greenwood's correspondent. He then asked him to cable to Cowdray 'his invitation to take in hand the floating of the entire new 5% Federal loan of $100,000,000 pesos'. The need for funds for the government was urgent, so the minister had indicated that if Cowdray was not willing to undertake the charge, he would approach Dr F. S. Pearson, although he suggested that the two contractors might be willing to take on the task together. Naturally Cowdray's first action was to consult the man who knew more than any other about the finances of Mexico. 'Needless to say we have no facilities for handling such a business direct,' he wrote to Limantour in Paris, 'but we do not want to

---

[1] Delbert J. Haff–President, 12 May 1913. SDF 812.00/7576. Josephus Daniels was subsequently ambassador to Mexico, 1933–42 (see *The Wilson Era: Years of Peace* (Chapel Hill, N.C., 1944), p. 181).

reply to that effect if we can be of any service in bringing likely people together. Our great interest, and naturally so, is to be of any use that it is possible to be to the Government.' He expressed his concern lest the commission might go to an irresponsible firm, and added that he was by no means certain that the loan could be placed at all, unless it could be done by Limantour himself.[1]

'You know probably that Noetzlin with Morgan, Kuhn Loeb, &c, on one hand, and Speyers with their group, on the other, have already been in touch with the Minister[2] for this same purpose', Limantour replied, after indicating that, since the individual in question had disagreed with him publicly when he was at the head of the Department, his name would have to be kept quiet. 'Moreover, the new Mexican Financial Agent is also trying, through the Hudson Consolidated, to form a syndicate to meet the Governments requirements.' He added that the government had tried too many doors without having a definite scheme in mind, and that they had exaggerated ideas of what terms could be achieved.

You are right when you say that it is almost impossible now to get money for Mexico by the way of a public loan; and therefore, I consider that the most practical scheme, while the Balkan crisis and the Mexican troubles will still last, should be the acceptation [*sic*] of drafts with an option on the future loan, at a reasonable price and the guarantee of the custom duties.

Limantour concluded his advice by advising Cowdray to speak to Hugo Scherer in London.[3] This he did, and cabled to Body to advise the minister accordingly.[4] This was Cowdray's last contact with the negotiations until September, when he was invited to subscribe to part of the loan.

Although Cowdray had in a sense used his efforts to secure a loan in England, he had done so by invitation, as an intermediary only, and contributed nothing to the actual working of the

[1] John B. Body–Cowdray, 9 April 1913; Cowdray–José Yves Limantour, 10 April 1913. Cowdray Papers.
[2] Then Toribio Esquivel Obregón, a Felicista, whom Huerta shortly afterwards replaced.
[3] Limantour–Cowdray, 11 April 1913. Cowdray Papers.
[4] Cowdray–Limantour, 15 April. Cowdray Papers.

operation. Nor at that time had the United States given any indication that they would be opposed to such a loan, nor even to recognition. It was also in this intermediary sense that Cowdray wrote to Captain Arthur Murray on 30 July to emphasize how much the Huerta government was in need of financial help, and how important it was for it to obtain the recognition of the United States. But this communication was merely filed, with a comment from Leslie that it repeated the 'usual thing' but that there was nothing the Foreign Office could do about it.[1]

When the Mexican Congress had fixed the date of the elections for Sunday, 26 October, and thus the apparent end of the interim government, Speyer once again pressed for recognition by the United States, indicating that it now appeared that the loan would be placed whether recognition was forthcoming or not. This time his communication was considered of sufficient importance for him to be summoned to an immediate conference with the Secretary of State.[2] The loan had become a matter of some concern. Yet the administration's attitude on recognition, which was to settle on a statement that they would be prepared to recognize a constitutionally elected President, was still not clear. The ambassador in Rio de Janeiro was told to inform Argentina and Chile, through the Brazilian government, that the United States government was 'not ready to consider recognising Mexico', but that they hoped that they would refrain from doing so until it was. Norway had waited for a long time, and gave up waiting on 23 May.[3] Nor was it just foreign representatives who were kept in the dark. Henry Lane Wilson was driven to cable to Washington on 9 June that, although he had been the President's personal representative at his post for three months, he had not been put in

---

[1] Cowdray–Captain Arthur Murray, 30 July 1913. FO 371/1674 file 6269/35448.
[2] Speyer–Moore, 31 May 1913, Telegram; Bryan–Speyer, 31 May 1913, Telegram. SDF 812.00/7651.
[3] Bryan–U.S. Embassy, Rio de Janeiro, Telegram, 31 May, 7 p.m.; Ambassador, Christiania [Oslo]–Secretary of State, 23 May 1913. SDF 812.00/7653, 7715.

David Franklin Houston, *Eight Years with Wilson's Cabinet, 1913 to 1920, with a personal estimate of the President* (Garden City, N.Y., 1926), p. 69, records that it was on this same day that 'Mexico loomed up at the Cabinet meeting ... as an ugly problem'. He personally opposed recognition. The cabinet agreed that Bryan should sound out the British and French ambassadors and warn them that the United States would not support a loan.

possession of the attitude of the administration on the question of recognition.[1]

The President seems then to have come to the conclusion that even if the ambassador was an imperfect instrument, he was at least the most obvious one. His relations with the Huerta government, distasteful as they were, could be put to service. Moreover, as ambassador, even in the absence of formal recognition, he enjoyed the right of direct access to the head of state, which the United States would lack if he were withdrawn. For he could not be replaced, since to accredit a fresh ambassador would be to accord formal recognition. The decision was taken to accept his offer, and the President provided a statement of policy for his personal information.

This Government does not feel that the provisional government of Mexico is moving towards conditions of settled peace, authority and justice, because it is convinced that within Mexico itself there is a fundamental lack of confidence in the good faith of those in control at Mexico City, and in their intention to safeguard constitutional rights and methods of action [it ran]. This Government awaits satisfactory proof of their plans and purposes. If the present provisional government of Mexico will give the Government of the United States satisfactory assurances that an early election will be held, free from coercion or restraint, that Huerta will observe his original promise and not be a candidate at that election, and that an absolute amnesty will follow, the Government of the United States will be glad to exercise its good offices to secure a genuine armistice and an acquiescence of all parties in the program.

It added that the United States could not acquiesce in anything that did not definitely promise 'peace, justice and recognised authority in Mexico'.[2]

Some of the doubt which this message shows may well have been due to a further letter from Judge Haff in which he indicated that the Huerta government was much more strongly based than he had believed, while liberty of speech and of the press continued to prevail under it.[3] It was also known that the government had in fact

[1] Wilson–Secretary of State, 9 June, 8 p.m., Telegram no. 280. SDF 812.00/7743.
[2] Bryan–Wilson, Telegram, 15 June, 12 noon. SDF 812.00/7743.
[3] Haff–President, 28 May 1913. SDF 812.00/7746.

succeeded in getting a loan, but on a very much smaller scale than it had expected, and one which left its ultimate value very doubtful.

On the other hand, by this time the Constitutionalists had captured Durango and in so doing had exhibited an irresponsibility and fury which made a very unfavourable impression.[1] In one direction, however, the doubt was speedily resolved. Hale's first report from Mexico, already quoted in part, indicated that in his opinion the ambassador's part in the *Decena Trágica* caused the government that retained him as their envoy to share in his responsibility. On 1 July the President suggested to Bryan that his recall should be arranged as quickly as possible.[2]

However, a temporary distraction was furnished by an incident that occurred while the ambassador was absent on a visit to Vera Cruz. A meeting of all other diplomatic representatives accredited to Mexico resolved to send identic telegrams to their governments asking them to intercede with the United States for recognition. On his return, Wilson was told by Stronge of what had taken place, and the ambassador informed the State Department, who were therefore prepared when the first note arrived in Washington on 10 July from the French government. At the same time, the ambassador made his last plea for recognition on his own behalf.[3]

Grey was more diplomatic than the French Foreign Minister. He sent for Page and asked his advice, stating that he wished the President to recognize the government of Mexico, and asking whether or not this was out of the question. At the same time he pointed out that British recognition, as that of other European governments, was purely provisional, and the whole question would arise again *de novo* after the elections. This statement seems to have puzzled Page, though probably not as much as the reply of the State Department suggests.[4]

Events now followed in quick succession. The ambassador's argument for recognition was finally rejected, and he was recalled

[1] Theodore C. Hamm–Secretary of State, Telegram, 21 June, 10 a.m. SDF 812.00/7919.

[2] William Bayard Hale, Memorandum, 18 June 1913, *cit. sup.* p. 137 note 1; Woodrow Wilson–Bryan, 1 July 1913. SDF 812.00/7864½. See also Woodrow Wilson–Bryan, 3 July 1913. Wilson Papers, File VII, Letterbook 5, f. 80.

[3] Wilson–Secretary of State, 8 July, 11 a.m., Telegram no. 311, Confidential; Moore–President, 10 July 1913. SDF 812.00/7992.

[4] Page–Secretary of State, 11 July, 7 p.m., Telegram no. 16. SDF 812.00/8026.

on 16 July, as President Wilson had recommended, for consulta-tion.[1] On 18 July Page was at last sent a copy of the memorandum written for Ambassador Wilson, but strictly for his own informa-tion.[2] On the following day, in reply to Grey's query on recog-nition, he was told that it would be better for him not to discuss the subject again until the President had been able to confer with Henry Lane Wilson.[3] Meanwhile, Page had suggested that growing excitement in the press about the possibility of joint intervention suggested that the question might be under official consideration. He was immediately told to express no opinion, but to report fully all that was said to him on the subject.[4]

Page was wrong about joint intervention, as he himself was able to report a few days later. The significance of the new interest of the administration in the British attitude to Mexico was that it coincided with a real move in Britain to bring the Mexican situation into some sort of order, while, at the same time, the United States government continued to give no indica-tion of their real attitude. Thus, on 25 July, Page had to give his own interpretation of the administration's position to Grey in default of an official statement. While this was well intentioned, it was also misleading.

Today I intimated to Sir Edward Grey my own belief (personal and un-official) that the President is unlikely at this late time to recognise the Huerta Government since the time before the election is now so brief [he reported], and I reminded him that the proximity of Mexico to the United States introduces conditions in our relation to that country that the British Government did not have and possibly could not fully measure.

To this he assented and declared that he had no wish to 'push'.

There is a widespread feeling here among intelligent men in both political parties that the British Government made a mistake in recog-nising Huerta [he added]. Opinion divides itself along financial rather than party lines.[5]

[1] *The World*, Thursday, 17 July 1913.
[2] Bryan–Page, Telegram, 18 July, 7 p.m. SDF 812.00/7743.
[3] Bryan–Page, Telegram, 19 July, 9 p.m. SDF 812.00/8026.
[4] Page–Secretary of State, 17 July, 7 p.m., Telegram no. 22; Bryan–Page, 19 July, 8 p.m. SDF 812.00/8067.
[5] Page–Secretary of State, 25 July 1913, no. 49, Confidential. SDF 812.00/8231.

This last statement was especially misleading, for if the feeling was in fact widespread—which is doubtful—there is no indication that it was shared by Foreign Office officials.

Henry Lane Wilson later maintained that the President's mind was already made up before his interview with him, and there can be no doubt that this was true. It was even decided in advance that he would not return to Mexico, and Nelson O'Shaughnessy would be left in charge of the embassy.[1] The manner of his actual dismissal, however, gave little indication of this. Ostensibly he was dismissed for disagreeing in public with the administration,[2] and if the disagreement occurred over the question of recognition, it still did not automatically follow that the United States would extend active disapproval to powers that also disagreed on this point. For that matter, if there was to be disagreement, it was by no means clear yet where it would originate, for, as Spring-Rice wrote to Grey: 'Altogether it looks as if the most incompetent government which America has ever had was embarking light heartedly in a policy which may have the gravest consequences/ [*sic*] that is a policy of securing a protectorate over the Caribbean sea and Central America.'[3]

[1] Wilson, *Diplomatic Episodes in Mexico, Belgium and Chile* (1927), p. 313.
[2] *The World*, Monday, 28 July 1913; Tuesday, 29 July 1913; Tuesday, 5 August 1913.
[3] Spring-Rice–Grey, 21 July 1913. Grey Papers.

CHAPTER 6

DECISION

On 16 May Spring-Rice first indicated the direction from which trouble was to come. The United States authorities were becoming 'anxious', he said, about the situation in Mexico, and a 'commission'—that is, the mission of Reginald Del Valle—had returned with an 'alarmist report'.

'Our recognition of President seems to have created unfavourable impression', he wrote. 'Although no new situation is expected at present general impression seems to be that existing régime cannot last and that it will increase difficulties of avoiding intervention . . .'

The minutes show clearly the problems of interpretation that are bound to arise from such a report.

We know that the state of unrest continues—or has even increased—in some of the provinces, but there is nothing in Mr Stronge's recent despatches to show that General Huerta's government (which in any case is only a provisional one) cannot last. It was largely owing to Mr Stronge's prognostication (somewhat guarded, it is true) of stability that we took a line of our own and recognised [wrote R. H. Campbell, and concluded:] It is conceivable that this telegram may be the result of a little pique on the part of the U.S. Govt. We have just concluded an arrangement with Guatemala about the debt without their help and in the face of their advice to us to delay our action and they may think that we are becoming too independent in C. America.

The debt settlement to which Campbell referred had ended the long-standing grievance of the Council of Foreign Bondholders, in the pursuit of which they had been consistently opposed by United States interests, since the Guatemalan default on the British debt had enabled them to consolidate their position with a fresh loan pledged on the same customs revenues. After a long period of unsuccessful bargaining, conducted by Sir Lionel Carden (of whom there will be more to say later), the Foreign Office had to decide whether or not to make a threat of force. They decided to do so, and, in accordance with their general Caribbean policy, gave notice to the United States of this intention on 28 April.

On 10 May Carden had duly handed to the Guatemalan government an ultimatum requiring a satisfactory answer within five days. The answer—entirely satisfactory—was received in a matter of hours. The sole reply from the State Department to the British Foreign Office had been a request to wait, for which no reasons had been given. To this extent, therefore, the Foreign Office were justified in ignoring it, but in the circumstances it was to prove an unfortunate decision. The Foreign Office were confronted with the possibility that in doing so they might well have tried the inexperienced United States President too far. Sir Walter Langley, the new Superintending Under Secretary of the American Department, suggested calling for information from Mexico. This was done, but Sir Edward Grey summed up the Foreign Office view when he added: 'We have only recognised a provisional President, & I think the whole diplomatic body, including the U.S. Minister [*sic*] paid him a complimentary visit. Is this not so?' And so it was.[1]

Stronge's estimate of the situation came without delay.

If the Mexican Government can obtain loan on reasonable terms it will probably succeed in reestablishing order throughout the country. Its difficulties are, however, greatly increased by the doubtful attitude of United States and especially by their postponement of recognition and failure to prevent importation of arms from across the frontier [he stated]. If this Government fails I can see no other which is likely to succeed, and I fear that intervention and perhaps dismemberment might ensue.[2]

Spring-Rice was accordingly instructed to inform the State Department of the British position. This can be summarized: having extended recognition to the provisional government only after it had been ascertained that it was legally constituted and had received the approval of all diplomatic representatives, including the United States Ambassador, which 'in itself constituted a certain measure of recognition', they believed that it would last if a

---

[1] Spring-Rice–Grey, 16 May 1913, Telegram no. 95. FO 371/1673 file 6269/22719.
[2] Stronge–Grey, 17 May 1913, Telegram no. 50. FO 371/1673 file 6269/22745.

loan could be obtained. Before Spring-Rice communicated this
to the Assistant Secretary of State, he was told that the attitude of
the Administration was 'still undecided'.[1]

Although informed of the need for a loan from the earliest days
of the new Mexican government, there was from the start no
question of the British government giving support to any loan
which the Mexican government might try to float in London. An
observation to this effect was the sole comment on a telegram
from Carranza threatening war if such a loan were supported.[2]

On 19 May Spring-Rice reported that France had recognized
Huerta without even informing the United States, much to the
annoyance of the French ambassador at Washington. 'It seems that
the reasons against recognition are based on the reluctance of the
United States Government to condone the various acts of violence
which accompanied the recent change of government, and also to
accept as legal the situation created on the Mexican frontier by the
chaotic state of affairs prevailing in the country', he wrote. To
the Foreign Office, the latter reason seemed only to be one more
argument in favour of recognition, much of the perennial concern about intervention being calmed by the ambassador's opinion
that the administration was 'entirely pacific'.[3]

On 28 May Spring-Rice cabled that the Secretary of State had
asked him if the British government was supporting 'the loan to
Mexico'. By now it was public knowledge that a loan had been
secured. He was told to inform them that they were not, and
had no knowledge of it.[4]

Suspicion of the government's position was not confined to the
United States. The Liberal M.P. for Newcastle-under-Lyme,
J. C. Wedgwood, asked for an explanation in the House as to why
Britain had accorded recognition when the United States had not,

[1] Grey–Spring-Rice, 21 May 1913, Telegram; Spring-Rice–Grey, 20 May 1913, Telegram
no. 102. FO 371/1673 file 6269/22745, 23200.
[2] Minutes on: V. Carranza–The President of the Cabinet of H.M. the King of England
[*sic*], Telegram (undated) received at Foreign Office, 23 May 1913. FO 371/1673 file
6269/24070.
[3] Spring-Rice–Grey, 19 May 1913, no. 127. FO 371/1673 file 6269/24127. It is significant
that the French government was scarcely criticized for this action in the subsequent
controversy.
[4] Spring-Rice–Grey, 28 May 1913, Telegram no. 112; Grey–Spring-Rice, 29 May 1913,
Telegram no. 168. FO 371/1673 file 6269/24663.

and while the landless *peones* of Mexico were still struggling for their rights. He also wanted to know whether Lord Cowdray had approached the Foreign Office in the matter. Sir Edward Grey replied accurately that he had not, but that his views had been sought, while he indicated that Stronge's telegrams had 'amply justified recognition'. Nor was Mr Wedgwood the only Member to be concerned. Mr William Young, M.P.,[1] whose interests lay in the North and were by this time endangered by the Constitutionalist advance, 'was much annoyed at the recognition of General Huerta & traced it to the influence of Lord Cowdray whom he denounced in the strongest language for his dealings with the Mexican Govt.', Sir Louis Mallet reported. 'He said that he meant to probe the matter to the bottom. I assured him that his suspicions were unfounded but was obliged to admit that Lord Cowdray among others had been anxious that HMG should recognize Huerta & had so informed us.'[2]

By 12 June Stronge was aware that the loan actually contracted was entirely insufficient for the government's needs.[3] Shortly afterwards, the Foreign Office received a long memorandum, drawn up by Hohler after an extensive tour of the country, which embodied the whole position as the legation saw it at the end of May, and is perhaps of particular interest in view of its authorship.

Hohler began by stating that the prevailing pessimism in the United States was to some extent justified, as there was no doubt that conditions in the North, from the government's point of view, were considerably worse. These conditions, however, were 'undoubtedly in great part due to the attitude of the United States', where the revolutionaries enjoyed almost complete immunity.

Meanwhile, the disappointed and angry adherents of the defunct Madero régime are working the press and public feeling in the United States with much energy and adroitness [he wrote]. The Hearst papers are all agog for more sensational revelations, and cinematograph shows

[1] See p. 19.
[2] *Parliamentary Debates*, Fifth Series, LIII, col. 332; minutes on Parliamentary Question, Mr Wedgwood, Thursday, 29 May 1913. FO 371/1673 file 6269/25135. See above, p. 142.
[3] Stronge–Grey, 12 June 1913, Telegram no. 54. FO 371/1673 file 6269/26982.

vividly depict the murders of Madero and Pino Suarez, and other outrages, real or alleged. They do not, however, depict the peculation of the Madero family, the ineptitude of his administration, or the tragic results to his country, of the indiscriminate and thoughtless dissemination of the most advanced democratic ideas, ideas dangerous and difficult of realization, even in the most educated and civilized communities of the old World, but which have wrought nothing less than havoc among the ignorant, semi-savage, three-fourths Indian population of Mexico.

A logical result of the non-recognition by the United States has been embodied in a statement made by President Huerta to the press that, while the Mexican Government will do all in their power to protect all foreign interests, whatever their nationality, yet, he is, of course, precluded from entering into negotiations with the United States Ambassador, and can only, by courtesy, listen to any representations he may have to make on behalf of his countrymen. In this respect, the United States Government have put themselves curiously in the wrong, as already reported, by inviting the Mexican Government, for instance, to join with them in recognizing the Chinese Republic.

The result, Hohler said, was that American interests were seriously affected, and hatred of Americans was being stirred up.

Huerta's government, he concluded, depended for its survival on obtaining the loan. This was being delayed by the 'factious opposition' of Maderistas in Congress. If it failed, the consequences were unpredictable. 'It is understood . . . (at least here in Mexico) that the Government of President Wilson is even more adverse to Intervention than was its predecessor, and this, notwithstanding the fact that its action has contributed so much to bring about the present critical situation.'[1]

There was much truth in what Hohler had to say. Mexicans were conditioned by long habit to regard the United States with suspicion. If the attitude of the United States was not friendly, it must be hostile. Recognition was therefore not just a question of ordinary diplomatic practice, as in the case of a European power. It was overvalued in Mexico, even by foreign diplomatists. Thus, whereas President Wilson was to come to believe that his moral disapproval could ensure the collapse of the Huerta government,

[1] Stronge–Grey, 27 May 1913, no. 148. FO 371/1673 file 6269/27492.

Stronge and many others believed that the moral support of the United States was essential to its survival. Both were wrong.

On 3 July Colonel House, President Wilson's personal representative, lunched with Grey at his house at 33 Eccleston Square. In the course of conversation, he took the opportunity of mentioning the Mexican situation.

I told him the President did not want to intervene and was giving the different factions every possible opportunity to get together [he wrote in his diary]. He wished to know whether the President was opposed to any particular faction. I thought it was immaterial, as far as our Government was concerned, which faction was in power, if order was maintained. I thought our Government would have recognised Huerta's provisional Government if they had carried out their written promise to call an election at an early date and abide by its decisions.[1]

It is generally agreed that this well-meant intervention seriously misled the British government as to the intentions of the United States. House had already been absent from the United States for some time and in his absence events had continued to move on. Nevertheless, there can be no doubt that House accurately reflected the situation as it had been when the administration took office. Furthermore, if Grey was misled as to the attitude of the United States, House was certainly accurately informed of the position of Great Britain. He understood correctly that British recognition of Huerta was provisional, and that Grey considered that a new situation would arise if the General were to become a candidate for the Presidency.[2] In these circumstances, the responsibility for any misunderstanding which might arise rested squarely with Washington.

By this time, Stronge, in common with other representatives in Mexico, had come to the conclusion that they should show their collective desire for United States recognition by the dispatch of identic telegrams to their respective governments. They were successful to the extent that steps were taken towards common

---

[1] As Professor Cline has pointed out, this was a mistake. Huerta had promised that Díaz could stand at the next election, not that he would hold an early election (Howard F. Cline, *The United States and Mexico* (Cambridge, Mass., 1963), p. 132).

[2] Charles Seymour, ed., *The Intimate Papers of Colonel House* (London, 1926), I, p. 201.

action between the European powers, which, though inevitably suspected in the United States, had not existed up to that time.

It was felt in London that the telegrams strengthened the British case for recognition, but Sir Louis Mallet for one doubted whether recognition by the United States at so late a stage could do any good. Furthermore, a report from Spring-Rice brought the news that on 22 June the United States–Mexican Arbitration Treaty had been allowed to lapse. This, it must have seemed, was a most ominous sign, coming from an administration whose Secretary of State had laid much emphasis for many years on the negotiation of treaties to forestall war. It was generally agreed in London that, in the light of this telegram, joint representations were unlikely to achieve anything.[1]

The furthest that Grey was prepared to go, even after learning that collective representations were favoured in Berlin, was towards making separate and unofficial approaches to see if provisional recognition could be accorded to hold things together until the Mexican election. This was in keeping with the advice of Spring-Rice that a joint approach was likely to do more harm than good with public opinion, while everything would wait for the administration to secure the passage of the Underwood Tariff and Federal Reserve Banking bills. It was for this reason that Grey consulted Page unofficially. Page's understanding of the essence of the inquiry differed considerably from Grey's.[2]

'I doubt whether we shall extract positive answer from Secretary of State', Spring-Rice observed pessimistically. 'American firms interested in Mexico have exerted strong pressure in favour of recognition, but in vain.'[3] On 14 July he re-emphasized the fact that the public in the United States were disposed to resent European interference on the grounds that the United States had most to lose in Mexico[4] and would have to shoulder the risk and

[1] Stronge–Grey, 4 July 1913, Telegram no. 55 and minutes; Spring-Rice–Grey, 28 June 1913, no. 152. FO 371/1673 file 6269/30792, 30871, 31286.
[2] Spring-Rice–Grey, 8 July 1913, Telegram no. 137; Grey–Spring-Rice, 11 July 1913, Telegram no. 272. FO 371/1673 file 6269/31640.
[3] Spring-Rice–Grey, 11 July 1913, Telegram no. 138. FO 371/1673 file 6269/31967.
[4] See p. 20. Cf. *The New York Herald*, 2 September 1913: 'Foreign Interests in Mexico', quoting figures given by Senator A. B. Fall in *Leslie's Weekly*, 14 August 1913, as justification of the view that the United States had a special interest. The figures in each case are almost identical.

cost of intervention, if it became 'necessary'. 'Owing to change of administration and frequent absences of Secretary of State, the State Department is in a chaotic condition,' he said, 'and seems to have no settled policy.'[1]

The first result of the discussion with Page was a most disconcerting telegram from Stronge, who for the past week had been emphasizing that relations between Mexico and the United States had worsened to the point of crisis.

Acting Minister for Foreign Affairs called yesterday, at President's request, to thank me for telegraphing to you respecting attitude of United States [it ran]. He had received a telegram from Mexican Embassy at Washington saying that British action had produced a deep impression.

'I suppose the "British action" means the conversation with Mr Page', Knatchbull-Hugessen correctly observed.

'I am afraid that the Mexican Govt. are endeavouring to make out that we are supporting them against the U.S. Govt: & I hope Mr Stronge has not been in any way instrumental in giving this impression', wrote Sir Arthur Nicolson, and he asked pertinently: 'How did the Mexicans know what he had tel[d]?'

'Mr Stronge cannot I suppose know anything of my conversation with Mr Page', added Grey. 'Tel to Mr Stronge "You must be careful not to give the impression that we can take action at Washington to influence the United States Govt."'[2]

Still no formal reply came, and, as we have seen, the Secretary of State had directed that none should be made. London was immediately informed from both Mexico and Washington when Henry Lane Wilson was recalled on 16 July. Spring-Rice drew attention to the fact that American recognition would endanger Americans in northern Mexico, and referred to a declaration

---

[1] Spring-Rice–Grey, 14 July 1913, Telegram no. 141 Confidential. FO 371/1674 file 6269/32635.

[2] Stronge–Grey, 12 July 1913, Telegram no. 58; 17 July 1913, Telegram no. 62. FO 371/1674 file 6269/32177, 32995. The Acting Secretary was Carlos Pereyra, subsequently a distinguished author of Latin American reputation, noted for anti-United States polemics, such as *Las dos supercherías diplomáticas norteamericanas* (Madrid, 1916) and *El crimen de Woodrow Wilson* (Madrid, 1917), and latterly for historical works, e.g. *México Falsificado* (Mexico, 1949). For his disputes with Henry Lane Wilson during this period, see Jorge Flores D., 'Carlos Pereyra y el embajador Wilson', *Historia Mexicana*, VIII, no. 29, julio 1958, pp. 95–121.

made by the President in May, of which no copy had been sent to London. He reported excitement at rumours of the British *démarche*, which the press were hinting would be backed by force if necessary, and stated that he was writing about them to the Assistant Secretary.[1]

It was not until after this that the Foreign Office heard of Henry Lane Wilson's request to the State Department for the President's views.

To this communication [Stronge had reported by mail on 28 June] he received a somewhat diffuse reply, stating that the United States Government were of opinion that the Huerta Government had not obtained general acceptance in the country, and that recognition should be made dependent on the holding of free elections and on the resignation of General Huerta, who should abide by the agreement he had entered into, and should not himself be a candidate for the definitive Presidency. It was further stated that the United States would be willing to use its good offices to bring about a peaceful settlement.[2]

Significantly, Stronge indicated that Huerta had not in fact bound himself as stated, as indeed was the case, and observed that the terms implied interference with the free choice of a President and the virtual recognition of the rebels' belligerency.[3] But Spring-Rice continued to follow the developing trend of opinion in the United States.

Impression seems further that there is an organised movement in favour of recognition of Huerta, to which several financiers and United States Ambassador were privy, and that active action of foreign representatives in Mexico was part of this plan, and an attempt to turn flank of United States Government, who has resisted a direct attack [he reported]. Sentiment of the Government seems opposed to recognition on the ground of insecurity of the present régime and bad effect on South American peoples of recognising a Government which attained power by unconstitutional and murderous methods.

This certainly ought to have warned the Foreign Office that they were running the risk of incurring administration disapproval.

[1] Spring-Rice–Grey, 17 July 1913, Telegram no. 143. FO 371/1674 file 6269/33135.
[2] Compare SDF 812.00/7743.
[3] Stronge–Grey, 28 June 1913, no. 183. FO 371/1674 file 6269/33209.

Spicer, however, misinterpreted the situation. 'The U.S. Gov^t do not seem to have any body of opinion behind them in their refusal to recognize Huerta, & it is difficult to follow the argument that they are withholding recognition on the ground of the insecurity of Huerta's administration', he commented.[1]

The tendency in London to see the new American policy in economic terms of a protectorate over northern Mexico is comprehensible since even Spring-Rice described it as being virtually identical with that of President Taft. He meant non-intervention and non-importation, with non-recognition added. Furthermore, they could see in Nicaragua the treaty on the point of being concluded which would constitute it a protectorate in all but name.

By 25 July Spring-Rice knew that President Wilson had personally taken over control as regards policy towards Mexico[2] after the inconclusive end of the Senate debate, which offered only the hint that the administration were in favour of stopping the export of arms to Huerta. Later, he indicated that there was 'little chance' of Huerta being recognized. 'Idea attributed to President is a commission of mediation to be sent to Mexico from US with knowledge & consent of the other American Govts. with a view to effect[ing] a settlement & ensur[ing] safety of foreign lives and property', he added, and said that it was unlikely that Henry Lane Wilson would be allowed to return to Mexico.

In his report on Wilson's recall Stronge re-emphasized the friction that had arisen between him and the Huerta government. He added:

... Mr Wilson has, I can well believe, much sympathy with the interventionists, but I do not think that, at any rate latterly, he has been working to bring intervention about, and I certainly do not believe that he is an annexationist. Possibly his ideal would be a nominally independent Mexico which should be controlled and practically governed from the United States Embassy.[3]

[1] Spring-Rice–Grey, 19 July 1913, Telegram no. 145 and minutes. FO 371/1674 file 6269/33378.
[2] Spring-Rice–Grey, 12 July 1913, no. 165 and minutes. FO 371/1674 file 6269/33682.
[3] Spring-Rice–Grey, 25 July 1913, Telegram no. 152; 25 July 1913, Telegram no. 149. FO 371/1674 file 6269/34507, 34389. Stronge–Grey, 17 July 1913, no. 201. FO 371/1674 file 6269/36772.

On 25 July, also, Grey had again seen Page, and the ambassador had given his unofficial indication that recognition was unlikely to be accorded. In Grey's words:

I said that I could not press any particular step on the United States; in the first place because things were so uncertain in Mexico that it was difficult to judge what the effect of any particular step would be, and in the next place, as he himself had said, the United States having a conterminous frontier might find it necessary to take into account conditions that specially affected them. But I hoped that they would agree in this, that it would be undesirable for the elections to be postponed beyond the date now fixed for them. We had recognised the provisional state of things in the hope of contributing to stability before the elections took place, but we did not regard the provisional stage as satisfactory, nor did we wish to see it prolonged.[1]

It was this long and carefully worded statement that Page reduced to the single sentence: 'To this he assented and declared that he had no wish to "push".'[2] Here Page was even more seriously at fault than he had been over the first interview. The point of that one would have been lost had Spring-Rice not been alert to seize an opportunity. In a private telegram he reported its curious consequences. We do not know if he was as fortunate in communicating the substance of the second.

Your remarks have had the effect of drawing the President's attention to the Mexican situation [Spring-Rice confirmed]. He seems to have asked the Secretary of State for details which the latter, who does not read reports, or allow Councillor [*sic*] to see them, was unable to give. The President sent for the Ambassador and asked to see all reports which had reached the Department.

I sent the Councillor privately your telegram. United States Ambassador had not grasped the meaning of the word 'provisional', which the President fully understands. Perhaps the matter might now be allowed to rest until the President has made his expected announcement. Even the mildest form of European intervention is resented.[3]

This was a stroke of good fortune, for Grey's summary had been sent by telegraph only as an afterthought. Had it been left to

---

[1] Grey–Spring Rice, 25 July 1913, no. 412. FO 371/1674 file 6269/35019.
[2] Page–Secretary of State, 25 July 1913, no. 49 Confidential. *Cit. sup.* p. 188.
[3] Spring-Rice–Grey, 26 July 1913, Telegram Private. FO 371/1674 file 6269/35019.

a dispatch, one more misunderstanding would have gone into the records uncorrected, as had so many before. Naturally Spring-Rice's advice to abstain from all further action was followed, while he continued to report the growing inclination of the administration towards a policy of mediation, and the pervasiveness of the belief that Huerta was only sustained by the organized pressure of cosmopolitan finance. 'It is of course impossible for me to gauge the truth of these surmises', he reported of the latter, 'but their prevalence would evidently account for much misconstruction of motives which might lead to regrettable consequences.'[1]

With the dismissal of Henry Lane Wilson on 5 August and the dispatch of John Lind to Mexico as special envoy of President Wilson, the proposals for active interposition in Mexico were translated into action.

John Lind was born in Sweden in 1854 and accompanied his parents to the United States when he was still young. He found his political home in the Democratic party in the state of Minnesota, and by hard work and ability rose to become governor of that state. He had been a keen and loyal supporter of Bryan in all his campaigns. This was remembered when the Great Commoner became Secretary of State and Lind was offered the post of minister to Sweden. Rightly or wrongly, he did not think it would be proper for him to accept.[2] It was for this reason alone that a man of his standing in the country and in the party was still available for an unofficial diplomatic mission, and one which the President, at least, knew was one of great delicacy. His other qualifications, unhappily, were less obvious, not to say absent.

'Lind is a politician who has been useful to the Secretary of State, and has the reputation of being honest but obstinate', Spring-Rice reported to Grey. 'He knows no Spanish and has no diplomatic experience.'[3] Nor was this a hostile comment. Lind's biographer was not able to find any better reason for him being

[1] Spring-Rice–Grey, 21 July 1913, no. 172. FO 371/1674 file 6269/35096.
[2] Woodrow Wilson–John Lind, 17 July 1913. Wilson Papers, File VII, Letterbook 4, f. 309.
[3] Spring-Rice–Grey, 6 August 1913, Telegram no. 162. FO 371/1674 file 6269/36547.

chosen for the task other than that he was 'silent',[1] and, in the event, it seems that this was one of the few occasions in his life when he did not live up to his reputation in that regard.

It is believed that his instructions are to negotiate with the rival leaders with view to pacification [Spring-Rice continued]. He will report to the President, who will make public statement as soon as he is ready to communicate with Mexican authorities as to the restoration of peace.

It is stated on good authority that the President is determined not to recognise Huerta or to sanction intervention, as recommended by the United States Ambassador, but hopes, without using force, to arrange through Lind for peaceful retirement of Huerta, recognition of provisional President, and constitutional election, with the consent of all parties. An informant tells me that the President's plan is almost sure to fail, because the parties will not accept the result of election, and troubles will continue as before.[2]

The mission was brief, stormy and abortive. It took place with full publicity in the world's press, and its course was watched with incredulity and even alarm in London and other European capitals. In the circumstances it is only charitable to say that Lind himself handled the brief surprisingly well.

Lind left Washington on the evening of 4 August to travel to Galveston, Texas, to board a United States warship for his journey to Vera Cruz. The terms of his mission were at once made fully known to the public, and could not do other than arouse strong feelings of hostility in Mexican government circles, sensitive to the implication—quite unintended—that the use of a warship implied a threat. For the sake of their prestige they could not do otherwise than protest, and on 6 August the Mexican Acting Secretary of External Relations announced that Lind would not be received if he did not come properly accredited.[3]

Meanwhile O'Shaughnessy, alarmed at the possible conse-

---

[1] George Malcolm Stephenson, *John Lind of Minnesota* (Minneapolis, Minn., 1935), p. 209. Houston calls it 'a singular choice (*op. cit.* p. 72).

[2] Spring-Rice–Grey, 6 August 1913, Telegram no. 162, *cit. sup.*, p. 201.

[3] *The World*, Thursday, 7 August 1913. The Secretary in question was Manuel Garza Aldape, Secretary of Public Instruction, acting Secretary of External Relations since the resignation of Carlos Pereyra on 27 July 1913. He was the chief advocate in Huerta's cabinet of a policy of defiance of the United States.

quences of the negotiations to Americans in general and not least to Lind himself, if newspaper reports that Lind was coming to insist on the resignation of President Huerta were not authoritatively contradicted, had telegraphed to the State Department. In reply Bryan ingenuously stated: 'You may say to the Minister of foreign affairs that Governor Lind comes on a mission of peace and that the President feels sure that his presence there will contribute toward a satisfactory settlement of difficulties. The Mexican government should await the President's communication and not give weight to misrepresentations of sensational newspapers . . .' This reply received a favourable reception in Mexico which it did not deserve.[1]

There is no doubt that Huerta and his advisers felt themselves to be in a strong position. As Stronge had reported on 2 August, the tide had turned in favour of the federal forces in the north, following the long build-up of the army there—a replica of Huerta's strategy of the previous year. The feeling was growing in the capital that the government could survive even without United States recognition.[2] Indeed, as was to become apparent only later, the internal resources of taxation in Mexico were as yet scarcely appreciated or exploited, though the successes of Orozco the previous year might have given some indication of their extent. But Stronge was concerned about the consequences of increased friction between Mexico and the United States, and on 7 August suggested that, if authorized, he might help to reduce it in the coming negotiations.

In London, this suggestion was regarded with scepticism. 'The action of the Mexican Govt. may cause a change in U.S. policy, leading either to recognition or intervention—at least it seems unlikely that President Wilson will persist in his present scheme in the face of this action', Leslie considered. 'I do not think it is a matter in which Mr Stronge should intervene, even privately, at present', Spicer concurred. 'The U.S. Gov^t refuse to recognize Huerta, & we could not possibly, after having recognized him

[1] O'Shaughnessy–Bryan, 5 August, 9 p.m., Telegram no. 387; Bryan–O'Shaughnessy, 6 August, 2 p.m., Telegram no. 333; O'Shaughnessy–Secretary of State, 6 August, 11 p.m., Telegram no. 397. SDF 812.00/8241, 8255.

[2] Stronge–Grey, 2 August 1913, Telegram no. 70. FO 371/1674 file 6269/35832.

ourselves, ask him to resign to please the U.S.—we should merely sacrifice our good position for nothing.'

'We are of course anxious that the provisional Mexican Govt. should not provoke the United States by any discourtesy but it would be better not to intervene unless asked to do so by both sides in which case you should report to me previously', ran the official reply.[1]

On 8 August, however, Bryan sent a circular to foreign representatives in Washington inviting their governments' assistance in obtaining a favourable hearing for his proposals. The difference between this suggestion and Stronge's was that Bryan wished the foreign governments to give such assistance *before* the terms themselves had been revealed to them, and, furthermore, to draw Mexico's attention to 'the situation which might arise should these good offices be rejected'.[2]

Grey instructed Stronge: 'You should . . . make it known unofficially to Mexican Government that a refusal to receive anyone sent on a mission by the United States Government or to hear what he has to say in a friendly spirit would in our opinion be a grave mistake and put Mexico in the wrong', emphasizing at the same time that he had no information on Lind's mission beyond the reports of Spring-Rice. He told the latter to inform the United States government, adding that, in deference to their request, he was breaking his normal rule not to intervene unless invited by both parties.[3] No clearer indication could have been given of the special consideration with which Grey viewed the United States.

On 9 August Lind arrived at Vera Cruz. There he met Hale and Admiral Fletcher, the commander of the United States squadron in Mexican waters. He conferred with them and then travelled overnight to the capital. From there, on 12 August, he reported to Washington that he had been received by the Secretary of External Relations, who, as a result of the cabinet changes by which Huerta had rid himself of the Felicistas, was by this time Federico

---

[1] Stronge–Grey, 7 August 1913, Telegram no. 71 and minutes; Grey–Stronge, 9 August 1913, Telegram no. 98. FO 371/1674 file 6269/36665.

[2] Bryan–Spring-Rice and others, 8 August, 4 p.m., Telegram. SDF 812.00/8284A.

[3] Grey–Stronge, 11 August 1913, 1.15 p.m., Telegram no. 101. FO 371/1675 file 6269/36935.

Gamboa. Gamboa's clash with Henry Lane Wilson and general anti-Americanism will be recalled from the account of the events of November 1910 (pp. 41–2). Not surprisingly, Lind found him 'officially a difficult personality to deal with'.[1]

From the beginning, Gamboa made it clear that the government regarded recognition as a prerequisite to all further negotiations. 'I explained the spirit in which the President's suggestions were proferred but stated that I was not prepared to discuss their terms except that the frankness with which he had spoken compelled me to say that the President did not contemplate recognition under existing circumstances', Lind reported. 'I deemed it advisable to make this point clear at our first interview.' He expressed his wish that the President's instructions might be sent soon and without advance publicity.[2]

Stronge reported that Lind had made a good impression on Gamboa, but that the latter believed that Washington felt themselves to be in the wrong. Stronge himself was confined to bed as the result of a fall from his horse, though he was still able to attend to business, and the President and Gamboa came to visit him the same day to ask if the British government would consent to transmit to Washington on their behalf a proposal that ambassadors be appointed reciprocally between the United States and Mexico, without conditions. Their excuse, which was a poor one, was that their chargé in Washington was only able to handle routine matters, but their motive was quite obvious. It was to secure action from Britain which would have the appearance of support for them against the United States. Stronge advised them that consent was unlikely to be forthcoming from London. It was duly refused.[3]

Before proceeding to state the President's terms formally, Lind expressed his doubts to Bryan. 'What course shall I pursue if

---

[1] O'Shaughnessy–Secretary of State, 12 August, 9 p.m., Telegram no. 422. SDF 812.00/8317. Gamboa became Secretary of External Relations on 11 August 1913. This appointment indicated the rejection by Huerta of Garza Aldape's policy of confrontation in favour of one of evasion. Both were equally moved by anti-United States views.

[2] John Lind–Secretary of State, Telegram, 12 August, 12 noon. SDF 812.00/8314.

[3] Stronge–Grey, 13 August 1913, Telegram no. 74; Grey–Stronge, 14 August 1913, Telegram no. 107; Stronge–Grey, 18 August 1913, no. 250 Confidential. FO 371/1675 file 6269/37558; FO 371/1676 file 6269/41049.

the President's proposal is spurned and I am given to understand that it is considered an unwarranted attempt to dictate in Mexican domestic affairs?', he asked. 'Such action is not likely but it is an eventuality that should be considered.'

Bryan simply directed him to communicate the terms at once, and then inform the State Department so that other nations could be told in confidence. 'President cannot advise as to next step until he knows how Huerta receives proposal', he added.[1] Lind acted forthwith and delivered the communication as a formal note. Two days later Gamboa's reply rejected the proposals sharply.[2]

On 17 August, Spring-Rice reported that Bryan had invited him to call upon him in Washington at his private residence. It was the day after Henry Lane Wilson had, from retirement, attempted to excuse his part at the ceremony congratulating Huerta on his succession, and the State Department had apologized for an insult he was incidentally supposed to have made about Britain. The Foreign Office were not particularly concerned —even after the apologies called their attention to it.[3] Now, on

[1] Lind–Secretary of State, Telegram, 13 August, 11 p.m.; Bryan–Lind, Telegram, 14 August 1913. SDF 812.00/8334.

[2] Lind–Bryan, 19 September 1913. Bryan Papers, Special Correspondence, Box 43, f. 198. Exchange first published in full in *Diario Oficial, Estados Unidos Mexicanos*, cxxvii, no. 50, Wednesday, 27 August 1913 (Poder Ejecutivo, Secretaría de Relaciones Exteriores, 'Nuestras relaciones con los Estados Unidos de América'), pp. 585–92.

Subsequently printed in English as *Mexican Affairs. Address of the President of the United States delivered at a joint session of the two houses of Congress. August 27, 1913*. 63d Congress, 1st Session. H. Doc. 205 (Washington, 1913).

[3] This incident was trivial from the point of view of Anglo-American relations, but some account should be given here. American newspapers published a statement, said to have emanated from the Foreign Office, attributing British recognition of Huerta to Henry Lane Wilson's speech of congratulation after the coup. Wilson issued a comment to the effect that his speech had been drafted conjointly with the other representatives, and casting doubt on whether the Foreign Office had made such a statement at all. Without checking whether or not this belief was true, Page was directed by Bryan to call at the Foreign Office and apologize. In fact, though the Foreign Office had been approached for a statement by the press, reporters had merely been referred to Sir E. Grey's answers to Questions in the House on 29 May and 7 July; the implications drawn by the press being their own. Henry Lane Wilson's account of the incident is, therefore, substantially correct, and Bryan was undoubtedly very much at fault. The pressure for a statement originated from the British press, who required material to answer the charge made by the *New York Sun* that British recognition had been due to 'the influence of powerful personages who own concessions in Mexico'. In this lies its only significance.

Sources: Wilson, pp. 323 ff.; Bryan–Page, 14 August, 9 p.m., Telegram and reply,

the face of it, Bryan wanted to go further, to make the attitude of the United States entirely clear and to enlist British aid.

He showed me instructions to Lind which have already been communicated to you and twenty six other Powers in strict confidence [Spring-Rice reported]. He asked that you should use your influence in order to obtain consideration for these proposals. I explained that you could not mediate unless asked by both parties or take sides in any way but that I was sure you would continue to urge Mexican Govt. in its own interest to abstain from taking any violent step of a nature to embitter the situation. I asked him what would be next step. He said that he hoped that Mexican Govt. would give a favourable hearing to his proposal and make a counter-proposal which could be discussed. If this course were not followed U.S. Govt. could bring pressure to bear in various ways, e.g. by allowing revolutionaries to obtain arms from United States. The latter assured U.S. Govt. that in that case they would soon drive Huerta out.

(This was an eloquent testimony to the real weakness of the Constitutionalist movement, which had by no means been starved of arms. In the event, they were not able to justify even this claim.)

'I asked whether U.S. Govt. were determined to get rid of Huerta', Spring-Rice continued. 'He said that President was convinced that if Huerta was definitely recognised as President the example to all South American Republics would be most deplorable, besides being directly opposed to principles enunciated by President on his taking office.'

The Secretary of State concluded by begging that any information reaching Grey from Mexico might be communicated confidentially to him. Spring-Rice assured him that he was sure that Grey would do all in his power to promote a peaceful solution.[1]

This telegram reinforced the warning given by Spring-Rice in a dispatch a few days previously concerning the dangers for President Wilson attendant on a 'moral' policy for Latin America.

SDF 812.00/8379A, 8380; Memorandum. Sir William Tyrrell, 15 August 1913, Spring-Rice–Grey, 15 August 1913, Telegram Private, memorandum and minutes, FO 371/1675 file 6269/38579; *The Morning Post*, Monday, 11, and Tuesday, 12 August 1913; *The Times*, Friday, 15 August 1913; *The World*, Thursday, 14, and Friday, 15 August 1913.
[1] Spring-Rice–Grey, 17 August 1913, Telegram (unnumbered) Very Confidential. FO 371/1675 file 6269/38021.

The danger is not that he will try to fish in the troubled waters of Mexico with the desire to hook additional territory for the United States; the danger rather is that by setting up, with the best intentions, a standard of 'morality' for Latin American Governments, he will fall into the same entanglements as did the Republican administration when, to quote Mr Knox's peroration three years ago, the United States vindicated its character as 'a nation resolute for righteousness' by aiding in the expulsion of Zelaya from Nicaragua.[1]

Stronge's view on the United States policy was bitterly expressed in his comments on the telegram. The situation was 'so grave' that 'such hypothetical considerations'—that is, as to the effect of recognition on other countries—'should give way to facts' while the proposal to arm the rebels would 'lead to indefinite bloodshed and misery'.[2]

The Foreign Office to a great extent shared these views. They did not see the Constitutionalists as a force that could provide an effective government; all the evidence was against it. But they could do nothing, even in face of Stronge's report on the terms made by Lind, which was their first indication of the actual nature of the exchange.[3]

M.F.A. showed me confidentially this morning correspondence exchanged with Mr Lind [he reported]. American Note opens with expression of regret that no serious efforts are being made in Mexico city to establish a Government which shall possess the respect and confidence of the rest of the country. After expressing friendly feelings of the U.S. Govt. towards Mexico, it puts forward two demands reported by Sir C. Spring-Rice and two others, that all parties now at once lay down their arms and make a general armistice: and that the result of the new elections be accepted peacefully by all parties.

Mexican reply was handed to Mr Lind yesterday. It is very courteous and conciliatory but quite firm in tone, refusing the assistance which in this form U.S. Govt. offer. It concludes by embodying the message transmitted to you ... [concerning the exchange of Ambassadors] ... which it says would be only method for restoring good relations.

[1] Spring-Rice–Grey, 3 August 1913, no. 180. FO 371/1675 file 6269/38075.
[2] Stronge–Grey, 18 August 1913, Telegram no. 85. FO 371/1675 file 6269/38450.
[3] Page's communication arrived the same day.

Then came a curious passage which does not harmonize with the attitude of Lind, as later understood.

Mr Lind went late last night to see the M.F.A. to thank him for the Note which he greatly appreciated. He said that it had quite brought him round to the side of the Mexican M.F.A., though he feared it would be impossible to change the mind of the people at Washington. He thought that a result of the Note might be either:

1. Increased encouragement permitted to revolutionaries
2. Recognition of revolutionaries as belligerents, or
3. Open intervention.

It is possible that he said this under instructions, as to myself he said that a warlike solution was unthinkable. U.S. Chargé d'Affaires informs me that all export of arms from the U.S. to Mexico has now been forbidden. Both Lind and Huerta have expressed to me their willingness to meet and they will probably have an interview today.

Sir Louis Mallet summed up the attitude of the Foreign Office for Sir Edward Grey.

I sent to you yesterday a list of the US demands as communicated to me by Mr Page, & I suggested a non-committal reply. It is clear that HMG should not support the US Gt but maintain an attitude of neutrality.

For a humanitarian like Mr Bryan the proposal to assist the revolutionaries with arms is as Mr Spicer remarks rather cynical but I do not know whether it means very much, as I believe that the revolutionaries have been obtaining all the arms they want throughout the struggle, from America.[1]

Grey himself only commented: 'We cannot after recognizing Huerta provisionally support a demand that he should resign before the elections.'[2]

In London it remained difficult to ascertain which of the many motives ascribed to the United States were correct. On the one hand, Lind told Stronge that they wished to enforce the terms of the *Pacto de la Ciudadela*. This was patently illogical, but particularly

[1] Stronge–Grey, 18 August 1913, Telegram no. 82. FO 371/1675 file 6269/38385.
[2] Minute on: Stronge–Grey, 18 August 1913, Telegram no. 84. FO 371/1675 file 6269/38328.

embarrassing to Britain.[1] On the other hand, John Bassett Moore told Spring-Rice that the United States wanted to ensure that Huerta was unable to draw the rest of the loan 'and thus exhaust Customs revenue which was the only remaining guarantee for indemnities'.[2] This made it very hard to take seriously Stronge's report that Lind was complaining that he found it very difficult to convince the Mexicans 'that the United States Government could be actuated by higher motives than those of mere commercialism'.[3]

For his part, Stronge did take care to comply with Grey's warning not to let the Mexican government think that Britain would back them against the United States. On 21 August he warned the President and Gamboa that European governments were not subject to influences inducing the sympathy of foreign representatives and resident foreigners, 'and, granting for the moment that arguments which Mexican Govt. might advance were good, they should remember that they were not engaged in a law-suit and that they had to count with American popular feeling'. He later reported that the Secretary agreed with him, but that there were 'other Ministers who advocated a strong policy and were trying to persuade President that he would be remembered in history as having successfully defied U.S.A.'.[4]

During this period Stronge, now evidently recovered from his fall, saw much of Governor Lind. The Governor's biographer represents him as an 'inspired caller' who had first urged recognition, then tried to arrange for Lind to see Huerta, explained that foreign representatives always became charmed with Mexico and tended to support the existing government, and deplored the fact that Henry Lane Wilson had misled him as to the real intentions of the United States government. After Lind had met Huerta, he says:

Through the British minister, Lind was informed that Huerta was very agreeably impressed and pleased by his call. The minister then called

[1] Stronge–Grey, 20 August 1913, Telegram no. 86 Confidential. FO 371/1675 file 6269/38609.
[2] Spring-Rice–Grey, 20 August 1913, Telegram no. 171. FO 371/1675 file 6269/38652.
[3] Stronge–Grey, 21 August 1913, Telegram no. 87. FO 371/1675 file 6269/38782.
[4] Stronge–Grey, 21 August 1913, Telegram no. 88. FO 371/1675 file 6269/38783.

Lind's attention to an item in the *Mexican Herald* stating that it had been proposed in Congress to afford rebels the opportunity to obtain munitions of war. The minister thought this a 'horrible proposition'. Lind thought it hardly worth while to discuss the proposition abstractly[!]. The United States was confronted with a situation that demanded action, he said, and there was no telling what might happen if the question were relegated to Congress. Lind thought the 'old gentleman tolerable only as a conduit for conveying Huerta's reflections'.[1]

This picture requires substantial modification. Lind clearly wished from the beginning to use Stronge as a channel for *his* reflections. While Stronge was prepared to assist towards reaching a peaceful solution, and to that end arranged Lind's interview with Huerta,[2] he fully appreciated something that Lind never understood: how utterly preposterous the government considered the demands that he had come to make, and, hence, as long as they remained unaltered, how minimal was the value of mediation. However, he was prepared to act as a messenger, if it would do any good, and telegraphed to London on 22 August for permission to do so.

'If the President Huerta can in any way consistent with his own dignity and that of his country make a public declaration or give definite assurances that election will be held at the date fixed and that he will not himself be a candidate for that term all further matters under discussion would be easily arranged' [Lind had told him].

In accepting these two points the President would merely be carrying out the promises he has already made and recognition of the new Government so constituted would speedily follow election.

Indeed the United States would, Lind said, 'withdraw all opposition to a loan' and would 'even facilitate it'.

The reply, drafted by Sir Louis Mallet, and sent on 25 August, summed up the Foreign Office doubts.

You have repeatedly said that Huerta is the only man who can deal with the situation and restore order, and in your telegram No. 89 you say that the revolutionary movement is on the verge of collapse; that,

---

[1] Stephenson, pp. 219–20.
[2] Stronge–Grey, 19 August 1913, no. 258. FO 371/1676 file 6269/41054. This action was approved.

if he falls, prolonged disorder and bankruptcy must ensue, and that there is no one who can replace him.

Would His Majesty's Government, in these circumstances, be justified in seeking to hold him to his undertaking not to stand as a candidate at the next election? Without further explanation it is a little difficult to reconcile your present proposal with the tenour of your previous telegrams . . .[1]

Developments taking place simultaneously in Washington suggest that it was fortunate that Stronge's telegram had been worded in so misleading a manner, though it is most unlikely that he would have been granted permission to act even as a channel of communication.[2] The American press on 22 August had carried an announcement that the President intended to send a Message to Congress about the Lind Mission. Recent speeches in the Senate had been critical of the administration, and a concerted attack had probably only been averted by consultation with its leaders. While it was publicly stated that intervention was definitely ruled out as administration policy, the effects of a Message could not be predicted with assurance.[3]

Even before this announcement was made, however, the reports of the administration's attitude had caused Judge Gerard to telegraph to Cowdray to ask him to use all his efforts to ensure that Huerta gave no further cause for offence. Cowdray left a copy of the telegram at the Foreign Office on 20 August, and was told: 'Stronge is doing all he can—of course unofficially and in a friendly spirit—with Huerta so as to cause as little irritation to Washington as possible.' At the same time John B. Body sent another telegram privately to Fred Adams in Mexico.

Chief has received confidential advice from Washington that Congress and people becoming irritated about Mexican situation [he warned]. Suggestion made from Washington that we advise Mexican Government take no arbitrary stand which might anger American people. Suggest you see Huerta do your best make him realise danger.

---

[1] Stronge–Grey, 22 August 1913, Telegram no. 91 and minutes. FO 371/1675 file 6269/38919.

[2] See p. 214. Minutes to Stronge–Grey, 25 August 1913, Telegram no. 95. FO 371/1675 file 6269/39429.

[3] *The World*, 18–21 August 1913.

Adams replied the following day.

Your cable August 20th of inestimable value [he reported]. It coincided precisely with policy Foreign Minister against other Members Cabinet. I have had interview this morning with General Huerta, Foreign Minister being present. President accepts your advice. He will do everything to gain time asking Washington to withhold reply Mexican note until he can send special representative to confer with them. Since interview Foreign Minister informs me that American envoy Lind agrees to support this procedure, consequently immediate danger rupture past.[1]

Lind was very well aware that the manœuvre was designed to gain time, though he did not know that the reason was to complete an internal loan for some £4,000,000 through the National Bank of Mexico which, it was hoped, would enable the government to suppress the northern revolutionary movement completely. His strategy, however, took no account of the delay. He planned to deliver his message through Stronge, obtain the statement he desired, and retire with his mission accomplished. It can only be supposed that he considered the fact that Stronge was to present the message would be sufficient to secure its acceptance. When he found that he was not able to use Stronge yet, knowing that President Wilson was not prepared to delay his Message to Congress later than Tuesday, 26 August, he delivered his message as a formal note, demanded a reply by seven o'clock the same evening, and, when he did not get it, departed by the night train for Vera Cruz.[2]

Stronge's reply illustrated the dilemma in which he had been placed.

I did not recommend mediation to H.M.G. and I did not propose to recommend acceptance of Mr Lind's proposals to President Huerta [he explained], but as there was a difficulty in reaching him I consented at the desire of Lind and M.F.A. to ask your instructions as to acting as channel of communication. An indirect message would have been less

[1] Cowdray–Guillermo de Landa y Escandón, 21 August 1913, Cowdray Papers; Enclosures with Cowdray–Sir Louis Mallet, 22 August 1913. FO 371/1675 file 6269/38984.
[2] Stephenson, pp. 220–2; Bryan–Lind, Telegram, 24 August, 5 p.m. SDF 812.00/8526; Stronge–Grey, 26 August 1913, Telegram no. 97. FO 371/1675 file 6269/39519.

irrevocable than the formal Note which has now, I understand, been delivered.

Lind was very anxious to avoid delay as the President of the U.S. is about to consult Congress which led me to think might have most serious consequences though obviously inclined to believe now that he may have exaggerated his fears.

Sperling commented:

I feel sure M[r] Lind could have found other indirect means of reaching Huerta if he had not wished to convey the impression that his proposals were supported by H.M.G. Even now, press messages from the U.S. continue to state that the U.S. attitude has the approval of other Powers. As far as we know there is no foundation for such a statement.[1]

Though Lind did not get the reply he expected by his deadline, one was sent after him to Vera Cruz. Its contents were not yet known when the President went before Congress to deliver his Message. The Message itself propounded no policy and consisted largely of a résumé of events as seen from the point of view of the United States, adding little or nothing that was new to the appreciation of the situation.[2]

Although Gamboa's second note was far more bitter and sarcastic in tone than the first (for the offer of a loan was regarded as equivalent to a bribe), it successfully created a diversion in the form of a statement that the President was debarred from being a candidate at the elections by law.[3] 'Accept my hearty congratulations', Bryan scrawled on a telegraph form well smeared with ink and emotion. 'Huerta's announcement that he will not be a candidate is the one thing necessary to the restoration of peace. The President desires you to remain there until situation is fully developed.'[4]

On 30 August Lord Cowdray wrote to Dr C. W. Hayes at Tampico:

---

[1] Stronge–Grey, 25 August 1913, Telegram no. 95 and minutes. *Cit. sup.* p. 212.
[2] *Congressional Record*, 63rd Congress, 1st Session, L, pp. 3803–4. See also note 1, p. 208.
[3] México, Secretaría de relaciones exteriores, *Boletín oficial*, XXXVI, no. 4, 31 August 1913, pp. 204–21 includes this reply in its original text.
[4] Bryan–Lind, 27 August 1913, 11 p.m., Telegram. SDF 812.00/8593. Bryan continued to believe this as late as 6 October. Spring-Rice–Grey, 6 October 1913, Telegram no. 183 Very Confidential. FO 371/1677 file 6269/45563.

Decision

The political friction between Washington and Mexico appears to be somewhat lessening so far as one can judge from the newspapers. The present position is that Lind is waiting at Veracruz to see whether Huerta will desire to re-open the negotiations. It is clear that there is going to be no intervention unless some untoward event arises: it is also doubtful whether any arrangement is going to be made by which Huerta will be recognised by the Washington Government. The outlook rather points to an arrangement being made under which Huerta remains until the new election takes place; that Huerta must not be a candidate for re-election and that the United States government will recognise the new President.

This, I think, is as satisfactory as we could hope, having regard to the fact that the United States could not, after the delay that has occurred, now recognise Huerta. I think the United States made a mistake, but that is neither here nor there.[1]

But Huerta, whatever claims had been made on his behalf or attributed to him, had still not given any guarantee that he would not emerge from the elections as President of Mexico. It was a question that sooner or later would have to be cleared up.

[1] Cowdray Papers.

CHAPTER 7

INDISCRETION

Throughout the period of the Lind Mission, Stronge had done much towards preserving peace. The suspicions voiced as to his motives by some sections of the American press at this time do not stand up to examination. Indeed, Nelson O'Shaughnessy, and afterwards Lind himself, paid tribute to his efforts.[1] Yet throughout the period after the fall of the Madero government he had to be, and had been, scrupulous in reflecting the policy of the British government.

Nevertheless it seems that by this time he was a sick man, having suffered seriously in health and strength from his experiences during the bombardment and ceaseless activity afterwards. This seems originally to have been the only reason why he applied for a two-month leave of absence and why it was decided to move him to a better climate and to replace him as minister to Mexico. The manner in which he was informed of the decision—the news simultaneously being released to the press—was certainly abrupt. As Hohler put it: 'In July poor old Stronge got a curt telegram from the Foreign Office directing him to leave as soon as possible for Chile, as H.M.G. wished to have someone in Mexico better acquainted with Latin-America, and Sir Lionel Carden had been appointed in his place.'[2] In the circumstances, he may or may not have been right to believe, as he said in his farewell speech, that he was going because 'his goodwill for the beautiful land of Mexico stood out perhaps too strongly for the taste of the interests represented here by him'.[3]

When Luis Riba heard the news he telegraphed to Cowdray: 'Very important that Strong [sic] British Minister be maintained in Mexico please do all possible towards this end Strong helping

[1] O'Shaughnessy–Secretary of State, 27 August 1913, no. 2041 Confidential, SDF 812.00/8693; Lind–Secretary of State, Telegram, 1 November, 6 p.m., Bryan Papers, General Correspondence, Box 29.

[2] Hohler, *Diplomatic Petrel* (1942), p. 186.

[3] Kardorff–Bethmann-Hollweg, 28 July 1913, no. A 40 GFM 12/16 f. A 16792.

Mexican Government greatly.'[1] There is no indication in the Foreign Office papers that Cowdray officially acted on this request. He did communicate the request from Fred Adams that Stronge should at least be retained until it was over, but that was at the height of the Lind crisis.

This second request certainly originated from President Huerta himself, and had already been embodied in an unofficial communication from the Mexican minister in London on 20 August. Grey's reaction was: 'It is not desirable to delay Sir L. Carden's arrival. The Mexican Govt want us to take an active "sympathetic" part, but though we do not wish to be unsympathetic this is not our policy nor would it in the long run be helpful to them if we allowed them to run us against the U.S.'[2] The indication is that this reaction was actually created by the intervention and the terms in which it was couched.

Huerta came in person to the farewell luncheon given by the British colony for the retiring minister, 'although some of his followers tried to prevent him'.[3] Stronge left the capital on the 14th, to sail from Vera Cruz on 16 September, and Hohler was left once more as chargé d'affaires. His first official act was to telegraph London to find out when Carden was due to arrive.[4]

There had been some doubt in London about the advisability of leaving an interregnum, so Grey had been prepared to accede to the Mexican request that Stronge at least be retained until Carden's arrival.[5] But Stronge was not willing to wait and, as Sperling minuted, Hohler had done 'very well' during his previous spell. Despite the apparent urgency felt about Carden's arrival, the Foreign Office had fortunately taken care to sound the Mexicans about their original plan to dispatch him from Galveston on H.M.S. *Hermione*, and Stronge had replied that it would be

---

[1] Luis Riba–Cowdray, Telegram, received 27 July 1913, Private and Confidential. Cowdray Papers.

[2] Adams–Cowdray, 28 July 1913, Cowdray Papers; Memorandum by Sir L. Mallet, 20 August 1913, FO 371/1680 file 39602.

[3] Hohler, p. 186. Stronge served as Minister to Chile from 1913 to 1919, when he retired from the service. Latterly he lived at Kilbroney House, Rostrevor, Co. Down, where he died 20 August 1924.

[4] Hohler–Grey, 15 September 1913, Telegram (unnumbered). FO 371/1680 file 42405.

[5] Memorandum by Sir L. Mallet, 27 August 1913; Stronge–Grey, 2 September 1913, Telegram no. 107. FO 371/1680 files 40511, 40592.

inadvisable.[1] Had they known what the circumstances of the arrival were to lead to, they might have felt it was less pressing.

Lionel Edward Gresley Carden[2] was born on 15 September 1851 and educated at Eton. His career started in the consular service in 1877 as vice-consul at Havana, and his diplomatic experience in 1883, when he was attached to Sir Spenser St John's Special Mission to Mexico to restore the diplomatic relations severed during the War of Intervention. As a result, he became the first acting chargé d'affaires for a few months in 1885, afterwards remaining in Mexico in various consular posts until 1898.

In the period between 1887 and 1895 he embarked on actions which were to prove a considerable handicap to him later. He joined in the general drive to invest in the development of the country, and by 1893 had invested a sum amounting to five times his annual salary. In that year the New Consular Regulations for the first time imposed a prohibition on investments of a speculative character. Carden took steps to divest himself of his shareholdings, though with little success evidently, for he had not yet rid himself of them in 1895 when it came to the attention of the Foreign Office that he had been engaged in the purchase of land in the region of the Isthmus of Tehuantepec. When he was questioned he claimed these were not speculations as the land in question was agricultural land and not subject to fluctuations. The Foreign Office, it is clear, were unwilling to think ill of him and accepted this contention. But he had not stated that he did not expect the value of the land to rise, and in view of its proximity to the Tehuantepec Railway he can hardly have expected not to make a substantial profit on it.[3]

It was in this connection that he might most noticeably have become associated with Lord Cowdray, then Sir Weetman Pearson. But for the moment this was not in question. In 1898 he was transferred to Cuba once more, as consul general, and at the

[1] Grey–Stronge, 25 August 1913, Telegram no. 115; Stronge–Grey, 26 August 1913, Telegram no. 98. FO 371/1680 files 37595, 39493.
[2] Biographical details from *Foreign Office List*, 1913; obituary in *The Times*, Monday, 18 October 1915.
[3] *The Times*, Tuesday, 10 February 1914; cutting and minutes with memorandum: 'Sir L. Carden's Connection with Mining Operations and Speculations in Mexico', by Gaston de Bernhardt. FO 371/2034 file 7392.

termination of the United States occupation in 1902 was trans-
ferred to the Diplomatic Service and raised to the rank of Minister
Resident. It was there that he acquired his reputation for anti-
Americanism, though, in view of the special position of the
United States, some friction might reasonably have been expected
between him and the American colony.

In 1905 he was transferred to Guatemala as Minister Resident to
Central America. With the enunciation of the Roosevelt corollary
and military intervention, and subsequently the experiment of
Taft with dollar diplomacy, it was not the place for him to shed
his reputation. He became identified with Foreign Office pressure
for the maintenance of British interests in the Caribbean, and was
individually credited with—above all—the successful debt settlement with Guatemala itself. It was for this that he was knighted,
and both events were very much present in people's minds when
his transfer to Mexico was announced.[1]

His stay in Guatemala of two normal tours had not been without its hardships, and above all in the effect of the climate on the
health of Lady Carden, an American by birth. With the conclusion of the negotiations, Grey had proposed to transfer him to
Brazil, which was considered healthier. In agreeing to Grey's later
suggestion that he should go to Mexico instead, he did so on the
clear understanding that it could not be for a period longer than
one year, and that he would then be transferred to Rio. There is no
doubt, therefore, that Grey deliberately chose him as his agent, for
his own reasons.[2] The appointment was interpreted in this light
by the United States government, who found it distasteful, and
recalled that on at least one previous occasion an indication through
the then American ambassador in London that the State Department considered him *persona non grata* had been brushed aside.
Because of this, President Wilson, though dissatisfied, rapidly came
to the conclusion that there was nothing he could do to stop it.[3]

---

[1] Corporation of Foreign Bondholders, *Fortieth Annual Report of the Council of the . . . for
the year 1913* (London, 1913), pp. 12–13; Hendrick, pp. 196–7; Notter, p. 246; Page–
Woodrow Wilson, 22 November 1913, Personal and Confidential. Wilson Papers Ac
3335 Box 86; Spring-Rice–Grey, 19 August 1913. Grey Papers.

[2] Grey–Sir Conyngham Greene, Tokyo, 23 January 1914, no. 15. FO 371/2033 file 3985.

[3] Woodrow Wilson–Bryan, 31 July 1913. Wilson Papers, File VII, Letterbook 5, f. 372.

Carden went to Mexico with very definite views on the situation. Sir Ralph Paget, the newly appointed Superintending Under Secretary, noted on one of Stronge's reports (27 August):

Sir L. Carden agrees with Mr Stronge that Huerta is the only man capable of dealing with the present situation & that nothing stands in the way of the complete pacification of Mexico except the action of the US. He does not think Huerta intends to stand for the Presidency but that the elections will either be postponed altogether on the ground that they cannot be held in certain states not at present under the control of the Gov^t or, if held wherever possible, that no new President will be elected until the vote has been taken in all the States. The latter course would appear satisfactory as Huerta would thereby carry on until the troubles are over & at the same time he would not fall foul of the U.S. by disregarding their demand that he should not be a candidate for the Presidency & should not postpone the elections.[1]

Whether this was really a 'trial balloon' or just an uncannily accurate piece of prediction is hard to say. That Huerta was likely to take some such course could have been deduced from his reluctance to give any undertaking which did not retain these two possibilities. It seems incredible, however, that Paget could have believed that President Wilson would be prepared to tolerate such chicanery. The whole tenor of his statements and Lind's communications had been hostile to the retention of Huerta as President by any device, and in particular by improper (if not actually unconstitutional) means. But these statements and communications had been neither clear nor explicit on any point except that Huerta must not be a *candidate*.

It is perhaps significant that Carden did not see Sir Edward Grey personally before leaving London, but wrote to him from the Piccadilly Hotel on 12 September:

It is a matter of great regret to me that I shall not have an opportunity of seeing you before I leave, but I have set down in the accompanying paper my views of the present situation and of the way in which it might be advantageously dealt with.

I have done this as [Sir William] Tyrrell [Sir Edward Grey's Private

[1] Minute to Stronge–Grey, 27 August 1913, no. 264 Confidential. FO 371/1676 file 6269/42006.

Indiscretion

Secretary] gave me to understand that it was highly undesirable that we should get into a groove and drift along without any definite policy, in view of the magnitude of the British interests which are at stake.

During the past 25 years the gradual extension of the Monroe Doctrine up to the point of implying a right of suzerainty over Latin America has by constant iteration come to be regarded by the world at large as a basic American policy [his memorandum began].

In this policy European countries have tacitly acquiesced, in the belief that the undisturbed influence of the United States in the Latin American Republics would conduce to their peace and good government; that the increased prosperity which this would bring would redound to the benefit of all the countries which had commercial relations with them; and finally that in recognition of the abstention of other nations from pursuing separate policies and of their co-operation with the projects of the United States Government the latter's influence would be exerted when asked for to obtain for them an equitable settlement of any just claims they might have against the Latin American Governments.

These expectations have not been realised.

The history of the period mentioned shows that the intervention of the United States Government in the domestic affairs of their weaker neighbours has only been effected by force of arms, whether by open war as in the case of Cuba, or by promoting or aiding revolutions, as in Panama, Nicaragua, Honduras and Mexico. In all these cases British interests have suffered severely through the destruction of property and the interference with trade and industry. Nor can it be shown that such interventions have had any effect which is likely to prove permanent in bringing about improved political conditions or removing the causes which have produced unrest in the past.

Moreover, the United States Government have given repeated proofs that, far from favouring the principle of the open door in Latin America, they view with jealousy the competition of European nations for the trade of those Republics: and all their influence has been and is being directed towards obtaining such special advantages for their citizens, by reciprocity conventions and otherwise, as will ensure for them in course of time a great preponderance if not a virtual monopoly in all matters connected with finance, commerce or public works.

Finally, American influence has been rarely if ever exerted in favour of the settlement of British claims against the Latin American Governments. Indeed, on the contrary, in the case of the Dominican, Nicaraguan,

Honduranean and Guatemalan Debts the aim of the United States Government has been to obtain for their own financiers so privileged a position as would enable them to force other claimants to sell them their credits at rates far lower than those which the debtor Governments were prepared to pay or had actually contracted with them to pay.

Thus far Carden was on firm and well-known ground, even if his observations were tinged with a certain degree of personal animus. But then he wrote:

The climax has been reached in Mexico, where the ineptitude and bad faith of the United States Government must be held to be largely responsible for the very great losses already suffered by British investors since the commencement of the Madero insurrection, and for the present imminent danger that these losses may culminate in the complete destruction of British interests of immense magnitude, as would undoubtedly be the case were an American force to cross the border.

Here there were serious inaccuracies. The losses already suffered by British investors were clearly in the main due to the existence of a state of revolution in Mexico. This the government of the United States, as such, had neither promoted nor consciously encouraged. There had been interference in the internal affairs of Mexico—some of it official—but it had been directed hitherto at the support and protection of American interests rather than at the destruction of British ones. No case of 'bad faith' towards Great Britain had actually occurred. However, the crucial point is that Carden, thinking he had Grey's support for an 'active' policy of commercial confrontation, did not consider whether it might produce the reverse effect to the one that was intended, given the existing geographical conditions and power situation.

The moment, then, would appear to have arrived for us to give the United States Government clearly to understand that, in view of their attitude towards General Huerta, while we should be glad to be able to co-operate with them in matters affecting our respective interests and policy in Mexico and Latin America generally, we can only do so with due regard to these interests on terms of perfect equality, and that we must reserve to ourselves the right to take such separate action, in case of necessity, as may appear desirable for their protection.

By adopting such a line we should avoid for the future being drawn into acquiescing in lines of policy of which we do not approve or about which we have not been consulted: we should leave ourselves free to afford effective protection to the great interests we have at stake which are being constantly imperilled by the ill considered or interested action of the United States: and we should regain the influence we used to have in Latin America and with it a considerable part of the trade which we have lost and are still losing.

As regards the present crisis in Mexico it would seem to be madness at such a juncture to contemplate substituting a new and untried man, for the present Provisional President, who from all reports is proving himself thoroughly competent to dominate the situation—and the interests of British and all other foreign investors would appear therefore to demand that he be given a free hand and be offered all possible moral and financial support.[1]

Carden's position in making these recommendations is not as clear as he no doubt intended it to be. Britain's moral position was weak as regards refusing to acquiesce in lines of policy about which her government had not been consulted or of which it disapproved. The government had not consulted the United States before deciding to extend recognition. On the other hand, since on this issue the Foreign Office had taken its own line, Carden would seem to have had less reason to press the case for this attitude in other eventualities.

Secondly, his analysis seems to ignore entirely the immense development of the United States in the previous twenty years. At the time of the Venezuela dispute, the United States' industrial production was little greater than that of the United Kingdom. Her navy was somewhat smaller than that of Chile. Her army was little more than one division. In 1913 the actual as well as the potential strength of the United States had developed out of all recognition. Even had this not been the case, distance alone would have made it impossible for Britain to deploy an adequate force in Mexico to protect her interests, if they were seriously threatened. Throughout the earlier stages of the revolution, the

[1] Carden–Grey, 12 September 1913. FO 371/1676 file 6269/43839. Carden had been taking a cure at Vichy for at least the latter part of his leave. It seems curious that he did not inform himself more fully of Grey's views during this period.

Admiralty had clearly recognized the limitations of naval power in affording protection even to British lives.

Thirdly, on grounds of influence, the British government had little cause for complaint, for its influence in Latin America was astonishingly great, and in few places more so than in Mexico.

Lastly, the analysis took no account of the possibility that there might be a government in the United States that was not in the first instance concerned to protect the commercial interests of its nationals; and, this being the case, considered that no other government had a valid case for expecting it to protect the interests of others.

Whether or not Carden considered that he had already received a mandate to carry this policy into effect, it is certainly significant that his exposition of it did not receive an immediate reply. The memorandum was circulated to the American Department, the Permanent Under Secretary of State, and the Prime Minister, Mr Asquith. It was a stormy month both in Balkan diplomacy and in domestic affairs, and the Mexican situation cannot have appeared particularly urgent.

The Prime Minister noted on the memorandum: 'Sir L. Carden's picture of American policy & methods in Mexico does not seem at all over-coloured.' Grey was to some extent prepared to agree with this but he was cautious about the implications that Carden had drawn from it. His reply, dispatched as semi-official on 17 October, sweetened the pill somewhat, but it remained entirely firm on the course that the Foreign Office intended to pursue.

Your memorandum does not appear to me to overstate the awkwardness of the situation [he began, after the routine acknowledgement] and I agree that the action of His Majesty's Government should not be made dependent upon that of the United States Government and that we should reserve to ourselves the right to pursue whatever policy British interests may require.

But it must be borne in mind that an attempt on our part to put pressure upon the United States Government, or to support one of these republics against the United States, is sure to precipitate the armed intervention by the United States that we desire to avoid. I cannot influence the United States Government as regards their attitude towards the Provisional President of Mexico; they have taken their own line in spite of all that European nations have done, and they lay it down that the geographical position of the United States requires them to take into account considerations that do not apply to European countries. This makes it difficult therefore to argue with them.

I am prepared, if it continues to be the only chance for the restoration of order in Mexico, to continue to recognise General Huerta. No financial support can of course be given him by His Majesty's Government.

I do not dispute the inconvenience and untoward results of United States policy, but while I am prepared to keep a free hand, His Majesty's Government cannot with any prospect of success embark upon an active counter-policy to that of the United States, or constitute themselves the champions of Mexico or any of these republics against the United States.

I shall be glad, however, to consider on their merits, independently of the United States, whatever steps you think practicable to protect the British enterprises and commercial interests in Mexico.[1]

But by the time that this statement, with its attendant warning, had reached Mexico, Carden was already at the centre of a crisis in which reason and argument stood little chance of making themselves felt.

This new situation was in part due to the development of internal strain within President Huerta's own cabinet, and in his relations with Congress. That is to say, the tensions deliberately provoked by the pro-Constitutionalists in Congress had brought about changes in the cabinet.[2] Furthermore, Gamboa, who resigned to contest the Presidential elections, was replaced by Querido Moheno, the sole surviving leader for the pro-government forces in the Chamber, with no previous diplomatic experience. He was appointed on 7 October, the day Carden reached Vera Cruz.

Hohler describes how it was that his arrival had such a pronounced catalytic effect on the situation:

[1] Grey–Carden, 17 October 1913 and minutes. FO 371/1676 file 6269/43839.
[2] Félix Fulgencio Palavicini, *Mi Vida Revolucionaria* (Mexico, 1937), p. 177.

I went down to Vera Cruz to meet Carden and was waiting on the quay when his boat came alongside, but unfortunately he had got off earlier in the pilot's boat and before I was able to catch him, he had had an interview with Lind at which he exposed his cards and criticised Woodrow Wilson, Bryan and the United States in general with utter frankness [he wrote]. He meant well, but his methods of pursuing his aims were unfortunate.[1]

Carden, on the other hand, says that when he landed, an invitation to lunch with Admiral Fletcher was conveyed to him by Hohler.[2] In any case, it was at this luncheon that Carden met Lind, and both then and later at Lind's hotel they had a very long conversation on all aspects of the situation. Carden reported only what Lind had told him—that Huerta must go (though there would be no objection to him coming back later), and that President Wilson was anxious to escape from the impasse.[3] Thus it is necessary to rely on Lind's account for the full significance of the conversation. There is, however, no reason to suppose that it is not substantially correct, for the similarity of the views attributed to Carden to those expressed by him to Sir Ralph Paget is striking.

Lind himself was in a peculiar position. In Washington the first belief that Huerta had given an unequivocal pledge by means of the Gamboa note had no sooner begun to wear off than it had been reinforced by an optimistic interpretation of Huerta's remarks at the opening of the Mexican Congress on 15 September. This interpretation had led the President and Secretary of State to ask Lind, who shared their views, to stay in Vera Cruz to await a summons to the capital for further talks. The Congress, however, had been rendered *hors de combat* by Constitutionalist infiltration and the report that Huerta intended to take advice[4] he had previously

---

[1] Hohler, p. 187.

[2] Carden–Grey, 21 October 1913, no. 320. FO 371/1678 file 6269/50684. Normally this nearly contemporary evidence would be preferred to a memoir written thirty years later but (*a*) the incident as Hohler describes it is a very unusual one, (*b*) Carden's form of words is so general that it need not exclude the possibility that Hohler's version is correct, though it would not normally be interpreted as such.

[3] Carden–Grey, 21 October 1913, no. 320, *cit. sup.*

[4] By Aureliano Urrutia, whom Huerta appointed Secretary of *Gobernación* in reward for the success of two operations performed on the General's eyes. After the fall of Huerta, Urrutia fled to the United States and continued to practise as a famous surgeon in his own clinic at San Antonio, Texas.

been given to act unconstitutionally and dissolve it aroused fresh
doubts in Washington.

Huerta himself helpfully told O'Shaughnessy that he did not
intend to remain in power through a subterfuge. Lind in Vera
Cruz, with nothing definite to report, slowly made up his mind
that all the evidence pointed to the conclusion that Huerta was
merely playing for time.[1] Furthermore, in his enforced leisure, he
was an obvious target for interested persons with points of view
which they wished to bring to the ear of the United States
government. Among these were agents of the Constitutionalists,
and, no less significant, Henry Clay Pierce's agent in Vera Cruz,
Mr Galbraith.[2] Before Carden's arrival, Lind had already gone so
far as to inspire a story in the press indicating that the United
States government was considering recognizing the belligerency
of the Constitutionalist forces. The reception given to his suggestion that the government should enter into negotiations with
the latter convinced him that Huerta had 'determined to hold on',
and that the elections would be voided.[3]

It was at this point that Lind reported Carden's arrival, observing that he had been received by Fred Adams, Cowdray's representative.

He impressed me as a man of great ability [Lind reported of his first
meeting with Carden]. He advocated the support of Huerta on the
score of expediency because he is a strong man, a strong man being
needed. Without entering into an argument I pointed out certain facts
in Huerta's career that do not indicate strength of character in the past
nor give promise for the future. I suggested that our situation was
different from that of European nations. They seemed content with any
solution that temporarily enabled them to resume the production and
shipment of oil and other products and to sell goods. We as neigh-
bors, while equally interested in the restoration of business, were

[1] Bryan–Lind, Telegram, 18 September 1913, 2 p.m.; Lind–Bryan, Telegram, 6 October,
5 p.m. SDF 812.00/8880, 9102.
[2] Lind made no secret of his meetings with Galbraith. His associations with the Constitutionalists would certainly have justified the Huerta government in shooting him as
a spy, though the picture of his activities by William Lemke, ed. *Crimes against Mexico*
(Minneapolis, Minn., [1915]), pp. 120–8, is highly coloured and its thesis that he was
acting for the St Paul lumber interests not proved. See also: Alberto María Carreño,
La Diplomacia Extraordinaria entre México y Estados Unidos (Mexico, 1951), I, pp. 275–7.
[3] Lind–Bryan, Telegram, 8 October, 2 p.m. SDF 812.00/9127.

compelled to consider the future and that the President had clearly indicated that he would sanction no attempted solution that rewarded treachery and assassination with office and power. In answer to the question as to what the United States proposed to do in case of no election, I simply said that that contingency had not yet been considered so far as I was advised. He then proceeded very adroitly to draw out my views to aid him as he said in forming a judgement of the situation. I confessed to him that the conviction had forced itself upon me that there could be no settlement that ignored the people of the north; that they are the most efficient part of the population, and that at times it seemed to me that the most expeditious way might be to afford them a fair opportunity to solve the situation and to pacify the country.

We parted [Lind continued]. I did not expect to see him again. He returned at six, in the meantime having been in conference with Adams. He desired to know whether I thought that the President's conditions had been [? met] if the elections are held as called. I said that I thought that would depend on outcome. If a new man is elected and seated: yes; if not: no.[1]

One is compelled to say that Lind's position was entirely untenable on any logical grounds, and the fact that it was also the view of the President and the State Department did not improve it. The government of the United States had called for a constitutional election. Under the constitution Huerta could not be a candidate, nor could he be installed if he were elected. But if democracy meant anything, the United States could not require that the people should not vote for him, nor that Congress should declare valid any election that was in fact void. By requiring of the Mexican government that a new man be elected or installed they were requiring the government to 'make' the elections in the traditional Mexican style. Accidents do happen and voters do vote for governments which an objective observer might regard as undesirable.

Carden's position, too, had its weaknesses. It was the attitude of a man concerned only to find a solution. He therefore gave the impression that he was not much concerned with principles, which was not necessarily the case.

[1] Lind–Bryan, Telegram, 8 October, 2 p.m. SDF 812.00/9127.

Carden may have expressed his innermost thoughts to Lind, but Lind did not express his to Carden. He reported them to Bryan. The fruit of his five weeks' meditation was as follows:

Summary of my views: (1) Lord Cowdrey [*sic*] through Adams controls Huerta Administration absolutely. (2) I believe election will be postponed. If not postponed it will be set aside as void. The only thing all parties fear is the possibility of rebel success. Intervention is deemed preferable by Huerta for political reasons, by Adams as affording security.[1]

There can be no doubt of the impact of these conclusions on Washington, where they were taken with the utmost seriousness.

The President instructs me to say he feels that the circumstances and influences disclosed by yours of October 8th, 2 p.m., make it highly desirable that you should remain and keep a close watch on affairs preferably, if you find it feasible at Mexico City itself [replied Moore on 10 October]. Your presence and constant moral pressure there might serve as a very useful corrective upon the inspired opinions of the new British minister who should be impressed as strongly as possible with our unchanged and unchangeable attitude towards Huerta and all that he represents. We demand a moral as well as a physical basis for government there. We thoroughly and entirely approve the course you have pursued in your interviews with the British minister and feel that the influence you are exerting will tell more and more, particularly in view of the revolutionary successes in the north. Hope it is your judgement also that you can be most effective just now at Mexico City.[2]

Copies of both these telegrams were sent to Page in London, with instructions to represent to Sir Edward Grey 'that moral considerations should be put before material at every point in the treatment of the Mexican situation and the re-establishment of genuine constitutional processes before the desire for order at any price'.[3]

If Carden came to Mexico with strong preconceptions, his arrival crystallized equally strong attitudes which both Lind and

---

[1] Lind–Bryan, Telegram, 8 October, 2 p.m. SDF 812.00/9127. Lind's general views on the Mexican situation had already crystallized into the form recorded in John Lind, *La Gente de México* (Vera Cruz, 1915).

[2] Moore–Lind, Telegram, 10 October, 11 a.m. SDF 812.00/9127.

[3] Moore–Page, Telegram, 11 October, 7 p.m. SDF 812.00/9127.

the administration in Washington had been forming. It is not without significance that Lind did not choose to follow the recommendation of Moore and move to Mexico City. From his vantage point at Vera Cruz he could see a picture of Mexico that omitted inconvenient details of reality—for example, that the chief move for the postponement of the elections came from the Constitutionalists.

Certainly no one man could control the administration of a country the size of Mexico 'absolutely', especially with so many rivals in the field. The power Cowdray could exercise in Mexico at this stage was not even sufficient to conclude the arrangements for the sale of his interest in the Tehuantepec National Railway, which had been on the point of completion at the fall of Madero. On the contrary, there is compelling evidence that the Mexican government were exercising considerable pressure on Cowdray, using his interests in Mexico as a hostage to secure active support from him, which would entail his entry into politics. The dividing line between tacit and active support might have been very narrow, but Cowdray was not willing to cross it.

Certainly Cowdray did buy the President's daughter a very handsome wedding present.[1] He did not, however, attend the wedding, as the American chargé d'affaires attended the wedding of her sister, some months later, on the very day he was given his passports. Cowdray made no secret of his personal view that the policy of the United States government towards recognition was wrong. But when on 4 September 1913 his firm was invited to take up a million pesos of the proposed $15,000,000 loan to be raised in spite of non-recognition, he was seriously concerned on two points. Was he bound to subscribe, and, if he was, would he be entering into politics? The solution was to agree to subscribe only on the same terms as anyone else and only if the loan were fully taken up.[2]

The strains of the past three years had affected Mexican credit to such an extent that the terms of the loan as announced on 12 September were far from encouraging. It is clear that had

[1] Adams–Cowdray, 28 July 1913. Cowdray Papers.
[2] Ryder–Cowdray, Telegram, received 4 September 1913; Cowdray–Aguilaco Mexico, Telegram, 4 September 1913. Cowdray Papers.

Cowdray not felt compelled to subscribe he would not have done so, and finding himself in such a position, he limited his investment to the smallest sum possible, although there is no doubt whatever of his sympathies in the matter. John B. Body expressed the position in a letter to T. J. Ryder in Mexico:

On receipt of your first cable dated September 4th stating that the Government desired us to subscribe $1,000,000 to the new loan, we had to give the matter very serious consideration, as to comply with the Government's wishes would mean our affiliation with the party in power, and our connection to a certain extent with Mexican politics, which, as you know, is what we have consistently endeavoured to avoid [he wrote]. On the other hand our sympathies are altogether with the Government, and we felt that, if necessary, we should strain a point to do our share in helping them bridge the difficulties with which they are confronted. Accordingly, the Chief telegraphed you that we would participate to the extent of $750,000, provided it should be absolutely necessary to go to this limit. At the same time the Chief advised you, that if possible our subscription should not exceed $500,000, and I judge from your cables that you will be successful in keeping within this amount.[1]

This is a very different state of affairs from the masterful control of the Mexican government imagined by Lind. The envoy's detachment from reality is even more sharply revealed by his enthusiasm for the bloodshed incurred in the Constitutionalist recapture of Torreón on 8 October.[2] These attitudes are of interest in view of the fact that it was the fall of Torreón that precipitated the long-threatened dissolution of the Chamber of Deputies.[3]

The Chamber's disputes with the Executive had come to a head after Senator Domínguez of Chiapas had delivered a violent indictment of the régime in the other House, and had thereafter disappeared from sight. The Senate was uneasy, but it was the Chamber that took the lead. They resolved to investigate the disappearance, to ask the Senate to do the same, to require the Executive to give all assistance and to respect Congressional immunity, and—and this was a challenge which could not be

<hr />

[1] Body–Ryder, 4 October 1913. Cowdray Papers.
[2] O'Shaughnessy–Secretary of State, 8 October, 12 midnight, Telegram no. 538. SDF 812.00/9134. [3] Cf. Lind–Bryan, Telegram, 9 October, 6 p.m. SDF 812.00/9143.

interpreted otherwise than as treason—'that said Executive be informed that in case the disappearance of another Deputy or Senator occurs . . . the national representation will be obliged to celebrate its session where it may find guarantees'.[1]

At 10 p.m. on 9 October the Mexican cabinet met in the dining-room of the President's house. Garza Aldape, the minister who had already advised Huerta to dissolve the Chamber for refusing to certify the appointment of a Catholic to the cabinet, repeated this advice. The remaining members were all, it seems, opposed to dissolution. Nevertheless, the President adopted the advice of Garza Aldape, and a list was drawn up of the deputies to be arrested. When the deputies arrived for the evening session, at which a petition was circulated calling for the deposition of Huerta, it was Garza Aldape who had the hall surrounded by soldiers, and, after trying in vain to bully the Chamber into rescinding their resolution, arrested the deputies already designated. An emergency decree was afterwards issued to make the whole proceedings official, but, needless to say, nothing could make them constitutional.

Nelson O'Shaughnessy learnt of the dissolution while it was actually taking place and lost no time in interceding with Moheno for the lives of the deputies. The latter gave what assurances he could, and accompanied the chargé to the penitentiary (much to the annoyance of Garza Aldape) to ensure that they were being properly treated.[2] No one else seems to have shown much anxiety about their fate.

'The city bears its usual aspect and the people whom I have met this morning do not seem to regard the Government's action with much concern', reported O'Shaughnessy the following day. 'Huerta has his back against the wall and may now be considered an absolute military dictator.'[3]

The reaction abroad to the dissolution was surprisingly slow.

---

[1] O'Shaughnessy–Secretary of State, 10 October, 10 p.m., Telegram no. 542. SDF 812.00/9167.

[2] Moheno, *Mi actuación política después de la Decena Trágica* (1939), pp. 43–55. Mexico. Congreso. Cámara de Diputados, *Diario de los debates de la Cámara de Diputados del Congreso de los Estados Unidos Mexicanos*, XXVI Legislatura, III (Año II, Periodo I).

[3] O'Shaughnessy–Secretary of State, 11 October, 12 noon, Telegram no. 545. SDF 812.00/9173.

In the United States the Secretary of State had been away for six days, and was not able to consult President Wilson before 9 a.m. on 13 October. Meanwhile the arrests stood little chance of publicity in the United States' press compared with the appalling tragedy of the burning of the *Volturno*, or even with the blowing up of the last dyke in the Panama Canal.[1] However, once Bryan had seen the President, the government of the United States acted, and within three hours a telegram had been dispatched to O'Shaughnessy, ordering him to deliver a magisterial note at the Ministry of External Relations.

'The President is shocked at the lawless methods employed by General Huerta and as a sincere friend of Mexico is deeply distressed at the situation which has arisen', the note was to run. 'He finds it impossible to regard otherwise than as an act of bad faith toward the United States General Huerta's course in dissolving the Congress and arresting deputies. It is not only a violation of constitutional guarantees but it destroys all possibility of a free and fair election.' This was the American case; in accordance with it the United States gave notice that neither the elections nor any President chosen by them would be recognized.[2]

Having thus rapidly charted its future course with reference to the Huerta government, the administration turned its attention to the attitudes of other foreign countries. The realization in Washington that one particular country appeared to be taking a line directly in opposition to that of the United States aroused increasing anger. That country was Great Britain, whose minister, Sir Lionel Carden, had presented his credentials to General Huerta at noon on the day after the coup.[3]

It was fitting that it was Lind, who had no responsible part to play at this stage, who should not only have been the first to record his suspicions concerning this coincidence of events, but in so doing seems to have initiated the whole dispute.

This morning [he telegraphed to Bryan on 15 October], I requested O'Shaughnessy to wire me as quietly as possible what Government, if

[1] Bryan–O'Shaughnessy, Telegram, 12 October, 12 midnight. SDF 812.00/9178A; *The New York Times*, Sunday, 12 October; Monday, 13 October 1913.
[2] Bryan–O'Shaughnessy, 13 October, 12 noon, Telegram no. 491. SDF 812.00/9180A.
[3] *The Mexican Herald*, Sunday, 12 October 1913.

any, besides England had recognised the Huerta dictatorship. I do not require the information but I took that means of conveying to Carden my view of his acts. I shall make no utterance upon the subject that will embarrass you. If I do I will stand for a disavowal and a reprimand. But I do want to smoke out England (Lord Cowdry [*sic*]). She is playing double. She contends to you that it was largely through mis-apprehension that Huerta was recognised as the Constitutional President ad interim. Later and the day after Huerta had ceased to function in the capacity in which he had been recognised when he had declared him-self a dictator and had assumed the legislative power of the Congress, Carden presents the greeting of the royal master and his credentials to the Dictator. This was no accident. I believe the whole was carefully planned. The dictatorship was deemed a necessity by Carden as you will note by my report of his conversation. The recognition of the dictatorship by England will be urged in support of the validity of such legislative action as Huerta may take as dictator.[1]

We have already dealt with the identification of Great Britain with Lord Cowdray and it is a question that must be raised con-tinually. It was to become an obsession with Lind. After his wife had returned to the United States he embodied it in a series of ever wilder, ever longer, and ever more rambling telegrams. Not only did he fail to produce evidence: he even admitted that his greatest efforts were unable to disclose any. Instead he reiterated his beliefs until for him they became moral certainties.

The telegram has other interesting points, however. First there is the certainty that his message to O'Shaughnessy would be com-municated to Carden. Lind had a deep distrust of the chargé, based upon real doubts of his friendliness with Huerta himself and his Republicanism, but also strongly tinged with a dislike of Catholicism.[2] Secondly, it shows Anglophobia, and a distrust of financiers, which was linked with a pronounced anti-semitism.[3]

---

[1] Lind–Bryan, Telegram, 15 October, 11 a.m. SDF 812.00/9218.

[2] Stephenson, *John Lind of Minnesota* (1935), pp. 228–9; Lind–Bryan, Telegram, 18 October, 3 p.m., Personal, reveals the latter trait in a peculiarly bigoted form. SDF 812.00/9264.

[3] Stephenson does not mention this. But see Lind–Bryan, 19 September 1913. Bryan Papers, Special Correspondence, Box 43, f. 198, where Lind states that he made the U.S. offer of a loan when he did because he 'wanted every Jew Banker or broker in the world to know definietly [*sic*] under what circumstances and to what extent the U.S. would tolerate a loan under existing conditions', and despite the fact that Hale advised him against it.

Lastly, it demonstrates total ignorance of the meaning of diplomatic recognition and the conditions under which it operates. And this really became the crux of the problem. Once the belief gained ground in the United States that the presentation of credentials was an act of formal recognition, or that by the internal action of dissolution Huerta had created a new government under international law and thereby required to be recognized afresh, it became extremely difficult to relate United States policy (let alone public opinion) to the facts of the situation. Only one man within the State Department attempted to do it, and his advice was entirely ignored.[1]

While Lind's ignorance was forgivable, that of the Secretary of State was not. In authorizing the dispatch of a telegram to O'Shaughnessy requiring him to inform other diplomatic representatives in Mexico that the United States expected their respective countries to withdraw the recognition they had already accorded to the Mexican government, he was calling upon those countries to perform a hostile act.[2] This is, of course, evidence that he did not share Lind's view that recognition had been ended by the coup, but it is clear that he did not exclude thereby the belief that Britain had put a special seal of approval on the dictatorship.

Two reports must have exacerbated the already bitter feelings towards Carden and the government which he represented. On the one hand, Page reported that he understood through a Liberal Member of Parliament that the cabinet meetings of 14, 15 and 16 October had been largely concerned with the Mexican question, and that financial interests had been urging intervention by the United States. On the other, O'Shaughnessy reported from Mexico:

The present British Minister is a firm believer that Huerta can settle the Mexican situation and lets it be known. The policy of Great Britain in Latin-America is purely commercial and forms of government matter little to her; she has no missionaries in Latin-America.

The British Minister has given me to understand in many conversations that he considers intervention as fatal to British interests and that

[1] I.e. John Bassett Moore (see below, pp. 251–2).
[2] Bryan–O'Shaughnessy, Telegram, 14 October, 12 midnight. SDF 812.00/9200.

our policy can only lead to it. Since his reception by Huerta on the eleventh after the dissolution of Congress, he is all powerful here and seems to have the full support of his Government.[1]

Feelings within the administration were mirrored in the press. The general and immediate reaction to the coup was that Huerta had destroyed his constitutional claim to rule. Many drew the (doubtful) conclusion that the President's policy had thereby been proved right, though not all were willing to say that the United States should do anything but ignore the change. The *Washington Post*, which held this last view, regarded the matter as one for the Mexicans only. No one seems to have thought that the coup might have been the result of the President's policy rather than a proof of his foresight, though the belief that the nation was solidly behind the President—expressed by *The World*—is obviously exaggerated.[2]

The New York Times paid particular attention to the aspect of the British attitude. After criticism of Wilson's announcement that the results of the election would not be recognized, it detected signs that Britain intended to follow the same line. On 17 October an accurate report from Mexico indicated that Britain would not support an aggressive American policy, but would not interfere. The administration were said to be 'disappointed' as it 'felt it had some reason to believe that the British Government would repudiate Gen. Huerta's declaration of dictatorship and decline to accord even provisional recognition to any Mexican government established as the result of the elections to be held this month'.

The following day the report changed. 'The attitude taken by the British Minister is arousing comment, as he had only recently arrived and is believed to be acting under instructions which appear equivocal', it said, under a Mexico dateline, while from Washington it added: 'In the opinion of some, and perhaps most, of the officials in Washington, foreign Governments should do

[1] Page–Secretary of State, 18 October, 2 p.m., Telegram no. 76 Confidential; O'Shaughnessy–Secretary of State, 20 October, 12 noon, Telegram no. 568 Confidential, for the Secretary of State. SDF 812.00/9260, 9289.
[2] *Washington Post*, editorial: 'The New Mexican Crisis', Monday, 13 October 1913; *The World*, editorial: 'The Man Who Knew', Wednesday, 15 October 1913.

nothing that would in any manner embarrass the United States; and it is said that the virtual support given to President Huerta by Great Britain's attitude is a manifestation of a disposition not entirely considerate.'

This attitude, *The New York Times* had already stated, was that the recent happenings were 'matters of domestic concern that do not call for any new policy on the part of foreign governments'.[1]

On 20 October *The World* announced boldly that the administration was 'none too pleased' with Britain. The administration considered that Britain had taken the position that her interests in Mexico were as big as those of the United States and she must look to the government for protection for them. The following day Page was reported by the same newspaper to have called at the Foreign Office to ask the British government to explain their policy in Mexico. 'According to reliable reports, the British Foreign Minister told Ambassador Page to-day that Britain's sympathy was with the United States, but that her financial interests in Mexico were so large and of such wide ramifications that Britain was forced to look to the controlling factor.'

The World then openly attacked Cowdray as having forced the appointment of Carden, accused him directly of having in the past supported Orozco, and implied that he had aided the overthrow of Madero.[2]

After such attacks pressure on Carden to give some sort of statement was bound to be exceedingly great. In deciding to speak to the press he must have been well aware of the risk he was running. Nevertheless he agreed to do so, and on the following day, 22 October, it was painfully clear that he had not avoided the trap.

Carden, it must be remembered, had no time for reflection or deliberation after taking over the legation such as Stronge had enjoyed before him. He reported the events of 10 October without comment. 'The consensus of opinion among heads of missions

---

[1] *The New York Times*, Wednesday, 15 October; Friday, 17 October; Saturday, 18 October 1913.
[2] *The World*, Tuesday, 21 October 1913.

present', he noted of the meeting for Moheno's statement the following day, 'appeared to be that the President's action was justified in the circumstances, and more than one expressed surprise that it had not been taken before.'[1] He did not claim to have advised the action, and quite obviously he had not done so.

With Spring-Rice seriously ill with Graves's disease, and the staff of the Washington embassy reduced to an abnormally low level, the Foreign Office first heard of Wilson's decision not to recognize the elections through the press on 15 October.[2]

The previous day Page, as we have seen, had called on Sir Arthur Nicolson.

Mr Page called today to say that though President Wilson was grieved, disappointed and distressed by the recent events in Mexico, he had no intention of changing his attitude—and indeed the coup d'etat had fortified his opinion that his attitude was the right one [Sir Arthur minuted]. Mr Wilson considered that Governments as human institutions should be founded on a moral basis.

Sir Arthur did not record that Page had said anything about the elections, and his opinion of the communication was no doubt much the same as that of Grey, who noted: 'It would require about 200,000 soldiers to put Mexico on a "moral" basis.'[3]

At the same time the British government did not consider taking any naval action, despite the example of Germany where Goschen reported that the decision had been taken to send a man-of-war to Mexico.[4] Carden, however, was much exercised by the prevalent reports that the United States was considering recognizing the belligerency of the insurgents. The matter was left to Grey to discuss with Page on 20 October, and after that, the Foreign Secretary telegraphed to the Washington embassy:

[1] Carden–Grey, 11 October 1913, Telegram no. 116; 12 October 1913, Telegram no. 117. FO 371/1677 file 6269/46369, 46370.
[2] Spring-Rice–Grey, 29 September 1913, Private Grey Papers, USA, 44; Gwynn, p. 193; minute to Carden–Grey, 14 October 1913, Telegram no. 118, FO 371/1677 file 6269/46830.
[3] Memorandum by Sir Arthur Nicolson, 14 October 1913, and minute. FO 371/1677 file 6269/47088.
[4] Sir E. Goschen–Grey, 16 October 1913, Telegram no. 178. FO 371/1677 file 6269/47120. The United States press, however, indicated that the whole of Europe was sending ships.

The American Ambassador has communicated to me the communications made by U.S. Govt at Mexico, which have appeared in the Press, saying that he had been instructed to inform me of the President's views.

I said in reply that we had but one object to encourage reestablishment of order in Mexico. Believing that the best chance of this pending elections was the recognition of Huerta as Provisional President we had so recognised him. His recent coup d'état produced an unpleasant impression; but we knew no more of it than was known to everyone. The elections were to take place in 6 days and we could not pledge ourselves in advance to refuse to recognize the result of them whatever it might be. We should wait till we saw the result & had a report from our Minister about them. We should then decide whether to recognize the result or not.

I said that we had heard the worst accounts of the so called Northern rebels: that they were merely brigands, whose methods were most barbarous, who sacked villages and committed crimes on non-combatants. To recognize them as belligerents would apparently make things worse. We had lately stopped the supply of arms from [British] Honduras; but if once we recognized belligerency I supposed that the usual practice must be followed in Honduras of allowing private individuals to supply arms to both sides at their own risk.

You should inform the Sec. of State of what I said to American Ambassador [Grey concluded]. The Ambassador communicated views of his Govt. without expressing any desire to influence our own policy and you should do the same.[1]

In fact this telegram crossed with one from the embassy indicating that the United States was not going to approach European governments for their co-operation. It was claimed that a report to that effect had been due to the indiscretion of the President's private secretary, while the rumours of recognition of belligerency were believed to originate from the Constitutionalists themselves.[2] The first half of the telegram was almost as misleading as Page's report to his government on his interview with Grey. Most of the space of the latter was devoted to a description of

[1] Grey–Spring-Rice, 21 October 1913, Telegram no. 273. FO 371/1677 file 6269/47486. Carden had protested violently against recognition of belligerency; O'Shaughnessy had done the same to the State Department.
Spring-Rice–Grey, 21 October 1913, Telegram no. 188. FO 371/1677 file 6269/48116.

what Page had said to Grey, and the overall impression of the Foreign Secretary's views was severely constrained by its concluding paragraph. This stated:

He granted that the problem of the United States with Mexico was very different from the problem of any other Government. His direct comment was meagre but the general impression he made on my mind very distinctly was his appreciation of the difficulties and an increasing respect for the President's policy. My inference is that he is under strong financial pressure which is irksome.[1]

Even from Page's report, however, it is apparent that the ambassador, though under the impression that he was conveying an indication of his government's desire for help in their policy, in fact did not do so. Indeed, he even emphasized that the basis of American policy was, in his opinion, bound to be *different* from that of a European government. Through an indiscretion in the embassy the Associated Press transmitted to the United States, in advance of Page's own report, the dispatch quoted above in which Page's inference was given as a statement by Sir Edward.[2] This did not help matters.

With Carden's interview, interest switched back to Mexico, where O'Shaughnessy had already indicated that Carden was pursuing a hostile policy and one that appeared to have the support of his government.

Von Hintze, however, recorded Carden's position much more accurately.

He proposes to support the Huerta Government alone *against* the United States [he wrote], yet doubts that Sir Edward Grey will follow him in that; for unhappily Sir Edward Grey has made himself very much dependent on the United States, also openly through his declaration on the Monroe Doctrine. On the possible American intervention he says: 'they dare not to come in; their troops are no more than what they were in 1847/'48: individually strong, but mostly town dwellers and loafers. I have seen them in Cuba during the war.' Later: 'Huerta is the only man capable of governing the country and the only one who has the support of the army: no one can hold his own against him.'

[1] Page–Secretary of State, 21 October, 4 p.m., Telegram no. 78. SDF 812.00/9310.
[2] Page–Bryan, 22 October, 2 p.m., Telegram no. 81 Confidential. Bryan–Page, Telegram, 23 October, 4 p.m. SDF 812.00/9315.

For this reason Carden believed Huerta would not exert pressure for his own election.[1]

The actual text of the Carden interview is very disputable, but as *The New York Times* claimed that their own reporter was present when the interview was given, the account of that eminently responsible journal seems dependable.[2]

Sir Lionel Carden, the British Minister, said today that he had made no representation to his Government regarding the advisability of intervention by the United States in the affairs of Mexico, but intimated that he was opposed to such action . . .

He emphatically refused to make any comment on the coincidence of his presenting his credentials to President Huerta simultaneously with the dissolution of Congress, merely saying that he had carried out the orders he had received. He said that it was not incumbent upon him to investigate what President Huerta had done the night before he presented his letters.

The minister was then understood to have said that he thought it unlikely that British recognition would be withdrawn from the government, and that the movement in the north was not, properly speaking, a revolutionary one.

When the opinion was expressed that this situation could not continue indefinitely, he said he saw no reason why it could not, as it took a long time for social unrest to be remodled [*sic*].

Mexico, he said, needed punitive and remedial methods—a strong man and statesman of no mean ability.

'It is ridiculous', he said, 'to suppose that such a man can be found in a haphazard election under the present circumstances.'

Then came the nub of the American complaint.

While professing not to criticise the Washington policy, he intimated that he considered its dealing with the situation here [i.e. in Mexico] superficially, without full knowledge of the real causes of the trouble, as complicating affairs rather than contributing to their solution.

[1] Hintze–Bethmann-Hollweg, 21 October 1913, no. A 82. GFM 12/16 f. A 22377.
[2] *The New York Times*, Wednesday, 22 October 1913. The newspaper's explanation of the authenticity of the interview was given on Saturday, 25 October 1913. As Carden *said* he spoke to only *one* reporter (see p. 243) variations in accounts *may* be due to sub-editing. *The New York Herald*'s version, similar to *The World*'s, was the one generally quoted in Britain.

Carden was then faced with comments on his actions taken from dispatches from Washington. He made no comment.

> He showed, however [said *The New York Times*], that he considered the Washington criticisms of his actions childish.
>
> He evaded all questions relative to intervention on the part of the United States. He said his Government had not asked his opinion on this matter, and he did not understand that the United States had any intention of intervening. Consequently he had done nothing to block the American policy.

The other account requiring special credence is that of *The Mexican Herald*, which Carden afterwards stated he did not repudiate, though he declined to make any further comment. It is substantially the same but with one significant difference. The paragraph relating to the United States read: 'The minister stated that he did not believe the United States fully realized the seriousness of the situation in this country. He also said that he did not believe that the necessary elements for the solution of the situation would be found by means of an election at the present time.'[1]

This was the version reported by *The World*, and *The World* forthwith damned Carden as a second Henry Lane Wilson.[2] The administration shared this view. Nor was it inclined, as was *The New York Times*, to forget the incident.[3] Bryan had apologized for Wilson's interview, and Carden was at least expected to apologize for Carden's interview.[4] As on the previous occasion, they made no effort to learn whether the criticisms had been made in the form reported, or even whether crticisms had been made at all, as *The New York Times* account seems to indicate they had not.

The uproar in the American press was reported in Britain on the

---

[1] *The Mexican Herald*, Wednesday, 22 October 1913. Carden's reported statement that he had not repudiated the interview was carried in its issue of Saturday, 25 October.

Note that Carden did *not* criticize President Wilson personally (cf. Hendrick, *The Life and Letters of Walter H. Page* (1924), p. 197, in reference to earlier interview allegedly given in New York on way to post and published by *The World*, which appears to be apocryphal).

[2] *The World*, editorial: 'Social Unrest', Thursday, 23 October 1913.

[3] *The New York Times*, Thursday, 23 October 1913.

[4] Woodrow Wilson–Bryan, 24 October 1913. Wilson Papers, File VII, Letterbook 7, f. 423.

morning of 24 October. Grey was out of London, but in a telegram to Sir Ralph Paget directed that Carden be informed at once: 'It is reported in press that you have given interview expressing opinion on Mexican situation & United States policy. I presume I can deny that any such interview was given. You should be very careful not to express any opinion till H.M.G. have considered result of election & made their attitude public.'[1]

Carden replied on 25 October:

I consented to receive reporter who wished to see me in regard to comments in the American press on my having presented my credentials the morning after the dissolution of Congress, as I considered that to refuse to do so might encourage the press in persisting to ascribe significance to what was merest coincidence.

At this interview no allusion whatever, direct or indirect, was made to United States interests or policy in Mexico.

The substance of this statement was thereupon released to the press. 'This will be sufficient as far as the Press is concerned, but let me have a copy when the American Ambassador comes to see me', wrote Grey. 'The American Press has been most unjust to Sir L. Carden & the U.S. Govt ought to know it.'[2]

The truth seems to be, however, that Carden still did not know what the policy of the United States was, and, wrapped up as he was in his own strong views on the situation, failed to recognize as such the leading questions which were put to him.

Meanwhile the main question remained unresolved. Ernest Scott, first secretary at Washington, had seen Bryan on 22 October and reported:

The Secretary of State gave no indications of his intention to recognize the rebels as belligerents. He said that the United States Government would probably refuse to recognise any results of the forthcoming elections and appeared to think that Huerta was playing for his own

[1] Grey–Sir Ralph Paget, Telegram, 11.45 a.m., 24 October 1913; Grey–Carden, 24 October 1913, Telegram no. 137. FO 371/1677 file 6269/48326. Carden himself had only reported: 'Editor of Daily Mail has asked me for my observations on certain statements attributed to me by the American press. In view of controversial attitude of press, I have declined to reply and have referred them to you' (Carden–Grey, 23 October 1913, Telegram no. 122. FO 371/1677 file 6269/1677).
[2] Carden–Grey, 25 October 1913, Telegram no. 123. FO 371/1677 file 6269/48628.

16-2

election as President. He spoke strongly of Huerta's methods and expressed surprise at our attitude as being likely to encourage him in his lawless conduct. Though invited to suggest some alternative for securing the re-establishment of order he was unable or unwilling to do so but said that no alternative could be worse than existing conditions.[1]

The explanation of this decisive statement was a curious one. Lind and O'Shaughnessy had both received documents, from Felicista sources in each case. They judged them to be authentic detailed orders from Huerta's government to state governors announcing the measures to be taken so that in the elections the majority of votes should be cast for Huerta, but that insufficient polling stations should function for the election to be valid.[2] It is scarcely necessary to say that these claims must be regarded with the highest suspicion. Lind was, no doubt, not in league with Félix Díaz, though the latter was staying at Vera Cruz, fearful of venturing as far as the capital. But that he had completely lost all sense of proportion is demonstrated by his efforts to persuade the State Department that the American merchantman *Morro Castle* had been detained by the government on a legal pretext purely as an insult, and that they should land forces to take the Customs House to recoup the cost![3] And he did have at least two very lengthy interviews with Díaz himself.[4]

On the eve of the elections Page invited the State Department to take the step they should have taken before making their statement of 14 October, and sound Sir Edward Grey as to whether the British government would refrain from recognizing the result of the elections until the United States had had time to consider them.

The excuse of an obligation created by the original recognition of Huerta will then be gone [Page explained]. I should get a favorable response or uncover the real reason for refusal and the situation would

[1] Spring-Rice–Grey, 23 October 1913, Telegram no. 190. FO 371/1677 file 6269/48345.
[2] Lind–Bryan, Telegram, 26 October, 10 a.m.; O'Shaughnessy–Secretary of State, 25 October, 9 p.m., Telegram no. 582; Lind–Bryan, Telegram, 28 October, 2 p.m. SDF 812.00/9392, 9390, 9441.
[3] Lind–Bryan, Telegram, 23 October, 6 p.m. Rush—Personal. SDF 812.00/9343.
[4] Lind–Bryan, Telegram, 23 October, 11 a.m. SDF 812.00/9355.

be clearer. There seems reason for this inquiry, if you should think it wise, in Huerta's reported boast published here this afternoon that he relies on British help in case we intervene.[1]

The approach was authorized. Before it took place two more very lengthy telegrams reached the State Department from Lind.[2] Their length, prolixity and repetitiveness are such that it would be wearisome even to try to summarize them at any length. Briefly, however, the first indicated that Lind considered the Huerta government was trying to bind itself to European aid through the wealth of its subsoil. This, he believed, harmonized with the policy of the British government to obtain a fifty or one hundred year contract for oil supplies for the navy, and he claimed that Congress had been dissolved because it had refused assent to these proposals. In fact, no such proposals had been laid formally before Congress. Moheno makes no reference to them, while attributing Garza Aldape's part in the dissolution to his own personal interests in two contracts requiring Congressional sanction, in one of which S. Pearson and Son could have been interested.[3] But neither had anything to do with minerals.

Lind had made a point of meeting Fred Adams, and was much impressed by his political acumen, which he considered far superior to that of Galbraith. He lost no opportunity of making known to him the views of the United States in the most forcible form.

Thus the gap between American and British viewpoints on the Mexican situation was actually continuing to grow while the report of Ernest Scott's interview was being considered. Bryan's charge that the British government seemed to be encouraging Huerta in his 'lawless conduct' clearly stung, but his plain speaking brought a fresh reality to the view from London.

There seems to be some confusion in the minds of the U.S. as to our attitude which has in no way changed [Spicer minuted]. Some time

[1] Page–Secretary of State, 24 October, 8 p.m., Telegram no. 84. SDF 812.00/9361.
[2] Lind–Bryan, Telegrams, 25 October, 2 p.m.; 27 October, 10 a.m. Personal. SDF 812.00/9401, 9415.
[3] Moheno, p. 78. These contracts were the ones for the Mazatlán Port Works (which Pearson's were considering) and the Matamoros–Topolobampo Railway.

ago we recognized General Huerta as Provisional President, & unless we had intended to withdraw that recognition, it was obvious that Sir L. Carden could lose no time in presenting his letters of credence. Huerta remains de facto Provisional President, & his coup d'etat is a matter of internal politics wh. does not affect our relations with Mexico, which have undergone no alteration.

'The U.S.G. seem to be suffering rather from nerves', was Sir Ralph Paget's opinion. 'They do not seem exactly to know what to do & what they mean to do themselves but they want us to do it with them.'

Sir Edward Grey's reply to Washington accordingly restated the British position.

I do not understand Secretary of State's statement that our attitude is likely to encourage Huerta in his lawless conduct. The statement I made to the American Ambassador here was that I would not decide whether to recognize the result of the elections in Mexico or not until after they had taken place. To reserve our decision can hardly be described as encouraging Huerta & I gather that U.S. Govt themselves have not quite definitely decided what their attitude after elections will be.[1]

It is clear that Carden himself realized the importance of avoiding offence to the United States at this stage, and was actually trying to remedy the situation in Mexico itself. On his advice Huerta held a conference with the representatives of foreign powers in which he explained his attitude towards the dissolution of the Chamber and reasserted that there would be full freedom at the polls. The very marginal utility of this act, however, was rendered useless by the press reports. These attributed to the President statements on 'Europe and the Monroe Doctrine' and the 'Cost of Intervention', calculated to increase feeling in the United States. 'You must be careful not to incur responsibility for Huerta's statement or policy', Grey warned the minister; 'it will apparently be his object, if need be, to create tension between European countries and the United States Government. Our policy should be one of reserve until result of elections is known, and we can consider what our attitude should then be.' This

---

[1] Minutes on Spring-Rice–Grey, 23 October 1913, Telegram no. 190, and Grey–Spring-Rice, 27 October 1913, Telegram no. 283. FO 371/1677 file 6269/48345.

warning held good even if, as was the case, the reported statements were quite apocryphal.[1]

The elections duly took place on 26 October. There was no open interference with the freedom of voting. In fact, the elections were so free that Lind himself was able to cast a ballot in Vera Cruz.[2] But very few who were entitled to vote took the trouble to do so, and, although the official results were not due to be made known for over a month, it was apparent as early as the day following the election that if the government wished to nullify the elections on the ground that the constitutional minimum requirements had not been met, they would be able to do so. The President had alluded to this possibility in a meeting with the diplomatic corps a few days beforehand. Furthermore, it was apparent that the majority of votes had been cast for the Huerta–Blanquet ticket, mainly by soldiers. To Lind and others this seemed to confirm that the whole conduct of the elections was a plot to defeat the demands of the United States, which it undoubtedly was, and that it had all been done on Carden's suggestion, which it undoubtedly had not. Grey's warning, therefore, was timely.

The warning was confirmed on 30 October.

Though I have not received expected communication of views of President Wilson I have the impression that the United States are quite irreconcilable as regards Huerta and contemplate intervention by force, if need be [went the telegram].

We have recognised Huerta as the only de facto Govt. in Mexico with which we had to deal and in hope of his restoring order, but there can of course be no question of our intervening on his behalf either inside or outside Mexico.[3]

Due credit must be given to Page for the accuracy of Grey's impression that the United States was 'irreconcilable'. He had not received the authorization he had requested from the State

---

[1] Carden–Grey, 23 October 1913, Telegram no. 121 and minutes; Grey–Carden, 27 October 1913, Telegram no. 140, and Carden–Grey, 27 October 1913, Telegram no. 130. FO 371/1677 file 6269/48431, 48952.

[2] Stephenson, p. 241. By taking part in a foreign election Lind presumably forfeited his American citizenship.

[3] Grey–Carden, 20 October 1913, Telegram no. 145. FO 371/1677 file 6269/49172.

Department, but in default of instructions had a most important, if unofficial, discussion with Grey on 28 October.

The American Ambassador spoke to me to-day unofficially and without instructions from his Government, but with much anxiety, of state of feeling that was developed towards this country, founded probably on misapprehension and certainly not justified by anything the British Government had done. Indeed, the object of his visit was to express most cordial thanks for my promise to wait before taking any decision about Mexican elections till I had received the promised communication from President Wilson.

... I said it was a most unpleasant thing that a British Minister should be attacked at all by a foreign press, and in this instance it was most unjust. Sir L. Carden had been perfectly right to correct the impression that he had anything to do with Huerta's coup d'etat, but it was monstrous to use his having done so to attribute other things to him. I resented these attacks upon him, and still more the way in which they had been manufactured.[1]

The substance of this discussion was transmitted by Page to Washington in a telegram the same day, indicating that Grey had wanted it brought to the notice of the President. From this report, however, it is apparent that Page took advantage of the occasion and once more 'went over the whole subject', but this time with a largely accurate impression of the administration's views.

He asked if British Government should withdraw recognition of Huerta what would happen [he reported]. I replied, 'in my own opinion he would soon collapse'. Grey said, 'what would happen then, worse chaos?' I said, 'that is impossible. There is no worse chaos than deputies in jail, dictatorial doubling of tariff, suppression of opinion and practical banishment of independent men. If Huerta fell there was hope that suppressed men and opinion would set up successful Government.' He asked, 'suppose that fails, what then?' I have replied [that] in case of continued and utter failure the United States might feel obliged to repeat its dealings with Cuba, and that continued excitement of opinion in the United States might precipitate this.

Grey protested he knew nothing of what British interests had done or were doing; that he wished time to think the matter out; and that

[1] Grey–Spring-Rice, 28 October 1913, 8 p.m., Telegram no. 291. FO 371/1677 file 6269/49181.

he was glad to await the President's communication. He thanked me cordially for my frank statements and declared he understood perfectly their personal nature. I impressed him with seriousness of American public opinion.

Some misunderstanding still remained. On the one hand, Grey now believed that the administration's view might be only Page's personal one, whereas formerly he had been led to believe that Page's personal views were the administration's. On the other, Page still had deep doubts both about the interests and about Carden, as his conclusion shows:

I think he has complete confidence in Carden; that he credits his disavowals, and thinks that he, Grey, cannot and ought not to do more with this aspect of the matter. I have hope that the President's strong statement and mutterings of popular disapproval in the United States may cause withdrawal of recognition of Huerta. But British investors of every sort would doubtless complain and this Government is now in sore straits because of domestic troubles. Strong influences in Cabinet if not elsewhere will have to be overcome.[1]

The Secretary of State endorsed Page's approach with enthusiasm.

You followed exactly the right line [he said]. Watch for New York Herald of yesterday containing full report of the President's speech at Mobile. It has been very enthusiastically endorsed in this country and indicates the President's line of thought. In conversations with British Chargé [*sic*] I have emphasised the same idea, namely, that the whole trouble in Mexico is due to the active influence of foreign investors who are denying to the people there the right to run their own government.[2]

It is very unlikely that Page was so naïve. But the Mobile Speech was undoubtedly received by him as a revelation, and was interpreted along the lines that Bryan had indicated, as later correspondence between him and Woodrow Wilson indicates.[3]

[1] Page–Secretary of State, 28 October, 7 p.m., Telegram no. 94. SDF 812.00/9442.
[2] Bryan–Page, Telegram, 29 October, 3 p.m. SDF 812.00/9442.
[3] Page–Woodrow Wilson, 22 November 1913, Personal and Confidential, *cit. sup.* p. 219: 'Yours, Mr President, with congratulations on the historic Wilson doctrine—no more territory, no more tyrants, no stealing of American governments by concessions or financial obligations (that's fixed now: no successor can set aside a righteous principle once clearly formulated).' Page was wrong: the banana proved more powerful than the ballot-box.

Its significance lies in what the speech was believed to contain, rather than what it did in fact contain.

In substance it was an address to the delegates of the Southern Commercial Congress, and it was particularly aimed at the Latin American delegates. The President spoke of 'concessions'; of the harm they did to the countries granting them, and of the day of emancipation which was at hand. He spoke of the high rates of interest demanded of their countries, the measures taken to reduce the risk involved in making the loans, and stated that the one cancelled out the justification for the other. He went on to indicate that the United States (on whose behalf he made a pledge of no further territorial conquest) was prepared, in the cause of furthering constitutional liberty in the Western Hemisphere, to assist its sister republics on terms of equality and honour. 'We have seen material interests threaten constitutional freedom in the United States', he said. 'Therefore we will now know how to sympathize with those in the rest of America who have to contend with such powers, not only within their borders but from outside their borders also.'[1]

The way in which this somewhat indeterminate statement was meant to be interpreted is well exemplified by Bryan's memorandum to the President linking it with the Monroe doctrine.

A new necessity for the application of the principle has arisen, and the application is entirely in keeping with the spirit of the doctrine and carries out the real purpose of that doctrine [he wrote]. The right of American republics to work out their own destiny along lines consistent with popular government, is just as much menaced today by foreign financial interests as it was a century ago by the political aspirations of foreign governments. If the people of an American republic are left free to attend to their own affairs no despot can long keep them in subjection; but when a local despot is held in authority by powerful financial interests, and is furnished money for the employment of soldiers, the people are as helpless as if a foreign army had landed on their shores. This, we have reason to believe, is the situation in Mexico, and I cannot see that our obligation is any less now than it was then . . .

[1] Henry Steele Commager, *Documents of American History*, 6th ed. (New York, 1958), II, pp. 269–70.

Bryan had already suggested that the United States should supply the capital needed in Latin America through a non-profitmaking syndicate which would carry with it no political control. He now repeated this proposal, adding: 'I believe it is perfectly safe and will make absolutely sure our domination of the situation.'[1]

The President, however, had promised only that the United States would sympathize; inherent in his whole philosophy was that the peoples of the respective republics must settle their affairs for themselves. Thus while his statement was hailed as a 'Wilson Doctrine'[2]—it could be regarded as the Wilson corollary to the Monroe doctrine—it was not backed up by machinery for giving the aid. There is no doubt either that this is what Wilson intended, or that he meant to give a clear warning to the European powers that he would oppose the extension of financial power in the Western hemisphere. In his first draft of the Mobile Speech he had been explicit where in delivery he had been studiously vague, saying: 'As in Cuba, the United States was willing to lend its assistance in the securing of independence from a foreign political power, so in Mexico this nation is willing to assist in maintaining Mexico's independence of foreign financial power.'

This was too bold, and clearly the President realized it. But equally his final draft was too cautious, though the difficulties of taking any practical steps at all were well put by John Bassett Moore in a memorandum to the President.

In handing me your memorandum, I understood Mr Bryan to suggest the inquiry whether, in connection with the course of the European Powers in recognizing the administration at the City of Mexico, the Monroe Doctrine might not be invoked, especially if it should be assumed that they acted under the influence of financial interests. I answered that the Monroe Doctrine did not appear to embrace this question. Recognition is an act performed in the ordinary course of diplomatic relations. As the independent States of America are not protectorates of the United States, we do not supervise their diplomatic

---

[1] Bryan–President, 28 October 1913. SDF 812.00/9469A (photostat).

[2] Policarpo Bonilla, *Wilson Doctrine: How the Speech of President Wilson at Mobile, Ala., has been Interpreted by the Latin-American Countries* (New York, 1914); J. Singer, *Die mexicanischen Finanzen und Wilsons panamerikanische Politik* (Berlin, 1914), pp. 18–29.

relations; and it has therefore never been considered necessary for foreign Powers to ask our consent to their recognition of an American government, or to explain to us their reasons for such a step. Nor can there be any doubt that the American Governments would themselves deeply resent any attempt on our part to assume such a supervision.

They would as surely resent the attempt on our part to prevent them from obtaining European capital for their industrial development or for their governmental necessities. It is an elementary and well known fact that the United States cannot today finance even its own needs. To say nothing of the money that we have borrowed for governmental purposes, we have from the beginning developed our industries and are still developing them with foreign capital, invested under what we here call 'grants' or 'charters', and what the Latins call 'concessions', the difference being one of language. Naturally, however, the conditions required by the investor vary with the risk. Whether a grant or concession might be of such a character as to raise a political question . . . would depend upon its terms. But, on the whole, in Latin-America as in the United States, the use of foreign capital has helped to develop industrial and financial strength and has thus contributed to political stability and independence.[1]

Nevertheless it was the President's view that became the official view of the administration, and the Mobile Speech became known as the expression of it. For this reason it is especially interesting to see how the Foreign Office reacted to it.

The President is very sanguine about the future of Latin-America after the opening of the Canal [noted Leslie]. His statement that the U.S. will never again seek one additional foot of territory by conquest is the most important statement in the speech, but this does not preclude the acquisition of territory by other means than conquest, or by a subsequent administration. The speech is a fine one to read, but its ideas do not seem very practical.

Spicer did observe the point on concessions, but remarked cynically: 'S. American Govts. will not welcome this declaration as the grant of concessions is generally accompanied by valuable pecuniary considerations.' Yet he did not remark on any connec-

[1] Moore–President, 28 October 1913, Confidential. Bryan Papers, General Correspondence, Box 29. Baker, *Woodrow Wilson, Life and Letters*, vol. IV (1932), p. 280. Yet the President was not prepared to explore with Bryan a way of carrying his views to their logical conclusion.

tion with the dispute over Huerta, while Sir Walter Langley went so far as to write: 'The reporter has read into the speech a reference to Mexico, but except as regards the statement respecting acquisition of territory it seems to have little connexion with the situation there.'[1]

The obscurity of the President's language was largely to blame for this misunderstanding. It was left to Page to explain how it was supposed to fit in with the facts of the situation, and to carry out the next steps in the United States programme. As far as Great Britain was concerned these fell into three parts: removing misunderstanding and gaining British support for the elimination of Huerta, crushing Cowdray, and replacing Carden.[2]

[1] Minutes on Spring-Rice–Grey, 30 October 1913, no. 224. FO 371/1678 file 6269/50866.
[2] Page–Woodrow Wilson, 22 November 1913, Personal and Confidential.

CHAPTER 8

NON-RECOGNITION

On 8 January 1914 Page wrote to Wilson:

We've travelled a long way since this Mexican trouble began—a long
way with His Majesty's Government. When your policy was first flung
at 'em, they show[d] at best a friendly incredulity: What, set up a moral
standard for Government in Mexico? Everybody's mind then was fixed
merely on the restoring of order—the safety of investments. They
thought of course our army w[d] go down in a few weeks. I recall that
Sir Edward Grey ask[d] me one day if you w[d] not consult the European
Gov[ts] about the successor to Huerta, speaking of it as a problem that w[d]
come up next week. And there was much unofficial talk about joint
intervention.

Well, they've followed a long way. They apologised for Carden
(that's what the Prime Minister's speech was); they ordered him to be
more prudent. Then the real meaning of concessions began to get into
their heads. They took up the dangers that lurked in the Government's
contract with Cowdray for oil; and they pulled Cowdray out of
Colombia and Costa Rica—granting the application of the Monroe
doctrine to concessions that might imperil a country's autonomy. Then
Sir Edward ask[d] me if you w[d] not consult him about such concessions—
a long way had been travelled since his other question!—They humili-
ated their admiral at our request. Lord Haldane made the Thanksgiving
speech that I suggested to him. And now they have transferred Carden.
They've done all we ask[d] & more; and, more wonderful yet, they've
come to understand what we are driving at, and have given one of
their financial Lords a tip that has cost him a long-shot more than his
Peerage cost in the beginning.

As this poor world goes, all this seems to me rather handsomely done.
At any rate, it's square and it's friendly.[1]

In return, Page suggested that the United States government
might do something about the Panama Tolls question.

This dispute had originated in the last year of the Taft administration, when Congress had insisted on resolving that United

[1] Page–Woodrow Wilson, 8 January 1914. Wilson Papers, Ac 3335 Box 86.

States ships should pass through the canal free of charge. The British contention that the Hay–Pauncefote Treaty imposed on them the obligation to share any such treatment with British vessels had then been rejected by the Department of State (with the support of somewhat strained legalistic arguments which gave much offence). The Democrats with their traditional appeal to Anglophobic elements had backed this position in their election platform. It was Wilson himself who studied the precedents and concluded that the United States was wrong on moral grounds. Two days previously, Wilson had written to Page in very much the same vein as the ambassador, and he, too, linked the two disputes.[1] History records that measures were taken, and the un-selfishness of the President's stand on Panama Tolls was greatly acclaimed at the time in Britain, and has been ever since in American text-books.

Nevertheless, the convenience with which Page's view of events fits into the pattern of international relations before the Great War must not be allowed to obscure the fact that it is sub-stantially incorrect. The truth is that the government of the United States deluded itself into believing that the British govern-ment was pursuing a policy actively hostile to its own in Mexico, and, having done so, deluded itself out again.

Woodrow Wilson, for one, must have known of the pressures exerted by the State Department on the Colombian government. The failure of the Murray contract was signalled from Bogotá to London, and not from London to Bogotá. The evidence that it had been supported up to the last by the Foreign Office went on record in the State Department files. It could not have been believed in Washington that Cowdray had been 'pulled out' of Colombia by the British government unless that was what they wanted to believe.

It is certainly true that the resources of the Anglo-Persian oil fields were by that time at the disposal of the Royal Navy, but Cowdray was fully able to fulfil his existing contracts from the Mexican fields and continued to do so throughout the War.[2] He

---

[1] Woodrow Wilson–Page, 6 January 1914. Wilson Papers, Ac 3335 Box 89a.
[2] Spender, *Weetman [Dickinson] Pearson, First Viscount Cowdray, 1856–1927* (1930), pp. 202–3.

was not, therefore, 'pulled out' of Mexico. Similarly, in London, Page received an unobtrusive education in the workings of parliamentary government, in many ways more significant than the lectures he gave Grey and others on democracy.[1] But the events following the Mobile Speech speak for themselves.

O'Shaughnessy reported from Mexico on 30 October that it was clear that the 'necessity' for Huerta's retirement had already entered the minds of many of his cabinet, including that of Querido Moheno. He repeated his warning that if suggestions from Washington were made in such a way as to salve Mexican *amour propre*, the aims of the administration might yet be achieved. From Vera Cruz, Lind followed this up with the advice that the statement must be absolutely definite, and the line of succession to the executive clear.[2] The terms, however, had already been dispatched to Mexico at 4 p.m. on 1 November.

Having received them, O'Shaughnessy was next faced with the problem of delivering them.

Last night came what is practically an ultimatum from Washington to Huerta [wrote Mrs O'Shaughnessy on 2 November]. He is to get out, he, and all his friends, or—intervention. N[elson] was at the palace until one o'clock in the morning. It is asking Huerta to commit political suicide, and he, unfortunately, does not feel so inclined. Also, he has a conviction that he is a sort of 'Man of Destiny' who can bring peace to Mexico. N. tried to convince him of the complete impossibility of standing up against the United States, and urged him again and again to give way . . .[3]

O'Shaughnessy then informed the State Department:

Huerta does not know the full text . . . but only that you insist on his resignation. The comminatory portions are unknown to him as yet. I have given the President's private secretary a translated paraphrase most carefully expressing the sense of your telegram for his own information and guidance. He informs me that he will again take up the matter with the President tomorrow and let you know by noon.[4]

[1] Page–Woodrow Wilson, 24 January 1914. Wilson Papers, Ac 3335 Box 86.
[2] O'Shaughnessy–Bryan, 30 October, 10 a.m., Telegram no. 592 Confidential for Secretary of State; Lind–Bryan, Telegram, 2 November, 5 p.m. SDF 812.00/9469, 9507.
[3] Edith Louise Coues O'Shaughnessy, *A Diplomat's Wife in Mexico* (New York, 1916), p, 32.
[4] O'Shaughnessy–Secretary of State, 3 November, 9 p.m., Telegram no. 598. SDF 812.00/9510.

Meanwhile, in preparation for an agreement which the State Department seem to have believed was inevitable, the text of the message was circulated to American embassies and legations, as well as to Lind in Vera Cruz. O'Shaughnessy's report seems then to have convinced the Secretary of State that secrecy really was of importance, and further instructions were sent out to withhold the message until news of its reception was received.[1] But these hopes were upset by an incident which Mrs O'Shaughnessy described on 4 November:

The extremely delicate negotiations N. has been having with the President's private secretary, Rabago, concerning Huerta's possible resignation, have leaked out, not from Mexico, but from the United States, and, we suspect, via Vera Cruz [she wrote]. At the somewhat early hour of two in the morning the press correspondents began to come to the Embassy. It is now 11.30 and they have been coming ever since.[2]

O'Shaughnessy naturally issued a denial that any ultimatum had been presented. It could not be concealed in Washington that negotiations of some sort were going on, and Bryan's similar denial was not entirely convincing. Considerable verbal complications arose from the fact that though the report had been published in the United States it took the form of a dispatch from Mexico.[3] This supported Bryan's suspicions that the report originated from Huerta's entourage as part of an effort to sabotage the discussions.

At this point Lind intervened to ask if he should go to the capital. The President decided that he should. His journey in itself would have been sufficient to confirm that something exceptional was expected to happen, but in addition, before leaving Vera Cruz, he confirmed for the benefit of the *Mexican Herald* that negotiations were taking place.[4] He informed

[1] Bryan–U.S. Embassies and Legations, Telegrams, 3 November, 12 midnight; 4 November, 6 a.m. SDF 812.00/9512A and B.
[2] O'Shaughnessy, *A Diplomat's Wife in Mexico*, pp. 33–4.
[3] Bryan–Woodrow Wilson, 4 November 1913. Bryan Papers, Special Correspondence, Box 43 f. 269.
[4] Lind–Bryan, Telegram, 5 November, 12 noon, Rush; Bryan–Lind, Telegram, 5 November, 7 p.m.; O'Shaughnessy–Secretary of State, 6 November, 10 a.m., Telegram no. 605. SDF 812.00/9568, 9596. *Mexican Herald*, Thursday, 6 November 1913.

Washington: 'It is my deliberate judgement that the time has arrived for fixing a very short definite time for such action as you require Huerta to take and the Embassy should be directed to deliver it as formulated and through regular channels.'[1]

Though it must be doubted that Huerta would have agreed to resign in any circumstances, Lind's entry on the scene was bound to be disastrous. Huerta countered his publicity and his ultimatum by disappearing among the numerous cafés of the capital, where even O'Shaughnessy had difficulty in running him to earth. Lind was not prepared to try. His worst suspicions of Sir Lionel Carden were easily confirmed when the latter said, in accordance with the views of his government, that no action would be taken before the results of the elections had been announced.[2] On 9 November Mrs O'Shaughnessy gave her mother an interesting picture of his views and methods.

There was an interesting conversation at lunch, only we four being present [she wrote]. Mr Lind repeated to von Hintze what he has, curiously enough, said to many people here—his opinion that the crux of the matter was the Anglo-American relations, and that the United States would never allow the dominance of British interests to the injury of American or Mexican ones; von Hintze, though he listened attentively, was non-committal and most diplomatic in his answers. It is always of absorbing interest to Germans to hear of possible difficulties between England and other nations, and *vice versa*, too, for that matter. A light springs into the eye; and I dare say von Hintze made a report to his home government on returning to the legation. He told Mr Lind he thought we had not sufficiently respected the *amour propre* of the Mexicans; that we were wrong in trying threats when what they needed was gentle coaxing. Mr Lind volunteered the surprising statement that it didn't suit us to have the elections held, anyway, as there would be concessions granted and laws passed that would render the Mexican situation difficult for us for fifty years. I really felt quite embarrassed.[3]

Mrs O'Shaughnessy was right. The German minister reported this conversation in detail,[4] as he also reported an equally remark-

---

[1] Lind–Bryan, Telegram, 7 November, 11 a.m. Personal. SDF 812.00/9611.
[2] Lind–Bryan, Telegram, 9 November, 12 noon. SDF 812.00/9623.
[3] O'Shaughnessy, *A Diplomat's Wife in Mexico*, p. 43.
[4] Hintze–Bethmann-Hollweg, 11 November 1913, no. A 91, GFM 12/16 f. A 23774.

able conversation with Carden. He said that Carden had become the 'acknowledged adviser for internal as well as external policy' to the government, and was a conspicuous contrast to his predecessors.

. . . Sir Lionel has without any doubt the right to have his own views on Mexico and to commend them to his Government [the minister wrote]. What appears less advisable to me is that he gives his steps a personal note—against the United States of America. He tells me that in Cuba, Guatemala and other Latin American countries he has always met the same opponents: the Americans. He has always found them people of bad faith, unbelievable crooks, swindlers . . . He has often attempted to reach an understanding with Americans; always they have broken their word ('they always went back on their word'). Sir Lionel thinks that now he has run the United States to earth in Mexico, 'now there is a chance of exploding that most foolish of all theories: the Monroe Doctrine'.

The instructions sent to Carden were unequivocal, but von Hintze makes it clear that he had, to say the least, misinterpreted them. He quoted the first sentence of Grey's semi-official letter as: 'If Sir Lionel Carden in his memorandum does not overstate matters, we ought to follow in Mexico a line of free and independent action, not openly in opposition to the policies of the United States nor openly hostilising [*sic*] them, but an absolutely free hand.'[1]

On the eve of Mrs O'Shaughnessy's dinner-party, Carden made himself even more explicit. Von Hintze had been arguing at length that 'agreement would be the best for United States, Mexico and all of us'. Carden replied:

'That may be true, but I can't see, how they will come to an agreement, as long as the United States insists upon dictating the inner policy of Mexico.'

'If I am not mistaken,' observed von Hintze, 'there are some symptoms of a certain tendency of giving in on both sides.'

'Not with Huerta,' said the British Minister; 'when he calls the new congress together, he will show his hand.'

---

[1] Hintze–Bethmann-Hollweg, 4 November 1913, no. A 89, GFM 12/16 f. A 23352. Compare Grey–Carden, 17 October 1913, *cit. sup.* p. 225.

'In view of the military unpreparedness of United States, they are likely not to make war—regular war—but just blockade the coast and the frontier and leave the rest to the Carrancistas', von Hintze suggested.

'The Carrancistas will never fight *with* the Americans against Huerta; they are afraid of the name of "traidores"', said Carden. 'Remember the catholic party: they called the French in (1863), and still today they are branded as "traidores".' And then he added a forecast so indiscreet that it is a tribute to von Hintze that it was never made known in the lifetime of either man. 'Then, if America does not make war, Huerta will *declare* war and will raid Arizona, Nuevo [sic] Mexico and Texas. That will *cow* the Americans.'

'Such a warfare would imperil to the utmost the lifes [sic] and properties of my countrymen as well as of yours—' protested von Hintze, 'it would be the worst that could happen, and for a long while.'

'May be,' the supposed nominee of the British interests said, 'but they live here and earn their living here, they must stand their chance.' And he showed, as the German Minister reported, 'that war would not be unwelcome to him for the opportunity "to explode the Monroe Doctrine"'.[1]

Lind, on the other hand, was expressing the policy of his government accurately, as Carden did not pretend to be doing. Preventing the Mexican Congress from meeting had now assumed in the eyes of the United States administration an importance second only to the removal of Huerta himself. This was shown clearly in the circular telegram sent to embassies on 7 and legations on 8 and 10 November, and drafted from a memorandum by the President. It directed them to make known to the governments to which they were accredited, confidentially and in advance, the President's 'clear judgement' that it was 'his immediate duty to require Huerta's retirement from the Mexican government' and that the United States must 'proceed to employ such means as may be necessary to secure this result'. While stating that the United States would not recognize 'anything done by Huerta since the assumption of dictatorial powers or . . . by the fraudulent legislature' which he was about to call together, it invited the powers to use their influence to 'impress upon Huerta

---

[1] Quotations in Hintze–Bethmann-Hollweg, 11 November 1913, no. A 91 (enclosure). *Cit. sup.* p. 258.

the wisdom of retiring in the interests of peace and constitutional government'.

But the United States government, whether from misplaced caution or inexperience, withdrew at the last moment from the path of frankness. President Wilson had originally wanted the British government to be given a special message which would say bluntly ('as strong and direct as the courtesies and proprieties of peaceful diplomacy permit') that 'the bottom was about to drop out when Sir Lionel Carden appeared upon the scene and took charge of its rehabilitation'.[1] But the message was not sent.

Lind's patience at his reception in the city of Mexico was wearing thin. He talked of intervention, believed that all the foreigners in Mexico had come to approve of the United States policy—which, as Mrs O'Shaughnessy wrote, was certainly only diplomatic camouflage on their part—and even came round to Henry Lane Wilson's view that many Mexicans would welcome armed intervention![2] Finally, on 12 November, he cabled to Washington that he had 'directed' O'Shaughnessy to deliver an ultimatum, that unless he was informed by 6 p.m. 'that Huerta had determined to dispose of the Congress by declaration of its illegality or dissolution or in any other manner he saw fit'[!]—he would 'entertain no further conversations with the administration'.[3] If Henry Lane Wilson had done this, he would have been accused of exceeding his powers. If Lind escapes this same charge, it is only because he had no powers to exceed.

Later in the day he telegraphed again. 'I assume that Huerta will decline to act on my suggestion. If he does I leave for Vera Cruz on the first train and further negotiations will be conducted there.'[4]

Nothing could have been more welcome to the Mexican government than Lind's departure! They were certain that the United States did not intend to intervene, and, as O'Shaughnessy had previously made clear, that was the only thing they worried

---

[1] Bryan–Page, Telegram, 7 November, 10 p.m. with 'Points' by Woodrow Wilson (undated). SDF 812.00/9625 A.

[2] Lind–Bryan, Telegram, 11 November, 9 p.m. SDF 812.00/9675.

[3] Lind–Bryan, Telegram, 12 November, 11 a.m. SDF 812.00/9677.

[4] Lind–Bryan, Telegram, 12 November, 3 p.m. SDF 812.00/9678.

about. But the United States government were not even willing to follow Lind's advice that the expiry of his ultimatum should be made the occasion for the severance of diplomatic relations; however, Bryan did instruct O'Shaughnessy that in the event of the *Mexicans* severing relations, he was to hand over the embassy to the Brazilian minister.[1] Once more, Huerta simply disappeared from view; Lind departed, and O'Shaughnessy remained.[2]

One further attempt was made to serve the unacceptable demands of the United States. O'Shaughnessy had succeeded in persuading Garza Aldape of the dangers he saw in the situation. He now undertook to transmit the demands that the new Congress should not meet, though he admitted frankly that he was afraid to do so because Huerta by this time flew into such a rage every time the name of Lind was mentioned that further conversation became impossible. The result was that on the morning of 16 November Garza Aldape's 'resignation' was accepted, and, sped on the way by handsome presents from the President for himself and his wife, he departed into exile on the liner *Espagne*. The same day the Congress met.[3]

These events were paralleled by an increase of diplomatic pressure on the British government. On the day after the circular telegram was dispatched to Page, Bryan spoke 'very earnestly' to Ernest Scott.

United States Government would not recognise any acts done by General Huerta since he made himself despot [ran the burden of the conversation]. They were determined that he should go, and go soon, and they were prepared to take any measures to make him do so. They would greatly prefer that he should go quietly, and they believed that this might be effected if the European Governments—Secretary of State mentioned French and German, but more particularly the

[1] Bryan–O'Shaughnessy, Telegram, 13 November, 1 p.m. SDF 812.00/(9702).

[2] 'The continual sparring for time on the part of the government and a persistently invisible President have got on his nerves', Mrs O'Shaughnessy wrote of Lind (*A Diplomat's Wife in Mexico*, p. 48). 'He hopes, by his sudden departure, to bring things to a climax, but climaxes, as we of the north understand them, are hard to bring about in Latin America.'

[3] *Ibid.* pp. 53–6; O'Shaughnessy–Secretary of State, Telegrams, 15 November, 9 a.m., no. 623; 15 November, 3 p.m., no. 624; 15 November, 11 p.m., no. 625 Confidential for Secretary of State; 16 November, 12 noon, no. 626 Confidential for Secretary of State. SDF 812.00/9755–9757.

British—gave him to understand that he would not get any sympathy or support from them. Secretary of State wished you to know that he had made a point of communicating the above to us before approaching any other Government.

Confidential. I strongly suspect that, unless we consent to take some such step in Mexico, United States Government will endeavour to lay on us the odium of having brought about armed intervention if they should find themselves forced to such action in the last resort. I venture to suggest that in the circumstances a continuation of our attitude of reserve no longer holds out hopes of a satisfactory solution and may be misinterpreted by the United States Government.

Faced with this threat, which he could not be certain was not the official policy of the United States government, Spicer did not waver.

If we act as the US wish—which means I suppose that we sh^d tell Huerta we withdraw our recognition of him—the U.S. w^d take care to see that as much odium as possible should fall on us . . . There seems no reason why we should make any departure from our present attitude of having recognized the de facto Gov^t, which however we have no intention of supporting actively.

Sir Walter Langley concurred with Spicer's opinion, and Sir Arthur Nicolson went even further. 'We cannot of course withdraw our recognition or in any way advise Genl. Huerta to retire—though we might say that he must not count on our support agst. the U.S.', he wrote. '*Our line has been so straightforward & logical that we need not fear publishing all that has passed.*'[1] [My italics.]

Page visited Grey the same day to communicate his message verbally. The memorandum of this interview went before the cabinet for consideration, and took some days to reach Washington, but its substance was embodied in a telegram to Carden which was repeated to Washington forthwith and in which the principal significance of the meeting lay.

American Ambassador has just informed me that the President of the United States considers it his immediate duty to require Huerta's

---

[1] Spring-Rice–Grey, 8 November 1913, Telegram no. 193 and minutes. FO 371/1678 file 6269/50822.

retirement, and that the United States must now proceed to employ such means as may be necessary to secure this result.

The President hopes that the British Government will use its influence to impress upon Huerta the wisdom of retiring in the interest of peace and constitutional government. . . .

I said that I did not see how Huerta's retirement was by itself to restore peace and order, which we desired to see established.

Our policy had hitherto been to recognise *de facto* Government as the only one with which we could deal, because we could not ourselves intervene in internal affairs of Mexico. I would say at once that there was no question of our intervening to oppose the United States. I regarded the communication as of so much importance that I must have time to consider it, and for reason given above I must know whether other Powers were being consulted in the same way.

Adding that though force had not been mentioned, the ambassador had given cause to suppose that it might be used, Grey asked Carden's opinion of the situation in Mexico in the light of this news.[1]

Page's first report of this interview left the impression in Washington that he had been met by a blank refusal. Discovering this, the ambassador hastened to correct the impression.

Sir Edward Grey was definite, positive, exceedingly friendly, even cordial, and he seemed to me to give all we asked [he explained]. I did not understand your instructions to mean that you wish him to take the initiative against Huerta and this he made plain, cordially and emphatically. He does not regard it as proper for his Government to take aggressive attitude because that would imply active British intervention; which the British Government does not regard as its duty nor does it regard such active intervention as desired by the United States. But if Huerta shows by word or act that he counts on British aid in any form he will be promptly informed that the British Government will not give it. This seemed to me wholly satisfactory.

And later in the course of the telegram he added: 'Sir Edward Grey left question of possible mediation between Huerta and the United States open till he should hear from other Governments, when it may be that they will voluntarily advise Huerta to retire.'[2]

[1] Grey–Spring-Rice, 8 November 1913, no. 644; Grey–Carden, 8 November 1913, 6 p.m., Telegram no. 149 Very Confidential. FO 371/1678 file 6269/50832.

[2] Page–Secretary of State, 13 November, 1 p.m., Telegram no. 104. SDF 812.00/9703.

There was much more to the telegram, which inspired the following reply from Bryan: 'Your November 13, 1 p.m. entirely satisfactory. We shall regard Great Britain's attitude as settled and in harmony with the President's plans.'[1]

Meanwhile, Carden had replied that Huerta was determined to meet force with force. After an interview with him, he added that he wished to do all he could to avoid a rupture, and would be prepared to accept British mediation, should the Foreign Office see fit to authorize Carden along these lines.[2] This telegram went to the Cabinet Room for Grey's attention, and the Foreign Secretary dealt with the proposal in a further conversation with Page on 11 November, when he said that mediation would only be undertaken at the request of both parties, and confirmed that he wished first to consult with other governments.[3] The previous evening, the Prime Minister, speaking at Guildhall, had taken advantage of the traditional speech on foreign policy to voice the official view of His Majesty's Government in unequivocal terms.[4]

I pass to another troubled theatre, Mexico, where also the commercial interests of this country call for our vigilant care [he said, after a review of the European situation and some observations on China]. Mexico is still in the throes of civil war. There never has been, I need hardly assure you, and there cannot be, any question of political intervention on the part of Great Britain in the domestic concerns of Mexico or any Central or South American State. It is no part of our right or duty—in that part of the world at any rate—to prevent revolutions, or to attempt to preclude the control or to put a stop to civil war. The utmost that we can do is to give what protection may be possible on the coast to British lives and property in times of urgent danger and crisis.

A rumour has found credence in some quarters that, at a moment when the Government of the United States were taking a line of their

---

[1] Bryan–Page, 13 November, 6 p.m., Telegram. SDF 812.00/9703.

[2] Carden–Grey, 10 November 1913, Telegram no. 137 Very Confidential. FO 371/1678 file 6269/51215.

[3] Grey–Spring-Rice, 11 November 1913, 8 p.m., Telegram no. 310. FO 371/1678 file 6269/51382. Cf. Edward, first Viscount Grey of Fallodon, K.G., *Twenty-Five Years, 1892–1916* (London, 1925), II, pp. 94–7, for positions as Grey afterwards saw them.

[4] *The Times*, Tuesday, 11 November 1913. *The Times* backed the Prime Minister's speech with a leading article and an authoritative statement of the United States policy. It is interesting to note, however, that while the Mexican minister (and the Japanese ambassador) were present at the dinner, Page was not.

own with regard to Mexico, we entered upon a new departure of policy deliberately, or at least if not deliberately, at any rate in effect, opposed to that of the United States and calculated to thwart it. There is not the vestige of foundation for such a rumour.

Here Asquith, hard pressed as he was by the internal political strains of the Ulster crisis, received the first enthusiastic cheers of the evening.

It was on March 31 of this year, before the present Administration in the United States had made, or indeed had had any opportunity of making, any declaration of policy, that his Majesty's Government recognized General Huerta as President *ad interim* of Mexico [he continued]. We did so because, having ourselves neither the will nor the power to intervene, we were bound to deal, as we should in the case of any Central or South American State, with whatever was for the time being the *de facto* Government; and because, according to the information then in our possession, there appeared to be no element except that of General Huerta and his supporters which offered any prospect of the restoration of stability and order.

That was on March 31. Very shortly afterwards, in answer to our inquiries, we were informed by the Government of the United States that, as regarded the recognition of General Huerta, no definite answer could be given except that they would wait some time longer before recognizing him. Since then there has been no new departure, no change of policy of any kind, on the part of his Majesty's Government. There has been a change of British Ministers, but it has involved no new policy. We have a right to assume, and we most gladly make that assumption, that in whatever policy the United States may adopt they will have regard to legitimate commercial interests in Mexico as well as to their own.

The Prime Minister concluded by saying that there had been 'from time to time . . . an exchange of views, without the least trace of friction, and on both sides with the most perfect cordiality', between the United States and Great Britain, but that their 'common resolve to attain and maintain a friendly and sympathetic understanding' was in no way impaired.

This speech has been enthusiastically received here by whole press and nation and a wave of cordial American friendship is now sweeping over the whole Kingdom [Page dramatically reported]. At many public dinners and gatherings intense satisfaction is expressed at cordial understanding as voiced by Prime Minister. We feel here that we have gained our whole wish and contention and the British Government and Nation understand that our whole contention has been granted.[1]

And generally, with the exception of *The World* and others, the American press echoed the encomium.[2] It was, by any standards, a triumph for Asquith; he said firmly that British policy had not changed, and was acclaimed for having changed it!

Grey, too, was working to eradicate two points of misunderstanding. 'I presume Huerta knows that we cannot support him in any way against the United States, but if not you should make it clear to him', he warned Carden, adding that Huerta was not likely to be willing to listen to the conditions that the United States would accept.[3]

Later, he dealt with the question of concessions. 'I have ... told the American Ambassador that Lord Cowdray has informed me that neither he nor any of the interests associated with him has obtained any concessions from the Huerta Government', he telegraphed to Mexico.

I added that I thought it reasonable that foreign Governments should not support or regard as valid concessions obtained from a Provisional Government under such conditions as exist in Mexico at the present time. I also added that Lord Cowdray had, I understood, very large interests acquired in Mexico before the Huerta régime, and that these were a legitimate source of anxiety.[4]

---

[1] Page–Secretary of State, 13 November, 1 p.m., Telegram no. 104 *cit. sup.* p. 264.

Cf. Richard Heathcote Heindel, *The American Impact on Great Britain 1898–1914, A Study of the United States in World History* (Philadelphia, Pa., 1940), p. 111: 'There was practically no approval of Wilson's Mexican policy in England . . . [it] was condemned as amateurish, muddled, idealistic, impractical, and sentimental throughout 1913 . . .'; also Allen, *Great Britain and the United States: a history of Anglo-American relations* (1954), who writes that even under a Liberal government the Foreign Office 'had by no means accepted the kind of international code of conduct which Wilson advocated; British calculations had national interests rather than international ideals in view'. But these attitudes did not preclude friendliness towards the United States.

[2] Spring-Rice–Grey, 13 November 1913, no. 230. FO 371/1678 file 6269/53137; article in *The World*, Wednesday, 12 November 1913—but see editorial, 'Democracy speaks to Democracy', of same date.

[3] Grey–Carden, 11 November 1913, 8 p.m., Telegram no. 153. FO 371/1678 file 6269/51383.

[4] Grey–Carden, 11 November 1913, 8 p.m., Telegram no. 154. FO 371/1678 file 6269/51384.

The Washington embassy was instructed to communicate the contents of this second telegram to the Secretary of State.

On 13 November Grey saw Page again, and informed him of the views of the French and German governments as they had been communicated to Washington. The former had endorsed the British view in stating that they would mediate only if asked by both parties. The latter had stated that they would be willing to consider the question only if the United States could propose a candidate for the Mexican Presidency, so that there was no lapse of executive authority there.[1] In view of Page's later sarcasm about this proposal, it is of interest to note his attitude at the time when Grey put it to him.

The Ambassador said that he thought this a very reasonable suggestion, and no doubt the President was giving the point his attention; but he observed that murders of foreign subjects might take place even while Huerta was there [Grey recorded].

I admitted this, but said that, as long as we did not intervene, if British subjects were killed and British property destroyed, we could not be held responsible for these events; . . . but, if we urged Huerta to get out of the way when there was nothing to succeed him, and worse disorder followed, in the course of which British lives were sacrificed, we might in a sense be held responsible.[2]

On the same day, Carden, increasingly worried by the rumours of impending doom current in Mexico City, again asked permission to mediate. Grey replied simply:

The only solution I can suggest would be that Huerta should come to an arrangement with the United States Government as to who or what they would recognise in place of him, but I am not sure that even this is feasible, and I see great risks in our becoming alone responsible for mediation, and so being separated from other Powers. Of course, if Huerta makes any proposal to you, you should report it.[3]

However, Carden, through O'Shaughnessy, had already offered the United States his services to support a settlement. He did not

---

[1] Sir. F. Bertie–Grey, 12 November 1913, Telegram no. 149; Goschen–Grey, 12 November, 1913, Telegram no. 195. FO 371/1678 file 6269/51490, 51493.

[2] Grey–Spring-Rice, 13 November 1913, no. 656. FO 371/1678 file 6269/51579. The telegraphic version condensed this considerably.

[3] Carden–Grey, 12 November 1913, Telegram no. 139; Grey–Carden, 13 November 1913, 8 p.m., Telegram no. 160; FO 371/1678 file 6269/51579.

do this on the instructions of his government; he even asked the American chargé to arrange for representations to be made to London for him to be empowered to act.[1] Page did not know of this. He assured himself that under the cabinet system of government the Prime Minister's speech was the most authoritative statement of government policy to be obtained and interpreted it as an apology for Carden's activities. He also reported Grey's statements to the State Department. However, he began to try to convince Grey that Carden should be removed from his post, at the very moment when O'Shaughnessy was trying to persuade the State Department to make use of his services.[2] His first efforts in this direction were interrupted by the departure of the Foreign Secretary to Windsor Castle for a spell as Minister in Waiting.

Fortunately at this moment the Washington embassy was in an exceptionally strong position to resolve outstanding problems. This was due to the fact that Sir William Tyrrell had chosen to visit Washington to spend part of his leave aiding Spring-Rice, whose condition was still serious. Through the good offices of Colonel House, who took Tyrrell for a British counterpart of himself, he was not only able to keep the embassy running efficiently but even to secure an interview with President Wilson on 14 November.[3] His report on this interview was as valuable to Grey as the interview had been to the President. It covers some ground that is already familiar but its distinction lies in its authority.

With the opening of the Panama Canal it is becoming increasingly important that the Governments of the Central American Republics should improve, as they will become more and more a field for European and American enterprize: bad government may lead to

[1] O'Shaughnessy–Secretary of State, 13 November, 12 midnight, Telegram no. 621; 13 November, 7 p.m., Telegram no. 619. SDF 812.00/9713, 9719.
[2] Grey–Spring-Rice, 13 November 1913, no. 657. FO 371/1678 file 6269/52448; Page–Woodrow Wilson, 22 November 1913, Personal and Confidential, *cit. sup.* p. 219.
[3] Edward Mandell House: *Diary*, 11–13 November 1913, quoted in Seymour, *The Intimate Papers of Colonel House* (1926), I, pp. 204–7; Gwynn, *The Letters and Friendships of Sir Cecil Spring-Rice: a record* (1929), p. 196, corrects above. See also Hendrick, *The Life and Letters of Walter H. Page* (1924), p. 201, for Page's letter to House calling his attention to Tyrrell's visit.

friction and to such incidents as Venezuela affair under Castro.[1] The President is very anxious to provide against such contingencies by insisting that those Republics should have fairly decent rulers and that men like Castro and Huerta should be barred [Tyrrell began]. With this object in view, the President made up his mind to teach these countries a lesson by insisting on the removal of Huerta. The mode of procedure which he proposes is that Huerta should convoke the Congress of last May, which he considers the only legal one in Mexico, and that he should proclaim a general amnesty so as to enable the contingents of the North to share in the election of a new President. If the latter refused to come in, they would be treated as rebels by the United States Government. The President assured me that, should Huerta agree to this, he would go almost to any length to enable him to save his face. After that, he does not propose to examine with a microscope what happens in Mexico, but he is under no illusion with regard to the capacity of the Mexicans for maladministration. Huerta, however, exceeded the limit of what is permissible. The President is confident that the Mexican Congress would and could elect a President capable of maintaining law and order.

The President did not seem to realise that his policy will lead to a 'de facto' American protectorate over the Central American Republics; but there are others here who do, and who intend to achieve that object. It seems to me that we have neither the intention nor the power to oppose this policy: the longer intervention is put off, the more distant the date on which this policy will mature. The Administration has, by its own mistakes, got itself into a difficult position, as it wishes to avoid intervention if possible. If we can do anything to help the President, he will be most appreciative.

The Prime Minister's speech, Lord Cowdray's statement to you, and his public announcement as to his share in financial assistance to Huerta, and your attitude towards new concessions . . . have created an excellent impression both on the Administration and on the public, and have done much to dispel the suspicions aroused by the attitude attributed to His Majesty's Minister in Mexico and to Lord Cowdray. Mr Hohler,

---

[1] Cipriano Castro was dictator of Venezuela, 1899–1909. He refused to meet claims for injuries to foreigners resulting from revolutionary disturbances, which led to a naval blockade of Venezuelan ports by Great Britain, Germany and Italy. This was ended by United States diplomatic pressure leading to the submission of the claims to arbitration (December 1902–February 1903). Subsequently, for the same reason, the United States suspended diplomatic relations with him (June 1908). Castro was overthrown in 1909 by his Vice-President, Juan Vincente Gómez, who remained as dictator until death in 1935.

who was on his way home from Mexico, confirms the accuracy of the reports current here as to the pronounced attitude of Sir Lionel Carden in favour of Huerta on his arrival in Mexico and his disapproval of American policy; but the President agreed that these questions have now assumed a historical interest only.—With all diffidence, I venture to submit that, if you could see your way to authorizing Sir Lionel Carden to move in the direction suggested in his telegram . . . [offering to mediate] . . . it would be highly appreciated by the President, who is a strong partisan of what Mr House described to me as a sympathetic alliance with England. In his opinion, the present is the psychological moment for promoting it.

As regards the Panama Canal Tolls, the President volunteered the statement, for your personal and confidential information, that he is in entire agreement with your view on the subject, and that he is determined to overcome the opposition of the Senate, which, as he told me, is partly due to the vanity of certain Senators and partly to the Hibernianism of others. With this object in view, he is even prepared to invoke the assistance of Republican Senators.

After noting that the President had expressed his hope that Grey's personal views would continue to be transmitted through the ambassador, and not, apparently, through the Secretary of State, Tyrrell concluded: 'He made on me the impression of great sincerity and force of character: every one is agreed that he is a man of his word, and the only man who counts in the Administration.'[1]

It is apparent from Tyrrell's account of this interview that he did in fact receive a clear account of the President's policy, and that the emphasis of Page's biographer on the celebrated phrase reported by House—'I am going to teach the South American Republics to elect good men!'—does Wilson an injustice. Certainly the President was, in Spring-Rice's words 'obstinate and secretive', but he was not a fool. For example, it did not take the interview to convince him that Grey was not dominated by the oil interests. Tyrrell indicates clearly that the President, though not Bryan, had already come round to recognizing this.

[1] Sir William Tyrrell–Grey (through Sir C. Spring-Rice), 14 November 1913, Telegram, Private and Personal. FO 371/1678 file 6269/52367. Compare this interview with that ludicrous conversation between Tyrrell and Bryan, described in Hendrick, pp. 202–4. Spring-Rice–Grey, 19 August 1913, Grey Papers.

Grey replied in terms equally cordial and frank, saying: 'The object of securing better Government, which the President has set before him, is one with which every one should sympathise, but I doubt whether there is any means by which the President can carry it out except direct intervention.'[1] The action to be taken, if any, was decided by a further telegram from Carden, listing the demands of the United States as O'Shaughnessy had made them known to him in confidence.

'I have reason to believe that Huerta is not indisposed to concede the essential points desired by the United States Government but he resents their general attitude and their disregard of the legal difficulties of conceding what they want as they want it. Personally Mr Lind also irritates him', he added.

Grey's reply, drafted in his own hand, was exceedingly subtle. It did not authorize Carden to negotiate, but gave him the information necessary to receive a proposal from the Mexican side. So British policy as regards mediation remained unchanged while the sense of Tyrrell's suggestion was met.[2] A copy of these instructions was transmitted through the Washington embassy and Tyrrell to President Wilson, who expressed his thanks. 'He would be very grateful for earliest possible communication to him of statement which Huerta proposes to make to-day to Sir L. Carden . . .', the reply added.[3] Thereupon Grey authorized the transmission of a copy of Tyrrell's telegram, suitably edited by the removal of the reference to Hohler, to Carden so that he could be fully informed. On 22 November he added a further warning of the need for haste.[4]

This crossed with Huerta's proposals. They were that when Congress had nullified the elections, new elections would be planned, and Huerta would then retire to devote himself to pacifying the country. He proposed that, since the old Congress could

[1] Grey–Tyrrell, 17 November 1913, Telegram, Private. FO 371/1678 file 6269/52367.
[2] Carden–Grey, 16 November 1913, Telegram no. 141 Very Confidential; Grey–Carden, 17 November 1913, 7 p.m., Telegram no. 167. FO 371/1678 file 6269/52130.
[3] Tyrrell–Grey, 18 November 1913, Telegram. FO 371/1678 file 6269/52477.
[4] Grey–Carden, 22 November 1913, Telegram no. 186, answering Carden–Grey, 20 November 1913, Telegram no. 147. FO 371/1678 file 6269/52908. Carden attended the Opening of Congress in accordance with general agreement of the diplomatic corps (excluding O'Shaughnessy).

not in any case be recalled and he could neither offer an amnesty nor propose cessation of hostilities, he would allow military action to lapse while the elections took place. These proposals were transmitted to Washington without comment.[1]

No reply came from there. On 26 November Page handed in at the Foreign Office a further statement of his government's views, which was at once recognized to be so uncompromising that chances of successful negotiations were ruled out. 'Whether they starve or force Gen[l] Huerta out the U.S. Govt say nothing as to who or what is to take his place', remarked Sir Arthur Nicolson—' & if there is noone or no strong Gov[t] to take his place there will be increased anarchy. The whole U.S. policy towards Mexico "smells of the study lamp" and is not practical.'[2]

Two days later Tyrrell took his leave of the President, who asked him if the Foreign Office expected a reply to their communication of Huerta's proposals, and indicated that he considered the proposals 'futile'. 'The US are not consistent—they were anxious for a statement from Gen[l] Huerta & when they get one they are inclined to take no notice of it. Their methods are certainly singular', Sir Arthur noted.[3]

The embassy was accordingly directed to find out if there was a reply, saying that it was inferred that there was no chance that the proposals would be accepted, but that the British government wanted to know what instructions to give Carden.[4] On 2 December they reported that the Secretary of State considered the proposals 'so absurd that he does not deem them worthy of any reply'. He added 'that Huerta knew quite well what was expected of him'. It was not just the bad manners of the whole proceeding that aroused surprise in London: there was also a reviving conviction that the United States government was using

---

[1] Carden–Grey, 21 November 1913, Telegram no. 149 Very Confidential; Grey–Spring-Rice, 24 November 1913, Telegram no. 355. FO 371/1678 file 6269/53067.

[2] Page–Grey, 26 November 1913 and minutes; minutes on Spring-Rice–Grey, 23 November 1913, Telegram no. 199 (transmitting report from Sir W. Tyrrell) show that Sir A. Nicolson was particularly irritated by so-called 'assurances' Wilson offered British investors. FO 371/1678 file 6269/53702, 53167.

[3] Minute on Spring-Rice–Grey, 28 November 1913, Telegram no. 203 (transmitting report from Sir W. Tyrrell). FO 371/1678 file 6269/53930.

[4] Grey–Spring-Rice, 1 December 1913, 1.15 p.m., Telegram no. 360. FO 371/1678 file 6269/53930.

professions of democracy to cloak the most sinister designs. Grey hastened to disentangle British policy from the possible embarrassment by directing Carden to make a formal report of the United States attitude to the Mexican government. 'We can do no more in the matter', he minuted.[1]

Thus the United States administration lost interest when they found out that the British government policy was not, after all, hostile to their own. Instead they turned to negotiating with the advancing Constitutionalist armies, through the agency of William Bayard Hale, and were concerned to learn that the Constitutionalists intended to trust no one but themselves. The suspicion began to dawn that the Constitutionalists understood no more of constitutional processes than the name, but it was sternly repressed.[2] In his State of the Union Message at the beginning of December Wilson at last revealed that his course was one of 'watchful waiting', though there were some who echoed Theodore Roosevelt's comment that it was really 'furtive meddling'.[3]

Militarily, the Constitutionalists were growing visibly in strength. On 15 November the forces of Francisco Villa captured Ciudad Juárez—bullets falling on the American side of the frontier without arousing more than a desultory interest.[4] To the south, Carranza's forces began to approach Tuxpam and the great oilfields. On 17 November Carden appealed for British ships to be sent to Tampico as well as to Puerto México (Coatzacoalcos), where a local rising appeared imminent. On 19 November the

[1] Spring-Rice–Grey, 2 December 1913, Telegram no. 204 and minutes. FO 371/1678 file 6269/54537. It is clear from this that the belief that Carden 'faced about and led a troop of European diplomats into the Palace of Chapultepec to urge Huerta to yield to the demands of the United States and give up the Presidency' (Samuel Flagg Bemis, *The Latin American Policy of the United States: an Historical Interpretation* (New York, 1943), p. 177) is not correct.

[2] Hale–Bryan, Telegram, 15 November, 7 p.m.; Bryan–Hale, Telegram, 16 November 1913. SDF 812.00/9759.

[3] Henry Cabot Lodge, ed., *Selections from the correspondence of Theodore Roosevelt and Henry Cabot Lodge, 1884–1918* (New York, 1925), II, p. 451 (Henry Cabot Lodge–Theodore Roosevelt, 15 January 1915). Text of Message in James W. Gantenbein, *The Evolution of our Latin American Policy* (New York, 1950), p. 566. 'Watchful waiting' did not *end* before this message, as is implied by Blum, *Woodrow Wilson and the Politics of Morality* (1956), pp. 88–9.

[4] T. J. Edwards–Secretary of State, Telegram, 15 November 1913; Lindley Garrison–Secretary of State, Telegram, 15 November 1913. SDF 812.00/9749, 9753.

Admiralty notified the Foreign Office that the ships had been dispatched, and that the Fourth Cruiser Squadron had been ordered from Barbados to Jamaica in case need arose for reinforcements.[1]

The same day, Cowdray was notified that his firm's properties at Tuxpam had been threatened with destruction by the advancing rebels unless they paid the sum of $100,000 forthwith. He called on Page and asked him to ask his government if they would be prepared to instruct their ships to give protection. Page telegraphed the request to the State Department, and received the reply that the Commanding Officer of U.S.S. *Louisiana* was being instructed by the Navy Department

to consult with the local American Consul and to endeavour to impress upon the revolutionists that the destruction of the great foreign industrial properties situated in the region of their operations, either wantonly or as an act of revenge, could not be regarded with indifference by the Government of the United States, and could not fail to be attended with the most unfortunate results, especially in the present condition of affairs.[2]

The way in which it happened that such a request could be met is not confined to the official diplomatic record. Contrary to general belief, few men can have been more disturbed than Cowdray himself at Huerta's dissolution of Congress and assumption of a dictatorship, which seemed to indicate that the state of disturbance in the country would be prolonged.[3] At the same time, it is clear this disturbance was not yet felt to be sufficiently great to be disastrous. The Aguila Company did not regard the emergency tax of three centavos a barrel on oil produced as much of an imposition, unlike their American rivals who complained of it bitterly. On any realistic estimate, the trade could well stand it.[4]

With the growing feeling against him in the American press, Cowdray followed his usual course. He ignored the calumny. He

[1] Carden–Grey, 17 November 1913, Telegram no. 142; Admiralty–Sir Arthur Nicolson, 19 November 1913, M-01963 Immediate. FO 371/1678 file 6269/52336, 52626.
[2] Page–Secretary of State, 19 November, 4 p.m., Telegram no. 111. SDF 812.00/9821. Page–Cowdray, 20 November 1913. Cowdray Papers.
[3] Cowdray–Limantour, 14 October 1913, Private and Confidential; Cowdray–Ryder, 18 October; Cowdray–Dr C. W. Hayes, 18 October 1913. Cowdray Papers.
[4] Lind–Bryan, Telegram, 15 October, 11 a.m. SDF 812.00/9218.

18-2

maintained this attitude until advice from Mexican sources impressed on him that a continued silence would do more harm than good. Ernesto Madero was in London to thank Cowdray for interceding with the Foreign Office, and through Fred Adams in Mexico on behalf of his three brothers who had recently been arrested by federal forces.[1]

. . . He thought you should take prompt and energetic action to refute the statements which were taking form about your rumoured financial assistance to the Mexican Government during the present crisis [Body wrote to Cowdray, who was out of town]. He explained that he had talked with several members of the constitutional junta in Paris who had called his attention to the part it was claimed you had played, and who said they believed it to be true. He replied that he knew you well enough to know that the statements were false, and he fears now that unless you make a definite refutation without delay it may develop into a serious matter and it would be very difficult later on to convince any new party coming into power that you had not rendered great financial assistance to the Government as is claimed.[2]

Accordingly, Cowdray issued a statement from his home at Dunecht near Aberdeen on 12 November.

In common with most of the Banks, and leading Houses in Mexico my Firm and Allied Companies subscribed for a small proportion—less than three per cent—of the Government loan made through the National Bank of Mexico [it ran]. Apart from this neither I, my Firm or allied Companies have in any way, directly or indirectly, assisted in a financial manner the present Provisional Government, nor, let me in justice add, have we been asked so to do.[3]

The accusations made against Cowdray in the American press had, unfortunately, ramified. This denial, limited though it was to the key charge from both the Mexican point of view and Cowdray's own, tended to be interpreted as a tacit admission of the others. Hence, on 17 November he made a further statement, and, in an interview with Page, made his position clear and asked

[1] Ernesto Madero–Cowdray, 25 October 1913, Telegram; Sir Walter Langley–Cowdray, 3 November 1913. Cowdray Papers. See also related correspondence in FO 371/1677 file 6269/48609, 49172.

[2] Body–Cowdray, 11 November 1913. Cowdray Papers.

[3] Lord Cowdray: Statement to Press: 'The Crisis in Mexico', 12 November 1913. Cowdray Papers.

the ambassador to advise his government, which he did. Cowdray denied having influenced the appointment of Sir Lionel Carden, having interfered in Mexican politics except to advise Huerta to receive the Lind mission, having applied for new concessions or having undertaken public works contracts with the exception of one granted under the Madero government, having sought or obtained an oil monopoly, or having taken part in the overthrow of the Madero government, which, he said, had specifically recognized the validity of his concessions.[1]

Despite this, he received a cable from Fred Adams the day after he had made a request to Page for protection at Tuxpam, saying: 'President requests me to assure Lord Cowdray that nothing can shake his confidence in the sincerity of his friendship both for himself and for Mexico and he recognizes fully his great services towards the development of Mexico.'[2]

Fred Adams was trying to locate the sources of the rumours, and reported on 21 November that O'Shaughnessy had told him

that his Government had been informed by Lind and believed that the new Congress had been called by General Huerta at instance Lord Cowdray for purpose giving him rights all national lands in exchange large loan. I gave absolute denial and challenged immediate investigation suggesting our local enemies be invited produce soonest evidence. He accepted and endorsed my denial to Washington am explaining Lind tomorrow fallacious benefit our existing concessions.[3]

Lind had just sent a peculiarly bitter report to Washington accusing Carden of having refused to act for a man of British origin because he was a Mexican citizen, and wondering what he would now do about the Aguila Company which was a Mexican company.[4] When he was challenged by Adams, he evaded the question, and in his report to Bryan, after discussing the question of protection for the Tuxpam oil properties, added:

[1] Cowdray–Page, 17 November 1913. Cowdray Papers; Page–Bryan, 19 November 1913, no. 174. SDF 812.00/9972. Lord Cowdray: Statement to Press, 17 November 1913. Cowdray Papers.

[2] Adams–Cowdray, 20 November 1913, Telegram. Cowdray Papers.

[3] Adams–Cowdray, 21 November 1913, Telegram. Cowdray Papers.

[4] Lind–Secretary of State, Telegram, 19 November, 4 p.m. SDF 812.00/9827. Lind was sending telegrams daily, many to the same effect. This one, however, is a quotation from an article written by an unidentified person which the Associated Press refused to handle.

I omitted to state to Mr Adams that I know that there is a provision in the Mexican Charter of the Aguilar [*sic*] Oil Company, that if the Company applies to a foreign Government for protection or for any purpose the Charter and all rights under it are forfeited. This is a fact and I mention it for your information. When I see Mr Adams again I will mention to him that I appreciate fully the delicacy of the Company's position.[1]

After a due interval to savour this knowledge, Lind saw Adams again and mentioned it. He also told him for the first time that the rebel General Aguilar had yielded to a communication from Admiral Fletcher, and undertaken to respect the oilfields. Adams duly expressed his gratitude.[2]

Cowdray telegraphed to Ryder:

Advise Galbraith verbally that unless Press attacks on Aguila Company ourselves through [Sherburne] Hopkins [and José] Vasconcelos cease we shall break understanding and go for whole trade. Absurd being friends Sales Department at Clay Pierce's suggestion when he maliciously attacks misrepresents us elsewhere with object inflaming Mexican American opinion against us.[3]

The attacks thereafter ceased. Pierce, his links with the Standard Oil now severed, and fighting for his own safety in the United States, was more vulnerable than ever. In the new year, the companies were to reach an agreement to split the Mexican domestic market fifty–fifty—marking an advance, not a retreat, for Cowdray.[4] Meanwhile, however, the full extent of Pierce's machinations was still not clear to his rival. It was made so by a cable from Adams on 25 November.

. . . Learned today from American Attaché that Galbraith has been month past assuring Lind that you are endeavouring by a loan to make General Huerta resistance to United States possible. That your action is directed against Monroe Doctrine that Carden's support General Huerta due sure influence [he reported]. Think Lind first believed but has since discovered error.

[1] Lind–Secretary of State, Telegram, 21 November, 12 noon. SDF 812.00/9869.
[2] Lind–Secretary of State, Telegram, 21 November, 6 p.m. SDF 812.00/9871.
[3] Cowdray–Ryder, 22 November 1913, confirmation of telegram. Cowdray Papers.
[4] Spender, pp. 170, 202–3; Middlemas, pp. 229, 232.

Adams went on to say that the American attaché suggested that Cowdray should see President Wilson, but for his own part he felt it was better to ask Ernesto Madero to do so.[1] Cowdray took this advice. He was too ready to agree with Adams that Lind had discovered his error, for this was far from being the case. Yet Adams himself was deceived by Lind's genuine friendliness towards him personally into believing that he was a reasonable being, even on the subject of Adams's chief.[2]

Page was not convinced when Cowdray explained to him confidentially that the Waters Pierce people were the 'head-devils' behind the whole affair.[3] He was jubilant over the failure of the Murray contract, and, attributing it to the influence of the British government, with which he was coming to have an increasing sympathy, he was content to believe that Cowdray had 'come to heel'. In the months ahead, Huerta, fortified by the recapture of Torreón, seemed as strong as ever to unprejudiced observers. During this period of waiting Page readily discussed all aspects of the situation with Cowdray, and considered that he had taken his setbacks outstandingly well.[4]

There remained, in United States eyes, the problem of Carden. In assessing the role of the minister at this period, however, some caution is necessary, for much of the direct evidence comes from the reports of von Hintze, and in some quarters these were considered not to be entirely above suspicion. Spring-Rice, as early as February 1914, came to the conclusion that he was engaged in an elaborate intrigue at the instigation of Holstein, 'grey eminence' of the German Foreign Ministry. He saw him as working to deny the supply of oil from the Mexican fields to the Royal Navy by stirring up Anglo-American conflict over them.[5] But it is not necessary to suppose that von Hintze's 'intrigue' went beyond

[1] Adams–Cowdray, 25 November 1913, Telegram. Cowdray Papers.
[2] Stephenson, *John Lind of Minnesota* (1935), p. 232.
[3] Page–Woodrow Wilson, 22 November 1913, Personal and Confidential, *cit. sup.* p. 219; Hendrick, *passim.*
[4] Hendrick, pp. 223–7; Page–Woodrow Wilson, 19 March 1914. Wilson Papers, Ac 3335 Box 86.
[5] Hintze–Bethmann-Hollweg, 23 December 1913, no. A111. GFM 12/17 f. A 712. For Spring-Rice's suspicions see: Spring-Rice–Tyrrell, 3 February and 17 February 1914. Grey Papers.

sympathetic listening and reporting for the observed results to be obtained, and there is internal evidence that it did not. The following composite picture is therefore offered as a logically satisfactory approximation.

To begin with, from the date of receiving specific orders to refrain from giving Huerta any indication of support, Carden had undoubtedly been punctilious in observing their terms. But he was not, and did not consider himself, bound not to try to reverse his government's policy. Indeed, it was his duty to do so, since he believed it to be wrong. From about 15 November he was speci-fically concerned lest the continued rebel successes lead to a sudden collapse of executive authority in Mexico itself, before the Con-stitutionalist army arrived to restore order.[1] However sincere this concern, and there is no reason to suppose that it was not, he began to use it as an excuse for action which might strengthen the case he was presenting in London. The military attaché, Lieut.-Col. Gage, was summoned from Washington to advise on the defence of the British community, and was told Carden's views. The minister then turned his attention to the commander-in-chief of the British Cruiser Squadron on the West Indian Station, Rear-Admiral Sir Christopher Cradock, to instruct him along the same lines. Admiral Cradock was invited to the capital, ceremoniously treated, and even taken to pay his respects to the President.

Sir Lionel has initiated him into his reports [von Hintze reported to Berlin]. Craddock [*sic*] told me that he could hardly sleep at night on account of all the dreadful things which Sir Lionel had prophesied in them. The British Minister said to me that he wanted to work through Craddock on the Admiralty, later through the Military Attaché whom he has requested from Washington (Lt.-Col. Gage) on the War Office; if from three places the same complaints came to London, they would probably convince Sir Edward Grey of what he is preparing here with his policy of the 'free hand for the United States'.[2]

The visit itself would have been sufficient to raise questions in Washington circles and in the United States press. But the inter-view with Huerta, which lasted an hour and a half, caused special

[1] Carden–Grey, 18 December 1913, no. 352. FO 371/2025 file 91/939.
[2] Hintze–Bethmann-Hollweg, 10 December 1913, no. A 106. GFM 12/16 f. A 25628.

irritation. The Admiral had departed from tradition in visiting the President in full dress, and the very length of the interview gave rise (as no doubt the President intended that it should) to the belief that it was an official indication of British support for which arrangements were being made.[1]

In fact, as Cradock's report to the Admiralty indicated, no political question was discussed.[2] Yet sentences purporting to come from that report were published in New York in *The World* on Saturday, 13 December. They were bitterly critical of the United States. O'Shaughnessy was moved to attempt to verify the report. Through the stenographer—an American citizen— who had acted for the Admiral, he secured a copy of the authentic text, which showed that *The World*'s version was an invention. In the fevered atmosphere of the time, however, he decided that in any case the actual report showed that Cradock and Carden were engaged in 'Machiavellian intrigues'.[3]

Cradock had, it is true, said that the situation was 'absolutely "without light"' and that the view was widespread in the capital that the United States policy of 'financial starvation' was designed to facilitate intervention. If this took place, and he had the slightest warning, he intended to send the legation 'clandestinely' a Maxim gun and ammunition. But this was merely for their own defence and the report contained no indication of British action hostile to the wishes of the United States.

However, Cradock became a marked man. He had in the meantime rejoined his ship at Vera Cruz and had led his squadron north to its station at Tampico. There he encountered Admiral Fletcher; who made haste to anchor before him so that, although he was the junior officer, he could receive the first salute. He then informed Washington that Cradock had waived his seniority in Mexican waters, forcing Cradock to protest strongly at this

---

[1] O'Shaughnessy–Secretary of State, 2 December, 9 p.m., Telegram no. 661. SDF 812.00/10018. The last previous British commander to visit a Mexican President (Madero) did so in civilian clothes.

[2] Cradock–Admiralty, 3 December 1913, unnumbered, with Admiralty–Nicolson, 1 January 1914, no. M-02188/13. FO 371/2025 file 91/296.

[3] *The World*, Saturday, 13 December 1913; O'Shaughnessy–Secretary of State, 15 December, 12 noon, Telegram no. 687; 15 December, 8 p.m., Telegram no. 688. SDF 812.00/10197, 10206.

attempt to trap him. On 9 December the Constitutionalist forces actually reached Tampico, which was besieged for four days. During these four days 'Admiral Fletcher used every artifice and stratagem to find any semblance of a pretext to land men', first by simply proposing to land and clear a neutral zone; then, when he encountered shocked disagreement from naval and consular officers, by taking refugees on board ships, one of which passed between the Mexican gunboat *Bravo* and the shore while shots were being exchanged; and, finally, by ordering the Constitutionalists to retire. No doubt to his great surprise, they did so. Certainly Cradock did not discover at the time what had led them to retire.[1]

As a naval officer, Cradock's interpretation of the situation seems to have been impeccable. But in the United States his efforts to avert a landing were criticized, and as senior officer his position was untenable. At the request of the Foreign Office the Admiralty removed the irritation by splitting the squadron and ordering Cradock to return to Vera Cruz. But not the least paradoxical fact was that they did so, not, as Page later thought, to accede to the American desire that their Admiral should have the right to command, but to ensure that the Americans should carry the full responsibility for any landing that might be made.[2] When, therefore, the following April, President Wilson slipped the last knot in the Taft leash, there was no non-American scapegoat left to take the blame, and Bryan, after the event, took care to lay it on Fletcher.

Meanwhile Page, with the full approval of Wilson, kept up the pressure on Grey for Carden's transfer. Obviously, it was a difficult request for Grey to satisfy in any circumstances, but impossible under pressure. On 5 January 1914 he considered that it

---

[1] Cradock–Admiralty, 13 December 1913, no. 157. FO 371/1679 file 6269/56338. *The World*, Saturday, 13 December 1913; Tuesday, 16 December 1913. Cradock–Admiralty, 19 December 1913, no. 396/427 Confidential. FO 371/2025 file 91/1194.

[2] The United States government did ask for Cradock to be subordinated to Fletcher. Bryan–Page, Telegram, 13 December, 7 p.m.; 15 December, 6 p.m. SDF 812.00/10169 A, 10237 B. Page was informed that the Foreign Office would arrange that there was no conflict of authority. Page–Secretary of State, 16 December, 5 p.m., Telegram no. 122, SDF 812.00/10222. But Admiralty–Nicolson, 16 December 1913, no. M-02103, Pressing and Confidential, FO 371/1679 file 6269/56806, states that Grey 'would prefer the American Admiral at Tampico to be the Senior Officer present in the event of a landing being considered necessary'.

was possible to give Page some indication that Carden would be proceeding to Brazil in the near future. How far, if at all, this represented a departure from his original intention to retain Carden in Mexico until August 1914 remains uncertain, for Page's report to Washington was 'leaked' to the press by a member of the cabinet, and the welcome it received made it impossible to do more than recall Carden for consultations. At any rate, the Japanese ambassador in London was told officially on 23 January that Carden would be returning to his post as originally intended, and this in the event he did. Spring-Rice later told Grey that he had said to Bryan 'that the attitude of the American press had made it impossible to recall Sir L. Carden but that he was going home to report as soon as possible'.[1]

Grey had sent to Hohler, then on leave in England, and asked him once more to take charge of the legation in Carden's brief absence.

I protested vigorously, but he retaliated by using most flattering language [Hohler records]. He declared I had rendered very valuable services in Mexico, and that by going out again I should be putting H.M.G. under a great obligation. He assured me I should not be kept there for more than two months. When the Secretary of State talks in this way there is nothing to be done.[2]

Almost simultaneously, Lind, finally permitted to leave Mexico, had a last meeting with President Wilson at Pass Christian.[3] The first week in January thus marks the end of the phase of Anglo-American conflict over Huerta, and the opening of the debate about the Constitutionalists. Since this merged with the general conflict of wartime diplomacy, as German commercial and strategic interests became increasingly involved, it marks also the end of the period that has a unity of its own.[4]

Some of the participants still had a part to play in the new phase.

---

[1] *The World*, Tuesday, 6 January 1914. It was Wilson's Secretary of the Interior, Franklin K. Lane, who revealed that Page had been informed confidentially that Carden was to be transferred (Baker, *Woodrow Wilson, Life and Letters*, vol. IV (1932), p. 298). Grey–Sir C. Greene, 23 January 1914, no. 15, *cit. sup.* p. 219. Spring-Rice–Grey, 31 January 1913, Telegram Private and Secret. Grey Papers.
[2] Hohler, *Diplomatic Petrel* (1942), p. 188.   [3] *The World*, Monday, 5 January 1914.
[4] Tuchman, *The Zimmermann Telegram* (1959).

On the British side, Carden had an unhappy fate. Grey showed his confidence in him by sending him back to Mexico, where he was still minister at the time of the Vera Cruz landings. When his year expired and he was finally recalled in August 1914, the war-time freeze of diplomatic promotion, due to the displacement of senior men from the Central Powers, had begun and the post in Brazil could not be vacated. He retired, a disappointed man, victim of what then seemed an injustice and one which many believed contributed to his death in October 1915.[1] Hohler remained in Mexico much longer than two months, in fact, until 1917. Having earned his niche in history on a world scale by securing the crucial Mexican copy of the Zimmermann telegram for British Naval Intelligence, he was transferred to Washington in time to see how his action contributed to America's entry into the Great War. He was knighted for his subsequent services, and died in 1946.[2] Spring-Rice, who remained in Washington through-out the war, was also very involved in Mexican affairs, while Cowdray remained a political force in Mexico until the sale of the Aguila Company in 1919, and a political force in Great Britain until his death in 1927.

On the American side, Nelson O'Shaughnessy remained until the customs house was taken at Vera Cruz, and he was given his passports. William Bayard Hale remained to conduct negotiations with the Constitutionalists, but was no more successful than Lind had been with Huerta. The fates of Doheny and Pierce have already been mentioned. Dearing became Assistant Secretary of State under Harding and Josephus Daniels became ambassador to Mexico under Roosevelt.

Huerta himself died a death as mysterious as that of Madero, following a long and dubiously legal incarceration in a Texas jail.[3] Most of his supporters went into exile for more than fifteen years before being allowed to return (like Félix Díaz in 1940) to the new Mexico that finally emerged from the years of turmoil.

---

[1] *The Times*, Monday, 18 October 1915, *cit. sup.*

[2] Hohler was the 'Mr. H' of Tuchman, pp. 101–2 and 157–8. His autobiography gives further details of his career up to 1918; details thereafter from *Who Was Who*.

[3] George J. Rausch, Jr., 'The Exile and Death of Victoriano Huerta', *Hispanic American Historical Review*, XLII (May 1962), p. 133.

CONCLUSION

It is easy to see Díaz in terms of extremes, either as he was seen by the *científicos* or as he has more recently been represented by the neomarxists.[1] For once, the truth does seem to be more vague and more complex. He was neither a superman nor a bandit, but an able ruler within the strict limitations of the military mind, and he was favoured by good luck and good fortune in the period and the country in which he ruled. Temporary exhaustion with war and politics facilitated a policy of 'the stick'; the natural resources of Mexico paid for the bread. However badly the resources were abused, there was still more left over than in many parts of the world. In an atmosphere of euphoria in which politicians so often dwell, and which leads them to attribute good luck to good management, the *científicos* drew up a doctrine of economic development by foreign investment which was as modern in appearance, and, no doubt, as effective in operation as its twentieth-century parallels, since in neither case has the money been available to make doctrinaire ambitions fully real.

Nineteenth-century man's situation was the more difficult in that tradition as yet prohibited the full exploitation of a country's taxation resources. These resources have been explored more fully under the pressure of war. On the other hand, for nineteenth-century man there were fewer inhibitions on seeking money where it could be found. The distinction between London, Paris and New York was not one of ideology, and it was not one that had a great deal of importance outside Latin America. The choice for Mexico to select European sources was a political one, due to fears of the relentless pressure of the United States which were something more than atavistic. The Mexican government made a deliberate effort to provide a counterpoise through British finance to American political influence, in short, and, as we have seen, by 1910 they had been more successful than is generally recognized.

[1] Both these views diverge from the views of the 'Wilson school' exemplified, *inter alia*, by: Hendrick, *The Life and Letters of Walter H. Page* (1924); Baker, *Woodrow Wilson, Life and Letters* (1932), vol. IV; and the memoirs of Josephus Daniels and Franklin K. Lane.

Conclusion

The curious thing is that this high level of British investment was not rewarded by a corresponding increase in British exports to Mexico. This might seem natural enough in the smaller Central American republics, where investment was largely in government securities. It was not so in Mexico, which was seen for industrial and commercial investment as being similar, if not superior, in potential to Argentina, Chile and Uruguay. The question therefore arises, and is particularly relevant today, whether foreign investment, or its modern equivalent the aid programme, really does further economic development, rather than hinder it.[1]

Dependence on foreign investment, however, poses the dilemma of choice between the foreigner and the citizen. Study of the resulting tensions in other areas appears to place the problem of corruption in the Mexico of the *científicos* in a more enduring setting. No doubt pressure from interests had much to do with the passage of the Mining Law of 1884, and United States mining and oil investors benefited from it. But the favoured position of Cowdray rested in quite another sense on the will of Díaz himself. It was coincidentally insured against the consequences of revolution by being related to a more enduring tradition than modern finance capitalism, but this was as much an accidental consequence of the political situation as the benefits received by his opponents.

However powerful Díaz might be, he could not wholly overcome the dictates of geography. Mexico would be a great power to her neighbours but for the existence of the United States. To the Americans the Caribbean had to be American for strategic reasons, but to the Mexicans it was Mexican for sentimental ones. The loss of prestige sustained by Díaz in his last years stemmed in large part from affronted nationalism. It was a self-defeating phenomenon, for its exercise created the opposition in the United States which nullified it. It is less surprising that the United States press and public should have expected the Mexicans to turn for aid to Japan than that they did not in fact do so. These too are signs of the general decay of the régime, owing to age, which was so patent to all foreign observers not bedazzled by the show of the centenary celebrations.

[1] Cf. Boris Goldenberg, *The Cuban Revolution and Latin America* (London, 1965).

Yet it appears that the revolution—that upwelling of affronted patriotism—was not foreseen, even by British observers who saw the decay. This seems surprising, especially in the perspective of the long series of Latin American revolutions which, since 1891, had been able to count on American sympathy, aid, and even active interposition. Military rule does not of itself impart legitimacy. The fact that a military ruler has lasted for thirty-five years is no guarantee that he will last a thirty-sixth. It necessitated only a very mild dissatisfaction among Americans on the frontier to enable a revolution to succeed. That the movement which did succeed was the one headed by Madero, and that it succeeded when it did, is, however, initially to be ascribed to the purity of its intentions and its leader's utter detachment from the realities of force which would have destroyed the hopes of many lesser men.

The United States official response to the Madero revolution exhibits the principal features characteristic of such movements in the Caribbean area. United States concern was voiced under the Roosevelt corollary. United States agents active in its promotion were detected in the lobby for arms importation and recognition. United States strength between the two was exerted to preclude other foreign influences. At the same time, its inconsistency illumines the handicaps which a conscientious nation inflicts on its decision-makers. Taft was foremost in the peace movement of the early years of the century—a movement for which the constitutional structure and conventional legalism of the American system made its leaders natural recruits. Under Taft this legalism became an obstacle to the realization of its own intentions owing to the clash between his natural impulse towards peace and his personal regard for the obligation to uphold the law as it stood. This became true also for the President's entourage. While their policy embodied philanthropy, it also exhibited something of its lack of humanity. When they sought to live by legal precepts, they became slaves to a system of law which had no basis and no sanction. Yet they did these things with idealism. In these terms perhaps Taft deserves more sympathy from historians than he gets. With allowances for normal human irritation, he emerges from the Mexican story as a consistent, sensible but unimaginative man of peace. If at times he felt the urge to violence, he restrained that urge, and he restrained the wilder spirits in and around the administration.

He stands, however, less in need of revitalization as a personality than his ambassador. Henry Lane Wilson was much more complex than the caricature drawn in the conventional mythology. There, the unpredictable and arbitrary behaviour of the ambassador has been attributed to his intemperance. Though to understand is not necessarily to forgive, it must be said that there was more to it than that. His excesses, whatever their nature, were related to a common centre of psychological disturbance. The picture, moreover, is not just one of a man detached from reality, but of a man becoming detached, because it was in the interests of others to detach him. The personality problem must be fairly related to the struggle for livelihood of a partisan appointee, at a time of profound change in his own country.

Others were not exempt from similar pressures. One can compare the detachment from reality of those Mexicans near to Díaz. It will give insight into the psychology of those long habituated to living under a dictatorship. One can compare, for example, the conduct of de la Barra as ambassador in Washington. In it one sees clearly his inability to understand the real meaning of democratic government, and is better prepared for its appearance in his role at the fall of Madero and the rise of Huerta. The same habit coloured the views of others, notably Manuel Calero, Querido Moheno, Gustavo Madero and Pedro Lascuráin, but it did so in widely differing ways.

The habit of autocracy even deceived the Mexican government collectively. They believed that, when they had the support of the United States government, they could call upon the immediate action of the executive power to which they themselves were habituated. In their disillusionment they found that they lost both the action and the sympathy which they might otherwise have commanded. Similarly, the habit of obedience blinded them to the real merit of the revolutionaries, their puritanical self-restraint and self-discipline in the early stages of the revolution, which was interpreted as weakness.

Conclusion

On the other hand, on the United States side of the frontier there were many who were prepared to take the views of the Mexican government as being in some way authoritative, separate from the real reliability of that government as a tainted witness. This too is not an unusual phenomenon, but this sort of double standard, however much of a relief to the democratic mind in a hostile world, is a dangerous measure of the real intentions of an autocracy. The revolutionaries that mattered were not the anarchists and out-of-work film actors from Upper California in search of publicity, but the peasants who captured their weapons from the mines and enforced the drink regulations during their stay.

The Madero revolution, forming as it does the base-line for all subsequent revolutionary movements, illustrates three continuing trends in State Department and Administration thinking which were to be characteristic of the whole period.

In the mobilization of 8 March 1911 the United States government automatically took refuge in the claim that they were acting under the pressure of European governments to forestall European intervention. There was no danger of any such move. But the disturbances in Mexico were automatically and crudely seen in terms of the Anglo-German blockade of Venezuela, despite the enormous physical and geopolitical differences between the two countries; to this extent the Taft administration acted less as the upholder of the Roosevelt corollary than as its prisoner.

There was some indication that territorial extension from the Gadsden strip into Baja California operated as a motive for Henry Lane Wilson's pressure for that mobilization. But both Wilson and the State Department disclaimed personal predilection for such a policy, the blame for the initiative being laid squarely on the other element of the diplomatic partnership. There can be no doubt that it was in everybody's mind. Taft once laid a curious charge against Bryan that he wanted to acquire Baja California, and the doctrinal claims of Henry Cabot Lodge on Magdalena Bay suggest that such an act of annexation was throughout these years one of the repressed motivations of United States policy-makers. Was it a factor in persuading Woodrow Wilson to order the pursuit and punishment of Pancho Villa?

Conclusion

In the support of Washington for de la Barra there was total failure to realize that the man on the losing side in the war of nationalisms in Mexico would always be the man with *gringo* support. Henry Lane Wilson saw this to some small extent. But he failed to draw the correct conclusion, that whoever became President in Mexico would inevitably be drawn into an anti-American position. To the extent that this was true, the best that the United States could hope for was a President who was not basically hostile; in other words, Madero, not Huerta.[1]

Thirdly, in their several reactions to the British landing from H.M.S. *Shearwater*, to the siege and capture of Agua Prieta and of Ciudad Juárez, the Taft administration—as did the Wilson administration that followed it—showed consistent reluctance to accept the consequences of civil disorder. They persisted in treating it as a childish habit which would disappear when the Mexican government was sternly reproved. This approach was dangerous and self-defeating. With Ambassador Wilson it led to the attempt of Cowdray and Bryce to secure his recall. British diplomatists and businessmen before them had realized the dangers sharply, and they gave proof of their understanding in the most decisive way, by rescuing Díaz from the city after his fall.

Madero was then bound by his own desire for democratic government to concur in the establishment of an interim government to hold elections. But, by definition, an interim government was a government in which the forces of the old dictatorship had sufficient foothold to fight for survival. It is not necessary to see de la Barra, as President, as a designing villain. He had not yet had sufficient provocation. It was enough that he was an able diplomatist who wished to be President and to secure a reputation in the only way he knew, by establishing peace and order. He therefore yielded to the army the usual tribute of a 'strong' policy.

The army had never been treated as insignificant under Díaz, whatever its fighting abilities, and politically its strength was overwhelming. The Maderistas in the interim cabinet were not well

[1] Due perhaps to their exactness in anticipating the United States reaction; compare the Japanese attitude towards Huerta after January 1914, when, under the influence of the Californian Land Act Crisis, they resorted to their favoured strategy of the 'double line'. Documents in FO 371/2033.

placed to resist this trend. They were well meaning, but a lifetime in opposition had made them cranky and unstable. Conservative resistance was only to be expected to their attempts to build up a new political machine, and the sole constitutional remedy was to maintain unity. The split in the revolutionary party, if it did nothing else, convinced the agrarian radicals that they had nothing more to hope for from the new government. In any case they did not give it a chance. For that, many of them were to pay the highest penalty, including Zapata himself.

Most observers were fully able to comprehend the significance of the agrarian discontent. It was perfectly apparent to the British diplomatists, and it was understood by Henry Lane Wilson as well as by Woodrow Wilson. They may not have heard of Mexican precedents but they had heard, for example, of Ireland. What is more easily forgotten is that they were as divided as British Liberals and Unionists as to what ought to be done about it. Moderate reform in 1911 might have diverted the current of revolutionary feeling into productive channels. By 1913, when the means to achieve it had been worked out, it was too late. The tragedy of the policy of Woodrow Wilson was that it was always concerned with providing the correct solutions to the problems of two years before.[1]

It was an impossible task, for it merely wasted the time of the Mexicans who had to solve them for themselves in their own way. Worse still, it enabled Wilson to be drawn by the domestic will-o'-the-wisp of the money power. It was not that which perpetuated Mexico's agrarian problems. The exacerbation of the agrarian situation and foreign domination of business were both essential to the régime of Díaz. They supported the régime and the régime supported them. Hard as the struggle between British and American interests was, it did not really affect much of Mexico. A large part of the country was still based on a subsistence economy and upsets in the modern sector, however large, were of little account there. With the disappearance of the régime the system to which it had given birth disappeared: the gold standard, the

---

[1] In 1916 Wilson justified his following his own inclination on the ground that he could obtain no accurate information from Mexico.

banking system and the prestige. Millions died of hunger and of disease. But the artifacts of the régime remained: the railway track and roadbed, the docks and harbours, the generating plants, despite accidental and deliberate damage at the hands of the Constitutionalists.[1] Otherwise a civilized respect for *pacíficos* was retained. The oil wells that had sprung up in the midst of chaos continued to produce. When Mexico was in the grip of *la Tormenta*, Mexican oil output continued to rise, reaching a peak in the first year of Obregón. It was able to fuel much of the first great motorized war in history.[2] Oil was too fragile an industry to be left to the coarse methods of a Henry Clay Pierce, and too important to be endangered by nationalism. It was taken into the international system, and so lifted out of domestic politics, until a new and stronger state could assert its claims to it.

This is not to say that it was not significant that Madero supported the extension of United States investment, while at the same time approving of Cowdray's efforts to dislodge Waters Pierce from its stranglehold on the Mexican domestic market. The two positions were not incompatible with the best interests of Mexico, and Madero was more far-seeing in his acceptance of international co-operation than he perhaps realized.

In a situation where hostility forms so basic a part of the pattern, a tolerant interpretation of human frailty is not only commendable but also rewarding. Businessmen, as private citizens, will have interests different from those of their governments, and governments will always be concerned lest they seek to develop political power. Those who claim the monopoly of power are jealous of any who seek to challenge it. Like other human beings, both learn from experience, and the participants in the Mexican situation were no exception. For example, the Taft administration had learnt much by the time that Madero was challenged by

---

[1] By 1916 the toll of trucks on the Mexican railways had been so heavy as to bring non-military services almost to a standstill. But the track and roadbed were for the most part intact. It must be remembered that the great lines over the northern deserts were not subject to the same hazards of climate that had left Lord Cowdray no option but to rebuild the Tehuantepec railway from the beginning.

[2] In the peak year, 1921, Mexico produced 193 million barrels, and this rate did not fall below 100 million until 1926 (Cline, *The United States and Mexico* (1963), p. 418).

Orozco, and, despite their inertia, Taft and Knox were prepared to agree to, and to further, provisions designed to help the Mexican government. This departure was both beneficial and improbable in the context of the unwavering solidity of their general policy. Then again, businessmen may dislike one another, and so may diplomatists. But the incompatibility of Wilson and Stronge does not necessarily imply that one was right and the other wrong in their estimates of the Madero government's chances of survival. One had a much better chance to 'make good' on his predictions than the other.

Nowhere does tolerant interpretation become more important than in the assessment of the *Decena Trágica*, but that is precisely where it generally has been most wanting. If here the effects of shellfire on the capacity to think coolly and rationally seem to be overstressed, it is because it seems more probable that the confusion which prevailed in these days of disorder, looting, rumour and bloodshed has caused its own understatement than overstatement.

In the Latin American context, of course, the *Decena Trágica*, extreme as it was, is not entirely unexpected, though in the completeness of the disillusion and betrayal of the Díaz faction it perhaps goes further than most such incidents. If diplomatists did believe that Díaz held the city, then it followed that by the rules of the game Madero was bound to resign. As he did not, they should have changed their minds when the true facts became known, but it was in the interests of several people to see they did not.

Here we have tried to give more prominence to the misdeeds of de la Barra and Lascuráin than has traditionally been the case, always with the aim of tracing the relationships between Stronge and Wilson. We have seen how Stronge independently pursued the line that what was needed was the resignation of the President, and seen that it stopped short at the resumption of firing, when Huerta finally resolved to make his bid for power. Ambassador Wilson we have not sought to judge again. The most depressing thing about his role, it seems, was that he genuinely believed that two men for whom good faith did not run outside their own immediate entourages, and probably not even there, could be bound by the mere act of placing their names on a piece of paper to live together in peace and harmony. A clear derivation from the prevailing nineteenth-century American concept of constitutionalism, this belief places the ambassador in ironic opposition to his namesake the President.

Paradoxically, the extraneous circumstances of the death of Madero and the vengeance of the *porfiristas* caused President and ambassador to exchange roles. The transition of power from Madero to Huerta was constitutional enough. What was wrong with it was that it was not peaceful, though in that respect it was ethically neutral within the norms of the society in which it took place.[1] In operating within these, the ambassador it was who was conforming to his environment; the President the man who sought to ignore it—and who in the long term was conspicuously and ridiculously unsuccessful. Of paramount importance was the fact that the British decision to recognize Huerta was taken in the context of traditional policy, and, in its independence, conformed to the customary obligations and privileges of a state in international law. Its departure from the domestic rule that recognition was not formally accorded to provisional régimes is fully explained within the limitations imposed by an exception made two years previously. It can be, and has been, established that in so far as the wishes of financial interests were expressed it was on the request of the officials, and the actions of the latter naturally took place in the light of the expected consequences to the former. There was nothing sinister about this. Due allowance must also be given to the success of de la Barra's diplomatic calculations, a classic instance of the successful blackmail of a great power by a small one. It admirably illustrates the thesis that, in considerations of power, the threat actually uses less more effectively than the employment.[2]

This consideration is equally applicable to the development of United States policy under the new Democratic administration.

---

[1] An excellent compact discussion of the normative and other roles of Latin American constitutions may be found in Martin C. Needler, *Latin American Politics in Perspective* (Princeton, N.J., 1963), pp. 124 ff.

[2] Daniel Cosío Villegas, *American Extremes* (Austin, Texas, 1964), pp. 28 ff., contains a discussion of the paradox of United States dependence on Latin America.

Conclusion

At its inauguration, this was an unknown quantity; unknown because unformed. It found its first expression in traditional generalities. The impression of continuity, as we have seen, was indeed the most forcible it could give, and that it was lost so speedily was more due to the side-effects of the demolition of the State Department machine and prime concentration, where concentration was employed, on matters of internal policy.[1]

Bryan's policy was one of peace. But Knox's policy was one of peace too. The Bryan policy differed in its revulsion from finance capital, an attitude then already a historical survival from the days of the free-silver campaign. Since then the New Nationalism had provided the justification and indeed the means for government to resume the first authority in the state.[2] Still, the assessment of 'dollar diplomacy' as a policy is biased by the suspicion that it was less the use of capital by government than the use of government by capital. This is not a distinction which it is profitable to make. It was both the one and the other. In the continuing trend of the expansion of the Western capital market it is hard to say which appeared the more ridiculous: the insistence of the Taft administration in participating in the Chinese Loan, or the insistence of the Wilson administration in withdrawing from it, while at the same time permitting the continuation on a large scale of State Department pressure for the economic and political subordination of Nicaragua to the United States.[3] The year 1913 alone was to show, despite hesitation in Nicaragua, the continuation of this trend in Colombia, Ecuador and Costa Rica, and every move that the Wilson administration made to get out of their moral difficulties only increased the extent to which American capital penetrated the Western hemisphere.

This resulted from the attempt to exclude European capital, not because it was European, but because it was capital. But the United States government could only take the decision to try to

---

[1] Bryan's insistence on continuing his lifelong custom of accepting invitations to speak on the Chautauqua circuit in return for fees caused much embarrassment to members of the administration.

[2] It should be said by way of qualification that it was not in a position to exercise it as early as the 1907 slump.

[3] The reader will recall the impressions of Foreign Office officials on this score.

exclude European capital because its power to initiate policy in external relations was absolute. It could not exclude its own capital, nor could it direct it in to fill the gap. It is not certain that it would have if it could, furthermore, since any real attempt to replace foreign investment on Latin America would have strengthened the pressure from investments at home, and that was just what the New Freedom sought to avoid.[1] Even at that, a standard of judgement was applied to Cowdray's relations with his government which was not applied to similar relations in the United States between business and Wilson's own government. Cowdray was judged as a Republican, not as a foreigner.

Of course, allowances must be made for Wilson's inexperience in foreign affairs. All the information he had to go on was vague. Much of it was tendentious.[2] It was reasonable, if dangerous, to develop an emotional rejection of Huerta. But given the criteria even of contemporary United States government, it was unreasonable to place real confidence in the Constitutionalists. In the long run, after two years of observation, among all the Constitutionalist factions, Wilson chose to recognize the least democratic.[3] Lacking a yardstick in judging Latin American affairs, he had taken the view that they should be made to conform in outward appearance to the standards laid down by the United States.

Now if this was applicable to political measurements, it had also to be applicable to economic ones, it seemed. The confusion here was in fact easier, for though Mexico had lost its appearance of political constitutionalism, it had not at the same time lost its simulacrum of being a state in the process of achieving a 'modern' economy. And Wilson, as he distrusted the power of finance, by definition had accepted its power as a fact, and desired to make use

[1] Other outlets were not available as early as 1914, but due weight must be given to Moore's contention that the United States could still have absorbed more.

[2] See note on p. 291 above.

[3] The yardstick of this is his acceptance of Villa at his face value as the 'sword of the revolution' who realized his own limitations and would leave politics to the professionals. The British, even before the Benton case, felt this view to be incompatible with the murder by him of an accredited envoy from Félix Díaz. When Bryan asserted to Hohler on his visit to Washington in February that the envoy was unwelcome and Villa had every right to 'kick him out', the British diplomatist replied: 'But hardly into the next world.' FO 371/2033.

of it for his own ends. It was a dangerous fallacy. Dangerous, not because the power of finance did not exist, but because, to operate effectively, it demanded the prerequisite of belief. Huerta did not believe in the power of finance, and so was not alarmed. Furthermore, there came to his rescue the essential strength of Mexico's backward economy: the ability of the traditional sector to absorb, though at some cost in civil disorder, those displaced from the modern sector, and the capacity of the economy to 'slough off' the modern sector and still survive. In addition, in Mexico, as in the United States, the resources of taxation had as yet scarcely been appreciated, and as the War came to develop the latter, so the Revolution developed the former.

The pressure of 'financial starvation'[1] was indirectly harmful to European countries dealing with Mexico. It was for this reason that in July 1913 the first British initiative for United States recognition was made. In the wake of the rejection of the Chinese Loan advantages, it was a reasonable enough inquiry, and it casts a harsh light on the essential reluctance of the human mind to accept simple and favourable explanations that the existence of an initiative was sufficient in itself to raise on both sides suspicions of double-dealing.

But there was more to it than that. President Wilson was silent, secretive and detached from the normal incidental contact of diplomacy. Walter Hines Page was excitable, misled by superficial resemblances, and given to reporting his own statements at length where he should have devoted the same time and energy to representing to his government an accurate picture of what was going on in Britain. John Lind was a racialist, bitter and unhappy in exile, with the alien's suspicion that those about him, whom he does not understand, are making fun of him. Bryan was a sincere man but he was wrong. All meant well, but their individual peculiarities contributed their own measure to the dispute. And the Mexicans too, and the British, were individuals, with their share—sometimes more than their share—of individual eccentricities and idiosyncrasies.

[1] Cradock–Admiralty, 3 December 1913, unnumbered, with Admiralty–Nicolson, 1 January 1914, M-02188/13. FO 371/2025 file 91/296.

Conclusion

It is the individual peculiarities which the formulae of diplomatic intercourse are designed to reduce to a minimum. By ignoring the formulae the United States government opted to attempt to form policy in the most unfavourable circumstances it could select. They nevertheless retained the assumption that others would still follow their initiative. As Mrs O'Shaughnessy rightly observed, Huerta, for one, could see no good reason why he should do so.[1] Understanding of this makes Stronge's—otherwise totally irrational—yielding to American pressure that he act as messenger somewhat clearer. Above all, it explains the role of Sir Lionel Carden.

The criterion for separating views on this issue is the degree to which the contestants equated power and force. To Huerta they were synonymous. To Woodrow Wilson, they were sufficiently so for him to reject the association with revulsion. Hence his reaction to the realization of a desire to exercise power, for a certain purpose, in Mexico was to turn to that 'non-violent' energy which fascinated him in domestic politics. He made use of financial starvation or, as we should now term it, sanctions. Then as now they damaged the social order in the target country quite extensively, but on the whole increased, rather than decreased, resistance among those political leaders for whose power Wilson was in competition.

But if he did not make use of military force at first it was at least largely because he realized, as Taft had before him, that he did not have it in his power to use. He had all the customary notions of his day about patriotism, racial superiority, and the duty of the great powers to act as policemen which in recent times historians have, rather unfairly, attempted to shuffle off onto Theodore Roosevelt.[2] The proposition that he might by judicious negotiation make use of the arms and lives of the Constitutionalists did not strike him with any sense of shame; at least, not in 1913. Fortified by the arrogance of time and distance he did not hesitate to order United States troops into action at

[1] O'Shaughnessy, *A Diplomat's Wife in Mexico*, p. 320.
[2] These were not a personal attribute in either case, but the small change of what passed for political thought of the day.

Tampico. His response, if current accounts are true, was instant and without the assurances that the action would be bloodless.[1]

It was not bloodless. The effect on the President was immediate, and perhaps permanent. Because he had wrongly wasted men's lives in a petty and unsuccessful endeavour, the President found himself psychologically debarred from venturing them even in the cause of freedom. In 1917, as in 1914, he found himself leading his country to war to uphold his word, and taking refuge in the meaningless phrases of Fourth of July rhetoric.[2] Even then, it seems, the President showed no hostility to war as such, only to deaths incurred *at his order*. However, this degree of conscience alone is enough to secure him an honoured place in the catalogue of rulers of the twentieth century.

But against this we must set that arrogance: the assumption of right. For the President was only as efficient as his sources of information, and the State Department knew its job so badly that it was incapable of producing an authoritative statement of the meaning of recognition in diplomatic practice other than that presented by John Bassett Moore. It is far from surprising that Moore took the earliest opportunity of escaping from the position of Cassandra. He had warned the administration that if foreign governments were weary of being used as shields, they were unlikely to view with favour an attempt to use them as spears. The administration had refused to listen.

It is not necessary, and not entirely fair, to summarize again the long list of erroneous assumptions, erratic actions and irritations created by these conditions. The last phase of open conflict stems from what went before, and merely reinforces and accentuates the diplomatic lessons to the point at which they become memorable and significant at a world level. To the significance of these, and their long-term effects, we must now turn.

That the crisis does have an intrinsic significance is generally agreed, within the general context of the last months before the

---

[1] Tuchman, *The Zimmermann Telegram*, pp. 49–50.

[2] Professor Link, in *Woodrow Wilson and the Progressive Era* ,pp. 281–2, places a more charitable interpretation on the speech of 2 April 1917, part of which he quotes. But see also Blum, *Woodrow Wilson and the Politics of Morality* (1956), pp. 130–1.

Great War. Yet, as von Hintze—one of the most perceptive observers of the time—wrote, it showed, above all, that 'the Anglo-American connection is not decided in Mexico',[1] and it proved, if it proved anything, that Anglo-American co-operation was already a reality. But it was assumed in the United States that it went further than this, and demonstrated to the stiff-necked British that in a quarrel with them within their own sphere of influence they would have to yield. But this had already been decided.[2] Nowadays many might wish otherwise, for hegemony has brought its own problems.

European influence in Latin America as a whole was not at stake, and hence its withdrawal was not a consequence of the dispute. Politically it was dormant only as long as the United States wished, and economically it revived in the 1920s as the almost automatic consequence of the continuing expansion of the Latin American economies.

But the enunciation of the principle of non-recognition was left as a permanent element in the foreign policy of a Great Power. It was not followed, admittedly, by great consistency in application, even by Wilson himself, whose enemies noted that he lost no time in recognizing the military government that overthrew President Billinghurst in Peru in February 1914.[3] It was abandoned in the years of the Republican ascendancy. But as revolutionary changes in the outside world came increasingly to develop a basis inimical to the United States—though not necessarily to its ideal—their government found itself once more turning to non-recognition as a device to enforce its views on good government on other countries. The device proved consistently unsatisfactory, and, even in the closest proximity to the limits of the United States, never had the desired effect without the backing of more forcible measures. In some ways it still deludes the present generation of policy-makers, suffering, ironically, from the con-

[1] Hintze–Bethmann-Hollweg, 16 December 1913, no. A 107. GFM 12/17 f. A 192.
[2] Campbell, *Great Britain and the United States*, pp. 191–2.
[3] Lawrence, *The True Story of Woodrow Wilson* (1924), p. 99. The parallel was immediately recognized in the Foreign Office. They had become accustomed to parallels there, in view of the repeated American allusions to the non-recognition of the Serbian coup of 1903 by the British government of the day. See minute by Spicer on Spring-Rice–Grey, 22 January 1914, no. 13 Confidential. FO 371/2034 file 5202.

sequences of Wilson's belief in his own success in excluding foreign influences.[1]

It was, of course, used for the best of motives, and within the respectable tradition pioneered as early as 1907 by the Central American agreement of that year. But it was among the Latin American countries that the first measures were eventually taken to declare it an inadmissible interference under international law. The responsibility for this reversal must rest largely on the unfortunate consequences of its application in Mexico: financial starvation, exacerbating the revolutionary temper by its burden on the lower classes; the arming of the Constitutionalists, which encouraged a devastating civil war; and armed intervention itself, to end all hope that non-recognition might be regarded as being a safe alternative to war.

The Wilson doctrine, as far as it referred to emancipation of the Latin American countries from foreign financial controls, did, on the other hand, mark an important step in the development of Great Power responsibility for the welfare of the smaller nations. It was a marked advance in theory to proceed from a duty to discipline to a duty to educate. Unfortunately the two concepts are not always distinct in the public mind. Wilson proposed, in any case, education without investment in educational materials, a defect in his scheme which the idealist Bryan saw and attempted to rectify. His scheme of finance without political controls foreshadowed the most enlightened aid schemes of our own age, for which, perhaps, the time was not yet ripe. But it went no further; like them, the political advantage was its progenitor, and its features can be discerned in its offspring.

Yet as far as the exclusion of non-American financial interests was concerned, the Wilson doctrine, which we have shown to be logically rooted in that of his predecessors, was far from being the rejection of dollar diplomacy—it was dollar diplomacy, as surely as was the policy of 'financial starvation'. In practice it became a further stage in the successful efforts of American business to

---

[1] Compare the response of President Kennedy to the Guatemalan and Ecuadorian coups of 1963, in which he was moved to recognition by considerations of expediency, with his general restatement of the Wilsonian position (Edwin Lieuwen, *Generals versus Presidents* (London, 1964), p. 100).

displace their European rivals, but it covered their efforts with the mantle of moral rectitude.

In all these ways, therefore, Wilson's policy accelerated the trend towards hegemony, failing to recognize the landmarks as they were passed. Fifty years later the resulting imbalance in Latin America has reached the point at which the dangerous tensions between citizens and their own governments find an easy outlet in attacks on the United States. This in the context of the habit of violence and the customs of revolutionary politics makes for uneasy relationships, and is a perennial source of danger to the economic growth currently seen as the first priority in the area. Americans are ill at ease in the Latin American political atmosphere. They are strongly conditioned to regard their own system as the inevitable outcome of political maturity, and the countries which have now still to share it as being bound in the future to achieve it.[1]

Worse still, since revolutions are essentially dramatic, they lend themselves to theatrical interpretation. They are, more easily than most political conflicts, and that is easily enough, seen in terms of ideal good and indefensible bad. But the typical revolutionary tradition can be represented as a series of intermittent periods of the unusual; the normal revolutionary situation being dynamic, not static.

In the Mexican Revolution, Madero was already a conservative when he came to power; that we can accept. But Huerta, in one sense undoubtedly a throwback to the *caudillismo* of Díaz, was in another a man anticipating the repressive phase of the intolerant Carranza or the counter-revolution of Obregón. Neither Republican nor Democrat in the United States, far removed as that country already was from its primeval 'revolutionary' fervour, really sympathized with the basic demands of the men who fought in Mexico. Taft wanted to remain in the days of Díaz; Wilson in the days of Madero. But at least in being removed from the revolutionary myth, their policy was not distorted by it. They saw the Mexican affair, not as a Revolution, but as a series of

---

[1] Implicit in the assumptions of, for example, Gabriel A. Almond and James S. Coleman, *The Politics of the Developing Areas* (Princeton, N.J., 1960).

revolutions. Had they done otherwise, it would not have been possible for it to assume the status of a Revolution, for the moral precepts inculcated by history tend to be inversely proportional to its accuracy.

In his desire for a moral world, with the United States in the van of the army of morality, Wilson was indeed not so far removed from Taft as he liked to think. What distinguished him was the personal feeling he brought to the matter. Wilson transformed his irritating ignorance of the conditions which gave rise to the counter-revolution into a personal vendetta against Huerta.[1] It is hard to imagine Taft doing the same. But his ignorance was no less great, and those who seem to feel it is necessary to find special arguments to justify the study of Latin American (rather than European or North American) history, politics or society might care to reflect on the implications of the fact that he was the first President of the United States to find himself face to face with what was to prove to be the main preoccupation of United States policy in the twentieth century.

For the Mexican Revolution, even in its first stages, was very much a twentieth-century affair. Even before 1914 wireless, telegraph, aircraft, motor-cars, telephone, electric power and the machine gun had all played their part, and in the ideological field the human mind operated in an atmosphere of guerrilla warfare, Great Power rivalry, socialism, poverty and race hatred. At the same time, of course, it was a distinctively Latin American upheaval. It was notable for the outstanding calibre of its participants, its legalism, its self-consciousness and devotion to international rights and duties, and its rhetoric. The characteristic role of the government in the national economy; the place of the leader, the chivalry and the casual violence of the conflict, all gave it a distinctive flavour. But, when all is said and done, in these few years other people and powers could have learnt much from it that they failed to learn, and have still to learn; and perhaps only in Latin America could they have learnt it so well.

For these reasons, the failure of the United States to accept the lessons it offered must be accounted remarkable. Threats were

[1] Blum, p. 36.

Conclusion

made, unbacked by either the will or the ability to make them good—and they failed. Information was gathered wholesale, but subjected to little consideration or thought. Vital decisions were forced by the accidents of the press. Very real personal feelings were ignored, and sensitive negotiations conducted in a glare of publicity. It was little wonder that the United States policy suffered in consequence.

In the circumstances, the success of the non-moral British policy must be assessed in terms of its limited objectives, the survival of its interests. It was, therefore, strikingly successful.

But on the British side, too, there were lessons to be learned, and they were not learned. Many of them were the same lessons. Others were peculiar to the British system. The Foreign Office, working with amazing coherence born of the discipline of a shared educational code, collected and interpreted information with effectiveness and speed. But the coherence of the machine did not mean that its parts were fully interchangeable. The spirit that had led to the appointment of the Marquess of Dufferin and Ava to Paris in 1892 was still at work when Carden was sent to replace Stronge in 1913.[1]

The American policy had the weaknesses of publicity, the British those of secrecy. The suspicion that Whitehall was continually engaged in a calculating plot to encircle the United States in the Caribbean was strengthened, if not created, by it. It was not so, as Page eventually realized, for the very lack of predesign in British policy of which, on moral grounds, he so much disapproved was incompatible with its having a real existence.[2] Even his President must occasionally have realized that other countries could not be expected to wait forever for the State Department to sort itself out. But as it happens, the last laugh was against the Foreign Office. Secrecy was maintained, yes, but at the price that for fifty years the United States version of the conflict was maintained unchallenged and unchallengeable.

This might not have been so serious had it not been for the accusations of bad faith levelled against so many of the partici-

[1] Sir Harold Nicolson, *Helen's Tower* (London, 1937), pp. 227 ff.
[2] Hendrick, p. 184.

pants; accusations which stood unrefuted, when, as Sir Arthur Nicolson himself wrote, the Foreign Office need not have feared 'publishing all that has passed'.[1] Only one set remains to be dealt with here, those of Sir Lionel Carden against the United States. They must not be allowed to pass by default.

Representative of a widespread view once, and one which is far from being extinct, they were natural but irrational. As I have indicated above, the government of the United States enjoyed, and enjoys, in its domestic affairs no such freedom of action as it commands abroad. To some extent, in the early years of this century, its power was new-found, and the more vigorously exercised for that. It was in the main legitimately exercised for the object of protecting American interests. Against it, the British government had but one remedy: to press back. If they did not do so for higher reasons of national security, as they did not, it is not for us to say that they were wrong, but it is there that the responsibility lies and not with the United States.

In both cases, however, the context of the times made the disputes personal and immediate: conflicts of individuals representing conflicts of nations. The crisis, therefore, was first and foremost a problem of individuals and not of ideas—like the Mexican Revolution itself.

[1] Minute on Spring-Rice–Grey, 8 November 1913, Telegram no. 193, p. 263.

BIBLIOGRAPHY

MANUSCRIPT COLLECTIONS

William Jennings Bryan Papers, Library of Congress, Washington, D.C.

Papers of James Bryce, Viscount Bryce of Dechmont, Bodleian Library, Oxford.

Papers of Sir Weetman Dickinson Pearson, first Viscount Cowdray, Archives of Whitehall Securities Limited, London.

Josephus Daniels Papers, Library of Congress, Washington, D.C.

Foreign Office Papers, Public Record Office, London.

German Foreign Ministry Archives, Public Record Office, London (on microfilm).

Sir E. (Viscount) Grey's State Papers, United States, Public Record Office, London.

Correspondence of Philander Chase Knox, Library of Congress, Washington, D.C.

Archivo de D. Francisco I. Madero, Biblioteca Nacional de Antropología e Historia, México (on microfilm).

Elihu Root Papers, Library of Congress, Washington, D.C.

The William Howard Taft Papers, Library of Congress, Washington, D.C.

United States, State Department Files, RG 59, National Archives of the United States, Washington, D.C.

United States, Records of the Department of State relating to Internal Affairs of Mexico, RG 59, National Archives of the United States (on microfilm).

Woodrow Wilson Collection, Library of Congress, Washington, D.C.

CONTEMPORARY PRINTED MATERIAL

Aguilar, Rafael. *Madero sin máscara* (México, Imprenta Popular, 1911).

American Academy of Political and Social Science. *Annals*, LIV, 'International Relations of the United States' (Philadelphia, Pa., 1914).

Anglo-Mexican Petroleum Products Co. Ltd. *Mexican Fuel Oil* (London [1914]).

Arnold, Channing and Frost, Frederick J. Tabor. *The American Egypt, a Record of Travels in Yucatan* (London, Hutchinson and Co., 1909).

Bell, Edward I. *The Political Shame of Mexico* (New York, McBride, Nast and Company, 1914).

Bibliography

Bonilla, Policarpo, ex-President of Honduras. *Wilson Doctrine: How the Speech of President Wilson at Mobile, Ala., has been Interpreted by the Latin-American Countries* (New York, March 1914).

Butt, Archibald W. *Taft and Roosevelt, the Intimate Letters of Archie Butt, Military Aide* (New York, Doubleday Doran, 1930).

Colina, F. de la. *Madero y el Gral. Díaz* (México, Guerra y Vázquez, 1913).

Commager, Henry Steele, ed. *Documents of American History*, 6th edition (New York, Appleton–Century–Crofts, 1958).

Corporation of Foreign Bondholders. *Fortieth Annual Report of the Council of the Corporation of Foreign Bondholders for the year 1913* (London, 1913).

Creelman, James. *Diaz, Master of Mexico* (New York and London, D. Appleton and Co., 1911).

Didapp, Juan Pedro. *Los Estados Unidos y nuestros conflictos internos* (México, Tip. 'El Republicano', 1913).

Dobson, Miles. *At the Edge of the Pit* (Pasadena, Calif., News Publishing Company, 1914).

Gamboa, Federico. *Mi Diario: Mucho de mi Vida y Algo de la de Otros*, v, Segunda Serie, ii (México, 1938).

'Hansard'. *The Parliamentary Debates*, Fifth Series.

Memorias del Gral. V. Huerta ([Barcelona,] 1915).

Lemke, William, ed. *Crimes against Mexico* (Minneapolis, Minn., Great West Printing Co. [1915]).

Lind, John. *La Gente de México, por el ex-representante personal del presidente Wilson en México. Traducido por la Secretaría de Instrucción Pública y Bellas Artes* (Veracruz, Tip. de la Sría. de I.P. y B.A., 1915).

Lodge, Henry Cabot, ed. *Selections from the correspondence of Theodore Roosevelt and Henry Cabot Lodge, 1884–1918* (New York and London, Charles Scribner's Sons, 1925).

Madero, Francisco Indalecio. *Las Memorias y las mejores cartas de Francisco I. Madero. Selección y líneas prologales de Armando de María y Campos* (México, Libro-Mex Editores, S. de R.L., 1956).

Madero, Francisco Indalecio. *La sucesión Presidencial en 1910* (México, Librería de la Viuda de Ch. Bouret, 1911), tercera edición: copia de la segunda.

Martin, Percy F. 'British Diplomacy and Trade', *The Quarterly Review*, ccxv (October 1911), no. 429, pp. 442 ff.

México. Congreso. Cámara de Diputados. *Diario de los debates de la Cámara de Diputados del Congreso de los Estados Unidos Mexicanos, XXVI Legislatura*, iii (Año ii, Periodo i) (México, 1913–14).

20-2

Bibliography

México. *Diario Oficial, Estados Unidos Mexicanos.*

México. Secretaría de Hacienda. *The Mexican Year Book: a Financial and Commercial Handbook, compiled from Official and other Returns, 1911* (London, McCorquodale and Co. [1911]).

México. Secretaría de Hacienda. *The Mexican Year Book: . . . 1912.*

México. Secretaría de Hacienda. *The Mexican Year Book: . . . 1913.*

México. Secretaría de Relaciones Exteriores. *Boletín oficial de la Secretaría de relaciones exteriores*, XXXIV–XXXVI (México, May 1912–October 1913).

Mexico, City of. Committee of the American Colony. *Facts submitted by the Committee of the American Colony to President Wilson and Secretary of State Bryan relative to the Mexican situation and the record of the Honorable Henry Lane Wilson in connection therewith* (Mexico [1913]).

Molina Enríquez, Andrés. *Los grandes problemas nacionales* (México, Imprenta de A. Carranza e Hijos, 1909).

O'Shaughnessy, Edith Louise Coues. *A Diplomat's Wife in Mexico* (New York and London, Harper and Brothers, 1916).

O'Shaughnessy, Edith Louise Coues. *Diplomatic Days* (New York and London, Harper and Brothers, 1917).

'Pirra-Purra' (pseudonym of Pedro Lamicq). *La parra, la perra y la Porra* (México, 1913).

Prida, Ramón. *From Despotism to Anarchy* (El Paso, Texas, El Paso Printing Company, 1914).

Seymour, Charles, ed. *The Intimate Papers of Colonel House* (London, Ernest Benn, 1926).

Simonds, Louis C. 'Victoriano Huerta—a sketch from life', *The Atlantic Monthly*, CXIII (Boston, 1914), p. 721.

Singer, J. *Die mexicanischen Finanzen und Wilsons panamerikanische Politik* (Berlin, Franz Siemenroth, 1914).

Toro, Carlos. *La caida de Madero por la revolución felicista* ([Mexico], 1913).

Turner, John Kenneth. *Barbarous Mexico: an Indictment of a Cruel and Corrupt System* (London, Cassell, 1911).

United States. Congress: *Congressional Record.*

United States. Congress. Senate, Committee on Foreign Relations: *Revolutions in Mexico: Hearing before a Sub-committee of the Committee on Foreign Relations, United States Senate, Sixty-Second Congress, Second Session, pursuant to S. Res. 335, a resolution authorising the Committee on Foreign Relations to investigate whether any interests in the*

Bibliography

United States have been or are now engaged in inciting rebellion in *Cuba and Mexico* (Washington, D.C., United States Government Printing Office, 1913).

United States. President, 1913–21 (Wilson): *Mexican Affairs. Address of the President of the United States delivered at a joint session of the two houses of Congress. August 27, 1913*)Washington, D.C., Government Printing Office, 1913).

MEMOIRS

Beaverbrook, William Maxwell Aitken, first Lord. *The Decline and Fall of Lloyd George and great was the fall thereof* (London, Collins, 1963).

Bernstorff, Johann Heinrich, Graf von. *The Memoirs of Count Bernstorff* (London, William Heinemann, 1936).

Calero, Manuel. *Un Decenio de Política Mexicana* (New York, 1920).

Churchill, Rt. Hon. Winston Leonard Spencer. *The World Crisis, 1911–1918* (London, Thornton Butterworth, 1931).

Creel, George. *Rebel at Large: Recollections of Fifty Crowded Years* (New York, G. P. Putnam's Sons, 1947).

Daniels, Josephus. *The Wilson Era: Years of Peace, 1910–1917* (Chapel Hill, N.C., The University of North Carolina Press, 1944).

Dumba, Constantin. *Memoirs of a Diplomat* (London, Allen and Unwin, 1933).

Furber, Percy N.: *I Took Chances From Windjammers to Jets* (Leicester, Edgar Backus, 1954).

Goltz, Horst von der. *My Adventures as a German Secret Service Agent* (London, Cassell and Co., 1918).

Grey of Fallodon, Edward, 1st Viscount. *Twenty-Five Years, 1892–1916* (London, Hodder and Stoughton, 1925).

Hohler, Sir Thomas Beaumont. *Diplomatic Petrel* (London, John Murray, 1942).

Houston, David Franklin. *Eight Years with Wilson's Cabinet, 1913 to 1920, with a personal estimate of the President* (Garden City, N.Y., Doubleday Page, 1926).

King, Rosa E. *Tempest over Mexico, a Personal Chronicle* (London, Methuen, 1936).

Knatchbull-Hugessen, Sir Hughe Montgomery. *Diplomat in Peace and War* (London, John Murray, 1949).

Lawrence, David. *The True Story of Woodrow Wilson* (London, Hurst and Blackett, 1924).

Lockhart, Sir Robert Bruce. *Friends, Foes and Foreigners* (London, Putnam, 1957).

309

Bibliography

Márquez Sterling, Manuel. *Los últimos días del presidente Madero* (*Mi gestión diplomática en México*) (Havana, Imprenta 'El Siglo xx', 1917).

Moheno, Querido. *Mi actuación política después de la Decena Trágica* (México, D.F., Ediciones Botas, 1939).

O'Shaughnessy, Edith Louise Coues. *Intimate Pages of Mexican History* (New York, George H. Doran Co., 1920).

Palavicini, Félix Fulgencio. *Mi Vida Revolucionaria* (México, D.F., Ediciones Botas, 1937).

Papen, Franz von. *Memoirs* (London, Andre Deutsch, 1952).

Pereyra, Carlos. *México Falsificado* (México, D.F., Editorial Polis, 1949).

Vasconcelos, José. *Ulises Criollo* (México, Editorial Jus, 1958), edición expurgada.

Vázquez Gómez, Francisco. *Memorias Políticas (1909–1913)* (México, D.F., Imprenta Mundial, 1933).

Wilson, Henry Lane. *Diplomatic Episodes in Mexico, Belgium and Chile* (London, A. M. Philpot, Ltd, 1927).

Winterton, Edward Turnour, sixth Earl. *Pre-War* (London, Macmillan, 1932).

SECONDARY SOURCES

Adams, Samuel Hopkins. *Incredible Era: The Life and Times of Warren Gamaliel Harding* (Boston, Mass., Houghton Mifflin Company, 1939).

Allen, Harry C. *Great Britain and the United States: a history of Anglo-American relations, 1783–1952* (London, Odhams Press, 1954).

Almond, Gabriel A. and Coleman, James S. *The Politics of the Developing Areas* (Princeton, N.J., Princeton University Press, 1960).

Alperóvich, M. S. and Rudenko, B. T. *La Revolución Mexicana de 1910–1917 y la política de los Estados Unidos* (México, Fondo de Cultura Popular, 1960).

Bailey, Thomas Andrew. *Theodore Roosevelt and the Japanese–American Crises* (Stanford, Calif., Stanford University Press, 1934).

Baker, Ray Stannard. *Woodrow Wilson, Life and Letters, vol. IV: 'President, 1913–1914'* (London, Heinemann, 1932).

Bates, J. Leonard. *The Origins of Teapot Dome: Progressives, Parties, and Petroleum, 1909–1921* (Urbana, Ill., University of Illinois Press, 1963).

Beals, Carleton. *Porfirio Diaz, Dictator of Mexico* (Philadelphia and London, J. B. Lippincott Company, 1932).

Bemis, Samuel Flagg. *The Latin American Policy of the United States: an Historical Interpretation* (New York, Harcourt Brace and Co., 1943).

Bishop, Joseph Bucklin. *Theodore Roosevelt and His Time, Shown in His Own Letters* (London, Hodder and Stoughton, 1920).

Bibliography

Blaisdell, Lowell L. *The Desert Revolution, Baja California, 1911* (Madison, Wis., The University of Wisconsin Press, 1962).

Blum, John Morton. *Woodrow Wilson and the Politics of Morality* (Boston and Toronto, Little Brown and Co., 1956).

Borchard, E. M. 'Calvo and Drago Doctrines', *Encyclopedia of the Social Sciences*, III.

Bulnes, Francisco. *The Whole Truth about Mexico—President Wilson's Responsibility* (New York, M. Bulnes Book Company, 1916).

Burns, Edward McNall. *David Starr Jordan: Prophet of Freedom* (Stanford, Calif., Stanford University Press, 1953).

Callcott, Wilfrid Hardy. *Liberalism in Mexico, 1857–1929* (Stanford, Calif., Stanford University Press, 1931).

Calvert, Peter A. R. 'Francis Stronge en la Decena Trágica', *Historia Mexicana*, 57, XV, no. 1, julio–septiembre 1965, pp. 47–68.

Calvert, Peter A. R. 'The Murray Contract: an Episode in International Finance and Diplomacy', *Pacific Historical Review*, XXXV, no. 2, May 1966, p. 203.

Campbell, Alexander E. *Great Britain and the United States 1895–1903* (London, Longmans, 1960).

Carreño, Alberto María. *La Diplomacia Extraordinaria entre México y Estados Unidos* (México, Editorial JUS, 1951).

Cline, Howard F. *The United States and Mexico* (Cambridge, Mass., Harvard University Press, 1963).

Cosío Villegas, Daniel. *American Extremes* (Austin, Texas, University of Texas Press, 1964).

Cross, Colin. *The Liberals in Power, 1905–1914* (London, Barrie and Rockliff with Pall Mall Press, 1963).

Cumberland, Charles Curtis. *Mexican Revolution: Genesis under Madero* (Austin, Texas, University of Texas Press, 1952).

Dangerfield, George. *The Strange Death of Liberal England* (London, Constable, 1936).

DeConde, Alexander. *The American Secretary of State, an Interpretation* (London, Pall Mall Press, 1962).

Dombrowski, Eric. *German Leaders of Yesterday and To-day* (New York, D. Appleton and Company, 1920).

Donaldson, Frances. *The Marconi Scandal* (London, Rupert Hart-Davis, 1962).

Downing, Todd. *The Mexican Earth* (New York, Doubleday Doran, 1940).

Dromundo, Baltasar. *Emiliano Zapata* (México, Imprenta Mundial, 1934).

Bibliography

Dunn, H. H. *The Crimson Jester, Zapata of Mexico* (London, George C. Harrap and Co., 1934).

Fabela, Isidro. *Historia Diplomática de la Revolución Mexicana*, vol. I, 1910–1917 (México, D.F., Fondo de Cultura Económica, 1958).

Feis, Herbert. *Europe the World's Banker 1870–1914* (New Haven, Conn., Yale University Press (Council on Foreign Relations), 1930).

Fleming, Peter. *The Siege at Peking* (London, Rupert Hart-Davis, 1959).

Flores D., Jorge. 'Carlos Pereyra y el embajador Wilson', *Historia Mexicana*, VIII, no. 29, julio–septiembre 1958.

Flynn, John T. *God's Gold—the story of Rockefeller and his times* (London, George C. Harrap and Co. Ltd, 1933).

Gantenbein, James W. *The Evolution of our Latin American Policy* (New York, Columbia University Press, 1950).

Gelber, Lionel M. *The Rise of Anglo-American Friendship* (New York, Oxford University Press, 1938).

Glick, Edward B. 'The Tehuantepec Railroad: Mexico's White Elephant', *Pacific Historical Review*, XXII, no. 4 (November 1953), pp. 373–82.

Goldenberg, Boris. *The Cuban Revolution and Latin America* (London, George Allen and Unwin, 1965).

Goldman, Eric F. *Rendezvous with Destiny, a History of Modern American Reform* (New York, Vintage Books, 1960), revised edition abridged by the author.

Granados, Ricardo García. *Historia de México desde la Restauración de la República en 1867, hasta la Caida de Huerta* (México, Editorial JUS, 1956).

Gruening, Ernest. *Mexico and its Heritage* (London, Stanley Paul and Co., 1928).

Gwynn, Stephen, ed. *The Letters and Friendships of Sir Cecil Spring-Rice: a record* (London, Constable, 1929).

Hackett, Charles Wilson. 'The Mexican Revolution and the United States, 1910–1926', *World Peace Foundation Pamphlets*, IX, no. 5, Boston, Mass., 1926, pp. 339 ff.

Hagedorn, Hermann. *Leonard Wood, a biography* (New York, Harper and Brothers, 1931).

Hannay, David. *Diaz* (London, Constable, 1917).

Harrison, John P. 'Henry Lane Wilson, el trágico de la decena', *Historia Mexicana*, VI, no. 23, enero–marte 1957, pp. 374–405.

Bibliography

Heindel, Richard Heathcote. *The American Impact on Great Britain, 1898–1914, A Study of the United States in World History* (Philadelphia, Pa., University of Pennsylvania Press, 1940).

Hendrick, Burton Jesse, ed. *The Life and Letters of Walter H. Page* (London, William Heinemann Ltd, 1924).

Hidy, Ralph W. and Hidy, Muriel E. *Pioneering in big business, 1882–1911: History of the Standard Oil Company, New Jersey,* I (New York, Harper, 1955).

Ilchman, Frederick Warren. *Professional Diplomacy in the United States, 1779–1939: a study in administrative history* (Chicago, Ill., University of Chicago Press, 1961).

Ise, John. *The United States Oil Policy* (New Haven, Conn., Yale University Press, 1926).

Jessup, Philip C. *Elihu Root* (New York, Dodd Mead and Co., 1938).

Katz, Friedrich. *Deutschland, Diaz und die mexikanische Revolution; die deutsche Politik in Mexiko 1870–1920* (Berlin, Veb Deutscher Verlag der Wissenschaften, 1964).

Langer, William L. *The Diplomacy of Imperialism 1890–1902* (New York, Alfred A. Knopf, 1951).

Lieuwen, Edwin. *Generals versus Presidents: Neo-Militarism in Latin America* (London, Pall Mall Press, 1964).

Link, Arthur Stanley. *Woodrow Wilson and the Progressive Era 1910–1917* (London, Hamish Hamilton, 1954).

Link, Arthur Stanley. *Wilson—the New Freedom* (Princeton, N.J., Princeton University Press, 1956).

McCaleb, Walter Flavius. *The Public Finances of Mexico* (New York and London, Harper Bros., 1921).

México, Fondo de Cultura Económica. *México: Cincuenta Años de Revolución, III: La Política* (México, Fondo de Cultura Económica, 1961).

Middlemas, Robert Keith. *The Master Builders* (London, Hutchinson, 1963).

Mowry, George E. *The Era of Theodore Roosevelt and the Birth of Modern America* (New York, Harper, 1958).

Munro, Dana Gardner. *The Five Republics of Central America* (New York, Oxford University Press, 1918).

Munro, Dana Gardner. *Intervention and Dollar Diplomacy in the Caribbean, 1900–1921* (Princeton, N.J., Princeton University Press, 1964).

Navarro, Moisés González. *La colonización en México, 1877–1910* (México, 1960).

Bibliography

Needler, Martin C. *Latin American Politics in Perspective* (Princeton, N.J., D. Van Nostrand Company, 1963).

Nevins, Allan. *John D. Rockefeller, the heroic age of American enterprise* (New York, Charles Scribner's Sons, 1941).

Nicolson, Harold. *Helen's Tower* (London, Constable, 1937).

Nicolson, Harold. *Sir Arthur Nicolson, Bart., First Lord Carnock: A Study in the Old Diplomacy* (London, Constable, 1930).

Notter, Harley. *The Origins of the Foreign Policy of Woodrow Wilson* (Baltimore, Md., Johns Hopkins Press, 1937).

Parkes, Henry Bamford. *A History of Mexico* (London, Eyre and Spottiswoode, 1960), revised edition.

Pendle, George. *Argentina* (London, Oxford University Press, 1961).

Perkins, Dexter. *A History of the Monroe Doctrine* (Boston, Little Brown, 1955).

Prida, Ramón. *La Culpa de Lane Wilson, Embajador de los E.U.A., en la Tragedia Mexicana de 1913* (México, D.F., Ediciones Botas, 1962).

Quirk, Robert E. *An Affair of Honor: Woodrow Wilson and the Occupation of Vera Cruz* (New York, McGraw-Hill, 1964).

Rausch, George J., Jr. 'The Exile and Death of Victoriano Huerta', *Hispanic American Historical Review*, XLII (May 1962), p. 133.

Rippy, J. Fred. *The Capitalists and Colombia* (New York, Vanguard Press, 1931).

Römer, Hans G. *Amerikanische Interessen- und Prinzipienpolitik in Mexiko 1910–1914: Ein Beitrag zur Kritik des Wilsonismus* (Hamburg, Friedrichsen de Gruyter & Co., m.b.H., 1929).

Rojas, (Lic.) Luis Manuel. *La Culpa de Henry Lane Wilson en el Gran Desastre de México* (México, D.F., Compañía Editora 'La Verdad' S.A., 1928).

Ross, Stanley Robert. *Francisco I. Madero, Apostle of Mexican Democracy* (New York, Columbia University Press, 1955).

Sherman, William L. and Greenleaf, Richard E. *Victoriano Huerta, a Reappraisal* (México, D.F., Centro de Estudios Mexicanos, 1960).

Spender, John Alfred. *Weetman [Dickinson] Pearson, First Viscount Cowdray, 1856–1927* (London, Cassell, 1930).

Stephenson, George Malcolm. *John Lind of Minnesota* (Minneapolis, Minn., The University of Minnesota Press, 1935).

Stimson, Grace Heilman. *Rise of the Labor Movement in Los Angeles* (Berkeley, Calif., University of California Press, 1955).

Bibliography

Tischendorf, Alfred. *Great Britain and Mexico in the Era of Porfirio Diaz* (Durham, N.C., Duke University Press, 1961).

Tuchman, Barbara W. *The Zimmermann Telegram* (London, Constable, 1959).

Ulloa, Berta. *Revolución Mexicana, 1910–1920* (México, Secretaría de Relaciones Exteriores, 1963, Archivo Historico Diplómatico Mexicano, no. 3).

Vagts, Alfred. *A History of Militarism, Civilian and Military* (London, Hollis and Carter, 1959).

Vagts, Alfred. *Mexico, Europa und Amerika unter besonderer Berücksichtigung der Petroleumpolitik — eine wirtschafts-diplomatische Untersuchung* (Berlin, Grunewald, Dr Walter Rothschild, 1928).

Viereck, George Sylvester. *The Strangest Friendship in History: Woodrow Wilson and Colonel House* (London, Duckworth, 1933).

Young, Desmond. *Member for Mexico: A Biography of Weetman Pearson, First Viscount Cowdray* (London, Cassell, 1966).

PERIODICALS

The Mexican Herald (Mexico).
The Morning Post (London).
The National Review (London).
The New York Herald (New York).
The New York Times (New York).
The Pall Mall Gazette (London).
The Quarterly Review (London).
The Spectator (London).
The Times (London).
The Washington Post (Washington, D.C.).
The Westminster Gazette (London).
The World (New York).

REFERENCE WORKS

Cokayne, George Edward. *The Complete Peerage* (London, St Catherine Press).

Dictionary of American Biography (London, Oxford University Press).

Enciclopedia Universal Ilustrada, Europeo-Americana (Barcelona, Hijos de J. Espasa).

Encyclopædia Britannica (London, Encyclopædia Britannica, 1963).

The Foreign Office List and Diplomatic and Consular Year Book . . ., ed. Godfrey E. P. Hertslet (London, Harrison and Sons, various dates).

Bibliography

Der Grosse Brockhaus (Leipzig, Brockhaus, 1931).

México, Secretaría de Relaciones Exteriores. *Personas que han tenido a su cargo la Secretaría de relaciones exteriores desde 1821 hasta 1924* (México, Publicaciones de la Secretaría de relaciones exteriores—Archivo Histórico Diplomático Mexicano, núm. 6, 1924).

Parker, William Belmont. *Cubans of To-day* (New York, G. P. Putnam's Sons, 1919).

Peral, Miguel Ángel. *Diccionario biográfico mexicano* (México, Editorial P.A.C., no date).

United States. Congress: *Biographical Directory of the American Congress 1774–1961* (Washington, D.C., United States Government Printing Office, 1961). 85th Congress, 2d Session, H. Doc. 442.

Who's Who, 1961–4.

Who's Who in America (Chicago, Ill., A. N. Marquis Co.).

Who Was Who.

Who Was Who in America.

INDEX

Abdul Hamid II, Sultan of Turkey, 45–6
Acland, Francis Dyke, 122, 164
Adams, Fred, 72–3, 212–13, 217, 227, 228, 229, 245, 276, 277–9
Adams, S. H., 26 n.
Adee, Alvey Augustus, 53, 168
agrarian revolt, 21, 87, 88–9, 104, 107, 291
Agua Prieta, capture and recapture of, 64, 66, 67, 290
Aguila Co., 50, 181 n., 275, 277–8; activities of, 25–6; structure of, 26; Lord Cowdray's interest in, 75; alleged corruption in, 97; connection with National Railways, 97; concessions granted to, 98, 99, 100; sale of, 284
Aguilar, Candido, 278
Aguilar, R., 101 n.
Allen, H. C., 5 n., 267 n.
Allen, W. H., 20 n.
Almond, G. A. and J. S. Coleman, 302 n.
Alperóvich, M. S. and B. T. Rudenko, 78 n.
American Smelting and Refining Co., 48
Ancona, Mr, 74
Ángeles, Felipe, 141, 142, 147
Anglo-American Oil Co., 24
Anglo-French Naval Conversations (1911), 2
Anglo-Japanese Alliance (1902), 3, 27
Anglo-Mexican Petroleum Products Co. Ltd, 173
Anti-re-election Party, 31, 32
Araujo, Manuel Enrique, 139 n.
Arbitration Treaty, lapse of, 196
Archbold, John Dustin, 79, 80–1, 82
Argentina, 7, 8 n., 185, 286
arms: supply to revolutionaries, 42, 44, 66, 71, 78, 80; ban on exports from U.S., 109, 113, 125 n., 177–8, 209; supply to counter-revolutionaries, 116; imported by Mexico, 177–8, 191, 199, 209, 211; supply to northern rebels, 239
army (Maderista), disbanded in *interinato*, 88
army (Mexican): cumbrous strategy of, 105; role in state, 105–6; effect on election results, 247; role under Díaz, 290
army (U.S.), *see* mobilization
Arnold, C. and F. J. T. Frost, 21 n.

Asquith, Herbert Henry, 1, 70, 224; speech on policy in Mexico, 265–7, 269
Associated Press, 135, 159, 240, 277 n.
Atrato region, plans for canal in, 174–5
Azcona, Juan Sánchez, 93 n.

Bachimba, battle at, 104, 105–6
Bacon, Augustus O., 171 n., 178
Bailey, T. A., 27 n.
Baja California, 47, 48, 60, 289
Baker, R. S., 136 n., 167 n., 177 n., 252 n., 283 n., 285 n.
Balfour, Arthur J., 1, 3
Ballinger, Richard A., 3, 38, 47, 48, 53
Bancaria, unpopularity of, 96
Barrett, John, 132
Basso, Adolpho, 154
Bates, J. L., 26 n.
Beals, C., 15 n., 17 n., 18 n., 21 n.
Beaverbrook, First Baron, 163 n.
Bell, Edward I., 17 n., 39 n., 62,64 n.,78–9, 83, 87 n., 94 n., 96 n., 106 n., 108, 110, 112 n., 113 n., 116 n., 117, 147 n., 155 n., 156 n.
Beltrán, Joaquín, 104, 106
Bemis, S. F., 274 n.
Bennett, J. J., 80
Benton, William, 296 n.
Bernhardt, Gaston de, 218 n.
Bernstorff, Johann Heinrich, Graf von, 40, 50 n., 57 n.
'Big Stick' policy of U.S., 9 n.
Billinghurst, Guillermo, 300
Bishop, J. B., 54 n.
Bismarck, Otto, Prinz von, 94
Bittenfeld, Herwarth von, 50 n.
Blaisdell, L. L., 40 n., 47 n.
Blanquet, Aureliano, 147, 247
Blum, J. M., 167 n., 274 n., 299 n., 303 n.
Body, John B., 72, 96–7, 141, 184, 276; denies allegations against Cowdray, 97; present at Cowdray's interview with Madero, 98–9; asks Adams to warn Huerta, 212–13; on Cowdray's subscription to loan, 231
Bonar Law, A., 2
Bonilla, Manuel, 96
Bonilla, P., 251 n.
Borchard, E. M., 8 n.

Index

Bowring, C. W., 181 n.
Bravo, Mexican gunboat, 282
Brenchley, Mr, 137
British Guiana, 6, 7
British Honduras, 6, 239
Brown, E. N., 72
Bryan, William Jennings, 171, 172, 175, 179, 185 n., 187, 201, 209, 214, 242, 243, 262, 265, 282, 283, 289, 295, 296 n., 297, 301; on U.S. recognition of Huerta, 165–6; advocates 'spoils system' for appointments, 168; instructs H. L. Wilson to mediate, 178; Lind's mission and, 203, 204, 205–7; criticized by Carden, 226; receives Lind's opinion on Mexico, 229; sees Wilson about Huerta's coup, 233; requests withdrawal of recognition, 235; accuses Britain of encouraging Huerta, 245–6; links Mobile speech with Monroe doctrine, 250–1; denies ultimatum to Huerta, 257; considers Grey dominated by oil interests, 271
Bryce, James, Viscount, 40, 93, 109, 124, 148, 290; views on mobilization, 49, 50, 51–2; defends U.S. attitude to arms trade, 66; aware of Cowdray's complaints against Wilson, 69; discusses Mexican situation with Taft, 69–70; asked about joint intervention, 122; refutes rumours of intervention, 125, 126; notifies Britain's decision to recognize, 165; replaced as British ambassador, 169; informed that U.S. not influenced by British decision to recognize, 173
Bulnes, F., 102 n.
Burns, E. M., 179 n.
Burnside, W. A., 93
Butt, Archibald W., 55, 57

Calero, Manuel, 96, 102, 110, 117, 122, 146, 288; *Un Decenio de Política Mexicana*, 87 n., 107 n., 118 n., 147 n.; joins de la Barra in legation, 141
Californian Land Act crisis, 290 n.
Callcott, W. H., 79
Calvert, P. A. R., 118 n., 175 n.
Calvo clause, 8
Campa, Emilio, 112
Campbell, A. E., 5 n., 7 n., 300 n.
Campbell, Sir Francis Alexander, 70
Campbell, Ronald Hugh, 70, 125, 190
Canada, trade links with U.S., 4, 5
Canada, W. W., 106 n.

Canfield, Edward, 77
capital, foreign: in Central America, 8–10, *see also* Guatemala; Venezuela; in Mexico, 17, 18, 19–21, 95–6, 100
Carbajal, Francisco S., 67
Carden, Sir Lionel Edward Gresley, 164, 190, 191, 238, 239 n., 248, 261, 263, 274, 298, 304, 305; appointed ambassador to Mexico, 216; connections with Cowdray, 218, 237; financial interests of, 218; early career of, 218–19; anti-Americanism of, 219; left London without seeing Grey, 220; opinion of Mexican situation, 220–4; considers Britain must put her interests first, 222–3; arrives at Vera Cruz, 225–6; criticizes President Wilson and Bryan, 226; meets Lind, 226, 227–8; Lind's opinion of, 227–8, 234, 258; presents credentials on day after coup, 233–4, 241, 243, 246; gives press interview, 237, 240–3; likened by press to H. L. Wilson, 242; replacement of, 253, 269, 282–4; criticized by von Hintze, 259; welcomes possibility of Huerta declaring war, 260; meets Huerta, 265; offers to mediate, 268–9, 271; attends opening of Congress, 272 n.; requests help of British navy, 274; attacked for not supporting Cowdray, 277; accused of intrigue, 279–81; instructed not to support Huerta, 280; recalled to London, 283
Cardenas, Francisco, 154 n.
Carranza, Venustiano, 101, 177, 192, 274, 302
Carreño, A. M., 227 n.
Carson, Sir Edward, 2
Carvajal, Francisco S., *see* Carbajal, Francisco S.
Castro, Cipriano, 270
Central America: U.S. interests in, 7–10, 28, 33–4, 269; foreign investment in, 8–10, 252, 295–6, 301; *see also* Guatemala; Venezuela
Cepeda, Enrique, 146, 180
Chamber of Deputies: dissolution of, 231–3; calls for deposition of Huerta, 232
Charbonneau, M., 83
Chihuahua, 44, 59, 62; Orozco extracts financial support from, 108
Chile, 7, 38, 75 n., 185, 286
China, recognition of, 194
Chinese, massacre of at Torreón, 71
Chinese Loan question, 9, 168, 172, 295, 297

318

Index

Churchill, Winston Leonard Spencer, 2, 173; announces Navy Plan, 173–4

científicos, 77, 96 n., 286; doctrines of, 16–18, 27; achievements of, 17–18, 285; role in downfall of Reyes, 29; accused of anti-Americanism, 41; influence of, 43; support Félix Díaz, 107

Ciudad Juárez, 47, 122, 290; captured by Madero's forces, 67–8, 71, 82; threatened for second time, 112, 116; captured by Villa, 274

Ciudad Juárez, Treaty of, 71, 88, 90

Ciudadela, Mexico City, see Decena Trágica; Mexico City, rising of Feb. 1913

Clark, Joshua Reuben Jnr., 44, 112

Cline, H. F., 195 n., 292 n.

Colina, F. de la, 29 n.

Cologan y Cologan, Bernardo Jacinto, 136, 140, 142, 145, 148; sent to request Madero's resignation, 142–3; received by Madero, 143

Colombia, 254, 295; relations with U.S., 4; oil concessions sought by Lord Murray, 174–5, 255; Standard Oil, 243

Commager, H. S., 250 n.

Committee on Foreign Relations (U.S. Senate), see Smith Committee

Comonfort, Ignacio, 11

Compañía Mexicana de Petróleo 'El Águila', S.A., see Aguila Co.

Comte, Auguste, 16

Conejos, battle at, 104

Constitution of 1857, 11, 16, 29; no re-election amendments annulled, 15

Constitutionalists, 177, 178, 193, 207, 208, 239, 280, 283, 296, 301; capture Durango, 187; infiltration into Congress, 225, 226; Lind contacted by agents of, 227; re-capture Torreón, 231, 279; recognition of belligerency of, 238, 239, 243, 270; State Department negotiates with, 274; military activities of, 274–5; agree to respect oilfields, 278; besiege Tampico, 282, 298–9; railways damaged by, 292

Converse, Lawrence F., alleges Madero helped by Standard Oil, 74

Corral, Ramón, 15–16, 31, 43, 63; accuses U.S. of fomenting revolution, 70, 81

corruption: allegations against científicos, 18, 286; allegations against Cowdray, 25, 26, 27, 73, 97, 176, 277, see also Cowdray, First Viscount; charges against Pierce and Doheny, 26

Cosío Villegas, D., 16, 294 n.

Costa Rica, 174 n., 254, 295

Council of Foreign Bondholders, 9–10, 190, 219 n.

counter-revolutionary movements, finance of, 106–8

Covadonga massacre, 127

Cowdray, First Viscount (W. D. Pearson), 22, 162, 180, 212, 253, 254, 270, 284, 290, 292, 296; civil engineering achievements of, 23–4, 33; friendship with Díaz, 24, 72, 73, 286; railway interests of, 24, 108, 230; oil concessions, 24–6, 76, 98, 99, 100, 255, 267, 270, 277; allegations of corruption by, 25, 26, 27, 73, 97, 176, 277; complains about behaviour of H. L. Wilson, 68–9; interest in Aguila Co., 75; contract with Standard Oil, 77; annulment of his concessions requested, 96; interview with Madero about concessions, 98–9; charged with assisting Orozco, 108, 237; arms trade and, 109; favoured Gerard as ambassador, 169; connection with British navy oil contracts, 173–4, 175–6; accused of involvement with F. Díaz, 179; accused of pressing for Huerta's recognition, 179, 182, 183; attempts to secure British loan for Huerta, 182–5; blamed for British recognition of Huerta, 193; reports on conditions for U.S. recognition, 214–15; asked to request delay of Stronge's departure, 216–17; connections with Carden, 218, 237; considered by Lind to control Huerta government, 229, 231, 234; subscribes to loan, 230–1, 276; accused of assisting Madero's overthrow, 237, 277; accused of forcing Carden's appointment, 237, 277; disturbed by Huerta's coup, 275; oil interests threatened by Constitutionalists, 275, 277; accused of financial support of Huerta, 275–6, 278; denies all accusations, 276–7; declares Waters Pierce to be behind accusations, 279

Cradock, Sir Christopher, 280–2

Creel, Enrique Clay, 48, 52, 108–9

Creel, G., 48 n.

Creelman, J., 15 n., 27 n.

creolism, científicos influenced by, 18

Cromer, Eldon Gorst, First Viscount, 5

Cross, C., 1 n.

Cuba, 8, 9, 34, 218–19, 221, 240, 248, 251, 259

Index

Cumberland, C. C., 17 n., 18 n., 29 n., 79, 83 n., 103, 106 n., 132 n.

Cunningham, E. B., 79

Cunningham, T. B., 79

Daily Mail, 243 n.

Dangerfield, G., 1 n., 174 n.

Daniels, Josephus, 183, 284, 285 n.

Dearing, Fred Morris, 52, 59, 91–2, 93, 96, 111, 113, 115, 145, 284; posted to Brussels, 168

debts, recovery of, 8–10, 11–12, see also Guatemala; Venezuela

Decena Trágica, 131–48, 177, 179, 180, 187; final assessment of, 293; see also Mexico City, rising of Feb. 1913

de la Barra, Francisco Léon, 48, 56, 138, 147, 179, 181, 288, 290, 293, 294; recalled to Mexico, 61; discusses Mexican problem with Taft, 61–2; informed H. L. Wilson of negotiations with revolutionaries, 63, 71; accuses U.S. of aiding revolutionaries, 64–5; named as interim President, 71; aware of Díaz's departure, 72; interinato of, 85–93; wishes to resign, 89–90; new policy of, 90–1; nominated for Vice-President under Madero, 95; Huerta employed by, 105; falsely reported as again being provisional President, 135; offers to mediate, 141; seeks refuge in legation, 141, 142; reports on meeting of senators with E. Madero, 143; resignation of, 148; reputation suffers as result of Madero's death, 156; had assured safety of Madero, 156–7; letter to George V a precedent for Huerta's, 159, 160; position in Huerta's régime, 161; final assessment of, 290

de la Torre, Ignacio, 154 n.

Del Valle, Reginald, 171, 190

Democratic Clubs, 31

Deputies, Chamber of, see Chamber of Deputies

Dewey, George, 120

Díaz, Adolfo, 37

Díaz, Félix, 74, 104, 106–7, 126, 148, 149, 179, 244, 284, 296 n.; financial support for, 107; and rising of Feb. 1913, 131–2, 134–5, 139, 140, 141; claims he held Mexico City, 140; negotiates for settlement, 147–8; candidate for Presidency, 148, 195 n.; motive for murder of Madero, 155; return to Mexico, 284

Díaz, Porfirio, 43, 62, 105, 154, 177, 291, 302; exchanges state visits with Taft, 4; Presidency of, 15–48; friendship with Cowdray, 24, 72, 73, 286; U.S. feeling against, 27; approves of democratic opposition, 31; fall of, 49–84; rumoured illness of, 50; on presence of Japanese navy, 51; resignation imminent, 64, 66; resignation requested by Cabinet, 68, 71; resignation accepted, 72; leaves Mexico, 72–3, 105, 290; later opinion of his régime, 91; posthumous view of, 285

Dickinson, Jacob McGavock, 53, 54 n., 69

Didapp, Juan Pedro: evidence to Smith Committee, 74–6; Los Estados Unidos y nuestros conflictos internos, 28 n., 76

Diedrichs, Otto von, 120

Dobson, M., 174 n.

Doheny, Edward Lawrence, 22, 23, 24, 25, 26, 77, 96, 182, 284

dollar diplomacy, 9, 36–7, 40, 169, 172, 219, 295, 301

Dombrowski, E., 121 n.

Domínguez, Belisario, 231

Dominican Republic, 9, 221–2

Donaldson, F., 174 n.

Dormer, Cecil Francis Joseph, 85

Downing, T., 21 n.

Doyle, W. T. S., 168

Drago doctrine, 8 n.

Dromundo, B., 89 n.

Dufferin and Ava, First Marquess of, 304

Dumba, C., 171 n.

Dunn, H. H., 89 n.

Durango, capture of, 187

economic development, foreign investment and, 285–6, see also investment, foreign

Ecuador, 295, 301 n.

Edward VII, King of Great Britain, 1, 5, 33

Edwards, T. J., 112

ejidos, 21

elections: (1910): re-election policy introduced, 12, 15; Anti-re-electionists request invalidation of, 32; (1911): 92; increasing freedom of, 94–5; (1913): date fixed for, 185; U.S. attitude to, 186, 228, 233, 236, 238, 242, 243, 244, 246, 258; lack of democracy in, 228; Constitutionalists anxious to postpone, 230; British attitude to, 239, 243, 244–5, 246; Huerta's supposed plan for, 244; conduct

Index

elections (cont.)
of, 247; results of, 247; nullification of, 272
Elguero, Luis, 97 n.
El Paso, 81, 112
El Salvador, 139, 139 n.
Escalón, Salas defeated at, 104, 114

Fabela, Isidro, 137, 144, 145 n., 150
Fall, Albert B., 171, 196 n.
Feis, H. G., 8 n., 20
Fell, Arthur, 57–8
Figueroa, Ambrosio, 140
finance: of revolution, 73–84, 95, 98; of counter-revolution, 106–8; sought by Huerta from foreign sources, 182–6, 186–7, 191–2, 194, 210, 213, 230–1, see also investment, foreign
Fleming, P., 136 n.
Fletcher, Frank Friday, 204, 226, 278, 281–2
Flores D., Jorge, 197 n.
Flores Magón brothers (Jesús, Ricardo), 47
Flynn, J. T., 22 n., 23 n.
Foreign Office: concern over Nicaragua, 33–4; pre-1910 attitude towards Mexico, 37–8; denial of involvement in U.S. mobilization, 49–50; decides against sending ship to Mexico, 63; against joint intervention, 122; ignores proposal to notify areas of disturbance, 123; considers withdrawal of legation staff, 125; receives account of Decena Trágica from Stronge, 139–50 passim; warns Stronge not to incur risks, 142; informed of Madero's death by Stronge, 156; concerned with legality of Huerta's election, 157–63; notifies Britain's intention to recognize Huerta, 165; believes U.S. withholding recognition until claims settled, 166; threatens force over Guatemalan debt, 190–1; sees non-recognition by U.S. as economic policy, 199; alleged statement following H. L. Wilson's congratulatory speech, 206, 206 n.; doubts stability of Constitutionalists, 208; wishes Fletcher to be solely responsible at Tampico, 282; efficiency of, 304; see also Great Britain
Foreign Relations Committee (U.S. Senate), 73–7, 109, 169 n., 178
France: naval agreement with Great Britain, 2; British diplomatic relations

with, 3; investments in Mexico, 20; recognition of Huerta by, 162–3, 164, 192; mediation conditions, 268
Furber, Percy N., 180, 181 n., 309

Gadsden strip, 289
Gage, Morton F., 280
Galbraith, James N., 57 n., 227, 245, 278
Galveston–Vera Cruz Cable Co., 140
Gamboa, Federico, 28 n., 42, 204–5, 210, 226; rejects Woodrow Wilson's proposals, 206; states that Huerta debarred from being candidate, 214; becomes candidate for Presidency, 225
Gantenbein, J. W., 274 n.
Garza Aldape, Manuel, 202 n., 205 n., 232, 245, 262
Gelber, L. M., 5 n.
George V, King of Great Britain: receives telegram from Huerta, 151; receives letter from de la Barra, 159, 160; receives autograph letter from Huerta, 165; replies to Huerta's letter, 180, 182, 183
Gerard, James Watson, 169, 212
Germany: investments in Mexico, 20, 283; alleged support of Orozco by, 108; recognition of Huerta by, 162–3, 164, 165; sends naval ship to Mexico, 238; mediation conditions, 268
Glick, E. B., 25 n.
gold standard, adopted in Mexico, 17, 21
Goldenberg, B., 286 n.
Goldman, E. F., 3 n.
Goltz, Horst von der, 50 n., 108 n.
Gómez, Juan Vincente, 270 n.
González, Abraham, 74, 179–80
González, Manuel, Presidency of, 15, 30
González Salas, José, 91, 103, 104
Goschen, Sir Edward, 165, 238
Granados, Alberto García, 91, 92
Granados, Ricardo García, 101–2
Great Britain: imperialism of, 1, 5–6; naval operations, 2, 9, 9 n., 64, 223–4, 274–5, 280–2; investments in Mexico, 19–20, 222, 235, 237, 285–6; overseas investments of, 19–20; absence from Mexican centenary celebrations, 33; parliamentary question on U.S. mobilization, 57–8; recognition of Huerta régime by, 150–2, 156–66, 179, 180, 182–3, 187, 188–9, 190, 191, 193, 195, 200, 203–4, 209, 223, 225, 239, 247, 249, 263, 266, 294; recognition of provisional Presidents by, 152, 157–65,

Index

Great Britain (*cont.*)
187, 294; parliament discusses recognition of Huerta, 192–3; unable to support U.S. against Mexico, 209; commercial interests and Monroe doctrine, 221; recognition of Huerta's dictatorship, 233–7; Cabinet discusses Mexico, 235; attitude towards elections, 239, 243, 244–5, 246; *see also* Foreign Office; navy

Greenwood, Hamar, 163–4, 183

Grey, Sir Edward (First Viscount Grey of Fallodon), 5, 34–5, 43, 57, 85, 122, 150, 151, 176, 191, 193, 220, 237; qualities of, 2; views on recognition of Huerta, 163, 187; informs Spring-Rice on British policy, 170; misled by Page on recognition question, 188, 200; misled by E. M. House on recognition question, 195; informed of Lind's appointment, 201–2; instructs Stronge *re* Lind's mission, 204; intervenes at request of U.S., 204; considers Britain unable to request Huerta's resignation, 209; refuses to let Stronge see Lind crisis through, 217; chooses Carden for Mexican appointment, 219; states Britain cannot take sides, 224–5, 247, 264, 265, 267; on British attitude to elections, 238–9; on dangers of recognizing belligerency of northern rebels, 239; opinions misinterpreted by Page, 239–40; presumes Carden did not give interview, 243; denies that Britain encouraging lawlessness of Huerta, 246; thinks U.S. considering armed intervention, 247; discussions with Page after elections, 247–9; not dominated by oil interests, 271; does not give Carden authority to negotiate, 272; role in Carden's transfer, 282–4

Gruening, E., 19 n., 39 n., 87 n.

Guatemala, 10, 190–1, 219, 221–2, 301 n.

Guggenheim family, interests of, 38–9, 40, 48, 56

Gulf Refining Co., 99

Gwynn, S. (ed.), 169 n., 269 n.

hacendados, 21, 87, 108

Hackett, C. W., 21 n.

Haff, Delbert J., 182, 186

Hagedorn, H., 52 n.

Haldane, First Viscount, 254

Hale, William Bayard, 136–7, 171, 182, 187, 204, 234 n., 274, 284

Hannay, D., 15 n.

Harding, Warren Gamaliel, 284

Harrison, Benjamin, 38

Harrison, J. P., 137 n.

Hay–Pauncefote Treaty, 255

Hayes, C. W., 214

Heindel, R. H., 267 n.

Hendrick, B. J. (ed.), 169 n., 219 n., 242 n., 269 n., 271 n., 279 n., 285 n., 304 n., 313 n.

Henry, Prince of Prussia, 33

H.M.S. *Hermione*, 217

Hernandez, Braulio, 74, 76

Hernandez, Luis, 79, 80

Hernandez, Rafael, 96

Hidalgo del Castillo, Manuel, 10

Hidy, R. W. and M. E., 22 n., 23 n.

Hintze, Paul von, 115, 124, 127, 136, 138, 142, 145, 146, 148, 258–60, 300; early career of, 120–1; reports on Carden, 240, 279, 280; discussions with Carden, 258–60

Hitchcock, Gilbert Monell, 77

Hohler, (Sir) Thomas Beaumont, 65, 67, 71, 91, 270, 272, 296 n.; *Diplomatic Petrel*, 25 n., 27 n., 45 n., 119 n., 139 n., 153 n., 216 n., 217 n., 283 n., 284 n.; early career of, 45–6; early dispatches on rebel activities, 46; suggested that mobilization concerned Japan, 50; considers H. L. Wilson an alarmist, 58, 60, 65; Wilson's opinion of, 61; offered legation guard by Japanese minister, 71; aware of Díaz's departure, 72; reports on finance of revolution, 83; opinion of *interinato*, 85–6, 91; protests about Zapata's 'pay-off', 89; interview with de la Barra, 89–90; considers Emilio Vázquez responsible for government's weakness, 91; reports Madero's denunciation of Huerta, 92–3; describes Madero, 93; views on Mexican elections, 94; opinion concerning Stronge, 119; opinion concerning von Hintze, 121 n.; absent during *Decena Trágica*, 139; account of *Pacto de la Embajada*, 148 n.; account of Wilson's party, 153–4; views on effect of Madero's murder, 157, 162; opinion concerning Huerta, 165 n.; memo. on Mexican situation, 193–4; reports Stronge's appointment to Chile, 216; becomes chargé d'affaires again, 217, 283; meets Carden, 225–6; subsequent career of, 284

322

Index

Holland, Philip E., reports Cowdray as assisting Orozco, 108

Holms, P. G., 58

Holstein, Friedrich von, 279

Honduras, 6, 36, 221, 222

Hopkins, Sherburne Gillette, 83, 98, 278; revolutionary activities of, 74–7; evidence to Smith Committee, 76–7

House, Edward Mandell, 195, 269, 271

Houston, D. F., 185 n., 202 n.

Huerta, Victoriano, 107, 116, 134, 140, 180, 227, 270, 279, 290, 298, 302; escorted Díaz in flight, 72, 105; denounced by Madero, 92, 105; appointed successor to González Salas, 103–4; emerges as Mexico's ruler, 104; physical appearance of, 104 n.; early career of, 104–5; distrusted by Díaz, 105; as military leader, 105–6; appointed successor to Villar, 131; attempts to recapture Ciudadela, 131–2; expected by Wilson to overthrow Madero, 133; detained in Palace, 139, 146, 147; distrusted by Madero, 139, 146, 147; sends troops to protect foreign colonies, 141; negotiates for settlement, 147–8; appointed Secretary of Gobernación, 148, 152; becomes provisional President, 148, 152; recognition by Great Britain, 150–2, 156–66 passim, 179, 180, 182–3, 187, 188–9, 190, 191, 193, 195, 200, 209, 223, 225, 239, 247, 249, 263, 267, 294; sends telegram to George V and Kaiser, 151; non-recognition by U.S., 152, 156–66 passim, 167, 171–3, 178–9, 182, 185–9, 191, 192, 194, 196, 198–200, 202, 203–4, 205, 207, 215, 225, 233; behaviour at Wilson's party, 153–4; Madero's death reflects badly on, 155–6; reported to have assured safety of Madero, 156–7; decreed by Congress to be President, 158; recognition by France, 162–3, 164, 192; recognition by Germany, 162–3, 164, 165; stability of régime reported by Stronge, 164, 190, 193, 211; sends autograph letter to George V, 165; character of, 165 n.; receives letter from George V, 180, 182, 183; financial problems of, 181–6, 191–2, 194, 203, 210, 213, 230–1; recognition by Norway, 185; meets Lind, 210–11; considered only person capable of keeping order, 211, 220, 223, 227, 235, 240; gives no guarantee will not stand for election, 215, 220; asks that Stronge remain until Lind crisis over, 217; strained relations with Cabinet and Congress, 225; dissolves Chamber of Deputies, 231–3, 275; dictatorship of, 232, 275; allegations that dictatorship recognized by Great Britain, 233–5; press reaction to coup, 236–7; supposed plan for rigging election, 244; explains reasons for coup, 246; retirement of, 253, 256–7, 258, 260–1, 263–4, 274 n.; threatened with intervention, 256; disappearances of, 258, 262; dictatorship not recognized by U.S., 262; agrees to accept British mediation, 265; plans for new elections, 272–3; visited by Cradock, 280–1; death of, 284

Hurst, Cecil James Barrington, 123

Ilchman, W. F., 168 n., 313

imperialism, differing aims of, 5–8

interinato, 76, 85–93; settled claims for Gustavo Madero, 83; inefficiency of claims commission, 89; new policy of, 90–1; see also de la Barra

International Workers of the World, 47

intervention, 8, 33, 36, 55, 64–6, 112–14, 122, 240, 246, 263, 272, 301; U.S. policy on, 113, 117–18, 121–2, 125, 147, 188, 191, 192, 194, 195, 202, 212, 215, 221, 241–2, 247, 261, 270; British policy, 125, 126, 264, 265, 268; H. L. Wilson's sympathy with, 199; urged by British financial interests, 235; as alternative to Huerta's resignation, 256, 261

Intervention, War of, 218

investment, foreign: in Central America, 8–10, 252, 295–6, 301, see also Guatemala; Venezuela; in Mexico, 17, 18, 19–21, 95–6, 100, 222, 249, 285–6, 291

Ireland, independence of, 1–2

Ise, J., 26 n.

Iturbide, Agustín de, 11, 106 n.

Japan: British diplomatic relations with, 3; U.S. Immigration Treaty with, 5; navy, 9 n., 51; U.S. fear of, 27, 29, 50 n., 51, 60, 115–16, 290 n.; minister offers Hohler a legation guard, 71

Jessup, P. C., 109 n.

Jordan, David Starr, 179

Juárez, Benito, 11, 12, 15, 67

323

Index

Justice, Department of, 79; unable to prevent Madero entering Mexico, 44; orders arrest of Madero, 44–5

Katz, F., 102 n.

Kennedy, John Fitzgerald, 301 n.

King, Rosa E. (Mrs Norman King), 89, 141, 181 n.

Kipling, Rudyard, 7 n.

Knatchbull-Hugessen, (Sir) Hughe Montgomery, 149, 159, 197

Knox, Philander Chase, 35, 36–7, 40, 47, 48, 55, 126, 138, 172, 208, 293, 295; threatened resignation of, 55; letter to Taft on Mexican situation, 56–7; correspondence with Archbold, 80–1, 82; suggests Wilson trying to force hand of State Department, 111; advises Wilson to leave Embassy if necessary, 133

Kueck, German consul, 108 n.

Kuhn Loeb, Messrs, 184

land, ownership of, 20, 21

Landa y Escandón, Guillermo de, 97 n., 213 n.

Lane, Franklin K., 283 n., 285 n.

Langer, W. L., 5 n.

Langley, Sir Walter Louis Frederick Goltz, 191, 253, 263

Lascuráin Paredes, Pedro, 117, 127, 140, 142, 144, 145, 154, 158, 288, 293; threatened by Wilson, 133; features in exchange of notes between Stronge and Wilson, 137, 138–9; recommended for interim Presidency, 138, 143; agrees Madero should resign, 142–3; breaks down during meeting with Madero, 143; becomes President and resigns, 148, 152, 159

Laughlin, Irwin Boyle, 157–8

Laurier, Wilfrid, 5

Law, A. Bonar, 2

Lawrence, D., 177 n., 300 n.

League of Nations, 103

legal code, remodelled by *científicos*, 18

Leslie, Edward Henry John, 43, 122, 185, 203, 252

Leslie's Weekly, 196 n.

Lespinasse, M., 87 n.

Letcher, Marion, 19, 115, 116 n., 179

ley fuga, 21, 134, 153

Libby, William H., 82

Lieuwen, E., 301 n.

Limantour, José Yves, 30, 50 n., 54, 59, 60;

exponent of *científico* doctrine, 17; early career of, 17; encourages European investments in Mexico, 18; absent from Mexican centenary celebrations, 33; returns from Paris, 48; negotiates with Maderistas, 48, 61; views on mobilization, 56; needed to secure cabinet changes, 60; criticizes government policy, 61; forms new cabinet, 62; assumed role of Díaz, 62–3; receives Corral's resignation, 64; concern over U.S. attitude to arms trade, 65–6; unaware of Díaz's departure, 72; advises on raising of loan, 184

Lind, John, 244, 272, 277, 279; charges Cowdray with corruption, 26; early career of, 201; lack of qualifications of, 201–2; mission to Mexico, 202–15, 277; in Vera Cruz, 202, 204, 213, 214, 226–7, 230, 256, 257; meets Gamboa, 204–5; meets Huerta, 210–11; meets Carden, 226, 227–8; dealings with Constitutionalists, 227; opinion of Carden, 227–8, 234; *La Gente de México*, 229 n.; considers Cowdray controls Huerta government, 229, 231; declines to move to Mexico City, 230; reports Britain's recognition of Huerta dictatorship, 233–5; Anglophobia of, 234; identifies Great Britain with Cowdray, 234; ignorant of meaning of diplomatic recognition, 235; meets Félix Díaz, 244; considered Huerta anxious to exploit Mexico's minerals, 245; meets Fred Adams, 245; votes in Mexican elections, 247; receives text of ultimatum to Huerta, 257; involved in negotiations with Huerta, 257–62; threatens severance of diplomatic relations, 261–2; attacks Carden for not supporting Cowdray, 277; leaves Mexico, 283; assessment of, 297

Link, A. S., 3 n., 167 n., 299 n.

Lloyd George, David, 176

Lloyd George, Richard, 176

loan, see Huerta, financial problems of

Lockhart, Sir Robert Bruce, 34 n., 310

Lodge, Henry Cabot, 60, 115, 274 n., 289

London Oil Trust, 22

Long, Boaz W., 168

Lonsdale, James Rolston, 57

Los Angeles Times, 46

Lower California, rebel activities, 47, 48, 60, see also Baja California

Index

McAdoo, William Gibbs, 181
McCaleb, W. F., 21 n.
McCumber, Porter James, 77
MacDonald, Sir Claude, 70
McKinley, William, 167
Macleay, James William Ronald, 19, 29 n., 41 n.
McNamara dynamite plot, 47 n.
Madero, Alfonso, 80
Madero, Ernesto, 30, 96, 108, 109, 143, 276, 279
Madero, Evaristo, 30
Madero, Francisco Indalecio, 79, 177, 237, 277, 281 n., 284, 290, 302; *La sucesión Presidencial en 1910*, 21 n., 29 n., 31; contender for Vice-Presidency, 29; physical appearance of, 29–30, 93–4, 94 n.; character of, 30–1; founded Anti-reelection party, 31; founded Democratic Clubs, 31; nominated for President, 31; arrested, 31–2, 67, 147; imprisoned, 32; fled to U.S., 32; revolutionary preparations by, 42–3; convinced that revolution a failure, 44; advances on Chihuahua, 62; attacks Ciudad Juárez, 67–8; terms accepted by government, 71; financed by Standard Oil, 74; triumphal entry into capital, 85–6; gives commission to Zapata, 88–9; submits to de la Barra's authority, 90; denounces Huerta, 92, 105; denounces Vázquez Gómez, 92; negotiates with Zapata, 92–3, 95–6; becomes President, 94; favours foreign investment, 95, 99, 100, 292; denies financial connections with Standard Oil, 98; discusses Aguila Co. with Lord Cowdray, 98–9; posthumous opinions of, 101–3; demands death penalty for Félix Díaz, 106; assisted by Pearson firm, 108–9; attitudes of Wilson, Schuyler and Stronge towards, 109–11, 114, 121, 125, 126, 127, 134; arrives in Mexico City, 131; appoints Huerta as military commander, 131; considered responsible for continued disturbances, 132; complains of Wilson's behaviour, 133; overthrow intended by Wilson, 133–4, 137–8, 144 n.; resignation of, 135, 137–8, 140, 142, 143, 144 n., 148, 149–50, 151, 158, 159; distrusted Huerta, 139, 146, 147; sends head of police to Ciudadela, 140; receives Cologan, 143; sends telegram to Taft pleading non-intervention, 143, 144, 146,
148, 149; murder of, 153–6, 163, 194, 294; murder not a factor in British recognition of Huerta, 158–63; final assessment of, 287, 288, 290; *see also* revolution; revolutionaries
Madero, Gustavo, 30, 76, 78, 81; embezzlement by, 83; bravery in rising of Feb. 1913, 131; arrested, 147; death of, 134, 154
Madriz, José, 28, 33
Magdalena Bay, 60, 62, 115, 289
Malkin, Herbert William, 151
Mallet, Sir Louis du Pan, 34, 44, 122, 150, 152, 193, 209; views on recognition of Huerta, 157–8; considers Madero's death should not influence recognition, 162; explains recognition position to H. Greenwood, 163–4; asks Cowdray's opinion about recognition, 164; considers U.S. recognition would be too late, 196; considers change in Stronge's attitude to Huerta, 211–12
Marconi disclosures, 174, 176
Márquez Sterling y Loret de Mola, Manuel, 135, 145 n., 154
Martin, P. F., 35 n., 38 n.
Massiglia, Count, 71
Maximilian, 12, 15, 106 n., 147
Maxse, L. J., 174 n.
Maycock, Willoughby Robert Dottin, 164, 165; advises against recognizing provisional President, 152, 159–60, 161; fails to prevent official recognition, 161–2
mediation, 132, 133, 178, 239, 268–9, 271, 272
Méndez, Luis, 96
Menelik IV, Emperor of Ethiopia, 45
Mexicali, disturbances in, 47
Mexican Central Railway, 23
Mexican Herald, The, 97, 125, 126, 135, 146 n., 211, 233 n., 242, 257
Mexican Petroleum Company, 23
Mexico City, riots and unrest in, 33, 41–2, 62, 71–2; military coup in, 104; rising of Feb. 1913, 131–48
Meyer, George von Lengerke, 53, 54
Middlemas, R. K., 23 n., 278 n.
Miller, Clarence, 84 n.
mineral rights, ownership of, 21–2, 23, *see also* oil industry
mines, closure reported by Wilson, 65, 68
Mining Law (1884), 21, 22, 23, 25, 286

325

Index

Miramón, Miguel, 106 n.
Mobile, Woodrow Wilson's speech at, 249–51, 252
mobilization on Texas border, 49–61, 63; purpose of, 54, 55, 58, 289; second occurrence of, 111–12
Moheno, Querido, 134 n., 225, 232, 238, 245, 256, 288
Molina Enríquez, A., 72 n.
Mondragon, Manuel, 107
Monroe doctrine, 6, 15, 36, 44 n., 56, 57 n., 64, 169, 176, 221, 240, 246, 278; Lodge corollary, 60, 115–16; 'Wilson corollary', 249 n., 251; criticized by Carden, 259, 260; Roosevelt corollary, 287, 289
Moore, John Bassett, 168, 180, 182, 210, 229, 230, 299; advice on U.S. policy ignored, 235; views on need for foreign capital, 251–2, 296 n.
Morelos, agrarian revolt in, 87, 88, 92
Morgan, J. P. and Co., 184
Morley, John, First Viscount, 70
Morning Post, The, 49, 207 n.
Morro Castle incident, 244
Mowry, G. E., 3 n.
Munro, D. G., 28 n., 174 n.
Murray, Alexander William Charles Oliphant, First Baron: connection with Marconi disclosures, 174, 176; seeks concessions in Colombia, 174–5, 255, 279
Murray, Arthur, 176, 185

Napoléon III, Emperor of the French, 11
National Bank of Mexico, 213
Navarro, M. G., 21 n.
navy (G.B.), 2, 9, 9 n., 64, 223–4, 274–5, 280–2; contract for oil fuel for, 173–4, 176–7, 245, 255, 279
navy (Japan), 9 n., 51
navy (Mexico), 282
navy (U.S.), 9, 28, 33, 50, 51, 52–3, 54, 171, 180, 202, 223, 275, 281–2
Needler, M. C., 294 n.
Nevins, A., 22 n.
New Spain, 10
New York Herald, The, 196 n., 241 n., 249
New York Sun, 206 n.
New York Times, The, 135 n., 147 n., 233 n., 236–7, 241–2
Nicaragua, 28, 33–4, 37, 40, 43, 74, 199, 208, 221, 295
Nicolson, Sir Arthur, 34, 49, 122, 162, 163, 165, 197, 238, 263, 273, 305

Nicolson, H., 34 n., 121 n., 304 n.
Noetzlin, Messrs, 184
Norway, recognizes Huerta, 185
Notter, H., 167 n., 219 n.
Nueva Era, La, 100, 101 n.

Obregón, Toribio Esquivel, 26 n., 184 n., 292, 302
oil fields, threatened by Constitutionalists, 274–5, 277–8
Oil Fields of Mexico Co., 180
oil industry: history of, 22–7, 292; agreement to split market, 278; see also Cowdray, First Viscount, oil concessions
oil industry (Colombia), Lord Murray seeks concessions, 174–5
oil requirements, British navy, 173–4, 176–7, 245, 255, 279
Olney, Richard, 6, 169
Orozco, Pascual, 44, 67, 74, 78, 106, 111, 114, 121, 203, 237, 293; defeated González Salas, 103; defeated by Huerta, 104, 105; finance of his counter-revolution, 107–8; U.S. supplies arms to, 116
Ortiz Rubio, Pascual, 44 n.
O'Shaughnessy, Edith Louise Coues, 17 n., 61, 62 n., 86 n., 87 n., 95, 104 n., 117 n., 147 n., 155 n., 169 n., 256, 257, 258, 261, 262 n., 298
O'Shaughnessy, Nelson Jarvis Waterbury, 168–9, 189, 202–3, 216, 227, 232, 233, 234, 235, 239 n., 244, 272, 272 n., 284; considers Carden hostile to U.S., 240; involved in ultimatum to Huerta, 256–8, 261, 262; involved in Carden's mediation plans, 268–9; reports rumours about Cowdray's concessions, 277; considers Carden and Cradock engaged in intrigue, 281
Otis, Harrison Grey, 46–7

Pacto de la Ciudadela, see Pacto de la Embajada
Pacto de la Embajada, 145, 148, 209
Page, Walter Hines, 196, 197, 206 n., 209, 229, 235, 237, 244–5, 253, 262, 271, 273, 276, 279, 282, 304; appointed U.S. ambassador to Court of St James, 169; thought Colombian concessions contract 'killed' in Britain, 175; opinion on recognition of Huerta, 187–8, 200; reports President Wilson's attitude to coup, 238; discussions with Grey, 239–40, 247–9; reports to Wilson on discussions

Index

Page, Walter Hines (*cont.*)
with Grey, 254; reports that Britain will not aid Huerta against U.S., 263-4; views on mediation conditions, 268; requests Carden's transfer, 269, 282-3; protection for Cowdray's oil interests requested of, 275, 277; assessment of, 297

Paget, Sir Ralph Spencer, 220, 226, 243, 246

Palavicini, F. F., 225 n.

Pall Mall Gazette, reports Huerta's 'proclamation' as President, 151

pan o palo, 16

Panama, 4, 221

Panama Canal, 5, 8, 233, 252, 269; possible rival to, 174; tolls dispute, 254-5, 271

Pan-American Union, 132

Papen, F. von, 50 n.

Parker, W. B., 136 n.

Parkes, H. B., 10 n.

Payne–Aldrich bill, 3

Pearson, Fred Stark, 20, 183

Pearson, S. and Son Ltd, 23, 50, 51, 60, 72, 84 n., 100, 108, 141, 174, 183, 230, 245, 276, *see also* Cowdray, First Viscount

Pearson, W. H. M., 58 n.

Pearson, Weetman Dickinson, *see* Cowdray, First Viscount

Peking, siege in, 125, 136

Pendle, G., 7 n.

peones, discontent among, 21, 32, 193

Pereyra, Carlos, 52-3, 197 n., 202 n.

Perkins, D., 6 n.

Peru, 300

Pierce, Arthur Clay, 97 n.

Pierce, Henry Clay, 22-3, 24, 25, 26, 97 n., 99, 227, 278, 284, 292

Pino Suárez, José María, 92, 95, 153-6, 159, 160, 163, 194

'Pirra-Purra' (pseudonym of Pedro Lamicq), 101 n.

Plan de Ayala, 104

Poinsett, Joel, 15

police, role under Díaz, 16

Porfiriato, 15-48

Porfiristas, replaced in *interinato*, 88, 90, 91

positivism, *see cientfficos*

Prida, R., 39 n., 67 n., 95 n., 107 n., 132 n., 145 n.

Priest, Henry S., 97 n.

Progressive Constitutional Party, 92

provisional Presidents, recognition by Great Britain, 152, 157-65

Puerto Rico, annexed by U.S., 8

Quirk, R. E., 169 n.

Rábago, Jesús M., 257

railways, 20, 24, 71, 83, 97, 218, 245 n.s 292; national ownership of, 17, 23; a, market for oil industry, 23, 97; Cowdray's interest in, 24, 108, 230; possible Japanese seizure of, 50-1; Board membership, 97

Rausch, G. J., 284 n.

'Reciprocity', 4, 5, 40

Rellano, battle at, 104

Remnant, James Farquarson, 58

revolution: early signs of, 42-5, 48; finance of, 73-84, 95, 98; finance of counter-revolution, 106-8

revolutionaries: advance on Chihuahua, 62; negotiations opened with, 63, 66; capture Agua Prieta, 64; posts in *interinato* held by, 88, 90, 91

Revolutionary Army of the South, 88, *see also* Zapata

Reyes, Bernardo, 29, 62, 86, 87 n., 92-3, 106, 118; loses Presidency to Madero, 94; gaoled after abortive revolt, 103; leads coup in Mexico City, 104; source of financial support unknown, 107; involved in rising of Feb. 1913, 131

Rhodes, Cecil, 22

Riba y Cervantes, Luis, 97 n., 183, 216-17

Richthofen, Baron von, 42 n.

Riesenberg, Mr, 83

Rippy, J. F., 175 n.

Riquelme, Hevia, 153, 154

Robinson, Albert Alonzo, 23 n.

Robles Pezuela, Manuel, 106 n.

Römer, H. G., 78

Rojas, L. M., 134 n.

Roosevelt, Theodore, 3-4, 5, 9, 53, 56, 115, 168, 169, 219, 274, 284, 287, 289, 298

Root, Elihu, 19, 109, 114

Ross, S. R., 29 n., 103, 132 n.

rurales: role of, 16; at Ciudadela, 131

Russian Revolution, 103, 120

Ryder, T. J., 96, 109, 231, 278

St John, Sir Spencer, 218

St Louis Post-Dispatch, 100

Salisbury, Third Marquess, 94

Sandys, Thomas Myles, 57

Santa Anna, Antonio López de, 11

Sargent, Orme Garton, 34, 35

Scherer, Hugo, 184

Schmucker, George B., 39 n.

Index

Schuyler, Montgomery, 117 n., 118, 124 n.;
change in attitude to Madero, 110–11;
proposal that U.S. cut supply of funds to
Mexico, 127
scientificism, *see cientificos*
Scott, Ernest Stowell, 243–4, 245, 262
Serbia, 300 n.
Seymour, C., (ed)., 195 n., 269 n.
Shanklin, William Arnold, 116 n.
Shearwater incident, 64, 290
Sherman, W. L. and R. E. Greenleaf,
104 n., 105 n., 155 n.
Simonds, L. C., 104 n.
Singer, J., 251 n.
slavery, existence of in Mexico, 27, 32 n.
Smith, J. V., 79, 80
Smith, William Alden, 73, *see also* Smith
Committee
Smith Committee, hearings on finance of
revolution, 73–7, 108
Society of the American Colony in Mexico,
70
South Africa, Dominion status granted to,
1
South American Journal, 19
Southern Commercial Congress, Woodrow
Wilson's speech at, 249–51, 252
Spectator, The, 174 n.
Spender, J. A., 23 n., 26–7, 75 n., 255 n.,
278 n.
Sperling, Rowland Arthur Charles, 34,
165 n., 214, 217
Speyer, James, 180–2, 184, 185
Spicer, Gerald Sydney, 43–4, 49, 70, 71,
118, 122, 123, 209, 263; considers
Madero's resignation an internal matter,
149; views on Britain's recognition of
Huerta, 151, 159, 161–2; his opinion of
Madero's death, 160; considers U.S. has
no support for its non-recognition policy,
199; considers Stronge should not
intervene, 203; considers coup merely
internal politics, 246; comments on
Mobile speech, 252–3
Spring-Rice, Sir Cecil Arthur, 158 n., 189,
190, 196, 197–8, 201, 271, 279, 283, 284;
appointed Ambassador to Washington,
169; poor health of, 169–70, 238, 269;
character of, 170; friendship with Grey,
170; difficulty in communicating with
President, 170; reports on anxiety in U.S.
over Mexico, 190; informs State Department on recognition situation, 191–2;

considers Wilson's policy identical with
Taft's, 199; reports on Page's misunderstanding of 'provisional' recognition,
200; reports on Lind's appointment,
201–2; discusses Lind's mission with
Bryan, 206–7; concerned over President
Wilson's attitude to recognition, 207–8
Stamfordham, First Baron, 151
Standard Oil Company, 22–3, 24, 106, 278;
complicity in revolution alleged, 74–84,
97–9; Madero denies connection with,
98; Cowdray receives aid from, 99;
enters Colombia, 175
State Department, 124; a political body, 37;
changes to merit system for appointments, 37, 167–8; attitude towards
Mexico, 37–8, 177; unable to prevent
Madero entering Mexico, 44; embarrassed by Corral, 70; suspicious of
Embassy reports, 111; authority misused
by H. L. Wilson, 113–14; diplomatic
exchange about frontier situation, 116–
17; attempts to keep Wilson on tight
rein, 133; publishes Wilson's telegram
denouncing mediation proposals, 133;
informed of Wilson's threat to land
marines, 144; mistakenly assumed to be
withholding recognition until claims
settled, 166; reorganization of, 167–8;
opinion on recognition misleadingly
reported by press, 171; persuades
Colombian government to withdraw
concessions bill, 174–5, 255; supports
U.S. firms against rivals, 175; attitude to
elections, 186, 228, 233, 236, 238, 242,
243, 244; urged to recognize Huerta, 187;
disapproves of Carden's appointment,
219; recognition of belligerency of
northern rebels, 238, 239, 243, 270;
negotiates with Constitutionalists, 274;
general policy of, 289–90; inefficiency of,
299
Stephenson, G. M., 202 n., 211 n., 213 n.,
234 n., 247 n., 279 n.
Stewart, Walter Annesley, 162
Stimson, G. H., 47 n.
Stone, William Joel, 64
'Stormy Petrel', *see* Hohler, Sir Thomas
Beaumont
Strong and Cadwalader Inc., 68, 97
Stronge, Francis William, 113 n., 123, 136,
187, 190, 193, 195, 198, 293, 298, 304;
early career of, 118; arrives in Mexico,

Index

Stronge, Francis William (*cont.*)
118–19; physical appearance of, 119, 137,
153; addiction to parrots, 119, 137, 153;
opinions of Hohler and Wilson concerning, 119; his opinion of H. L.
Wilson, 120; concerned over anti-
Americanism in Mexico, 121; opinion
of Madero's government, 121, 125–6,
127; British support of Mexico against
U.S. requested of, 122, 205; quarrels
with Wilson, 123–4; intercedes for F.
Díaz, 126; exchange of notes with
Wilson, 137–9; account of *Decena
Trágica*, 139–50 *passim*; unwilling to
attend Diplomatic Corps meeting, 141;
told Ángeles of whereabouts of de la
Barra, 142; unlikely to have seen
Madero's telegram to Taft, 144, 146;
exceeds duties as representative, 144–6,
150; not implicated in overthrow of
Madero, 147; reports on negotiations
with Madero, 148–9; warned not to
meddle in internal politics, 149–50; did
not finally encourage Wilson, 150;
reports on Huerta becoming provisional
President, 152; reports on Wilson's
recognition of Huerta, 152; reports
Madero's death, 156, 160; explains
legality of Huerta's position, 159; considers Madero's death may prevent
recognition, 162; considers Huerta
régime stable, 164, 190, 193, 211, 220;
fears consequences of U.S. attitude to
Huerta, 191; concerned over friction
between Mexico and U.S., 197, 203–4;
reports Wilson's recall to Washington,
199; role in Lind's mission, 202–15
passim; health fails, 216; tributes to work
of, 216–17; transferred to Chile, 216,
217 n.; leaves Mexico, 217
Stronge, Sir James Calvert, Fourth Baronet,
118

Taft, Henry Waters, 97, 109
Taft, William Howard, 80, 97, 171, 172,
177, 255, 282, 289, 293, 302–3; general
policies of, 3–4; policy towards Latin
America, 4, 172; public opinion against,
4; visits to Mexico, 4, 41; advocate of
dollar diplomacy, 9, 36, 219; 'trust
busting' by, 27; attitude to foreign
policy, 35–6; appoints H. L. Wilson, 38;
orders mobilization, 49, 51, 53–4; left

Washington for Georgia, 51, 54; orders
navy to proceed north, 53; on need to
protect American lives and property, 55,
112; discussions with de la Barra, 61–2;
requests Americans to withdraw from
Douglas, 64; receives complaints about
H. L. Wilson, 68–70; unconcerned at
capture of Ciudad Juárez, 71; favours ban
on arms trade, 109; Proclamation on
non-intervention, 113; threatens invasion
of Mexico, 113–14; interview with
Calero, 117–18; opinion on intervention, 117–18, 121–2, 125, 147; defeated
at polls, 126; orders concentration of
forces during 1913 uprising, 132; receives
telegram from E. Madero, 143, 144,
146; final decisions on U.S. policy
towards Mexico, 167; tolerated change
to merit system for appointments, 168;
prepared to negotiate for alternative to
Panama Canal, 175 n.; final assessment
of, 287–8
Tampico, besieged by Constitutionalists,
282, 298–9
Tehuantepec National Railway, 24, 50–1,
58 n., 108, 218, 230, 292 n.
Terrazas family, Orozco financed by, 107
territorial extension, as motive for mobil-
ization, 289
Texas Co., 99
Thompson, David E., 57 n., 70
Times, The, 156, 207 n., 218 n., 265 n.,
284 n.
Times South American Supplement, 20
Tischendorf, A., 20 n.
Tormenta, la, 292
Toro, Carlos, 107
Torreón: capture of, 71; recaptured by
Constitutionalists, 231, 279
Tower, Reginald Thomas, 38 n.; reports on
outbreak of riots, 42–3, 44; on implica-
tion of Japanese–American war, 50–1
Treaty of Ciudad Juárez, 71, 88, 90
Troxel, C. R., 79, 80, 81–2
Tuchman, B. W., 1 n., 50 n., 283 n., 284 n.,
299 n.
Turner, J. K., 21 n., 27 n.
Tuxpam, threatened by Constitutionalists,
274–5, 277–8
'Twenty Inch Gun' note, 6–7, 169
Tyrrell, Sir William George, 171, 220–1,
272, 273; interview with President
Wilson, 269–71

Index

Underwood Tariff bill, 196
United States of America: trade with Mexico, 4, 40; Republican rule ended, 4, 35; Democratic party gains control, 4; Arbitration Treaties with G.B. and France, 5; imperialism of, 7-10; naval operations, 9, 28, 33, 50, 51, 52-3, 54, 171, 180, 202, 223, 275, 281-2; investments in Mexico, 18, 19-20, 24, 70, 95-6; charged with aiding revolutionaries, 64-5, 70; non-recognition of Huerta, 152, 156-66 passim, 167, 171-3, 178-9, 182, 185-9, 191, 192, 194, 196, 198-200, 202, 203-4, 205, 207, 215, 225, 233; business interests favour recognition, 196; growing power of, 223; non-recognition policy of, 300-1; see also arms; Justice, Department of; mobilization on Texas border; State Department
Urrutia, Aureliano, 226 n.
Uruguay, 286

Vagts, Alfred, 22, 23 n., 79
Vasconcelos, José, 83 n., 278
Vázquez (Gómez), Emilio, 88, 90, 91, 92, 94; resignation of, 91; abortive revolt of, 94 n., 104
Vázquez Gómez, Francisco, 48, 74, 79, 80, 88, 92, 102; stands for Vice-President, 31, 32; Memorias Políticas, 54 n., 67 n.
Vazquista, see Vázquez Gómez, Francisco
Venezuela: boundary dispute, 7, 223; naval blockade of, 9, 270 n., 289
Vera Cruz (City), 24, 33, 131, 142, 187, 281, 282; Porfirio Díaz stays in, 72-3; disturbances in, 104, 106, 107, 110; Maderista sympathies of, 154; Lind's arrivals at, 202, 204, 213, 214; Carden's arrival at, 225-6; Félix Díaz stays in, 244; landings at, 284
Veracruz (State), 24, 87
Vice-Presidency, creation of, 15
Victoria, Guadalupe, 11
Viereck, G. S., 177 n.
Villa, Francisco ('Pancho'), 274, 289
Villar, Laureano, 131
Volturno disaster 233

Wainwright, Richard, 53
Washington Post, The, 36, 236
Waters Pierce Oil Company, 22-3, 75, 76, 77, 96, 97, 99, 292; financial involvement

in revolution, 78-9, 82, 84 n.; behind attacks on Cowdray, 98, 179, 279
Wedgwood, Josiah Clement, 192-3
Westminster Gazette, The, 156, 169 n.
Wickersham, George W., 68, 69, 80, 81, 82, 97, 109
Wilfley, Lebbeus Redman, 39, 70
Wilhelm II, German Emperor, 121, 151 n.
Wilkins, James H., 179
Wilson, Francis Mairs Huntington, 36, 40, 56, 111, 113; advocate of dollar diplomacy, 40, 172; concern over Americans involved in revolution, 59; suggests evacuation of El Paso, 112; remains Assistant Secretary of State, 168; resignation of, 168
Wilson, Henry Lane, 50 n., 81, 82, 126, 151, 156, 177, 180, 191, 205, 210, 261, 289, 290, 293; Diplomatic Episodes in Mexico, Belgium and Chile, 38 n., 78, 86 n., 110 n., 134 n., 148 n., 153 n., 189 n.; early career of, 38-9; character of, 39, 69, 288; admitted exceeding his powers, 41, 114; asks for suppression of Mexican newspaper, 45; concern over revolutionary outbreaks, 48, 53, 54, 56, 57; on leave in U.S., 48, 52, 53, 57, 91, 110; discussion with Díaz over Japanese navy, 51; accused by Hohler of being alarmist, 58, 65; considered instrumental in securing mobilization, 60; opinion concerning Hohler, 61; informed of negotiations with revolutionaries, 63, 71; considers possibility of Díaz resigning, 66-7; at centre of Anglo-U.S. conflict, 68-70; 'common defence' policy not adopted, 70-1; unaware of Díaz's departure, 72-3; accuses U.S. of financing revolution, 78; informed of financial negotiations with revolutionaries, 80; exaggerated reports of disturbances, 85, 86-7; opinion of interinato, 85, 86-7; did not predict downfall of Madero, 86; reports arrival of Madero in capital, 86; comments on new policy of interinato, 90; sympathetic to Madero, 93-4, 125; hopes de la Barra would be Vice-President, 95; threatens disclosure of Standard Oil's connections with revolution, 97-8; challenged Constitutionalist view of Madero, 102-3; favours methods of Díaz, 109-10; opinion of Madero government, 109-10, 114, 125, 126, 127, 134; party defeated at

Index

Wilson, Henry Lane (*cont.*)
polls, 111; misuses authority of State Department, 111, 113–14; and El Paso situation, 112–13; emends diplomatic note, 114–15; opinion about Stronge, 119; opinion of Stronge about, 120; quarrels with Stronge, 123–4; denounces Barrett's mediation proposals, 133; increasingly involved with Huerta, 133; threatens Lascuráin with U.S. power, 133; unwilling to withdraw from Embassy, 133; intends overthrow of Madero, 133–4, 137–8, 144 n.; dismissal of, 135, 171, 189, 201; claims he is acting on behalf of Diplomatic Corps, 135–6; opinion of Hale about, 136; exchange of notes with Stronge, 137–9; seeks protection for foreign colonies, 139–40, 142; asked to persuade Madero to resign, 140; offers to mediate, 141; accused of using Diplomatic Corps as cover, 144; threatens landing of U.S. marines, 144, 145; reports overthrow of Madero before it happened, 146–7; presides over meeting between Huerta and Díaz, 147–8; supports provisional President, 152; gives party attended by Huerta, 153–4; receives conditions for recognition, 156; accepts official explanation of Madero's death, 157; reports Britain's attitude to provisional President, 159; remains at Embassy in Mexico, 168; denounced for part in February coup, 171; recalled to Washington, 171, 187–8, 197, 199, 290; helps Mexican government to restore order, 178; reports on *Decena Trágica*, 179; urges U.S. to restrain G.B. over recognition, 180; summoned by Huerta over non-recognition, 181; asks for President's view on recognition conditions, 185–6, 198; return to Mexico unlikely, 199; apologies made for supposed insult to G.B., 206; understood agrarian revolt, 291; assessment of, 293–4
Wilson, John Lockwood, 38, 68, 111
Wilson, Thomas Woodrow, 102, 171, 175, 191, 261, 267 n., 273 n., 279, 282, 283, 289; little interest in foreign relations, 167; policy towards Latin America, 169 n., 171–2; fails to attend public functions, 170; policy on recognition, 172–3, 186, 194, 198, 207–8; and Colombian concessions to Lord Murray, 174–5; indecision over arms trade, 177, 191; sends Hale to Mexico, 182; suggests recall of H. L. Wilson, 187, 188; policy on intervention, 194, 195, 202, 212, 270; takes charge of policy towards Mexico, 199, 200; sends Lind to Mexico as special envoy, 201; Message to Congress on Lind mission, 212, 213–14; dissatisfied with Carden's appointment, 219; against Huerta remaining President by subterfuge, 220; criticized by Carden, 226; asks Lind to remain in Mexico, 229; shocked by Huerta's lawless methods, 233; decides not to recognize elections, 236, 238; speech at Mobile, 249–51, 252; 'Wilson doctrine', 249 n., 251; action on Panama tolls, 255; requests Huerta's retirement, 263–4; interview with Tyrrell reported, 269–71; informed of Carden's instructions, 272; 'watchful waiting' policy of, 274; final assessment of, 291, 294, 296–7, 298–9, 300–3
Winterton, Sixth Earl, 58
Winthrop, John, 53
Wood, Leonard, 52 n., 53, 55, 56, 57 n., 175
Wood, Thomas McKinnon, 32 n., 57, 58, 122 n.
Woodcock, Mr, 140, 142
World, The, 20 n., 49, 50 n., 56 n., 57 n., 70 n., 73 n., 77, 97, 106 n., 107 n., 112 n., 114 n., 116 n., 134 n., 135 n., 171, 172, 173 n., 174 n., 188 n., 189 n., 202 n., 207 n., 212 n., 236, 237, 241 n., 242 n., 267, 281, 282 n., 283 n.
World War (1914–18), 103, 299–300

Young, D., 23 n.
Young, William, 19–20, 193
Yucatán, unrest in, 21, 32

Zamacona, Manuel, 69 n.
Zapata, Emiliano, 88–9, 92–3, 96, 104, 105, 107, 141 n., 291
Zelaya, José Santos, 28, 75 n., 208
Zimmermann telegram, 284